PRIVILEGE INTERRUPTED

PRIVILEGE INTERRUPTED

my brother's keeper

MR. LOUIS A. FAZIO, JR., O.P.

with Matthias J. Mahoney

W. Brand Publishing

NASHVILLE, TENNESSEE

Privilege Interrupted: My Brother's Keeper by Louis A. Fazio, Jr. – First Edition

Cover Design by: JuLee Brand | designchik

Cover image from Author's personal collection

Available in Paperback and eBook formats

Paperback: 979-8-89503-024-0

eBook: 979-8-89503-025-7

Library of Congress Number: (applied for)

CONTENTS

DEDICATION

Louis

I wish to dedicate this book to my beautiful mother, who was devoted to me and her family and who sadly passed on October 30, 2002.

Further, I wish to dedicate this book to all mothers of children with unique needs. These needs are gifts. Some enjoy opening the gifts and fully embracing them, while some do not.

Matthias

For all those caring for others with great needs: May you never lose the spark of love that inspires your caring heart and may you always know how much Our Father in Heaven cherishes your love and dedication. I pray for your strength and your peace.

Dear St. Faustyna, secretary of Divine Mercy, be the patron of our work. May our writing touch souls and open pathways of grace for all who read our stories. Pray that I may be a worthy intern in your office.

Dearest Mother, I pray that this work meets your expectations to reflect the fulfillment you promise to deliver. I entrust these words and all who read them to your motherly care. Immaculate Heart of Mary, pray for us now and at the hour of our death!

On a brisk Sunday morning in the autumn, 2011, Louis Fazio rolled into the sanctuary of First Unitarian Church in Salt Lake City. Serving as the minister, I was startled by such a brazen entrance, not usually associated with people of disabilities. He came flying into church with his University of Utah banner flapping in the breeze. He parked his motorized wheelchair in an appropriate place, making sure he was not blocking anyone's view. He flashed a smile.

I waited to see who brought him to church, soon realizing that Louis came on his own steam. He sat attentively waiting for church services to begin. Louis made it clear from the onset that he was a thoroughly independent human being who exuded confidence. He would have to. He did not live nearby and thus navigated the Salt Lake transit system on his own. He was a man about town.

It would be fair to say that Louis rolled into my life as well that day. Following the service, I made a beeline toward him, still having to wait my turn to speak because congregants were swarming him. Who is this guy? He was a paraplegic and an extrovert. Meeting him was a novel experience. Building and sustaining a valued, yearslong friendship with Louis has been like a gift from the gods.

When Louis first told me he was writing a book about his life experiences, I listened carefully. As always, he was the captain of his own ship. He invariably knew the dangers and limitations of trying to make his life accessible while refraining from any moralism. He wanted to avoid any self-pity while recounting his life challenges from the perspective of someone with cerebral palsy. He wanted to speak honestly about his personal story while also bringing a unique lens to examine the impact of needed laws to help people with disabilities gain dignity and a fairer shot at life. Ultimately, his goal was to produce a manuscript that would transform attitudes of those who, to the fast tempo of modern life, are quick to dismiss people with disabilities as irrelevant. If anyone could inject credibility into a personal story of perseverance and courage, it is Louis. I told him that, and after a huge reflective sigh, he said, "I need to do this."

Louis Fazio's book, *Privilege Interrupted: My Brother's Keeper* chronicles his quest for a purposeful life and his relentless pursuit of dreams. A wrenching overcomer's narrative, Louis reveals being institutionalized in childhood as a noncontributing member of society, while feeling discarded, unsupported, and unworthy of the care and attention he needed. What was the role of faith in steering him past the darkest days of doubt and self-worth? How did the love of friends help move him forward in his relentless drive to attain success as understood by the able-bodied masses? What did it mean to pursue higher education and a career with high earnings while confined to a wheelchair his entire life?

Louis takes us on a journey not only of his own indomitable spirit, but he shows how every human being is endowed with gifts of meaning. Louis, and leaders in the disability movement, refuse to be crushed by unmindful citizens who fail to understand the worth of people who cannot move their limbs. But the soul of a person resides in the mind, and by the grace of his articulate speech, Louis moves the conversation forward with new ideas and advocacy for the disabled. The mountain to attain equality is steep for everyone who has experienced oppression.

Privilege Interrupted: My Brother's Keeper offers certain metrics by which we measure if our own commitment to justice is as strong as we like to think it is. Although we identify with Louis in his struggles to be seen as an equal human being, the tussle is exhausting. Would we have made it to the finish line ourselves?

Louis underscores the role of confidence in fearful situations, forcing us to examine our own stamina in facing mean-spirited impulses in many adverse situations. We might be inclined to confess our lack of fortitude in these situations, which makes Louis not just a guide in the journey but also a mentor. His courage is inexhaustible.

Louis has written a tribute to equality and a paean to the human spirit. He forces us to stop our assumptions about others by opening channels of love and understanding. We feel our own sensibilities grow and develop as Louis acquaints us with the issues and problems faced by people who could well be ourselves. *Privilege Interrupted* never flinches in the face of the human condition. Louis's story is universal, making us realize the inhumane tendencies that haunt our society.

Rev. Tom Goldsmith

INTRODUCTION

My name is Louis Anthony Fazio, Jr. I was born into privilege, but in many ways, that privilege was interrupted by the circumstances which compelled me to write this book. I have lived all my life with a mobility-limiting disability; I've faced institutionalization and endured the effects of a toxic family environment. I've struggled through personal financial crises and addictive sexual behaviors, all while living as a gay man in America and trying to remain devout in my Catholic faith. I didn't lose hope, and it is my prayer that by reading my unique account you will be inspired to persevere through whatever challenges you face. I also hope that together we can broaden the conversation around disability—privately, publicly, and politically—and that stories like mine will help inspire a kinder, more hospitable world for everyone.

When I was born three months premature in 1964, the attending physicians made an error with the oxygen levels I was given in my incubator. Because of this, my brain was damaged, and I was diagnosed with cerebral palsy, which I have lived with since. After many years of physical therapy and surgery, I am still unable to walk and am confined to my wheelchair.

My disability has had a huge impact on my entire life. It permeates every facet of my existence like a foul stench festering in the refrigerator. It affects my relationships, my health, and my career. It changes who I spend my time with, what activities I can do, and the places I can go. Everything from cutting a piece of chicken to visiting the john is changed by having cerebral palsy.

In my developmental years, I would go to the store a lot with my mom. This was the late '60s to early '70s, when the stares of fellow shoppers made me feel like the K-Mart Blue Light Special; which, on a certain level, made me feel unique. But on another level, it made me feel like the Hunchback of Notre Dame.

It might be tempting to say that my life has been defined by my disability, but this would be rolling too far. Though my disability has changed what I do day-to-day, it cannot tell you what kind of a person I am. This sounds obvious enough, but you might be surprised how many people are quick to judge my character without a second glance. People can look at me and come up with all kinds of assumptions about my mental capacity, whether or not I have a job, whether I ever want to be in a romantic relationship, etc.

For as many assumptions that are made, there are nearly as many that are forgotten. Many people don't allow themselves to get close enough with a disabled person, as though the condition were contagious. People can look from afar in safety but seldom come up close. Even today, I can still feel the veiled stares of passersby. The looks of those gazing upon something too different to look away from, but too foreign to approach.

If you were to get to know me, you would find that I do a good job of staying on top of my limitations and am quite an outgoing fellow, too. I enjoy going to football games, concerts, museums, and parks. I have gone sky-diving just once (though I hope to go again soon), and some day I'd like to take a donkey down into the Grand Canyon. I volunteer at the VA one day a week, and in Utah I pioneered the genre of sit-down comedy. My disability can't tell you any of these things. It can't tell you about my political views, my intense relationship with God, or about my rocky relationship with my family.

A goal for my story is to fuel productive conversation about disability; I also hope that it strengthens people's faith, whether Catholic, Protestant, non-denominational Christian, Muslim, or Jew. I also welcome those of Eastern faiths to read this book, to reflect from your own perspective on how we can all come together in this time of division within our American society.

I ask in my book, with Matthias Mahoney, the questions that many may ponder but may be reluctant to answer: Who is my brother's keeper? What privileges have been interrupted? Not to say that privilege has been extinguished—by my faith, my Father, and Jesus, the privilege of eternal inheritance will never be extinguished. Only we can deny our inheritance in Jesus. He loves us all unconditionally.

My hope and my goal for this book is to be as honest as possible, so that others who read it in this generation and beyond will realize that no matter if you have a disability and whether that disability is hidden or you can see it as plain as day, or if you are man or woman, the dignity of the person is what matters, along with your faith in God. At least in my case; that will carry you through. I hope all who read these pages will learn something about my experience that will help them with their own. I wish you a continued journey of faith and learning, no matter what your faith or how you learn.

It is also my goal to present both Matthias's and my unique perspectives: care recipient and caregiver, an old man with a young soul and a young man with an old soul, a gay man and a straight man. There are few memoirs out there that speak from both sides of these coins. We both hope that our raw, messy, and beautiful walk (and roll) together may bless you and inform your reflection on life, suffering, love, and sacrifice.

If I have tapped your interest, please come along with me on the journey of *Privilege Interrupted: My Brother's Keeper.*

my childhood

According to my mother, the day I was born, I was put on hold. A Beatles fan, my mother was one of the 73 million people watching them make their historic debut on *The Ed Sullivan Show* that evening, February 9, 1964. Although my birth was imminent, Mom waited to see the full performance and *then* she went to the hospital.

To this day, I wonder about the special connection between The Beatles and my birth, since the beat of Ringo's drums and the sound of their voices heralded me into earthly existence—but only after they exited the stage.

Another notable event that occurred the year of my birth: the founder of the independent living movement, Ed Roberts, gained his B.A. degree from the University of California Berkeley. He was the first student admitted to the institution who utilized a power wheelchair.

No one was really cognizant of whether I had cerebral palsy or a "birth injury" until about the age of six months, when I wasn't meeting typical developmental markers. My aunt Marguerite and my mother had been pregnant at the same time, and it became evident that I wasn't developing in the same way my cousin Tracy was. It was noted that I could not sit up or crawl or roll like my cousin did.

My mother, being somewhat concerned, took me to Dr. Lezik, the pediatrician. She told the story that at my first visit, I reached out from my mother's arms to touch artwork that the doctor had on the wall. I guess Dr. Lezik complained about it, and my mother's response was, in her true style, "My son is a fan of fine art."

After a battery of testing, it was determined that I had spastic cerebral palsy, with the cause suspected to be the attending physician's error with the oxygen levels I was given in my incubator. Because of the damage to my brain this caused, I had no control (and still have no control) of my legs and limited control of my arms and hands.

This diagnosis meant that another Fazio had the haunting of a severe medical condition.

In 1945, my father's family experienced the tragic loss of my father's eldest sister Sylvia to leukemia. She was just 19 at the time of her passing, and my father was 17.

As the family story goes, after Sylvia's passing, the doctor told my grandfather, Frank, that the best thing he could do for his wife, Jenny, was to get her pregnant. So, sure enough, it wasn't long until my Aunt Marguerite was born.

Still, my grandmother's shadow of grief carried over and was hard for her to shake. I always wondered why my relationship with her was not always optimal. In fact, at one point my grandmother said to me, "Do you know what they do to little boys who fall on Grandmother's kitchen floor? They put them away." I, being all of nine or 10 at this time, did not realize what was meant by those words. As an adult, I now know. Those words weren't meant for me but were only a projection of Grandmother's pain.

Life in the Fazio home could be volatile, and my father suffered my grandfather's version of spare the rod, spoil the child. My grandfather, according to my father, beat the hell out of him on many occasions.

My father did not appreciate the authoritarian approach, so, at 17, the year that Sylvia died, he set his sights on the Army. My grandparents, as my grandmother Jenny will tell you, were surprised by the enlistment, only learning of it after noticing the U.S. Army pin on my dad's lapel.

"How could you! You're underage!"

"I got Uncle Freddy to sign me in." Dad then left home in Pittsburg, Pennsylvania, for Ft. Bragg in North Carolina, to join the 82nd Airborne and become a paratrooper.

On one of his first training jumps, the chute failed to open and he plunged, only the tiny drogue chute slowing his descent. This particular jump was his undoing, breaking every bone in his body except his neck.

For the next two years, during the Korean War, he called Walter Reid Army Hospital in Washington, D.C., home. Interestingly, Ingrid Bergman's first husband, Petter Aron Lindström, operated on him during his stay. He was eventually discharged from the Army due to his disability, and the metal plate in his back remained for the rest of his life, which at times was painful.

He strongly disliked entering any hospital thereafter. I've often considered whether my father's conflicting feelings about his own injuries and my disability were interconnected.

I should add when talking about family that I had an older brother. He was unnamed and buried in Mt. Carmel Cemetery, along with Aunt Sylvia. My mother knew he had already died in the womb months before the due date and made the conscious decision to carry him to term. He was born in 1962, approximately two years before I was. I like to think that he is waiting for me in Heaven, with open arms, and that we, the Fazio boys, will keep the rest of the Fazio family in line.

When I came along, Grandmother Eva Vujevich (Mom's mom) came to the aid of my mother and father by having them move in with her on Malcolm Avenue in Pittsburgh.

Grandmother and Grandfather Vujevich had been potato farmers in Croatia and had come to America for a better life. They embodied and instilled in their children the values of kindness, hard work, and service to family, each stepping up to help in seasons of need. At 18, my mother and her twin brother, Steve, had worked together to help support the family of five children after their father's passing. Likewise, my grandmother was there for us.

My grandmother was a very caring individual and did the bulk of my care so that my parents could pursue their careers unrestricted by caring for a child with a disability. This was a tremendous help for the family, as my parents valued their work and the independence it allowed.

In fact, my mother was a trendsetter in that she had been the primary breadwinner in the first five years of marriage to my dad—unusual for the early '60s. She later told the story of my dad's career kicking off on the day of my birth, when he was hired by Butler Auto Auction after a string of odd jobs. Meanwhile, my mother taught at Park Terrace Middle School and was given permission by the principal to leave early three to four days a week to pick me up from my grandmother's house, then drive me to Easter Seals for physical therapy.

If it weren't for the principal's understanding and my grandmother's kindness, my mother wouldn't have been able to keep her job as a teacher.

I know my grandmother worshipped me; I was the apple of her eye. Maybe that had something to do with the fact that I was her first male grandchild. I especially remember her smile. Her smile for me was a smile of love. My Grandmother Eva knew that her grandchild had a disability, and she knew what my mother was facing.

I don't think the dynamic of disability was quite the same for Eva, compared to my father's mother, Jenny, who lost her beloved daughter Sylvia to leukemia. The impact of disability left its mark in different ways for both sides of the family.

In retrospect, I believe that love existed, but it was contaminated, at least on my father's side, by the hurts and tribulations of their human condition.

This difference between my grandmothers' attitudes toward disability even led my mother to suspect that my dad's mother, Grandmother Fazio, attempted to have me killed. It was a time of potential tragedy. Grandmother Fazio was going to take me to her home in Penn Hills to babysit me.

My grandmother was *always* interested in what my mother had to wear and just *had* to see what she bought. However, she always said that my mother spent too much money on clothes. This day, she left me and my dog Fritz, the miniature dachshund, in the car with the ignition on, while she went inside to see my mother's new clothes. As many three-year-olds can be, I was precociously curious, and somehow, while I was sitting on the front seat, put my grandmother's car in gear. We lived on a hill, and the next thing I remember is my dog Fritz and I rolling down a hill as my mother and grandmother ran after the car, my mother yelling, "My son's in the car! Please stop the car!"

There was a Black gentleman doing yardwork on our neighbor Schreiber's lawn. He heard my mother scream for help and raced to the car. Fortunately, the driver's side window was down; he reached in and turned off the ignition just prior to the car going over the hillside. My grandmother was taken to the hospital because she was dragged by the car in her futile attempt to stop it.

For the longest time, my mother thought my grandmother had something to do with the car not being in gear. But, as an adult, I know my mother's theory is just not possible. I am the culprit who caused the car to careen down the hill on Pennhurst Dr. This was my first—and certainly not my last—interaction with my Heavenly Father saving my life.

My mother, until the day she died (or until the day the gentleman who saved my life passed, I'm not certain who passed first), remembered him by sending him a card every Thanksgiving for saving my life. My mother was a very kind soul.

A couple of years after the incident in my grandmother's car, our nuclear family grew. On March 14, 1968, my younger brother Frank was born. Little did I realize, his entry into the family unit would lead to my exit.

"they put them away."

In the first two years after Frank's birth, yelling matches frequently erupted between my father and mother. My mother always said that my father was the one who pushed for the decision, and not nicely—then it happened. It was August or September of 1970.

One day my mother told me we were going to visit Uncle Ed and Aunt Carole, her brother and sister-in-law. When we got in my father's Cadillac, I was kind of excited because I was getting to go see my uncle and aunt. I didn't know much about them, but I liked them.

Driving on the Turnpike seemed like forever; it was a five-hour ride. We arrived at my aunt and uncle's place at Valley Forge, a suburb of Philadelphia. As a six-year-old, I didn't know that this was a battle site of the Revolutionary War. I also didn't realize that this was the start of my own type of revolution.

I enjoyed seeing my Aunt Carole, Uncle Ed, and cousins Margaret (whom we affectionately called Peggy) and Madeline.

I was acutely tuned into the ebb and flow of the family dynamic. From a very young age, I could always sense tension. I had a primal awareness that Uncle Ed and Aunt Carole's place was not our final destination. This was just a cover. My dad had to take the day off for the next Monday, and he rarely ever took a day off, so, I knew that this was a big deal. *Where were we going?*

At my aunt and uncle's place, Peggy and Madeline slept on the sofa bed out in the TV room so that Mom and Dad could sleep in their room. I slept in the guestroom. The next morning, we said goodbye to my uncle, aunt, and cousins, as they went off to work and school. I still wasn't sure where *we* were going but felt a growing anticipation. We rode for about 30 minutes before we arrived at a place that reminded me of a medieval castle, gray and cold.

My parents took me inside the Home of the Merciful Savior (HMS[1]) and explained they were going to leave me there and that it was going to be my new home. I couldn't quite understand why my parents would leave and why this would be my new home. We were in a large dining room full of people at a bunch of tables. My parents sat me at a table with about four or six other children.

This is where my parents left me. I cried, and I could see the tears in my mother's eyes. I asked, "Why do you have to leave me?"

I remember a stranger's voice saying to my parents, "It's better that you go so that Louis will stop crying."

I thought to myself, *They don't know me. How do they know I'll stop crying? Where's my mother going? And my father?*

The next thing I knew, a voice from an overhead speaker came out of nowhere, announcing that it was 8:00 p.m. and time to go to bed. My six-year-old self thought, *I already have a place to sleep! Why do I have to sleep here? I want to be with my mom and dad.* They were nowhere to be found.

I was taken to a large room with multiple beds. I was to sleep in a bed that I had never seen before. This was the bed that I would sleep in for the next three years. In fact, as it got dark, I thought, *Where am I? What is this place?* It seemed as though I would cry forever.

The next days, while observing my surroundings, I wondered, *Who are all these people?* There were white people with special caps with a black stripe. *Who are they?* And there were big rooms with tubs and Black people who would help with baths. But there were no yellow ducks with me in the bathtub; it was just in and out.

I remembered that Mom used to give me bubble baths—but there were no bubble baths here. *Where did that go?* Then I thought, *Maybe I did something wrong. I'm in a type of prison. I'm not allowed to go out. Did I make Mom or Dad mad?*

Mom called every day, and asked how I was. She said she loved me. I looked forward to the phone call, but I wasn't really sure why she couldn't come and see me. When I would ask, she would just say, "It's too far away." But she tried to reassure me, telling me I would spend every other weekend with Uncle Ed and Aunt Carole.

I enjoyed the Saturdays when my uncle picked me up and drove me to his home in Valley Forge. One of the weekends, I got a package from my mom: It was a big Winnie the Pooh that she'd sent for my birthday. We kept it at my aunt and uncle's house because I think they were afraid someone would take it from my new residence. So, at their home every other weekend I had Winnie the Pooh, their pet cats, and the neighbor's skunk, which kept me occupied.

Even at such a young age, I began to learn to adapt and make the best of things. When I was with my aunt and uncle I didn't think much of my new place of residence, other than being glad to not be in that prison. At times I still wondered, *What did I do wrong?*

My time in Valley Forge was full of love and adventure. Aunt Carole and I would take the dog, Fluffy, out for walks or take a photo with the neighbor's pet skunk. I also annoyed Peggy and Madeline by getting into their room, causing havoc that only a young boy can. The girls would scream for their mother, "Get Louis out of here!" and Aunt Carole would come to retrieve me as I scurried along on all fours.

At that time of my life, I could crawl, and I made Dennis the Menace look like a choirboy. I liked going to my aunt and uncle's home, and I soon realized that it was my place of family.

I did get to see my parents during this time period, during the summer, and on major holidays—Thanksgiving and Christmas, specifically. My uncle and aunt took me home. They would load up the car—a green station wagon, to be exact, late '60s model—with me, my two cousins, two dogs, and at one point, two cats. We were a zoo on wheels.

Back at the HMS, it was rare that my mother could come and visit, because she had my brother, Frank, and eventually one more child to care for. Further, the economics of going across the state were not always feasible. On the rare occasion she came to see me, I would watch her from a window as she disappeared from view to board the Philadelphia Subway.

As I got more used to things at HMS, I would go into the day room and watch the Philadelphia Warriors (which was the roller derby team for the city of Philadelphia) and/or *Sanford and Son*. Those were the two shows I remember.

I recall one young man who was our physical therapist. He was cool. Physical therapy wasn't always fun, because that is when I had to learn how to fall and let go of my crutches onto a mat, which, to me, felt like falling from a three-story building.

I smiled when he was around. Then suddenly we didn't see him again, until one weekend when I wasn't with my uncle and aunt, he came back. A friend of his who worked there brought him back, and he wrestled with us; we all had fun. I don't think he was supposed to be there, but they snuck him in. That was one of the most fun times I'd had just being a kid. To me there was nothing wrong with me; I was just who I was.

In my loneliness and loss, I learned I must create my own happiness. I learned quickly that part of this happiness was achieved through playing with my penis. Even at that age, I played with myself, and a tingling sensation came that made me happy.

Another thing that made me happy was being asked by Nurse Mansfeld if I would like to come up and let all the residents know it was time to go to bed. I became the announcer for the 8 p.m. declaration, "It's time for everyone to go to bed now."

I didn't enjoy the repercussions when I did something bad. Mrs. Mansfeld would come with a ruler and smack me across the knuckles in the darkness of the night, right before bedtime. Sometimes I didn't really remember what I did that was bad, but I figured I did something bad because why would you smack someone across the knuckles for doing nothing?

Interestingly, when Neil Armstrong walked on the Moon in July of 1969, I was in the infirmary. Nurse Anderson was on duty. By this time, I became a pro (in my eyes anyway) and realized that there were benefits to truly being sick. I had the room to myself and got to watch the Moon landing. That's the cool thing when you were sick: you got your own room, right next to the nursing station, as opposed to the crowded dorm-style rooms.

Dr. Chance was the doctor at the HMS. Occasionally, he gave us medical exams. I felt like a guinea pig on steroids: I would be in my underwear, poked and prodded, while the doctor grunted as he noted his observations. Most of the time I liked to run away from him!

And then there was going to the dentist. I didn't like going to the dentist there because they put an apparatus in your mouth to hold your mouth open. All they said was, "Don't cry; it'll be over soon." I thought to myself, *Well, who are they to say "don't cry" if they're holding your mouth open with this creepy, goofy looking thing?*

HMS was the place where I learned how to read. My teacher, Ms. Laughlin, helped open the world to me. Even though I was shut off from the world, my spirit could take off beyond the walls around me because I now knew how to read. In fact, Ms. Laughlin gave me a guinea pig whom I named "Fluffy". I would eventually bring Fluffy home with me on my last day at the Home of the Merciful Savior.

As residents of HMS, we rarely left the premises (other than for holidays and weekends with family). However, on one occasion we did get to go see Santa Claus. Of course, there were no accessible vehicles, and so we got to see Santa Claus at the local mall like this: We were put into a box truck—there were about maybe five or six of us back there—our wheelchair brakes locked, and the back of the box truck was shut. The driver was up in the front with the aide, and we were left in the dark. There was no light. Nothing until we got to the mall.

We were just kids wanting to see Santa; we didn't really care how we got there. Santa didn't see our disabilities. I think we even got to sit on his lap. And then we were done, back into the box truck we went. I know that in the truck we didn't say much because it was dark. But we were excited, because we got to see Santa! I don't recall how we were selected to see Santa, since not everyone got to go.

Memories of my time at HMS were of sadness sprinkled with happiness, and that of difference. I quickly grew to understand that there are many types of individuals.

Whether you have a disability or not, looking back at this experience with the eyes of an adult, I saw how our American society excluded those who were different, including marginalized groups such as Blacks, Hispanics, and other non-whites.

There were white individuals within the institution of HMS in the late '60s and early '70s in positions of authority. The non-white workers did the grunt work and cared for those of us with physical or mental disabilities. Most of whom I was exposed to had both developmental disabilities and physical disabilities.

The Home of the Merciful Savior was originally named The Home of the Merciful Savior for Crippled Children, and still is located on Baltimore Avenue in Philadelphia, Pennsylvania. Opened in 1882 by Helen Innes, she and her husband, an Episcopal minister, had a young boy with disabilities in their custody. Unable to find a suitable home for him, she set about founding one herself and soon began providing a home for children from any city and any state for no fee. Later, the Home of the Merciful Savior expanded to include a school. The focus of HMS evolved its mission and purpose over the decades.

During the '40s and '50s, HMS was especially serving children with polio, but as the Salk vaccine became more available, their focus shifted to children with cerebral palsy. By the '80s, as powerchairs were becoming more user-friendly and more widely available, the HMS was an innovator in communication programs and "augmentative approaches to traditional speech" and took the name "HMS School for Children with Cerebral Palsy". During my residency, the name (The Home of the Merciful Savior for Crippled Children) was indicative, in my view, of American society's perception of disability at that time.

I left HMS in the summer of 1973 with my father. I was able to use my walker to leave, wearing my long-leg braces, and I remember exiting at what seemed to be a quickened speed. I was wearing my University of Nebraska helmet, given to me by Uncle John, who played for the University of Nebraska. Nurse Anderson hugged me goodbye.

Instead of heading to the entrance of the Pennsylvania Turnpike to go west to Pittsburgh, my father made a detour. My dad was a ladies' man of his time, a hyper-sexual Italian American in the early 1970s. He took me to a topless bar. I suppose he wanted to bond with me—at the tender age of nine. This experience began the psychopathology of addiction that I would struggle with well into adulthood.

I returned to visit HMS in 2007. This time, I did not make a detour to the topless bar of the early 1970s—I went to Jim's Philly Cheesesteak instead. Ms. Wilson was still employed at HMS, now approaching retirement. She was 17 or 18 years old when she originally took care of me. Upon seeing me, now a man thirty-four years later, she exclaimed, "Louie! Oh my God, Louie!"

One of the staff social workers pulled me aside asking, "How did you get to see Santa Claus?" I told her the story of how we were corralled like cattle into the box truck with no windows. The staff had heard rumors throughout the years about how we got to see Santa Claus. According to them, no one could say for sure from a first-person residential perspective whether or not this was true. I recounted that it was indeed true.

A disabled person was categorized as underprivileged; that was how it was done back then. There was no public access to transportation; such luxuries were reserved for the privileged and wealthy. Society was not set up for "alternative" folks. My experiences at the Home of the Merciful Savior are imprinted on my soul.

what is a home?

My childhood home was on Tall Timber Drive in the quaint Pittsburgh suburb of Allison Park. This was where my family lived from 1970 to 1979. "Home," for me, might be an overstatement, since I was away during much of this time, either in institutional-residential care (HMS), in day school, or hospitalized to undergo numerous surgeries from '73 to '78.

In our early childhood, my brothers came to know me through photos Mom showed them of me every day I was away. I am five years older than Frank and seven years older than Ed, who was born on December 7, 1970 (the infamous Pearl Harbor Day).

Ed and I both had premature births. I weighed 3 lbs. 2 oz, and Ed weighed 2 lbs. 2 oz. In fact, as my father told me, they did not expect either my mother or brother to live. Ed was a fighter, but he also had technology on his side. I've always wondered whether I would have ended up with cerebral palsy if the technology of the 1970s had been around when I was born. Nevertheless, Ed and I will at least always have our early births in common.

My relationship with my brothers was very fragmented; even when I was home it seemed they had more of a relationship with each other than with me. The Fazio boys seemed to be only two. They would often go out and play with their friends while I was left behind.

But we had some good times together. One day my mom took us to the A&P grocery store, and as typical little boys, we got into everything. My brothers pushed me in my manual wheelchair when we came across the Pringles potato chips display. Pringles were a brand-new product, and my brothers and I thought the tubes of chips would make nice bowling pins. We didn't have a bowling ball, but we did have something that rolled. . . me. We didn't expect the whole display to topple over; but when it did, my brothers were nowhere to be found, and I was in the middle of all the fallen Pringles.

Then I heard a voice over the intercom say, "Mrs. Fazio, please come to the front. Your boys are at it again." Like a good brother, I blamed my siblings for the mess, though I can't say I was entirely guiltless.

Another area of fraternal fun was when we would be in the pool together. As a young boy, I was in fairly good shape and was able to hold my own in the water. This spelled mischief. My brothers and I would play Marco Polo, tag, and just horse around. The pool was one of the places where the buoyancy of the water created an illusion of normality: a place where I had even footing.

My mother felt the need to carry a wooden spoon to keep us in line in the car. We traditionally traveled across town to visit my Grandmother Vujevich. On the way home, if we behaved ourselves, we would tradition-ally stop at Eisley's on West Liberty Avenue for an ice cream cone. I think this was a strategic move by my mother because she realized that she would have to put up with three boys who were relentless in their fighting with each other.

One time, however, the strategy did not work. We were just about home when Ed, being more mischievous than ever, decided that he really didn't care about my mother's warnings of getting whacked by the wooden spoon or dealing with my father's wrath at home. Ed boldly took the wooden spoon and threw it out the front window as the car sped on. Even more incensed, Mother slammed on the brakes and took matters into her own hands.

In retrospect, my brother would have probably rather dealt with the spoon. My mother had the patience of Mother Teresa until she'd had enough. Ed now has four children of his own to handle. God does have a sense of humor.

We had babysitters when our parents went away and once for our father's business trip for the Auction. We promised to behave, but once we were alone with the sitter all bets were off. On one occasion, Ed (who always seemed to instigate the havoc) threw eggs over the roof; on another, he tried to squirt one sitter with the hose. My brothers and I didn't have a lot in common, but the babysitters provided us common enemies. We were no angels.

Frank did not get along with my father or my father's family and was very much a mama's boy. He suffered much of the physical and emotional abuse served by my father. Frank was a very intelligent individual and a very good student. I think he had a problem accepting that his older brother had a physical disability, from my recollection. Although, we do share something in common: we both went on to graduate from the University of Arizona. We actually did some crazy things together like when he came to Tucson to visit and went to my psychology class with Dr. Poole, entering the auditorium on roller skates. It was a big hit, as he rolled down the aisles of the lecture hall.

In 1973, when I was nine years old and having left the Home of the Merciful Savior, I became a "day student" at the D.T. Watson Home, where I would have school during the day and go home at night, except for when I had orthopedic surgeries. D.T. Watson was, for the most part, a great place. There are a few memories I wish to forget, but for the most part, the people who staffed D.T. Watson were compassionate and caring individuals who practiced with great faith the care and education of disabled children in the 1970s. Looking back, I was fortunate to come from a place of privilege, because it cost approximately $4,000 a year (1970's dollars) to send me to there. That's no small potatoes, considering my mother's parents were potato farmers.

This caused strain at home, as publicly, my father always said, "Oh, I'll do anything for my son," but, privately, he gave my mother a hard time when it came to the cost of my care.

Compounding this frustration, my dad always wanted me to be able to walk. My father did everything he could to somehow ensure that I would walk. This motivated the innumerable orthopedic surgeries, the purchase of a pool (so I could exercise), and Dantrium™ drug trials at the Butler, Pennsylvania VA. He even considered brain surgery for me. The only thing he didn't do was pray. He left the praying to my mother.

My mother's relationship with the Trinity was extremely important, not only for her personal growth, but it seemed to be a guardrail and the glue that kept the family unit together. The presence of the Church in our lives was driven by her. My father respected the fact that my mother went to church. That was her role, in his eyes. He looked to my mother for that type of support, no matter how dysfunctional things were. Even if he was not an active participant, he made it abundantly clear to us (the boys) that we were to obey our mother, especially with respect to our formation in the Catholic faith.

I received my sacraments of Baptism, Confession, and Communion. My mother would carry me up the stairs of St. Ursula's Catholic Church so that I could participate in the sacramental education of CCD (Confraternity of Christian Doctrine). In fact, my mother was a CCD instructor.

I truly believe that my father was hurting inside and did not know how to establish a relationship with God. Religion for my father was about appearances, not deeply felt convictions. Our family was rotting from the inside out, we were rotten to the core, in spite of my mother's genuine light of faith. From the outside we looked like a Norman Rockwell rendition of the ideal family, including family piety.

I believe that my father attempted to murder me.

One evening in 1973, my dad came home angry, as he often did, from work. This was a Thursday night, and I was watching *The Brady Bunch*. I heard him say to my mother, "I'm going to take Lou out to the water for exercise."

"I don't think that's a good idea. You don't seem to be in the right mood or frame of mind." Mom sounded concerned.

Unmoved by my mother's comments, my father said, "C'mon, let's go."

So, we were off to our backyard pool. Even though it was wintertime in Pittsburgh, there was a dome over our pool so that I could use the water year-round. That night, my father and I went into the pool for about half an hour. We got out of the pool, and my father placed me in my manual wheelchair with my back to the water. The next thing I heard was *splash!* And that was me and my wheelchair careening nine feet underwater to the floor of the pool.

I remember my father yelling, "Help! Help!" and my mother, who could not swim, screaming as she saw me lying on the bottom of the pool. Fortunately for me, our neighbor, Dr. Lou Scotty, heard my father and mother screaming and came running.

Supposedly, from my mother's recollection, my father, upon seeing Dr. Scotty, jumped into the water. I remember seeing my father through his goggles, looking to see if I was still conscious. He pulled me from the nine-foot depth.

My first utterance was, "I don't have to go to the hospital. I'm OK. God saved me." You see, even at the age of nine, I had been in and out of the hospital so much, I certainly didn't want to go back.

After my near drowning, I began to realize that the family I was in was dangerous. This realization was hard to understand as a nine-year-old. Traumatic events like this and my father taking me to the topless bar would shape who I would become forevermore. In retrospect, these experiences provided some explanation for my family's dysfunction. We were trapped.

Life went on. The grace of God continued to play a role in my childhood and adolescent development. My experiences after my father's attempt to end my life were also shaped by a newfound spirit that lifted me to greater heights. At D.T. Watson, I learned about the gifts of music and theatre. Joanne Pascarelli, who herself had polio and walked with crutches, was our teacher and one of my heroines. She was a stickler for making sure that our theatrical productions were of the utmost quality. I remember vividly, if we screwed up, she pounded on those piano keys and gave us the most ominous look and told us we could do better. My first performance was the music of Nat King Cole, one of my last was part of the *Star Wars* trilogy in 1978.

Mr. Larry Powell also left an indelible mark on my development. Not only for my disdain for math—he used to slap me on the back when I'd get something wrong—but he himself had cerebral palsy and walked on crutches. I admired him, since he and Mary Joe, who also had a disability and worked as a receptionist in the front office, were living fairly "normal" lives. I sometimes overheard them converse about putting things in crock pots or what one had done over the weekend. It helped me to imagine possibilities.

Toward the end of the school year in 1978, things again were changing. We rode in a mini school bus, rather than the green station wagon that had been used to transport us. At that time there was no funded special technology; therefore, the bus had no lift. My wheelchair had to be hoisted up the bus stairs by staff members and placed behind me. I also trained to move through cafeteria lines similar to what we would encounter in the outside world. We were being prepared for the culture that awaited us. Mainstreaming was on the horizon, and we were some of its first pioneers.

A notable field trip was to Point State Park Community College. I had a couple thoughts as we toured the campus. The first was *I'm glad to have been considered for this trip.* The second was, *I can see myself going to college—but not in Pittsburgh.* I knew that then. Finally, even though, overall, I had great respect for the staff at the D.T. Watson Home, my last thought was, *Thank God I'm getting out of here!*

While I attended D.T. Watson, my brothers only saw me when I came home at night (unless I was staying there for orthopedic surgeries), which didn't improve our bond at all. I personally feel that my disability also played a definite role in how our sibling relationship—or lack thereof—evolved. From my view, the conflict came from my father's feelings toward me. I think my brothers sensed my father's total lack of acceptance of my person and disability. Also, I think there was a bit of jealousy on the part of my brothers because my mother spent an inordinate amount of time around me whenever I was home.

As we got older, things began to change between us. There were lots of activities Frank and Ed didn't get to do because they had a brother with a disability. I think my father didn't like taking me around because he felt embarrassed of my condition. It was a part of the culture back then to want to conceal things like that. Our family often stayed home, and everything was centered around our house; everyone came to us. My parents thought that it was easier for everyone from extended family to friends to come to us, especially in the winter months, than for us to go to them. Our house became the center point for everything.

We had a huge basement. So, instead of having us go out, Dad created an arcade of massive proportions. My father was very talented; he built trainsets that would rival any science and industry museum, with the tracks going every which way. There were multiple trains on different tracks; they could go over each other, around, and everywhere.

I played with trains. We also had pinball machines, a ping-pong table, shuffleboard, and pool tables. The basement covered the whole area of the house—1,936 square feet—so it was huge. That was our playground, and my father's gallant attempt to provide amusement for the family, since he felt it was too much of a burden to do things in the traditional sense. This way, we never had to leave the house in the evening. The games were fun, but they soon lost their charm. I could see my brothers wanting to get out more, but my disability was holding them back.

Money remained a charged topic that my parents continued to fight over. The cost of my care, the cost of the disability, was always an issue with my father. One of the worst physical arguments my father and mother had was during the Christmas season of '77. At that point, my father was bringing in most of the income since mother had left full-time teaching and was only substituting.

My father and mother planned their annual Christmas party. Forty or 50 people would attend. My dad was a businessman and strived to put a good spin on things. Publicly, money was no object. Parties like this were a great opportunity for my brothers and me to ask for things, especially money—because the coffers would open. "Oh, you want $20? *Sure!*" As opposed to when we were alone, and it was just the nuclear family, "Hell no! I'm not gonna give you $10! Make it on your own. You boys have too much as it is."

I could always sense when things were tense at home. The evening after the big Christmas party, my brothers and I played *Monopoly* in the family room, while Mom and Dad sat at the kitchen table discussing the holiday expenditures. Mom was mandated to go over each line-item purchase, and I sensed a high degree of tension as we played.

We were accustomed to hearing our parents argue and yell, but this seemed particularly intense. I was 13 at the time, Frank eight and Ed seven. So, I said to Frank, "I think it's time for us to go to bed, guys. Frank, can you help me to bed, and help with Ed?" He did, and the next thing I remember my parents were screaming and *thud.* Mother screamed for Frank, so I told Frank to go help Mom.

Frank went into the bedroom and Mom later explained that the *thud* had been my father throwing her onto the floor, then he had put her across their king-sized bed and attempted to choke her. When he saw Frank, he stopped and ran out of the house.

My parents separated for a while, and I remember my Uncle Marion came for one evening. They went to the basement for a discussion, and everything was going to come back to some sense of normalcy.

That was our normal, but the abuse still went on. I was my mother's confidant, being the oldest of the brothers. We had this relationship where she told me more as young child than I think you should. She would say to me privately that my father was an NG: no good. I knew of his suspected affairs and even met one of his girlfriends. I witnessed and was subject to a lot of psychological abuse, and some physical abuse.

My father downplayed the issues and my mother rationalized staying with my father, believing that a good Catholic could not divorce. She also seemed to feel that she had built the marriage financially and wouldn't walk away from her investment, despite my pleas for her to do so. She would say, "Half the money is mine. We are staying together for the children."

I felt bad for my mom and there was nothing I could do. I felt powerless and somewhat responsible for their behavior, because a lot of times they were fighting over me. I longed to do anything to ease the situation for my parents, but I couldn't stop their fighting nor plug the money leaking from their accounts to pay for all my needs.

I've heard plenty of stories about people's disabilities bringing families closer together. My experience wasn't like that. Growing up with a disability in the '60s and '70s was difficult for everyone, but I was reminded often how much money my existence cost my family. My needs did not make us destitute, however, to give the reader an idea, my father's gross income in 1982 was $39,000, which equates to approximately $130,000 in 2025. The cost for D.T. Watson at that time was $3,000 to $3,500 a year (approx. $10,000 to $11,700 in 2025 dollars). The cost for my schooling was less than about 9% of their income. But for my father, it seemed like every cent he had.

The summer of 1978 was when my sense of self came into greater clarity. It was an amazing, confusing time. I was 14, and my mother gave me the book called *Love and Sex in Plain Language* by Eric W. Johnson. The first thing I did was express a sigh of relief. My dad was fairly nonexistent, at least when it came to my upbringing, so Mother was the driving force. With the book to inform me, I thought to myself, *Thank God, I'm not getting the sex talk from my mother!*

The next thing I did was scan the table of contents for homosexuality and masturbation, the two areas of my sexual being that I was dealing with. I saw sketches of men doing the activities I was curious about, and I started wondering what it would be like to have a boyfriend. Still, I wasn't ready to admit to others (or myself) that I was attracted to boys.

When D.T. Watson began serving individuals with learning disabilities or alternative learning situations in their day program, I noticed two of the guys were quite cute. Sitting with one in the back of the station wagon while riding home from school, he and I investigated each other's anatomy while the driver in the front eyeballed us in the rearview mirror. We would talk to each other during the night over the phone and ask questions such as, "Do you have any clothes on?" or some even more provocative. That was my first experience expressing my sexuality.

An awakening came the last week of June 1978, when I exited D.T. Watson and was finally emancipated from the institutionalization and day student program that our American culture found fitting. This was the week I was outfitted with the tools that would serve me from that point to the present day. I was introduced to my first power wheelchair, an Invacare, which I would ride into my independent future. I also began academic preparations for high school with my mother who faced one of her biggest challenges by becoming my partner in my educational pursuits.

This was an unprecedented time of transition. No longer would I be separated from my peers. I would now become one of the public masses, if you will. Fortunately for me, I had my mother as an advocate. As I have stated earlier, my mother was an advocate from the beginning, but what became even clearer, in retrospect, was her commitment and love for me, to academically achieve. This had profound effects for the rest of my life. My personal aspirations were to achieve higher education. I was driven by my mother's passion for education. I saw firsthand in her and her twin, my uncle Steve, what education could achieve. I had the opportunity to take hold of my own destiny.

high school

In 1979 I got the chance to finally sit with my peers in mainstream school. I wasn't sure what to expect; I remember talking to my dad about why I couldn't go to school with my neighborhood friends, and my dad said, "Well, when you can walk you will be able to go." So, the smartass I was replied, "How the hell am I ending up in high school when I still can't walk? God hasn't come down and healed me. What happened?"

Well, what happened was Public Law 94-142, section 504 of the Rehabilitation Act. Not divine intervention, but perhaps legislative intervention inspired by God. These laws were the beginning and the precursor, if you will, to the Americans with Disabilities Act of 1990. Public Law 94-142 gave me and others the right to be educated alongside our able-bodied counterparts in the least restrictive environment possible. This began the shift to community-based intervention from institutionalization, which had haunted the disability community for hundreds of years. This was our time of enlightenment.

The summer before high school, my mother spent countless hours helping me prepare for grade level placement testing. This testing would ensure that I was ready to compete with my peers in relation to my chronological age. Previously, while at D.T. Watson and in special education, I had been on an ungraded system. Now, I was to be placed with my peers on a graded system that eventually would foretell my educational future.

Fall 1978, I began attending 9th grade in Hampton Township. However, the most impactful experiences would come at a completely different high school in Timonium, Maryland. My father had taken a new job with a different automotive group in Baltimore, Maryland. The relocation of the family to Maryland, disrupting my 9th grade year, posed a challenge. Would I be able to enter the 10th grade at Dulaney Sr. High School, or would I have to go to Cockeysville Middle School to complete the 9th grade? My mother was keenly aware and orchestrated a battery of tests over the summer of 1979. I achieved grade level placement and began the 10th grade at Dulaney Sr. High School in Fall 1979.

Public Law 94-142 gave those of us with disabilities our desegregation. Bill, Jackie, Dan, and I were the first group of students with physical disabilities to mainstream at Dulaney. Not all students with disabilities who began mainstreaming at this time were welcomed. But in our case, as far as I knew, we were welcomed—with only some trepidation.

Bill, Danny, Jackie and I had Carolyn Wallenburg, who was hired by Baltimore County School System, to act as our academic support person. Carolyn, and then later Mrs. Rigley, was stationed in a room off the library, where she would help us with various homework assignments, testing, and so on. During this time, there was no such thing as assistive technology. Carolyn would write what we said, with no assistance in relation to content. We had to know our studies because in many instances, she didn't know the subject anyway.

Even with our newfound support and opportunity, this time of high school had its confusion. I wasn't quite sure what was going to happen. My friends began to work various part-time jobs as grocery store baggers, car washers, ice cream scoopers, etc. *What was I going to do?*

Would society allow me to work? How would I find a job? I asked my mom, "Do you think I could get a job?" And my mother said, as she always did, "You can do anything you think you can." That would bode well for me in the years to come.

Two classes stick out in my head from the beginning of my high school experience: Biology and Ms. Clem's World History. I enjoyed history, so it didn't seem like it was going to be much of a problem for me. I remember watching movies on the Holocaust, talking about WWI, WWII, the Treaty of Versailles.

Then there was Ms. Heiney's Latin class. We had to take a foreign language, so I picked Latin. In retrospect, I'm glad I did, because it helped me with the SAT. My verbal score is what would get me into the University of Arizona along with being in the upper third of my class. My mother and I spent countless hours at the kitchen table doing my homework. Mother was pulling out her proverbial hair when it came to my Latin. Verb conjugation—*amas, amat,* and *carpe diem*—is about all I remember. I think I got a "B" in the class, thank the Lord!

The other nailbiter was math. My father, who had only made it to seventh grade before later getting his GED, would vigorously complain and say, "Ann! How long are you going to be working with him at this kitchen table?"

We worked late from 6 p.m. after dinner into each evening. The nights he worked, I'd think, *Thank God he ain't here so I don't have to hear him complaining about Mom helping me with my homework!* I was driven by the memory of him coldly telling me when I was 12 years old, "It's gonna be either you or I that leave." I was determined that it would be me who would leave for college to prove him wrong, and for that matter my Grandmother Fazio, who had called me retarded.

We went home to Pennsylvania for Christmases during my high school years, and I'd stay with my Aunt Carole and Uncle Ed. On holiday I tagged along with my cousin Peggy to college parties when I was a sophomore and junior. Drinking, smoking pot, and whatever else you might think of, went on but in a civilized manner.

During these stays, my mother, knowing I was a bit explorative, would call the house and say, "How's Louis?" Aunt Carole was always covered by saying, "He's fine!"— even if I was drunk and throwing up at the time. That's why I chose to stay with Aunt Carole and Uncle Ed instead of my parents during holidays: It was a hell of a lot more fun!

I felt privileged, because Peggy never did really see my disability. She only saw her crazy cousin Louis. In fact, one night, she carried me on her back when I was too drunk to function with my chair and the snow. She just gave it up and said, "I'm gonna carry you!" All I can remember is us falling in the snow and making it home to her house and my aunt helping me over the toilet as I heaved more than a little.

Will was one of Peggy's friends during her high school and college years, and he does not know this, but, he was one of the first individuals I had a crush on.

The intersection of being disabled and gay merged for me in high school. That is when I began to ask God why he gave me two issues that, to me, were humdingers. I still wanted to experiment with individuals of my own gender. I had that feeling long before high school, but now it came to a head like a zit on prom night.

For a while, I kept it under wraps. I did not date a lot, being mostly consumed with homework. However, I had my first relationship with a guy around the age of 16. He would come over and we would fool around. I'm a romantic at heart, and he was my first knight in shining armor. He was also passionate and would help me with my personal care. I loved him for it, and still to this day think of him with great fondness.

By this time, my mom had stopped doing my personal care because she felt awkward. She would get me up and ready for school, but she no longer showered me, so that was left either to my father, who wasn't home a lot of the time, or my friends from high school.

My parents found out I was gay, officially, during my late high school years. I made the decision to have a discussion with them, a brief one at that. Sexuality was not really spoken of in the household, but I think they suspected for many years prior, either through behavior or action that they were informed about or witnessed themselves.

My father was a ladies' man, to say the least. So, to have a son who was disabled *and* gay, the *Mona Lisa* cried, and he became even more distant in our relationship. I feel as though my father struggled to come to terms with my disability, which he never truly did, let alone coming to terms with my sexual orientation. He was proud, in his own way, of my accomplishments. But there was a bit of cognitive dissonance—and indifference—if you will, in our relationship.

High school was also when I realized I had a voice. Mr. Capisio taught U.S. Government, which was foundational to my understanding of the power of our Constitution. Mr. Sledge, along with my speech instructor, Mrs. Holleran, gave me the understanding of the power of the word. Mr. Sledge taught college-prep English, and Mrs. Holleran taught speech and rhetoric.

I began to learn how to effectively use the power of speech and to this day am very cognizant of it. It is a privilege that not all have, but all have access, at least in this country, if they know how to gain it. This goes all the way back to how I used the dictionary as a child. I didn't read until I was in first grade. The way I learned was not only from Mrs. Laughlin, or by listening to my mother (who had an extensive vocabulary), but by reading the dictionary.

The power of words, written and spoken, is something to be reckoned with. I realized, specifically in high school, how important the verbal delivery of the word was. That was my most powerful weapon and/or gift, and I had a sense, even back then, that it was a gift from God.

I was often excused from class to teach seven periods about disability and being mainstreamed. I would share with other classes in my high school what it was like to have a disability and to come from a special education background. Mr. Don Leshke, who was a disability advocate, frequently accompanied me for these talks. As an aid for these talks, I would use a reeled projector to show a movie produced by the Maryland Governor's Commission on the Employment of the Handicapped. The gist of the film was that people are people, good or bad, no matter if they are in a chair or not.

I also did a bit of volunteering with an organization called The Brotherhood of Men, mentoring younger individuals with various issues. I learned about grassroots efforts of pioneers like Ed Roberts, the Father of the independent living movement; Harvey Milk, one of the first openly gay activists to hold civic office; Joni Eareckson Tada, who currently speaks on a global stage; and many others who have gone before, like President Franklin Delano Roosevelt, who hid his disability for fear of public backlash. These were leaders of men, women, and children.

Ed Roberts especially had an impact on me. Mr. Roberts was the first individual admitted to UC Berkeley to use a power wheelchair. I was one of the first individuals to attend Dulaney Sr. High School who used a power wheelchair. This parallel in education began the process of feeling the responsibility of speaking for those who, through no fault of their own, could not speak for themselves.

Starting my junior year, I was on Mr. McNamara's debate team. I wasn't the greatest, but I was on the team. I enjoyed the experience. I think that's what Ed Roberts wanted us to learn back then in the early '80s; we had a voice and to use it.

High school was also a time of just downright craziness and fun, from rites of passage like senior skip day to prom, which was yet to come. The summer prior to my senior year, I went to Ocean City, Maryland for senior week, which shocked my parents. I informed them at the breakfast table; I didn't ask them. My poor mother. She expressed concern about logistics, asking, "How are you getting there, and who's gonna dress and shower you?" I explained that my friends Danny and Kevin were going to drive us and they would help me with my care.

Danny had a minor case of cerebral palsy, which caused his walking gait to be awkward, at best, and his knees to be constantly bent. But he was certainly capable of getting around and driving. Kevin, one of my AB (able-bodied) friends, was not physically limited in the least. (AB/DB is not a singing group, but an acronym for *able-bodied* and *disable-bodied*.)

This trip to Ocean City provided my first opportunity to do whatever the heck I wanted. For a 17-year-old, this posed several issues. For one week, Kevin, Danny, and I enjoyed the nightlife of Ocean City, and during the day we enjoyed the sun on the beach. I think we drank a little, but not to excess. What I remember most about this senior week was the freedom it gave me to express and learn more about myself.

I really wanted to go into the ocean. I met a lifeguard, and after making friends with him, I wanted to see if he would take me out into the ocean; he did! And I got to go for the first time out of my chair into the ocean to body surf with him on the waves.

Also, my hormones were racing. Being a gay guy, I was in heaven. I had this guy, who was a lifeguard, holding onto me for dear life! What more could a gay guy ask for? If memory serves me correctly, we went into the water more than once. I'll always remember his kindness.

Even in high school, I had a sense of the compassion *of* others and compassion *for* others. Ocean City will always be in my heart as a place of awakening.

Later that summer we went on our one and only family vacation during the whole time of my childhood with the Pattersons to Busch Gardens, Virginia. This was the only time my father took us, usually my mother would take us places.

In January the last semester of my senior year, my parents informed me that they were moving back to Pittsburgh from Hunt Valley, Maryland. Originally, they were not supposed to move until I finished high school. However, my father reneged on that promise and said that we would be moving April 15, 1982. I was supposed to graduate in June that year. It would mean that I would not be able to graduate with the class I had spent three years with. I was appalled by this and felt betrayed. Not only by my father—I was accustomed to his betrayal—but for the first time, I felt betrayed by my mother.

By now having grown accustomed to speaking out against perceived injustice, I spoke out, reminding my mother that I would soon be 18 years old. This fact was undeniable to my parents, so I made it a point to tell them—remember I was a smartass–"Well then, technically, I don't have to move with you."

They replied in unison, "Yes, that's correct."

"Well, I'm not gonna go," I informed them that I would ask my friend John Faillace if I could live with his family from April to June so that I could graduate with my class.

John's family considered this, then he got back to me, saying that his parents had some concerns. One was architectural. They happened to live in a split-level home. So, where would I sleep? The other one was that the bathroom was on the second level. How would I shower? They also wanted to first meet my parents before agreeing to let me stay.

From an early age, I lived by the motto, "I'll figure it out." This was no different, except this time, I was truly able to figure it out because I was 18. My mother agreed to meet John's parents, while my dad (as expected) left it up to Mom. John's mom, Mafalda, who went by "Meff," was very gracious. She already had a plan for how it could work. My mother, being the overprotective mother of a person with a disability, expressed her overarching concern, "Are you sure? Is it going to be too much?"

Meff said, "No, we want to do it, so that Louis can finish high school with his peers. We will turn the screened-in patio off the living room into Louis' bedroom and put a refrigerator in there."

Even though it was difficult for me, I kept my mouth shut, since I saw the events going in the favorable direction.

I thought, *Ooh, that's a good idea.*

My mom asked, "Well, how about showering Louis?"

I was a little concerned about this myself. But, knowing the fact that John and I were good friends and that he didn't mind helping, I thought that there was a good chance that the plan would work. Sure enough, Meff echoed our plan that two to three times a week, John and his dad, Joe, would take turns helping me shower, first carrying me up the stairs.

I was truly grateful that John's family was willing to take on this role, and I believe my mom was thankful as well. On April 15, 1982, I awoke with excitement and said, "See you later," to my mom and dad and joined my new home and family, the Faillaces.

While living with John's family, I got to attend senior prom with my date, Paula Sooter. You might say, "He went with a woman? But he's gay." That's because it was just what you did back then. Even if you were gay, at least in my case, you still wanted to fit in.

Paula was a really cool girl with a disability herself. She walked with a cane. I was honored to have her as my date. John helped us to get there, Paula and I rode in the back of a pickup truck, with he and others in the front seat. Back then, there weren't as many accessible vehicles so you made your own. We had a great time and danced, which I love to dance, and it was one of my fondest memories of high school. Pretty tame, compared to some of the stories that swirled about, but it was my senior prom, and thanks to John and his parents, I got to experience it.

Graduation June 1982. Out of the 612 students, only five students did not graduate, due to unforeseen circumstances. Four were involved in a horrendous automobile accident, killing all of them. The fifth was abducted, and never to be seen again. His name was Jaime; I wish to pay him honor here.

I was a graduation speaker. That speech was mostly about my mother and a few anecdotes about how the elevator broke down, which prohibited me from making it to class. I spoke of what Dulaney High School meant to me as well, but most of that speech was about my mother's role in my education.

My mother was a licensed teacher and educator. From that perspective, I was privileged. Privileged, to have a mother willing to sit with me, every night, for three hours a night in my early high school years, to ensure that I passed such subjects as Latin, mathematics, chemistry, biology, world history, U.S. History, college prep English, the SAT. She was there by my side, as I climbed the academic ladder, coming from an ungraded system, called "Special Education," into a system that had expectations and markers of success and failure. I spoke of how my mother made sure that I succeeded in that transition.

I graduated in the upper one third of my class, which for me, was quite an achievement. But I am here to tell you, if it were not for my mother, I would not have had that same level of success.

The high school years were part of my human experience that led me from the hills and equestrian valleys of Pennsylvania and Maryland to the parched desert of the Southwest: Tucson, Arizona. Summer 1982.

college in the desert

In July 1982, I began a new life as a college student at the University of Arizona. When I arrived in Tucson for orientation, I had so much anticipation of what was ahead of me. I honestly didn't think much about what I was leaving behind. I was just grateful for the privilege to become a college student and thought to myself, *if only all the naysayers could see me now.* I thanked God, I know, because without Him, and without my mother, this certainly would not have been possible.

We landed at the Tucson International Airport, and we were dropped by limousine at the then Plaza Hotel, where my mom and I stayed, just off the University of Arizona campus. I met Melissa Veto Morrow, the director of new student orientation, who became one of my mentors.

I remember during orientation, dancing to Kool and the Gang's "Celebration" on the University campus, and it certainly was a celebration. I finally felt free to be myself—to discover who that was—and come into my own, both as a person and as an individual who became part of the University of Arizona. Behind me were the days of institutionalization at the Home of the Merciful Savior for Crippled Children and D.T. Watson Home. I felt privileged, finally feeling the chains of underprivileged existence being lifted.

My mom was as proud as the NBC peacock, and I could tell that even she, who was my greatest advocate, was, in her own way, shocked that this was about to happen. On my mother's side of the family, college was a big deal. Although my other brothers would follow, Frank going to University of Arizona as well and Ed going to Penn State University, I was her first son to achieve such a goal. Carrying this honor, I felt the responsibility to achieve.

Honestly, I was not always sure if I could do it. But I kept telling myself, *Yes, you can.*

Thankfully for me, at the time the university had the Disability Student Service Center located in the basement of the Education building. When my mother and I first went to this office, she was astounded that the director, who was in a wheelchair, had achieved his doctorate and many of his staff were in chairs or had other disabilities of their own. I saw pride in her face and a sense of the potential opportunity that awaited her beloved son.

One of the first orders of business was to set up not only my schedule of classes, but my personal care. Gene Chida was the support specialist who helped in that regard. Gene himself was in a wheelchair and was married, and my mother found that absolutely remarkable. At that time, I could still care for myself at night, so Mother asked Gene how much it would cost for my morning care on a monthly basis. Gene said, "Ah, Mrs. Fazio, I think $100 a month would be fair." So that began my personal care journey. And I shared a dorm with my first care assistant, John, at Papago dorm, located adjacent to the Arizona stadium.

Papago was World War II housing that had been converted to dormitory space. There were two bunkbeds in the room; I slept on the bottom, and John had the top.

John was my roommate for a semester, and Paul, who was an electrical engineering computer major, began to assist me in the second semester freshman year.

Paul was a pretty fun guy to be around. In fact, although my concentration was social sciences, we had some elective classes together.

In choosing my major, it felt as though, at least at that moment, I was beginning my identity separate from my family of origin. I was leaving behind their idea of who I was and forging ahead with the vision of who I would become. The major I chose was that of Rehabilitation Counseling, with a minor in Psychology. My decision focused on answering these questions: *How could I apply the knowledge that I would receive to help others avoid what I endured? How could I apply my life experiences to improve segments of our society that were marginalized?*

Paul and I ended up taking a psychology course together, along with his friend Kevin. Intro to Psychology was taught at the main auditorium (now named Centennial Hall), which held about 500 students. Paul, Kevin, and I sat up toward the top of the bottom level of the auditorium. Dr. Pool was our instructor. I dutifully listened to Dr. Pool's lectures while Kevin and Paul, being engineering majors, weren't so interested. They didn't cause much of a ruckus usually, but one day, Paul and Kevin were more gregarious than usual and decided to have a little fun—at my expense. They thought it would be funny to interrupt Dr. Pool's lecture about Freud or human behavior by activating my wheelchair horn during the lecture. How's that gonna get Louis in trouble? Well, when the able-bodied friends hide underneath their chairs so that the professor sees only Louis sitting in his wheelchair with the horn intermittently going off. At the second blow of the horn, Dr. Pool stopped his lecture and said, "Mr. Fazio"—I was surprised that he even knew my name out of the 500 students—"Do you find my lecture interesting?"

I said, "Oh yes, Professor, I certainly do."

He said, "Well, why then does your horn continue to go off on your chair?"

I did not have a really good answer to this question, other than to say, "I'm not quite sure," because I wanted to protect the two fool friends of mine, laughing underneath their seats beside me.

"Well, don't let it happen again."

I said, "Okay, Sir, thank you."

About 20 minutes went by, and again, the blast of the horn.

This time, Dr. Pool was not so nice. "Mr. Fazio, did I not ask you to ensure that your horn did not go off again during my lecture?"

Realizing that the two fools beside me didn't care if they made me look like an ignoramus, I decided the gig was up and exposed them, "Yes you did, Sir. And the culprits are sitting right beside me, hiding underneath their seats."

The story ended by all three of us getting reprimanded, and my being embarrassed beyond belief.

While living in Papago, my freshman spirit was ever-present, even when I wasn't in class. My friend, Frank, who lived in Papago with me, was a business and finance major and fairly conservative, as he is to this day. I, on the other hand, was not as conservative and tended to have a wilder demeanor.

Case in point: the infamous shower scene. Frank protested my idea asking, "Why would you do this? This is crazy." But help me he did.

That day, I took all the clothes and towels out of another guy's closet while he was in the shower and brought them to Frank's room. To make matters more interesting, I got ahold of a guy with a camera and had him line up some girls in our hall outside the shower. He readied the camera; there was no hiding anything. So, when the recipient of the prank came out of the bathroom, he yelled and had to streak out of the shower down the hallway (which I thought was awesome because he was pretty good looking). The girls were lined up, whistling at him, and the cameraman took his photo. He was very embarrassed.

He didn't know for a while who plotted this prank, but eventually someone spilled the beans, and unfortunately it came back to me when I was using the bathroom. Back then, my quadriceps were strong enough that I could transfer myself from my chair to the toilet. One day, I had just positioned myself on the commode with my chair in front of me when all of a sudden, I see my chair moving. The guys (the one whom I pranked and his buddies) grabbed me off the toilet, put me in my chair, and blindfolded me. They pulled me out to the parking lot, duct taped my hand to the joystick, turned the chair back, set the chair on high, and then sent the chair in circles until I threw up . . . a lot. They said, "We told you we were gonna get you back!"

Needless to say, I never pulled a prank like that again.

In my second year at the university, I decided to move from Papago to Babcock, which at the time was an upper division and athletic housing dormitory. This is where—for me, anyway—life resembled *Animal House* meets the University of Arizona, or even better, *The Revenge of the Nerds*, which was filmed on the University of Arizona campus.

Babcock was a great place to live and where I learned more about the responsibilities of being an independent young adult, while also managing to have a lot of fun. I kept up my academic studies without much trouble, but my Babcock years tested that goal.

One incident was being a human football for two of the university's great football players, Keith Moody and Gary Parish. This was around '83-'84, when I weighed about 115 pounds, so being a human football for those guys wasn't out of the question. There was a pool at Babcock that is still there today.

One particular Saturday, it became our playground. Gary, myself, and Keith decided that I, with my lifejacket on, would become their pool football. Gary and Keith would take turns bringing me up onto the diving board and jumping off with me on their shoulders. At the end of this activity (which we thought was a heck of a lot of fun), it seemed like there was more water out of the pool than in it. My Resident Assistant, Maryanne Schiavone, whom I still talk to this day, remembers this event vividly because this is one of the few times that I was written up by the head resident, Lee Byrd, for, shall we say, "behavior unbecoming a University of Arizona student."

During this time, if one might've said, "Louis can be a little crazy," they would've been correct, because shortly after the pool experience, I had another that was a little more serious in nature.

One night, when I returned from the Bashful Bandit, a local spot where I'd gotten quite drunk, I was screaming and hollering in the dorm. This landed me on probation. Bruce, one of my dormmates, questioned Maryanne about her decision to discipline me this way, though I don't remember this because I was three sheets to the wind.

"He's in a wheelchair," Bruce said, "why are you putting him on probation?"

To this, Maryanne replied, "Everyone is equal. There are no exceptions to the rule. Anyone who comes in after

10 p.m. drunk and causing trouble, male or female, one legged or two legged, gets put on probation."

I liked that. That was very important. There was no preferential treatment. But it was not the last time I got into trouble.

The Wildcat House was a nearby dance club off Stone and Speedway where all the U of A Cats went to growl—or meow, if you will—me included. My favorite drink at the time was a screwdriver. Well, thank God I had a screwdriver, because, as the night would have it, I was about to get screwed. I decided that I would dance and drink—which I don't do any longer. After having a good ole time, I left around 1:30 a.m., but I didn't get too far from the Wildcat House before I noticed blue and red lights behind me summoning me to pull over. Well, pulling over in a power wheelchair while under the influence can be kind of interesting.

The police officer approached my chair and said, "Do you know why I am stopping you?"

I, being a smartass, said, "No, not really, Sir."

"Well, let me tell you." And he proceeded to tell me that I had jay walked.

At this point I wasn't in much trouble yet, but now I was about to be. I told him he was full of it, and that I in no way could jay-walk because, if he didn't realize it, I couldn't walk. This did not bode well for me, and he promptly told me that I should watch what I say.

I then realized that he could not get me into his police car (back in the '80s, there weren't that many accessible vehicles), so I thought I was pretty safe. Well, think again! That wasn't the case on that Saturday evening. The officer had his own strategy of teaching me a lesson, one that I still remember to this day.

He said, "Young man, here's what you're going to do. You're going to follow me back to your dorm"—I had told him that I lived at Babcock—and I thought, *well, there's not much he can do.*

In hindsight, again, as you will see, I was wrong. We get to Babcock at about 2:30 a.m., that Saturday night. I thought, *Great! I didn't get a ticket! I didn't get arrested! He's just going to let me go into my room and sleep this stupor off!* No, that wasn't the case. As soon as we hit the parking lot, the whole dorm was awakened by the Tucson Police officers blaring siren and lights. Again, I thought, *There goes my clean record: a splash in the pool and now this!*

Sure enough, it is an experience that I am still, to this day, remembered for. The moral of the story is: *Don't drink and drive.* Today, they would have probably arrested me for DUI. So, in essence, I think I got off easy.

When you have a disability, whether physical, developmental, mental, or whatever, and when it's noticeable (because some are not), your life can be very structured and with less autonomy. I, on the other hand, was privileged. Even though both of my parents could be overbearing, they still attempted to give myself and my brothers as much independence as possible. And this included faith. My father didn't go to church, so it was up to my mom to provide the foundation for faith. I grew up as a cradle Catholic and had only been to Catholic Mass.

When I went to college, I explored a bit. I went to houses of worship of different faiths, and I still do this today because I think that no one faith has the monopoly on God. So, my autonomy of faith was heightened in my college years.

Some of my experiences exploring were good. Others were not. Regarding my disability, one gentleman from a Protestant denomination once asked me, "Do you know why you have your physical disability?" To which I replied, "No, tell me why." Then he told me, "It's because you don't have enough faith."

Needless to say, I never went back to that congregation, and being the smart-aleck that I was at times, I abruptly told the gentleman that he was full of horse feathers (but I didn't say "horse feathers").

A church I did go to for numerous years in college was Mountain Avenue Church of Christ, because my roommate Paul went there and they had a lively relationship with the Bible, which the Catholic Church of the '70s and '80s didn't seem to be encouraging for the laity.

During this time, I also tried to figure out what it meant to believe in God while knowing I was gay. I was always seeking acceptance, and I thought that faith would provide it. Much to my dismay, that wasn't always true. My experience was sometimes very disappointing.

The Newman Center, with Fr. Tom DeMan, was a place that I would go, but in retrospect I didn't take advantage fully of the resources available at the time. My faith was strong, but in many ways, I did not fully actualize my relationship with God. I knew I believed in God with all my heart. I was just trying to take the route of Baskin Robbins and sample the ice cream of the day. There are so many flavors to choose from. Also, being on the U of A campus, there were lots of options, and I was searching for total acceptance of my person among these various religious congregations.

After my sophomore year, I started working with Student Orientation for Melissa Veto Morrow, the Director of Student Orientation who had first welcomed me to the university. I was a new host, and one of the first, if not *the* first, person with a physical disability to hold that position.

That summer, I found myself in youthful exploration as it relates to my sexuality when I met Susan, a secretary on campus who filled in at the disability resource center. When I met her, I was 20, and she was 37. It tends to be that women who are heavier set are more attracted to me. She fit that bill. Because of this, she and I started talking. One thing led to another, and we began an intimate relationship. While I knew that I wasn't attracted to females, it became clearer through our relationship.

My mom would call almost every day, and she developed a pretty good relationship with my roommate. So, it wasn't long until she found out about Susan. I denied it telling her I didn't know what Jerry was talking about.

So, my mother sent my brother Frank from Pittsburgh for a visit.

Susan had a green station wagon, so we picked Frank up from the Tucson International Airport. There was immediate tension. In fact, when we were driving back to campus, my brother called Susan "Miss Piggy" (*to her face*) and called me "Kermit". She didn't like that, so she threw him out of the car and made him walk the rest of the way to the dorm. I locked him out when I got there.

Only a day or so later, the three of us had a huge fight in the parking lot while Jerry was on the phone giving my mother real-time commentary. Other people noticed, too. It was some spectacle, I'm sure.

Susan is one of the few women whom I dated, and my mom did succeed in putting a wedge in our relationship. But she didn't know (nor did my brother) that during this time Susan had told me that she was pregnant.

We broke up, and I believe she moved back to Texas. She told me in the end that she was never pregnant. But I honestly am not sure what the truth was. I could, potentially, have a son or daughter that I don't know about.

A funny thing about the relationship with Susan was that when it ended, one of the last things she said was,

"Don't hide in the closet," just as I was literally coming out of my closet.

Looking at this with some objectivity, it was a real learning experience for me and part of the process of accepting my sexuality.

My freshman and sophomore years I studied but didn't give it as much attention as I did during my upper division courses. I think my junior and senior years, I grew personally and academically. These years were full of more academic development and more buckling down on my degree. I could see the light at the end of the tunnel.

The Centennial Celebration for the U of A took place in 1985, which I was honored to be a part of. Being an orientation host, there was a sense of pride for the university and a sense of privilege to be a student at that time and to remember the history of the University. There was a sense, walking (rolling, in my case) across campus, that the university was on the move, and that we remembered our history.

Senior year: that was a good year. We did the Capstone project, and I did my practicum at Pima Community College. I have a lot of respect for my supervisor, Deborah Gateley McKeen. She was in a wheelchair herself, and she was married to an able-bodied individual. I looked up to her and wanted to emulate her. This was one of the times when I knew that I could do something with my life. Of course, Debbie and my vocational rehabilitation counselor, Roxie Meck, she herself also in wheelchair, were people whom I saw as role models.

During this time, I applied to be a page for the State House of Representatives at Arizona. I didn't get it because of my writing deficit at the time, and they didn't have computers. But I tried and was able to meet with four or five senators who wanted to meet me specifically, even though I didn't get the internship to be a page for the House. I thought, humbly, at that time, *Well, what's so special about me?* I think they were impressed that I applied. They thanked me for my application, asked about my vocational pursuits, and wished me well.

I did not graduate in Spring of 1986 as initially planned; I took an extra semester. Summer vacation and the fall semester of 1986 were jam-packed. I went to Las Vegas, hiked Sabino Canyon, and had some adventures with my friends.

After returning from Vegas, my friend, Greg Taylor, who was part of the University wrestling team at that time, and I decided to make one of my crazy dream-ideas a reality. I told Greg that I wanted to climb Sabino Canyon. *How would we do this?*

Babcock, again, was a backdrop for my idea. Summit Hut, a climbing store which is still in existence today, was also part of the plan. Greg and I went to Summit Hut and rented a climbing backpack. For those of you who are climbers, you know that the backpack is tied to a frame. Well, Greg's idea was that I would become that backpack, and he would carry 130 pounds of dead-weight. Thank God he was a wrestler!

Do you think he could do it?

We needed to train. How would that happen? Again, Babcock became the backdrop. Here comes the train-ing. We decided that we would use the stairs of Babcock as our training tool. Greg took a day on a weekend and put me in the frame of the backpack, and then, from the floor of my dorm room, picked me up in the frame, and placed me on his back. This gave new meaning to "He ain't heavy, he's my brother." Greg had me up, to my amazement, and now we just had to tackle the stairs together. We climbed the stairs and then descended. We climbed the stairs again and then descended. This process repeated itself until Greg felt confident that we could do this at Sabino Canyon.

At this point in my life, I was much more limber, and I weighed next to nothing, so this was feasible. However, I was still dead weight. My spirit, on the other hand, was alive and well.

The day came for the hike. We took the rental car and drove to Sabino Canyon. I was anxious to see if we could do it. Divine intervention intervened, and we achieved climbing Sabino Canyon. In fact, the trams that still run today stopped to watch this climb by two individuals who were unknown to most.

Greg and I finished climbing Sabino Canyon and then jumped into the waterfall pools below.

There were so many moments in Babcock. My university years are moments that will be etched in my memory as experiences of growth.

I was also greatly impacted by my friendship with Steve Kerr, who went on to have a remarkable NBA career as both a championship-winning player and coach. I still occasionally have the pleasure of being in contact with Steve.

I remember fondly my U of A days with Steve and the guys. They would pile me into one of their cars, and we would travel to Bobo's Restaurant, an American diner that has served Tucson for at least 45 years. Bobo's was part of an experience of being included, being part of something, and being with my friends.

Steve was a resident at Babcock when I was, and he was popular, but unassumingly so. His girlfriend, Margot, was in a sorority and was also popular. I did not know Margot as well as I did Steve, but I do know that she had good taste in her decision to marry him.

I got to dance at his wedding with his mother. Steve has overcome a lot, from loss to physical challenges. He lived in Beirut, Lebanon, where his father was tragically assassinated back in 1984, coming off the elevator, where he served as president of the American University. Steve does not know this, but he is one of my heroes and has inspired me to keep going through my adversity and purposeful suffering. It has always given me the sense of privilege to call him my friend.

When I was able to spend time with Steve, I knew I was in the presence of a man with great compassion. Even at the time, when both of us were only babes in this world, I had a sense that he was a man of character, similar to that of Martin Luther King, Jr. And, in fact, he had spoken quite eloquently directly to power.

When Steve was a student athlete in the mid '80s, playing in the PanAm games, he injured his knee. I don't know if he's going to remember this or not, but my recollection is this.

He said, "Sweet Lou,"—that's what he called me—"my NBA career is in jeopardy."

"Why?" I asked.

"Because I hurt my knee."

"So, what does that mean?"

"I won't be able to play on the professional level."

I honestly don't remember word for word what I said next, but it was something like this: "You won't be able to play, only if you don't think you will be able to play! Can you get us into McHale center, before it is open?"

"Yes," he said.

"I want to meet you there."

"For what reason?"

"I'll let you know when I am there."

The day came. We met each other. We were alone in the arena. I then told him to go to the floor of McHale, and that I would stay on the concourse level where we entered. I told him to run or walk up to me. He did. He repeated this more than once. Again, the moral of the story: I asked him how his knee was. He said it's okay, or something to that effect.

The rest is history. I am in no way a healer. I do believe I am a motivator. Steve went on to play in the NBA for both the Phoenix Suns, the Orlando Magic, the San Antonio Spurs, the Cleveland Cavaliers, and the Chicago Bulls. Steve is all of 6'1" and is one of the best three-point shooters the NBA has ever seen. But I will say, without hesitation, knowing Steve personally, the reason that he is one of the best three-point shooters in NBA history is certainly not because of his physical stature. It's because of his heart. This hero for me (which he doesn't know he's one until he reads this) loves me unconditionally for no other reason than my humanity. Now head coach for the Golden State Warriors, Steve is a warrior among warriors.

This is another gift of the University experience, that it leaves an indelible mark in the souls of all who attend by affording the opportunity to meet many special individuals.

One of the courses I took during my final semester of senior year was on rehabilitation in the prison system taught by Dr. Ken Fisher. Steve and I—not Kerr, one of my classmates—were partnered up and were to do a research project on folks with disabilities and incarceration. This was what we wanted to learn about, for both males and females.

We went to Florence, AZ, which is between Phoenix and Tucson. At the time, Arizona State Prison (now with "Complex" added to its title) in Florence was one of the largest, if not the largest, co-ed facilities. Steve and I went early one morning. Not having access to a wheelchair-accessible van, we drove in his car (I was a lot skinnier then, so I could ride in the passenger seat. We brought my manual wheelchair and folded it to fit in the back.).

Our goal was to interview three or four individuals on their incarceration experience and having a disability. So, we did just that. We met one lady, who held up a convenience store, who had a mental disability. We interviewed another gentleman. He was an amputee, and the interesting thing about his story was his telling me, "I just don't understand why they won't give me my arm back!"

I said to him, "Oh, yes, I think that's terrible that they won't give you your arm back! I'll ask the warden for you." We were there eight hours, and in the sixth hour or so, we went to the warden's office, and I asked about this gentleman's arm, "Warden, I have a question. Why don't you give so-and-so his arm back?"

"If the gentleman would like to claim his arm, he may do so, but if he does, that will add to his sentence. It will add to his drug possession charges. His wooden arm was where he had been caught hiding drugs when he was apprehended."

We collected our notes, and we were supposed to be sent on our way.

The warden asked us, "Do y'all need a guard to walk you out, or are you familiar with where you're going?"

"No no, we know where we're going; we don't need a guard."

As it turns out, we really didn't know where we were going. The Florence facility was a big facility. Steve had been pushing me in my manual chair the whole day. I said to him, "Steve, I think we're los, Bro."

We approached the work release gate, and we came up, and the guys were whistling, hooting, and hollering at us (two young dudes, fresh meat, I guess), so we went up to the guard and asked, "Can you let us out?"

"Who are you guys?"

"We're from the University."

"Well, how do I know that?"

"We're telling you the truth!" Just as we tried to explain ourselves, the radio came in from the warden's office about two students from the U of A out by the gate.

Steve chimed in, "They're talking about us!" So, we showed him our IDs, and we were allowed to go.

Finally, graduation, December 1986. It took me an extra semester, but I made it. I wasn't always sure I was going to make it, but thanks to people like Bonnie, who did a lot of my notetaking, I made it.

My parents came to my graduation, along with my Uncle Ed and Aunt Carole. This time period was one of reflection and excitement. I think there were approximately 5,000 of us who graduated that year, both in May and then December, at the McKale Center. I felt like I had my whole life ahead of me.

Debbie, my practicum supervisor for that final semester, felt that I would be a good counselor for the Disability Resource Office at Pima Community College. At that time, Pima was smaller, and there was one room dedicated to Disability Student Services. So, it was just her and I.

I would help her with students and whatever task was needed. I worked with people with Lupus and other physical and developmental disabilities. I remember saying to myself, "I enjoy this." So, Debbie worked on getting me hired on as a beginning counselor.

They were going to hire me the Spring of 1987 and pay me $5 an hour. Back then, that was okay, because minimum wage was $3.75 an hour, which was what I had made as an Orientation Host.

This was my plan, so I stayed in Tucson and moved out of Babcock dorm to live in my own apartment on Drachman Street. I also needed a personal care assistant, but I struggled to find someone reliable to be in-home with me. I ended up living again by myself and having folks come in to assist me.

I enjoyed the flexibility of having someone come over while also having privacy. However, there were definite periods of loneliness. This was when I began to realize that I, too, struggled with not truly understanding how my sexual orientation, disability, and everything else about me made sense, except through my relationship with God.

I began to have a conflict of conscience. I wanted to be a good person in the eyes of God. But I also wanted to be able to be who I was. Considering I had just recently gotten out of a relationship with a woman, I wasn't quite sure who I was.

In late January 1987, my father called me and offered this proposition: "How would you like to work for the company that I work for?" My father offered to put a good word in for me to get into the management training course at Cox Enterprises in Florida Auto Auction, Orlando, which was one of the largest auto auctions in the system.

My immediate reaction was, "Hell no!"

My father's response to that was, "I wonder who's going to pay your bills."

I then said, "Well, I have an interview with Pima Community College, Downtown campus."

"How much are they going to pay you?"

"I think $5 an hour for 40 hours a week."

"Well, I think you should look into working for Cox Manheim."

"I don't know."

My dad said, "I have a trip for the general managers out to Phoenix, with Mr. Warren Young Sr.,"—who was then the president of Manheim—"I would like you to come out and meet him during the general managers' meeting."

I said, "Okay, Sir, I'll set it up with my friend John," who could drive me to Phoenix. We drove to Phoenix to meet my father and his fellow general managers, Mr. Young and Joe Greco, Sr.

I had already met Joe and had known him since I was nine years old. Joe worked for my dad at Butler Auto Auction, Gibsonia, Pennsylvania, somewhere around 1973, when he started as his accountant.

Joe had replaced Mariel, who was my father's bookkeeper for years. Mariel died of a form of cancer. I remember going to visit her in the hospital, as a little guy, and I knew that my dad had a great respect and love for her. That was one of those times when I saw my father's humanity.

After the meeting I told my father, " I would like to stay here in Tucson."

"I don't think that's possible. Manheim's Florida Auto Auction of Orlando is a much bigger option, and they will be able to sustain and support some of your disability-related needs."

This was before the Americans with Disabilities Act of 1990. So, in hindsight, my dad was pretty sharp. However, the ignorance of youth still prevailed, and I fought my father tooth and nail about staying in Tucson versus being uprooted, leaving my friends, and moving to Orlando, Florida.

Basically, I was a spoiled brat not thinking of the big picture of life after college.

My father was a stern man, so our conversations were pretty one-sided when I told him, "Okay, I'll consider it, but I need to go visit the Auction." So, that's what I did. I went to visit the Auction in February.

I was there for a few days; everyone was very nice. Joe was there, too. Honestly, I wasn't quite sure what I could contribute. I honestly think they didn't know either. They thought I had a pretty good knowledge of computers. I guess so, for the time, which helped me. But I still wasn't sure how I could fit into this organization.

My mother was involved in this as well. The first offer I received from Cox Manheim was for $12,200 to start basically as a manager trainee. My mom said, "Nope. Don't accept that."

I thought, *Well, okay.* I still hoped I could stay in Tucson, so I called my mother, and she said, "I'm going to talk to your dad and see what can be done as far as your starting salary."

The final offer came in at $16,200 a year.

I thought about it, and my dad asked me what I was going to do. I told him, "I appreciate it, but I'm going to turn it down."

He said, "You're what?"

I said, "I'm going to turn it down and wait to see if I could get a job here in Tucson."

My dad, in his forthrightness and candor, said, "Good luck to you. I think you're making a mistake. How are you going to pay your bills?"

I had just turned 23, so I thought I knew everything about the world. I also prayed about this situation. And, after all the wrangling with my father and praying to my Heavenly Father, I decided I would take it.

the grand experiment

In March 1987, I left Tucson, Arizona and embarked on a journey to Orlando, Florida. There, my first days were spent at the airport Holiday Inn, and Tommy from the Auction, would come and pick me up and take me to the Auction location. As maintenance manager, he outfitted a retired company van with a lift for me to make my daily trips to the Auction.

Despite this professional opportunity, it was a time of profound loneliness because I had left my friends behind in Tucson. The first night I was in Orlando, I was supposed to have assistance from an agency, but as fate would have it, they did not have anyone to assist. I decided that I would ask someone whom I met at the hotel bar to assist me in going to bed.

Being 23, I was pretty fearless, and my boundaries were not always intact. As it turns out, the guy who helped me go to bed wanted to do more than just help me go to bed. For me, this was a learning experience because even though I agreed with the initial intimacy and sexual contact, I didn't agree to his anal penetration. I was raped.

Male rape is not as common as female rape, or it is underreported; in fact, I didn't report my rape. Even now, to this day and time and space, it is difficult to articulate my feelings. I would not be truthful to say that I was not a willing participant, but when someone says stop, the person should stop. And he didn't.

I haven't shared much about this incident, except in recent years. It's something that will always stay with me, as part of me, and it certainly has shaped me.

The morning after my rape, I suppressed it and moved on. When Tommy came to pick me up, no one was the wiser. No one at the Auction ever knew that I was raped. I put my game face on, as I had done on many occasions when I would suppress something. It was the first day of my first "real" job in the world outside of the University of Arizona, and I had big shoes to fill.

My initial hire wasn't really about what I knew, in my opinion, it was about *who* I knew. (Or was it?) My name was a double-edged sword. Because I was my father's namesake, the expectation of my ability was extremely high. My father had worked for Manheim since their acquisition of Butler Auto Auction in 1968, and he had already begun working for the auctions in 1964, the day I was born. Through the years, my dad built a reputation for being somewhat of a showman and later an icon of the auto auction industry. He was president of the Pennsylvania Independent Auto Dealers Association, and he was well respected in the industry. In 1987, he was still the general manager of Butler Auto Auction. In 1989, he was promoted to vice president of Factory Fleet Operations. I would have to fight to not be encompassed by my father's shadow.

Many times, people would whisper as I rolled by, "That's Lou Fazio's son." I don't think Cox had ever hired a manager-trainee who happened to have a severe disability. Their whispers would mean one of two things: either *watch what you say around him* or *he's just where he is because of his father.*

In 1987 when I first had the opportunity to work for Manheim (Cox) we didn't have the ADA. But I had Joe Greco, who compassionately directed others to ensure that I was integrated into the Auction. Joe took the time to listen to my mother, who came with me, prior to the start of my employment, to find apartments. He had Tom drive me and my mother throughout Orlando in the company's green station wagon to look for one.

The apartment we found was in Altamonte Springs. It was in an area that my mother felt comfortable with (and I did as well), and I could roll to the grocery store in a nice environment. It was also close to the Church of the Annunciation. The apartment complex was called "Timberlake." They offered accessibility prior to ADA. It had a roll-in shower, one bedroom, and the rent was affordable with my salary. It was $385 a month. The challenge: it was 45 minutes away from the Auction. *How was I going to get there?* I had to be at work by 8 a.m. So, this is when the Auction embraced me once again, not being told by a law for reasonable accommodations.

John Saullo and Steve Robinson, along with Scott Keener, found me Bob Bentz and his wife, Flo. Bob lived in Longwood, which was adjacent to Altamonte Springs. Bob would come and pick me up every day, Monday through Friday, at about 7:15 a.m. so that we could get to work by 8 a.m. Bob worked as a jump cart driver, in our outside operations area, on what we termed "the field". That is where all the cars are parked, numbered, and stored. A jump cart driver is a person who would ride around on a golf cart with a radio and, for the cars that had bad batteries and needed to be moved, Bob was one of the guys to call. His wife Flo worked in our main office in the Title Department. We would meet every day at about 5 p.m. to go home.

As the years went on, we got to know each other fairly well. Bob would take my shoes off when I got home. I was in better physical shape back then, so, it would help me do other things that I needed for myself before the person who helped at night would come. In fact, I even helped one of my neighbors across the hall who was also severely disabled, who worked for AT&T in their IT department. I helped him warm up things in his microwave if his personal care assistant was late.

This compassion of others ensured my success. As things changed in our culture over the years and as the corporate culture became more prevalent, as opposed to the stand-alone independent culture, a lot of these qualities would be sadly suppressed. From 1987 to 1989, I was in the management training program, and pretty much stayed to myself. I would be on the phones, eight hours a day, inviting dealers to come to the sale, or I was doing calls on late bank drafts where the dealer owed us money, or I was in the Title Department.

I also served in what was termed the "Limo Department". That department was headed by Kevin Bonner. People were careful around me because they knew I was connected to Joe Greco and Lou Fazio, Sr. Their ties went *way* back. So, while also working in the Limo Department, I was watched with skepticism. *What is this guy going to do? Is he going to tell on us? Is he going to expose us?* I know this sounds like something out of a spy movie, but that's what they considered me: a spy. I was a direct line to the general manager. Dolly Rice, who supervised me in what was known as the "call girl" department (later to be termed "Sales and Marketing"), said one day, "You have lots of power." Everyone knew that I did. I, of course, tried to downplay it. It was all about integrating into the culture.

Each Auction ran independently and was strongly steered by the general manager. The culture was very independent. The general manager, Joe Greco, had a lot of power. The corporation, Cox, did not interfere with the operations of the Auctions at that time. They were considered independent entities, and they were run as such. FAAO (pronounced, "fay-oh", Florida Auto Auction of Orlando), as we were known back then, was the granddaddy of the auctions.

The only competition with us in volume and sales percentage was Manheim Auction in eastern Pennsylvania, Philadelphia area. They had many more lanes than we did, but let me tell you, Joe Greco was a man on a mission, and he was determined to overtake them. We grew exponentially from when I first started, expanding from seven to nine lanes. When my career ended, we had at least 23 lanes.

Let me explain why auction lanes are so important. Back then, we didn't have internet to the level we do now. We didn't have virtual auctions. It was rubber-meets-the-road and very personable. The lanes were where the cars went through to be sold, just like cattle, if you will. Each car was numbered by our lot personnel as it came into the Auction. The Numbering Department worked with our outside operations team to make sure that each car had a number and a lane. The more cars being sold at the facility on a weekly basis, the more lanes were needed to sell said cars. Pretty simple equation and procedure, right? But it took painstaking hours and a lot of manpower for this operation to run seamlessly on sale days.

Our primary sale day was Tuesday, and our factory car sale day was Thursday. We had the factory sales for General Motors and Chrysler. Every other week, General Motors and/or Chrysler would run their cars on that particular day. Those cars also had to be numbered and placed properly to be ready for sale. This also required many acres for the cars to be stored as they were unloaded off the transport trucks. We were a huge operation in this little city called Ocoee.

The auction process included many frontline employees who were dedicated to making certain that the dealer was taken care of while they were at our Auction. This is the formula that made Cox billionaires. Interestingly, today, Cox's main source of revenue is not its communication holdings, but its over one hundred Auctions that they now own. Many of these Auctions were independent when they were acquired by Cox.

In '90 or '91, Kevin Bonner began to phase out of his supervisory role over the limo department, primarily due to his emphysema. He had worked as an iron worker and smoked a lot. I had a great deal of respect for Kevin. He also knew that I was well connected.

One sale day, Kevin became ill and could not come into work. That began my upward rise. Joe Greco's assistant said Kevin wasn't coming in that day, and would I be okay? I said, "Absolutely. No problem here. We are ready to go and serve the dealers." So, from that exchange, I took the reins and never looked back.

The Limo Department was responsible for picking up dealers and customers and bringing them to the sale day with the company fleet of vehicles which numbered over 100 at the time. We were also responsible for coordinating efforts with the "call girls," inviting dealers (our customers) to our location. I ended up also supervising that area for a time. Our customers, the dealers, were usually from out of town and tended to be high rollers, so they brought great revenue to the Auction.

However, it wasn't an easy road; I had to prove myself and show that I had what it took, separate from my father. Even though my father had no influence over my day-to-day operation or location, he still was in corporate management and was a force to be reckoned with. I had the responsibility of 15 people who were a lot older than me, except for a few. And, for the most part, they didn't like me.

One person who didn't particularly care for me was Gary. Gary was a little older than me and hoped he would become manager when Kevin left. Quite frankly, this is where my father's influence did help. Honestly, I had my college degree, Gary did not, and I also had the backing of my boss on top of the influence of my father. In 1991, I was given the title of Public Relations Manager, after being supervisor of the Limo Department for approximately a year and a half. I still felt the pressure to establish my own professional identity.

My early years of management were difficult. Joe Greco was a fantastic general manager with high expectations. I had known Joe Greco to be a kind and compassionate man of great heart, the same man who had helped me secure this job to begin with. That being said, the five years I worked for Joe, frankly, on many occasions, had my stomach turning. Here are some stories to illustrate my point.

On Fridays, we were responsible for all fleet cars within the company Auction fleet. That included all management vehicles as well. The Limo Department was tasked with maintaining these vehicles. We would literally take each vehicle into the lanes and wash them by hand. I would help my crew as best I could from my wheelchair. One gentleman in my department was Larry. Larry didn't like me and thought that he would pull a fast one. I asked him to go and get Joe's car, a black 1989 Cadillac Fleetwood, his pride and joy, to begin the washing process, by hand. I thought I made myself pretty clear, but again, as fate would have it, I guess it wasn't clear to Larry.

Larry took Joe's car and ran it through the mechanized car wash at the local gas station. I, back in my office, saw the lanes, thinking everything was sailing right along, with no problems. Then I heard over the loudspeaker PA system, "Fazio! See Joe in the Main Office!" I thought, *I wonder what he wants; he usually calls me on my office phone.*

I went to Joe's office; he shut the door. "Have you seen my car lately?"

Trust me, when Joe had a certain look, you only said, "Yes Sir" and "No Sir." My voice trembled as I replied, "No Sir, I didn't see your car lately, but I sent Larry D. to wash your car."

"Walk with me to the lanes."

I should have realized that something was up, because most people cleared a path as Joe and I walked to the lanes. And, sure enough, I was right. When we got to Joe's car, my head began to throb, because his beloved Cadillac Fleetwood was now covered in swirl marks going throughout the paint. I couldn't quite hear my thoughts over his yelling.

He then asked me, red-faced, "What the hell are you going to do about it?

I had to think on my feet. Thank God I was sitting down. I said, "But Sir, what I told him was—"

He stopped me and said, "*You're* the manager; it doesn't matter what you told him!"

"Yes Sir. I'll take care of it."

"My whole car is going to have to be repainted."

From that experience I learned that Larry didn't like me and wanted to get me into the proverbial doghouse. I learned that I could not always be a marshmallow. From that day on, I thought, *I'm not going to let this happen again.* Over the next couple of years, I was pretty much a hard ass. Rumor had it that they even called me "Little Hitler". They were afraid they would go to the woodshed.

Go to the woodshed? That's what my office came to be known as. It was endearingly termed this by Bill Ingles, a driver for me in the limo department. Bill was in upper management himself from his previous career and had since retired. He called my office the woodshed because this is where the rubber hit the road when my folks didn't do their jobs. Joe Greco even called me into his office to tell me to take it easy on my folks, because he had been getting reports that I was a hard nut. So, I figured Joe's training paid off, but maybe I should've held back a bit.

Larry was eventually released for being insubordinate, and I continued under the tutelage of the Joe Greco School of Management. No university class could teach me the value of customer service like Joe did. It was all about the customer, the dealer, and quite frankly, the employee.

In 1991, during one of our anniversary sales, which happened every second week of July, I had three to four years under my belt, working hard as I could to please Joe and to stay out of his way as much as possible. By now, my department had expanded, as well as my responsibilities, with a team of 20-25 individuals who helped me carry out the frontline customer service activities, along with a part-time administrative assistant or secretary. My first administrative assistant was Kay.

Kay was an older woman, in her late 70s, who had retired from the corporate world and worked at the Auction for extra money in her retirement years. Joe asked our operations manager of the time, John S, to find someone to help me administratively. Kay became that woman.

As it turns out, Kay's daughter was secretary to Attorney General John Mitchell under the Nixon administration. The Auction had another connection to

Watergate beyond Kay's daughter: one of our dealers, Mr. Eugenio Martinez. One day I was watching television and there was a documentary on the individuals who broke into the Watergate Hotel. To my astonishment, it was Mr. Martinez being profiled as one of the plumbers (infiltrators) of the Watergate Democratic Committee Headquarters who had a hand in the whole affair and operation. I was like, *Oh my goodness! That can't be!* Sure enough, I asked Mr. Martinez directly, whom I saw almost weekly. And he said, "Yep. That's me."

Kay was the first of four individuals who served as my administrative assistant throughout my career. She had a sign on her desk that said, "Mine is not to question why, but to just make sure the train keeps rolling." She knew that when Joe was a-callin', it was time for everyone else to shut up and keep their head down. I ended up doing *something* that wasn't what was supposed to be, and Joe's voice did not need the PA system.

In the early years, I did not want to remain with Cox, Manheim. The first year for instance, I didn't know anyone, so I was coming home, going to bed, getting up, and going to work. The American Dream, but sometimes it felt like a nightmare. I thought to myself, *I went to four years of college . . . to get yelled at?* However, those first five years of my employment were the most foundationally beneficial. I grew because of those five years, and though they were some of the most grueling, they were also some of the most memorable.

Joe, I know, stood up for me in those first years when people were saying, "Louis is just where he is because of his father." There were many nights and days when I was managing that I worked more than 60 hours a week, and I got paid for 45. So, the argument of, "He's just where he is because of his father" didn't hold much water with me. Especially when Joe would just downright chew my ass out!

When I asked Joe Greco if he would contribute any-thing to the book, he looked at the draft for this chapter and responded, "What about the fact that you were a part of a team that took a 500-car, five-lane, 22-acre auto auction in 1980 to an 8,000-car, 25-lane, 250-acre auto auction in 1992? The World's Largest Auto Auction. On an Anniversary Sale we registered over 12,000 units, and sold 73%, a record still standing today. We also had the only Factory Sale with Chrysler, Ford, and General Motors on the same day.

"We had dealers attending weekly from over 35 states. I did not realize that I scared you so; I thought you knew that you were on my team, no matter what. We sold for Toyota, Lexus, Volvo, Mazda, Chrysler, Ford/Lincoln, General Motors, Kia, Mitsubishi, Subaru, Land Rover, Infinity, Hummer, Avis, Budget, Hertz, Thrifty, Dollar, General. Handled $65,000,000 in sales every Tuesday. AND WE HAD FUN!!"

Sadly, in 1992, Joe was let go. I will only say that he was a general manager of heart, care, and compassion, both for his employees and customers. I knew Joe since I was a little boy, and I personally hold the utmost ad-miration for him. According to Joe and my father, upper management was worried that the employees would not work for anyone else.

I believe Joe's departure changed the Auction. He was not always an easy man to work for, but he taught me many things and stood up for me when fellow em-ployees would challenge me.

Tony Gerardo took over Joe's position and was a good man, but in my view, in the year and a half that he was at the helm, he was there just to hold it together. Like I said, the Auction was never the same, as the spark was not quite the same either.

Then we had Robert D. Mowers, the general manager from Riverside Auction, California. He was promoted to general manager of Manheim Orlando, FAAO. They called "Rob the Bean Counter." He could make Abe Lincoln cry, on both the $5 bill and the penny. In his first management meeting, he instructed all of us to cut staffing by 10% across the board. He viewed the Auction differently and had a vision of what would make a better Auction. Florida Auto Auction of Orlando, was, at that time, in the '80s and '90s, No. 1 in the auction system for Manheim Cox. But things were beginning to shift.

There was a culture of caring when I first arrived there at Cox. Ike Henderson, the general manager before Joe Greco would supposedly send cards to each individual dealer for their birthday. Joe Greco kept that spirit going. But now it was slowly eroding, becoming a culture more about the bottom line, the IBD culture (Income Before Depreciation). When Rob Mowers came to us in 1994, I believe he struggled and was conflicted with controlling the costs and honoring the service of the employee.

One example: the Anniversary Sale, which took place every second Tuesday of July. We would give it our all, and, traditionally, we would get bonus checks for that sale, management and employees alike. Well, after the Greco era ended, instead of getting bonus checks, all the employees got were Mickey Mouse watches. One could say a Mickey Mouse watch is fitting in Orlando. But I think our employees missed the extra money.

That being said, there were ways the culture was changing for the better. In 1994-1995, we were offered a supplemental benefit: long-term care insurance, administered through John Hancock. This was offered only for one year. I seized the day, *carpe diem,* and added it to my benefits. Thank God I did—and I do thank God. Little did I know that I would need to use it sooner than I thought.

Another thing for the better was that we were becoming more diverse. When I first started working for the Auction in Ocoee, Florida, there were very few, if any, Black individuals working for the Auction and were either drivers or worked in the office. There was a definite demarcation between those who worked in the field on the big lot that encompassed 300+ acres, and those who were in the office.

When I first started working, down south in Ocoee, Florida, I was told, "Watch what you say because you never know who you might be talking to." And I thought, *What did that mean?* Well, going up from Ocoee up the road there was a sign, back in 1987, that said the following: "If you're Black, don't let the sun set on your back." Being a 23-year-old at that time, I was naïve and didn't much think about race relations. But in fact, that sign said it all.

During my tenure at the Auction, early on I was tasked with hiring for our upcoming Anniversary Sales in July 1987, '88, and '89. I hired hundreds of people. I thought to myself, *you know, we should be hiring a more diverse population.* However, I didn't see a lot of diversity coming to apply, at least in the early years. So maybe that sign did what it was supposed to do: keep diversity away.

By 1990 or so, we became more diverse. As a hiring manager, I always tried to follow the advice and words of Dr. Martin Luther King, Jr. "Do not judge a person by the color of their skin, but by the content of their character." That is one thing that I learned in my early years at

Florida Auto Auction Orlando that no college class could teach: the day-to-day results of structured racism.

In 1989, we had the great fortune, on the corporate level, of having Darryll Ceccoli become president and CEO of Manheim Auctions. He empowered me in my career. My biggest issue of the time was the cost of my personal care and getting to and from work. Fortunately for me, I was part of the management team, which afforded me the privilege of a company vehicle. I also had lobbied for personal care assistance to become part of my compensation.

In 1994, under Rob Mowers, my personal care became part of my compensation. It was an additional $20,000 per year paid by the Auction to individuals who assisted me. Many may say Rob was a man of the bottom line, but Rob and Darryll Ceccoli coordinated the effort to make my personal care part of my compensation, which I will forever be grateful for. Rob himself had severe back problems; I think this is why he had great empathy for me.

This brings up the point of "reasonable accommodation". In my humble opinion, that was more than reasonable. That is why I worked my hardest with honor and pride. Darryl Ceccoli would later call this "the grand experiment". He meant that I was breaking new ground. My disability was pretty "severe", but if someone truly took the time to look at my abilities, they could see that the "experiment" was worth it.

Rob stayed with us until 1996, when Charlie White came aboard as the new general manager. To this day I still talk to Charlie over Facebook. Charlie was a man of vision, and he attempted to bring back the Joe Greco era of customers and employees as the backbone of the Auction's success.

Charlie always said, "You gotta have fun at what you do!" I took that to heart. In 1997, the University of Arizona basketball team was in the Final Four. I watched them play at a restaurant bar with my department (we would have quarterly dinners together, as a way of saying "thank you") and the Wildcats won. It was Saturday; they would be playing the Jayhawks in the championship game the following Monday. So, I asked one of my team members, Mike, if he could go with me to the championship in Indianapolis.

I was determined to go, and for those who know me, if I'm determined to do something, look out because I'll move every mountain there is to make sure it happens. This is one of those times the mountains began to move. Mike and I were on a plane that Monday morning headed for Indianapolis. The only thing was, we didn't have a ticket to the game. However, I did not let Mike know that until we got to Indianapolis. Mike happened to ask, "Do you have our tickets," and my response was, "No, but I'm sure we'll get them."

Knowing the type of person I was, Mike just shook his head and didn't say much about it until we got to the ticket booth. He was curious what my next move was going to be. I asked the attendant, "Do you have a ticket for the upcoming game this evening?" After she stopped laughing and called me crazy (or asked what type of drug I might be on) she said, "I'm sorry Sir, we're sold out."

I said, "Are you sure?"

"I'm sure."

"OK, I'll figure it out," I said or something to that effect.

Then Mike asked me, "I know you're crazy, but what are you going to do now?"

"We're gonna go to a scalper."

Sure enough, that's what we did. Mike was like, *Oh my God.* Outside the arena, the first guy I went to I asked, "How much are you selling your tickets for?"

His response was "$250 per ticket."

This was quite a bit higher than the going rate for the ticket, at least double, so I said, "No, I think I'll shop around."

I went to the next guy, and he was even a little higher per ticket. I thought to myself, *I was never really good at math, but $250 per ticket sounds pretty good.* So, I bought two $250 tickets. Part of my challenge was over, but there was more to come.

After my haggling with various scalpers, Mike and I decided to go to the Spaghetti Factory to eat dinner and to have enough time to go back to the room, freshen up, and get ready to leave for the 9 p.m. tipoff and for me to prepare our entry into the RCA Dome, since the tickets I'd purchased were not wheelchair accessible, but I didn't care. At least I had tickets, and, in my mind, possession is nine tenths of the law.

"We got the tickets, now we just have to stay in the arena. Just let me do the talking."

Mike responded, "OK, I have no other way."

I told Mike that we should look like we know what we are doing. I'd gotten things that looked like press passes which were actually conference attendee-type badges, with lanyards, that I put around our necks. And I used my wheelchair to my advantage.

We went to the accessible entrance, which happened to be on the floor-level of the arena; this was good for my plan. Plus, there were a lot of people, so the next part of the plan was to act like we knew what we were doing and where we were going, for that matter.

I headed toward the floor, and Mike followed. We sat in an open seat on the floor, and I said to Mike,

"We're here buddy. The only thing we have to watch out for is security."

My premonition of trouble wasn't that far behind. Sure enough, security asked for our tickets. "This isn't your seat."

My response was, "Oh really? I didn't know that." A little white lie. I then asked the security person where our tickets were, as far as seating was concerned. And he pointed up to what seemed like Mt. Everest. I said, "But Sir, I can't sit there, that isn't an accessible area."

He said, "Well, young man, you're going to have to go back to the ticket window and see what they can do for you."

I asked for the elevator, and he pointed it out to us. We headed over. This was about 20 minutes before tipoff.

Mike said, "Louis, we're gonna miss tipoff!"

"No, I think we'll be okay."

We get back to the Arizona ticket window with about 18 minutes to tipoff. As luck or Fate would have it, the person that told me earlier in the day that there were no tickets left for sale was the same person who was manning the Arizona ticket window. In all honesty and candor, I said to myself, *Oh shit!* But, knowing we traveled this far, and the fact that I truly wanted to see this game, I had to keep plowing ahead. So, I was ready.

When the lady asked me, "Weren't you the young man I told there were no tickets?"

I said, "Yes ma'am, you certainly were."

She asked, "Well, how then did you get a ticket?"

I said, "Do you want me to tell you the truth, or do you want me to lie?"

"Never mind." I think she figured out that I had scalped the tickets, which is illegal especially if you pay over face value!

She said, "Well, I hate to tell you this, but I absolutely don't have a place for you to sit."

I said, "But I'm bringing my own chair! Can you not just find me a spot?"

"But what are you going to do with your friend?"

I thought, *Well, he can sit on my lap.* But I actually said out loud, "Can you please just help me out? Considering how far I've come and the tenacity I've had to get to this game, since I'm coming from Orlando? You could even put us in the press box!"

About five minutes before tipoff, the ticket agent, who I think had a bit of comical empathy for us, came back to us and said, "Well, I guess I am gonna put you in the press box." And, sure enough, that's where Mike and I sat for the NCAA Final between the Jayhawks and Arizona, free drink, food, and all. So, it was well worth the investment.

The Arizona Wildcats, much to my pleasure and excitement, won in overtime, 84–79, as we were pounding back free drinks and food. As you may or may not know, *I love to eat.*

a love triangle of sorts

I was lonely. I was somewhere new, starting my job as a manager-trainee for Cox Manheim at Florida Auto Auction of Orlando. I would go to work in the morning, go on the walkway to public transit, and then come home, put something in the microwave, wait for the person to come put me to bed, and do that whole routine again the next day.

On the weekend, maybe I'd read something, walk around or go to church at the Annunciation Catholic Church with Fr. Calvary. I struck up a friendship with the youth director named Terry. He was a few years older than I was; I was in my early 20s. As fate would have it, Terry ended up helping me a time or two with my personal care. He is also gay, so that helped me. His sexuality was not publicly known at the time for fear of losing his job with the church or his later career with various public-school systems as an administrator.

Terry was an example for me. Here was a man who was gay and who belonged to the Church, even worked for the Church. Terry's parents, Anne and Bill Sullivan, became an integral part of my life. They were also originally from Pittsburgh. Through their love for each other, they had a large family. Two of their sons, Terry and Jim, are gay. This was a Godsend for me. My family was not as accepting. God was once again interweaving the framework that would allow me to thrive while providing the needed support that I so desperately craved.

Bill and Anne were and are a great example of the beatitudes. They are also one key reason that I remained a practicing Catholic. God has always been present to me. Jesus has placed people to protect me in my darkest moments, such as Anne and Bill.

Bill worked at FAAO as a limo driver in my department. Bill was a man of few words, but he had great character and conviction. He also ended up living close by when I lived on Bridgewood Trail in Pine Hills, a suburb of Orlando. Anne and Bill would have me over for dinner. I would roll to their manufactured home, or Bill would pick me up by leaving his car in my driveway and we would take my minivan to their home.

While I was thankful for my relationship with Terry, I didn't have a close friend in Orlando until I met Jeff. I became kind of tied to his hip. We did everything together.

I met Jeff Eckert in 1988. Jeff was 18, and I was 23. We were like oil and water at times, and our tempers would flare, but we ended up being good friends. The first time I met Jeff was at the Auction in the lanes. He was walking through the lanes since he was a driver for the Auction, and I was rolling through the lanes myself. That day, I had to go to the bathroom quite badly and knew that it might not be so pretty if I didn't ask someone for help. Our paths crossed, and I asked him if he could help me use the restroom. He said, "Sure!"

He would always smile. I had seen him a couple times before, and I would think, *Wow, I want to meet that guy, because he always has a smile on his face!* After that first meeting, we ended up going to dinner at Olive Garden in Winter Park. Jeff stayed overnight; he actually had to call his mother to let her know where he was, considering that he was still living at home.

This was the start of many interesting times ahead. Jeff was a cyclist; he lived in West Orlando. So, I asked

Jeff if he would like to come over one weekend to my apartment in Altamonte to hang out, and I even asked if he would like to race wheelchairs. In this case, the chair and the bike. Obviously, we both knew who would win, considering my chair went about five miles per hour, and he went up to 35 mph—it was the beginning of a friendship.

Jeff's family became my adopted family. When I had my wisdom teeth pulled, I stayed at their home to recuperate. I met his sister Kathy, along with his mother Maureen and his stepfather Mike Mannion. Having them in my life was very important since I was extremely homesick for Tucson. Jeff's family was interwoven with my life from this time on.

Jeff also became one of my drivers and began to help with my personal care. He also began to work directly under me in the limo department. This was very helpful because I wouldn't have to ask any other managers to enlist Jeff's services; I oversaw his hours.

I liked the fact that Jeff was a friend before he became my caregiver. At least in my experience at this time, personal care assistants don't usually become your friends, because the relationship is transactional. They're your acquaintance, and they spend a lot of time with you, at least in my case: three hours per shift, six hours a day, 42 hours per week. The fact that this time is transactional has taken me a long time—still to this day—to cope with and evaluate. It has caused me to cross boundaries because when you spend so much time with a person, and if you like the person, you begin to think, "They're my friend." However, that is not always the case, sometimes they're just there to help you. So, if it works, I like to have my friends help me because then they're my friend *and* they help me! Not always doable, but that seems to be what I like best. Does this model cause problems? Yes.

In my friendship with Jeff, we pushed the boundaries. Sometimes I was his supervisor, sometimes I was his friend, and he was sometimes my caregiver. But that's not what Jeff saw; he saw something different. From what I know now (and I don't want to speak for him, but I'll try to put myself in his shoes), I was this guy who was clingy, in a wheelchair, wanted to be around him 24/7, and quite honestly, didn't give him that much time to breathe! This became even clearer to me when he met Jenny.

To be honest, when Jeff started dating Jenny, I felt like we were getting divorced. There's been no one quite like him since. I mention this because I don't think I'm the first person to feel this who happens to have a physical, developmental, or mental disability or challenge.

I don't think Jenny really knew whether she was supportive of my friendship with Jeff or not. I think she was as nervous as I was, maybe because we both had pretty strong personalities.

For example, when Jeff and Jenny first met, we were all supposed to go to Cirque du Soleil in Orlando. I ordered the tickets and decided where we were going to sit. I had us all sitting together in one area, and in hindsight, I think Jenny wanted to be closer to Jeff, which caused definite friction between us because I had Jeff and myself together and Jenny off to the right. Needless to say, this seating arrangement caused some issues. In fact, Jenny said, "Louis, do you realize what you did?" And I think I remember saying that I didn't think I did anything wrong. It was pretty much a given that Jeff and I would sit together, and anyone else could take a hike, including, from my view, his then-girlfriends.

When I met Jenny's parents, they were very gracious, but I do believe that the family in general would rather have had me roll back a few paces—maybe over a cliff.

No longer was I the center of Jeff's life. There was now someone who occupied the center, and I had to learn how to be content with occupying a much less significant role. Our friendship continued while life circumstances caused challenges along the way. The opportunity for reconnection would have to wait.

a conspiracy: the grim reaper approaches

In 1990, I had the opportunity to attend a Cursillo, which is an opportunity for one who is Catholic to experience God, Jesus, the Holy Spirit, and His brothers in Christ on a much more personally engaging and intimate level. The closest comparable retreat for our Protestant brothers and sisters is Walk to Emmaus. My friend, Jim Byrne Sr., was vital to my being able to attend the Cursillo, after speaking about it with me on various occasions. He asked if I would ever consider attending. I said I would.

The time then came when I could attend a Cursillo weekend. Jim graciously acted as my personal care assistant and served as part of the team in the kitchen so that he could be available for me in the early mornings and late evenings for my personal care. This also provided the flexibility if I needed him to assist me with the bathroom throughout the day.

This weekend brought me closer to the Trinity: God, Jesus, and the Holy Spirit. One of the big events was listening to others' testimonies on how Jesus had affected their humanity and their earthly lives. One activity that still remains with me is that of receiving letters from loved ones and friends in relation to what you mean to them and how they truly value you as an individual.

This was a surprise for all of us to receive these letters of encouragement. The other surprise was at the end of the retreat, family members and friends would come to the concluding Mass. My spirit was on fire. My soul had a sense of awakening. This was the mustard seed of my adult faith formation.

I began attending catechism class for confirmation students. During this time, I also faced the question: *How can I be same-sex attracted and have such a strong faith?* It did not seem to add up to me. I was in my early thirties. I had struggled with being same-sex attracted and my faith since a very early age. How could God love this about me?

My answers came in the form of the Cursillo, my friendship with Jim, and my confirmation. I took the confirmation saint name of Jude. Jude is the patron saint of hopeless causes. I definitely felt like I was a hopeless cause. God, Jesus, and the Holy Spirit were working within me. I just had to be willing.

I was confirmed at St. Andrew's Parish in Orlando. Fr. Andrew O'Reilly played a vital role in my confirmation. He is a missionary of the Society of the Precious Blood. God was definitely calling me during this time. Between the Cursillo and my confirmation, my relationship with God and Jesus and the Holy Spirit was growing. I even began serving as a lector at St. Andrew's Parish on a regular basis, thanks to my friend Maureen, who dutifully served as a lector alongside me and assisted in making the text bigger every week that I read.

I wondered, *What is God calling me to do?* Maybe He was calling me to the priesthood. It came to a pinnacle in the mid-1990s. I kept feeling the desire to see if I could become a priest. I asked myself and God, *Are you nuts?* I've said that before—to myself *and* God. I have learned that no, God is not nuts. So, in 1998, I found myself discerning the priesthood actively, to the point that the then-bishop of Orlando considered the option of placing me at an accessible seminary in California.

I told my father of my intention and discernment. He was actually quite pleased. He felt that if I were being called to the vocation, the Church would be able to assist me for the rest of my life. Surprisingly, my mother was not so much in favor of this possibility. She questioned whether or not it would be a good idea. I, too, was questioning the veracity of my discernment. My mother knew of my sexual orientation, and I don't believe she felt it would be appropriate. But she never expressed that thought to me directly.

Through much contemplation, I decided not to pursue the call to the priesthood, due to my active participation in same-sex sexual activity, which is an act of "grave depravity", according to Church teaching (CCC 2357).[2] I humbly felt at that time I would be doing a disservice to God and His Church.

Also, during this time, I began to have issues surrounding my disability that necessitated having orthopedic surgery to once again release my hamstrings bilaterally. I further chose to experiment with the Baclofen pump created by Dr. Leland Albright to reduce spasticity primarily in children. But, as my privilege would allow, I chose to try this for myself at 34 years old. So, I had it inserted during my orthopedic surgeries for my hamstrings. For six months I would be in post-op rehabilitation at Harmerville Rehabilitation Center, up in Fox Chapel outside of Pittsburgh.

During my absence from Manheim's Florida Auto Auction of Orlando—now called Manheim Orlando—my occupational struggles began to take root. The team that was acting on my behalf in my absence began painting a narrative of my faults and inadequacies as a leader aimed at ousting me from my position during my medical leave of absence. My father got wind of this and learned that the conspirators seemingly had the support of the Auction upper management.

Did Charlie White know about this situation? To this day, honestly, I don't think he did. In all honestly, I can't say for certain what the motives or objectives of my team were, either. But I knew that Charlie might have been weighing the financial perspective. I had a driver that drove me for the Auction, not to mention my yearly personal care costs upwards of $20,000. Being an expensive employee due to my disability, I could understand, in hindsight, why this coup narrative might have occurred.

So, it was a rough occupational life. I truly did not know whom to trust.

When I finally returned to work post-surgery, the family atmosphere I had tried to create was not there, so much so, that by 1999, approaching the new millennium, I felt it was time for a change. I loved doing what I did at Manheim's Florida Auto Auction, but I didn't feel comfortable.

As fate would have it, Rob Mowers, whom I'd worked for in the past, was leaving his post as regional vice-president for the Western region to become general manager of Manheim's Central Florida Auto Auction. So, in early 2000, I joined him and Manheim's Central, about a half hour to the south. By this time, I felt that if the team didn't need or want me anymore, I would go to a new team.

I became Dealer Service Manager, and I supervised the Limo Department at this auction as well. For a brief while, I supervised the Sales Department as well. In essence, I supervised 75 people, including another supervisor and one manager.

Working with Rob and the team at Florida Central Auto Auction lasted for about a year. In the end, I wasn't happy there. I felt like my talents were not being fully utilized. Whether that's true or not, I asked Rob if I could transfer back to Orlando. I'm not quite certain Rob ever truly understood why, considering part of the issue with Manheim's Florida Auction in Orlando was the coup. The work conflicts I experienced were tiring me out physically, emotionally, and psychologically.

To recharge, I looked forward to visiting my cousin Peggy, who was living in Washington state. Unfortunately, my trip never happened. My mother informed me that Peggy had been tragically killed on her way from work one rainy night, when she had pulled off the roadway to wait out the storm. When she re-emerged back onto the roadway, she unknowingly placed herself in imminent danger as a motorist plowed into her from the rear, killing her instantly.

This event changed my uncle and aunt's trajectory forever. It also left me without the cousin whom I so admired and loved. We seemed to have had a spiritual connection of sorts. I will only know the truth when we meet each other on the other side of the veil.

My father and I didn't spend much time together at this time, even though he was Florida-based and remodeling the Manheim Central Auto Auction. I remember he came to my house maybe once during those two years.

"I have something to tell you," my mother said with a tone that made me uneasy; it was the code phrase for me to brace myself. "Your father had a stroke. You need to come home."

He was in a coma, completely unconscious. It was the weekend before September 11, 2001, the date that changed our country forever, and also a time, in my view, that would change our family forever.

I did not immediately go home to Pittsburgh. On 9/11, the Tuesday after my father's stroke, I headed over to the Auto Auction when my phone rang; it was my mother. I immediately asked how my father was, but she was more acutely concerned at that moment about a possible terrorist attack from the skies over Pittsburgh. The plane that she was most concerned with happened to be United Flight No. 93, which ultimately crashed in Shanksville, Pennsylvania. That flight did go through Pittsburgh airspace, and if not for the heroism of the crew and the passengers on board, they might have (as many have speculated) crashed into the White House.

Right after September 11th, I transferred back to Manheim's Florida Auto Auction. Charlie White and I began to have a better relationship that shattered the narrative my conspirators attempted to promulgate in 1998. Charlie, aka "Boss," as I liked to call him, developed an amicable understanding which I believe enabled him to see through my coworkers' thinly spun fabrications about me.

I gained a new position when I returned, becoming the community relations manager, with public relations as my primary responsibility. Interestingly, my office was to be on the second level of the newly expanded part of the Auction, so I had to rely on the elevator which got stuck on a few occasions, stranding me in my office. Eventually, the decision was made that I would move my office to the front of the building on the first floor, which was much more practical.

I was not in my new position long before I finally did fly home to Pittsburgh to visit my father, a month or so after his stroke. This was the beginning of more turbulent times to come. I remember going to my father's hospital room at North Allegheny General Hospital, rolling out of the room, and saying to the nurse, "Are you sure you gave me the right room? That isn't my father."

"Is your father Louis Fazio, Sr.?"

"Yes ma'am."

"That is your father."

I remembered my father as a strong man of huge presence. Instead, I saw a man who seemed quite vulnerable, who could not even open one of his eyes, sitting on a chair, drooling. To say I was shocked would be an understatement. A friend had come with me from Orlando, and I said to him, "I can't believe that's my father."

My father's precarious situation also brought with it financial issues related to inheritance. While I was still in Pittsburgh, my mom had asked me to come to Mars National Bank to add her to one of my father's bank accounts. My name was on this account. I wasn't even aware this bank account existed. I concluded that this account must obviously have been set aside for my care and disability-related needs. *Why else would my father have put my name on one of his bank accounts?* She wanted me to take $40,000 out of this account to give half to each of my brothers. I told her, "I don't think that's a good idea," and I refused to do it.

Several days later, I eventually reneged and agreed to allow Mom to do what she wanted to, and I would give my brothers $20,000 each. However, in order to secure the account, I insisted that it require both my signature and my mother's. I figured that this would prevent anyone (i.e., my brothers) from just taking money from this account. My mother was not pleased.

"What do you mean we need two signatures? It's my money!"

"But Dad put it aside for me and my care. Why are you being such a bitch?"

"Excuse me?"

This devastated my mother. I called my own mother a bitch. I know the devil is real, because in times of distress, especially distress of faith, the devil does his best work. The weight of my regret burdens my soul to this day. The woman who gave me birth and life, I had questioned, even disparaged.

Ed learned about this, and it did not help tensions between me and my brothers. My mom was the glue that held the family together, but even in relation to her, there was a source of tension. My brothers were jealous of the closeness I had with my mom.

In retrospect, I don't know if my financial reluctance was the right choice or not. My mom was trying to ensure family cohesion. But I was so overwhelmed at that point, praying by my dad's hospital bedside, praying to St. Jude, praying for forgiveness for cursing at my mother, and praying for my dad to recover.

My mom was overwhelmed as well. I wasn't even aware of the fatal burden that she was carrying, in addition to the many financial complications and my father's situation about which she hadn't told me.

I put my mom's name on the account, coming to this agreement: I would give each of my brothers $20,000 and there would be $60,000 left. I used the $60,000 to pay off my house in Orlando because I knew Mom would be living with me.

My mother indicated that if my father was not getting any better, we would have to make the decision of whether we were going to pull the plug or not. He was in the Allegheny General Hospital in Pittsburgh. My head was spinning faster than any merry-go-round or top I knew of. I thought to myself, *Pull the plug? What the heck does that mean? We're not pulling a plug from a socket or an outlet, are we? We're pulling the plug on our father.*

Granted, he was a son-of-a-bitch at times, but he was still my father.

I went back to the hospital room. This time the nursing staff knew me, since I had instructed them earlier to ensure that my father's blinds were open, and that the CD player by the window please be on playing his favorite artist's music, Frank Sinatra. They said they would.

I held my dad's hand and said to him, "Dad, we're gonna pull the plug if you don't come out of this coma. If you can hear me, please squeeze my hand." I knew that, like me, my dad's not a quitter; he might be down, but that doesn't mean you can count him out.

So, sure enough, he squeezed my hand. At that time, the neurologist came into the room, and said, "Who are you?"

I said, "I'm his son."

"You need to come back more often; this is the most activity we've seen out of your father in weeks."

I said, "Yes doctor, thank you." And, sure enough, my dad started to come around.

My dad was soon interacting with doctors and family members and began a year's-long recovery. He was transferred to Harmerville Rehabilitation Center in Fox Chapel; ironically, I also went there for rehab three years earlier after my orthopedic surgery. In fact, some of the staff still remembered me. Now it was Lou Fazio, Sr.'s turn.

The patriarch who hated hospitals, who would not usually come to see me when I was hospitalized, was now a patient himself.

My dad didn't want any nursing home care and begged my mother to bring him home. She did so, and took care of him, all of 2001 and 2002. Aunt Betty and I agree that my mother's care was the main reason my father recovered as well as he did and lived so long after his stroke. Little had I realized what else she had been dealing with.

By early 2002, I returned to Orlando and began my new work as Community Relations Manager. My father was recovering, and exciting paths lay open to me ahead.

January 2002, I received a phone call from my mother. It was not my father who was in medical trouble now. She let it be known that she had been struggling with multiple myeloma, a form of bone cancer for about four years. I hadn't known how sick she truly was. She wanted to protect me, something my mother was famous for. I just figured she was in declining health from old age and the stress of caring for my father. Now that I was given the truth, it was too late. The woman I love, my mother, was dying.

This was the woman whose statement at my birth was, "Since I don't have an average child, I'm not going to be an average mother." This was the woman who, in the 1960s and '70s, when there was no ADA for accessibility, would, with her 5'1" frame, out of true love, lift my manual wheelchair and put me into the car and out of the car to go shopping at Joseph Horn's, Coffman's, or Gimbal's, never once complaining, and me just knowing that she loved me.

This was the woman who would pray behind closed doors twice a day and was totally selfless toward me. She was my biggest advocate.

During those last months of my mom's life, I think she lost the sparkle in her soul due to her trials and tribulations. It is said that God does not give us more than we can handle. I always question that maxim when it comes to my own journey, and I wonder if my mother questioned it as well. Hopefully, I can ask her that question in

Heaven; I hope my mom will be waiting for me, to escort me to the other side.

My mom died October 30, 2002. I was at work, in an off-site management training seminar. The Human Resources Department sent someone to tell me that my brother Ed had called and told them that my mother had passed away. As best I can recall, she died at 4:45 in the afternoon.

I broke down and left the conference room. Tammy, my administrative assistant, was there and tried to comfort me but I really did not want any comfort at the moment. Jeff called, and I talked to him and asked him if he would go to my mother's funeral. He said "yes." I told him I'd pay for his travel expenses to go with me.

We went to Pittsburgh. Fortunately for me, Darryll Ceccoli and Charlie White were very supportive. I later found out that Darryll had told Charlie that whatever I needed, he was to make sure it was taken care of, which he did. Darryll, who had a great deal of admiration for my mother, also attended the funeral.

I was not scheduled to speak at my mother's funeral, but that was amended. Much to Aunt Barbara's surprise, I ended up doing one of the readings and eulogizing my mother at the funeral mass. I expressed her unselfish love, not only for me, but for her other three offspring. Darryll Ceccoli came up to me afterward and said, "The words you expressed were those of love."

My mother's death changed my person. I no longer had my protector, my advocate, and my companion on this life's journey. She was taken, and I questioned, to the deepest depth of my faith, why she had to be taken. Even to this day, I think of my mother daily. Though she has gone from this earth, I know she is there for me, because of the strength that I have, and the people who have been placed in my life to ensure my care and safety.

My Uncle Steve, my mother's fraternal twin, provided his gift to his sister by singing *Ave Maria* at her funeral. This piece was an offering of love which lifted my mother into the Heavens, where I know we will meet again.

not many like me at the table

After my mom's death, the world took on another interesting lens: a world without her. Mom left in 2002, 20 years after I graduated from high school, 16 years after I graduated college, and 15 years since I began working for Cox.

My earthly advocate was now an advocate from Heaven. No longer was my advocate overbearing and telling me what I should and should not do—lovingly, though overbearingly. I was further on the path of being orphaned by the hand of God, or was it the hand of man?

I was angry with God. In fact, I did not understand why God took my mother, and it took several years for me to receive an answer. In a practical sense, I still continued to go to Mass, attending St. Andrew's Catholic Church and then transitioning to Holy Family Catholic Church. But I also began to fall deeper into the darkness of sexual addiction, unknown to many on the outside.

During this time period, I moved from Bridgewood Trail to another house in Windermere, Florida where the likes of Tiger Woods and other celebrities lived. My economic income was stable at the time, and my house was a four-bedroom, two-bath home that was worth well over $240,000. I had to pinch myself a couple times!

Around this time, I was sexually assaulted again. An individual whom I cared for and who "cared" for me went a little too far. I was raped in the guest room of my home.

Sexual assault at the hands of someone I knew and respected was psychologically traumatic. I made the conscious decision to suppress it, not allowing it to surface until years later. This was compounded when I had to be admitted to Winter Park Hospital.

During this particular stay, I was again faced with sexual assault while being given a sponge-bath by a CNA. She was soaping up the water. When it came to my private area, she rubbed until I had an erection. One of the other nurses saw what was happening and said, "I don't see a thing."

I never reported this incident. To this day, it still causes me great pain. As in other occasions, I suppressed what had just happened to me and continued my life, the wounds of sexual assault mounting.

Personally, I was enduring a lot of pain. Professionally, I launched the latter part of my career with Cox Automotive. Under my position as community relations manager, I was also responsible for representing the Florida Independent Auto Dealers Association on behalf of Cox Automotive and the Florida region. This meant I would spend greater time on the road, which came with having a driver since my disability prevented me from driving alone.

My rise in the ranks also paralleled, to some degree, my father's path. My father had been, at an early point in his career, the Pennsylvania Independent Auto Dealers Association President while working for Butler Auto Auction. Our paths would intersect decades later, but eerily, the paths of father and son were already intertwined by our quality of charisma and a people-centered ethic. At times we honored this in each other while realizing we were our own individuals.

The Department of Community Relations (and my role as its manager) was new. I needed a new administrative assistant, one who could help me project the Auction as vibrant, innovative, and as a downright great neighbor to the surrounding community. I needed to find someone to help me be the face of the Auction and Cox to the community. That was my vision. It was my time to shine. So, I set out on the hiring process. The person who would be my partner in this endeavor had to be a person of great skill but also a person of great compassion. I found that person in Darlene.

Darlene came to us from a legal background as a legal secretary. She was crackerjack at her job as my administrative assistant. When I hired Darlene, I knew that she would go to greater heights, not just as my administrative assistant, but that she would be a great asset to Cox Automotive and Cox in general. I can say beyond question that Darlene was one of my greatest hires.

Individuals like Darlene are like diamonds in the rough. She was a leader within the Department of Community Relations. Her leadership skills and professionalism were noticed by Charlie White. This era began Darlene's role as a conduit between the administration of the community relations department and the administration of the Auto Auction. Charlie White was savvy. He came to me and said, "Louis, I need you to do me a favor. I need to have Darlene as the administrative assistant to me." I agreed.

Darlene now was on her ascent, rightfully, to prominence. I told Darlene more than once that eventually she would be in management. And in fact, today, that is exactly where she is. She now serves as the Office Manager for our Jacksonville location.

I loved my role as a community relations manager. I became more involved in political and community affairs and began to work on a regional basis for the Florida region of auctions, stretching our connections from just Orlando to the cities of Ocoee, Winter Garden, and the town of Windermere. I represented Cox at various funerals of dignitaries. I served on numerous boards such as the Health Central Foundation, the West Orange Chamber of Commerce, Share the Care, and the American Cancer Society. We adopted Maxey Elementary, a local high-risk elementary school, due in part to its racial and ethnic makeup. Through various drives and benefits, we brought them up to an "A" rating under the FCAT grading system, having started at a "D." This is the time where I helped facilitate and build a house for a wounded warrior veteran in Oakland, Florida, a small town in West Orange County.

I became somewhat of a local celebrity: I interacted with Jeb Bush in the Governor's Mansion. I danced with the likes of Mary Wilson from The Supremes. I went to parties where millionaires and people of great influence called me by my first name and sought the money I controlled in the name of Cox. I would hear from leaders and people of influence and power about the charities that they were trying to promote.

I began chairing the diversity board meetings. My interest in politics began to bud. I was well connected with the likes of the Ocoee mayor, Scott Vandergrift; the Winter Garden mayor; and the Windermere mayor, all of us sitting together on the West Orange Chamber of Commerce Board of Directors. I was named Auction Man of the Year by the Florida Independent Auto Dealers Association. I even became a notable face to watch for on local television. One of the local network affiliates ran a story about me running my first 5K.

You may ask, "How is this guy in a power wheelchair supposed to *run a 5K*?"

In 2004, I was looking for ways to raise money for the school nurse program, which supplied school nurses for West Orange County's public schools. Corey Perry was a physical therapist at Health Central Park Nursing Home where I would do physical therapy on an outpatient basis a few times a week. During one of our sessions, I said to him, "I have an idea. I want to get up in a walker and walk. Do you think that's possible?"

He said we could give it a try.

Corey started by having me practice standing with parallel bars. After weeks of standing in the parallel bars, we devised a suitable mechanism by which I could walk with a four-arm walker with a sling to give me added support. We started walking throughout the gym and then throughout the nursing home.

I told him I would like to do the Ocoee Founders' Day 5K. As strategic fate would have it, I would become Health Central Foundation chairman of the next 5K. Under my leadership and the help of many, including Cox Enterprises, we raised well over $50,000 for the Health Central Foundation because the initiative became a company-wide one. Each Auction contributed to my 5K, and I truly felt honored to be working for such a company.

The first time I ran it, it took me over four hours. I would run it four more times. The last time, which I think was around 2008, my father was there. They blocked off the streets early, and I ran it in an hour and 45 minutes. It was always about putting a face on the brand called "Manheim".

Now, the City of Winter Garden seemed to have a better relationship with us at that time. And, in fairness, we encompassed two cities that grew to love us, not just for our money, but for being part of the community.

Cox Automotive now staffed a diverse population of employees. As president Ceccoli stated, "The Grand Experiment". I was part of that grand experiment which was why I always remembered in my role as community relations manager to be one of inclusion of all.

This was further exemplified in the Martin Luther King Day parade, where both the Cities of Ocoee and Winter Garden came together to honor Martin Luther King, Jr. Or, when I was chairman for Relay for Life, West Orange County, where we made over $200,000 for the American Cancer Society. Or, when I represented Cox at Florida Hospital and their children's neonatal unit. I was always honored to be in the role. The team members I had along with the other employees that served as communications ambassadors were part of that vision as well.

In 2005, I traveled to corporate headquarters, as I typically did. But this time, we were in our new building, on Peachtree Dunwoody Road in Atlanta. During that visit to Cox HQ, I stopped by the Cox Museum, which was inside our building.

The Cox HQ building lived up to the Cox name in its style and presence while honoring its past and looking forward to its innovative future. Those were the thoughts that raced through my mind as I was honored to be part of the Cox vision and drive toward the future. I thought about James M. Cox and my hero FDR, running against Warren G. Harding in 1920 for president, and the story of visiting President Wilson in the White House after his massive stroke. It is documented that he had great compassion for his circumstance and was moved by his station in life.

Mr. Cox was someone whom I had never met but was someone I admired from our company and country's history. He was governor of Ohio, and he founded the chain of newspapers that continues today as Cox Enterprises, a media conglomerate. Many do not realize, including my co-author, that Cox owns over 100 Auctions in the United States and Canada. I honestly always chuckle when they come to the realization and say "Wow, you were part of a *big* company! The same one that provides my internet?"

I felt privileged to be part of a company that was moved by my station in life, and propelled me, despite my disability and the expenditures surrounding it, to the rank of management. As some people would tell me, there weren't many like me at the table, and I was keenly aware of this opportunity and privilege.

When I returned from my corporate visit, I was energized to represent Cox with even more vigor and optimism. I was in management many times during my career working 60-80 hours a week, though my paycheck did not reflect that. It was about promoting the Cox creed of inclusion.

I felt like inclusion was a hallmark within my career, including for those who had similar (or potentially dissimilar) circumstances that made them unique, whether LGBTQ, disabled, or a person of color. I saw Cox as breaking new ground by also promoting more women into positions of executive authority.

We were trying to change culture, to make it more inclusive. In fact, I was honored to have, as part of my benefit package, a company vehicle (which managers did have)—but I also had a driver, and considering the hours that I was putting in, I had *two* drivers, along with the fact that my personal care was covered as part of my benefit. Those individuals were paid as independent contractors. This was not an easy benefit to acquire; it took me numerous letters to the corporate office through Darryl Ceccoli to obtain this benefit. But, with the help of Rob Mowers, our general manager in 1994-1995, this became part of my benefit package, from 1994 onward.

There weren't many like me at the table. My peers saw me as a trailblazer. I was the face of Cox in West Orange County. I was the beacon of hope for Maxey Elementary. If you gave me a charity, I'd make it financially flourish. I was not only economically independent; I was wealthy. Under the auspices of Cox, my disability-related needs were all covered. These 7 years, between October 2002 and March 2009 were the peak of my career, a time of enlightenment, yet also a time of spiritual loneliness and drought which pervaded my life's landscape.

that wasn't moses

In 2004, my friend Noel and his wife Melissa stayed with me while their new house was being built in east Orlando. This is when I was living in the Windermere area, an upscale gated subdivision called Belmere off Roberson and Maguire roads.

One night coming home, we were off Roberson Road, heading toward the back gate of my community, when a unique thing happened. Noel's two children, six-year-old Cameron and eight-year-old Dylan, were in the backseat of my vehicle, a 2003 Pontiac Montana. Noel was driving. The pickup truck ahead of us unexplainedly lost its mattress from the bed of the truck, landing on the roadway ahead. We had no choice but to run over the mattress. The combination of the mattress, the roadway, and our catalytic converter spelled disaster: the minivan caught on fire. Fortunately for us, we were close to the back gate of my subdivision. The car was engulfed so quickly that I said to Noel, "We're on fire, pull over!"

Noel was in shock, but his parental instinct kicked in, and he handed his two young sons over the wall of the subdivision to neighbors, watching in disbelief. It was dusk. At this point, he said to me, "I'll come back to help you."

I said, "Just put the ramp out. Put the ramp out, and I'll get out!"

Well, it wasn't that easy. Somehow, my chair got stuck in my seatbelt, and I could not move. Noel came back and said, "C'mon Louis, come on! What's the problem?" He tried to get closer to the car, but it was too hot.

I said, "I can't get out of the seatbelt, get back!"

He took his shirt off and began fanning the flames in an attempt to get closer to the car, to no avail. I heard a helicopter overhead, and police radios, along with firemen and EMS, calling over a megaphone that there was still a person in the Pontiac Montana. That person was me.

Miraculously, from my point of view, I extricated myself from the seatbelt.

People were yelling, "It's going to blow, it's going to blow!"

"Fall out the side door," Noel said, as he watched.

I had no intention of falling out the side door. I did have the intention of removing myself from the car. So, I decided to do something that, to this day, still gives me chills.

I decided to go across the burning ramp into the flames. But before I did so, I said one thing, "Jesus, protect me."

The next thing I knew, I saw two hands, as God is my witness, and the two hands parted the flames, signaling to me, in all my humanity, that it was safe to go through. I was between this universe and the next. I remember people echoing, "Run! Run!"

As I came off the ramp and hit the ground with my front wheels, I felt the earth tremble below me. The tremble was from the ensuing explosion behind me. The fire had hit the gas tank, just after I had gotten off the ramp.

This experience forever shaped my life, as many of my life experiences have. It also reconfirmed my faith in a higher power, and in my case, my God. This was also observed by others, specifically, Noel, my friend, who at the time, I'm not sure went to Church—but he did that night.

He said, as we were walking home, "You know, Louis, when you were coming out of the vehicle, it looked like Moses parting the Red Sea."

"Noel, Bro, that wasn't Moses, it was Jesus."

This story was later published in a trade magazine for the Florida Independent Auto Dealers Association.

God showed me again that no earthly power is more influential and more earth-shattering than His own. The question is, was I smart enough to realize it?

The van accident with Noel and his children reignited my desire to find out and to ask God why my mom had to suffer and leave her earthly body. His answer was simple: she needed to rest. The woman who gave so much of herself, for not only me, but all her children, in the end of her bodily journey, was suffering anxiety and was a shell of the person she once was.

This made me think, does giving of one's self mean one should drain one's own humanity to give it to another? Or is there a way of supporting humanity so neither are drained?

This reminds me of families and folks with disabilities. From my lens, I see a few types of families: those who cherish their family member who happens to have a physical or intellectual disability; those who are indifferent or conflicted like my father; or those who throw their family member aside and have nothing to do with them.

It's interesting and unique to think that I've experienced all these types of situations personally. What does that mean about humanity?

"the golden child has fallen"

For the majority of my career with Cox, I imitated my father's work ethic. This meant I hardly ever took vacation time off to relax. I was the son of an icon of the auto auctions industry. Any vacation or flex time I did take was to handle disability-related issues, with few exceptions. I was typically working 60 hours or more a week, especially in my role as community relations manager. It was Charlie White's encouragement that helped me to seriously consider my work-life balance. "You need to learn how vacation helps you be more productive."

Thus, during the latter part of my career, I grew amenable to taking more time off for leisure. For example, I took time out to spend time with my brother Ed, and my sister-in-law Christine, and my nephew Tio. They came to visit Orlando. Tio at that time was about five years old. We went to Discovery Cove on one of our outings, where we all got to swim with the dolphins. We also went into the lazy river pool where Tio enjoyed being in the water. This was one of the times where, even during fun, there seemed to be a bit of tension. His wife Christine picked up on his distant demeanor, but I was in the dark.

My other brother Frank and his wife Helga and their daughter Nina lived in Delmar, California, just outside of San Diego. My relationship with them really did not consist of much substance. The last time I'd had any face-to-face interaction with Frank and his family had been during my mother's funeral in November 2002. Beyond that, we exchanged an occasional card or two for the holidays for a few years after my mother's passing.

In 2005, after Charlie White left, Allan Wilwayco became our general manager. The office of Community Relations was still in existence, but it was Charlie's baby, not Allan's brainchild. This was the beginning of the end, in my opinion, for the Community Relations Department. We would organize the Christmas party and/or the Spring and Summer picnic, while still doing community related things, but not with as much targeted purpose.

That was an interesting thing I learned about leadership: each leader brings something different. Under Allan's leadership, the community relations department became more of an employee-engagement department.

The Auction became a training site for continued education for independent dealers around the state in 2006. My role became that of host for the training school, in the name of Cox and Manheim. Terry Myers was the dealer training school representative from the Florida Independent Auto Dealers Association (FIADA) that handled the dealer training seminars at our location. Terry and I began to build a closer relationship as I continued to serve on the Board of Directors for the FIADA.

My role began to grow less attached to the auction facility. My professional autonomy was ever-increasing.

This was also the beginning of my fall from grace.

I was on a trip to the Annual Capital Connection with the West Orange Chamber of Commerce in February 2009 with one of my personal assistants. We traveled to Tallahassee. The person this year was one whom I had taken with me to do my personal care and assist with administrative needs. Like in years past, we shared the same room, but this time it was a bit different. Because we had gone on other personal trips together, I had a sense of security with him and confidence.

In fact, the year before we had gone on a personal trip to Arizona to visit the southwest where I had gone to school. This personal assistant and I were gaining a sense of understanding and empathy, because he also visited my mother's gravesite with me in 2008 and made a comment of how cold my father was in relation to the gravesite visit. Those comments gave me a greater sense of closeness to him. We even visited the Home of the Merciful Savior where I had been institutionalized from the age of six to nine and also visited the D.T. Watson Home.

The relationship between my personal assistant and myself began to blur, culminating in our sexual encounters. This was a very confusing time for both of us.

In retrospect, I look back at the situation and say to myself, *That was not a very good idea.* On the face of it, I was this person's supervisor; however, on his side of the power dynamic, he was related to a senior employee at the Auto Auction.

I was heading down a destructive path, but I didn't know how to stop. This was a flaw of my own. I'd had other relationships at Cox that I'm not exactly happy about, including one long-standing one, for over 10 years. I cared a lot about the individual, but it also made me wonder why this person entered into a sexual relationship with me.

Back to the trip, when my personal assistant and I got back from the Capital Connection trip, he was not comfortable and was very standoffish. We both felt awkward and not much was said between us. There was a sense that I was used, and so was he.

I didn't think much of the relationship after this trip, or what ramifications it could have for my employment.

Upper management at Cox already knew I was gay, and I knew of copious other situations like my own which typically flew under the radar. I worked through the end of March as usual.

Then on March 30th, I was summoned to the conference room on the second floor of the Auction by the human resources director. She left the room, leaving only HR corporate there: two individuals. They interrogated me relating to the relationship with my personal assistant, and I answered very honestly.

They said, "We don't need to do an investigation; thanks for your honesty."

They told me that I had to take the next two days off, and to *not* tell anybody about the meeting, including my driver. I agreed to that.

The following Monday corporate called me at home before I left for work and told me of their decision: I was being laid off, and they were going to offer severance. I was told that my personal assistant was traumatized by our encounters and this was going to be a stain on the reputation of Cox Enterprises, so there was nothing else to do but let me go.

At that point I was reeling. I didn't tell anyone. I kept it a secret for over a year. The only person who looked at the situation was one attorney from Winter Park. He asked me, "Do you want your job back?" I guess he felt that there was something wrong with how Cox handled it. I told him, no, I was so afraid to go back into that environment. I had held a high-profile position in the community. I just wanted to crawl under a rug.

I felt so degraded, so ashamed, that I couldn't face anyone. *Plus,* with being let go, my whole department of Community Relations closed; five other people lost their jobs, too. I felt like a wanted man, a fugitive. People knew I was gay, but my father and my brother Edward worked for Cox, too. There was a lot at stake. It was not a good feeling.

I have not stated who these individuals are, for the very purpose of protecting their right to privacy. I must say that this time period in my professional and personal life was one of anguish, and also one of self-reflection. I came back to my Maker, with greater force than ever before. My Aunt Marguerite, reflecting upon my situation, said, "The golden child has fallen."

Looking back on this now, some decades later, it's sad, reflecting on Jerry DeBellis's comment of, "It takes people a while to get used to you." Officially, my department closed because of the economics of the situation, to the best of my knowledge. Unofficially, my department was closed because I'd had a relationship with a subordinate. I wasn't the only one who had relationships with subordinates. It was commonplace in the company's culture. It appeared to me, however, that I was the only one who had a relationship with a subordinate where the subordinate was the same sex and was perceived as a victim.

I spoke to Darryll Ceccoli about this. He told me that what I did was wrong, but that he perceived the punitive action taken against me to be inequitable. In his position as president of Cox Automotive Manheim, he had seen similar cases that were handled far less severely. He recommended I sue and assured me that he would help me.

With the further benefit of hindsight, I can now see that Cox had been targeting me. In my final months at Cox, Allan Wilwayco asked a very poignant question, "How did the benefit of the coverage of my care begin?" Corporate was apparently asking Allan why this expenditure or benefit was in place.

I responded by forwarding him this email from Darryll Ceccoli.

-----Original Message-----
From: Ceccoli, Darryll (MAN-Corporate)
Sent: Friday, December 05, 2008 11:04 AM
To: Fazio Jr., Lou (MAN-Orlando)
Subject: Personal Care Assistant

Lou,

Good to hear from you and glad you are doing well.

Regarding the issue of a personal care assistant being provided to you, here is my recollection.

While I was president of Manheim, which would have been 1996 or before the question of providing a care assistant for you came to me from yourself, in writing and from Rob Mowers, GM of FAAO.

I recall a discussion of the matter with Barb Osborne, HR; Bob Gartin, CFO, Mike Langhorne, controller and John Stower, regional ops.

We agreed to provide you that benefit and we did not put a time limit on this practice.

Documentation is somewhere, but if it cannot be found I'm sure the recollection remains with others as it does with me and should suffice for the authorization of the continuation of a care assistant provided to you.

Take care, say hello to Sr. and have a good holiday.

Darryll

I retained this email to show the support I had received, specifically from Darryll and his team, and Rob Mowers. This email I believe shows that in the 2009 situation, the powers that be were looking for a way to get rid of me.

And they started at the end of 2008. Unfortunately, the new regime at Cox saw no value in my dedication and service. I was a line item to be eliminated.

I'm not saying I did no wrong. I was hurting, which caused a lot of my inappropriate and unsafe behavior. From this experience and my work with people in relation to sexual assault, I have come to realize that human sexuality is a very complex matter. I've also come to realize, through some very high-profile cases, that we must remember the human dignity of the person. I was sexually assaulted three times; two of those times were by men, one was by a female professional. I won't forget that. It is stuck in my mind.

the land of zion

My dismissal from Cox was not the only source of strife at this time. My father was ill, owing to complications from his stroke back in 2001 and his chronic smoking habits. At this point, I also had to have orthopedic surgery for my hip, which caused me immense pain. The stress created great physical problems for me. I ended up hospitalized at Florida Hospital because of kidney stones and UTIs.

After recovering from the battle with the kidney stones, I decided to move to Salt Lake City in August of 2009, where the meek of heart should not go, and the rugged frontierism of the land would challenge me physically, spiritually, and intellectually. I reconnected with Jeff. He had moved to Salt Lake City in the mid-to-late '90s and married Jenny. Now he was a physical therapist, having graduated from the University of Utah with his doctorate. He recommended that I see Dr. Kubiac to perform the necessary orthopedic surgery on my left hip. This began my journey westward. My plan was to stay in Salt Lake only for six months at the Marriott Residence Inn located in the heart of Salt Lake City, sell my house back in Windermere, Florida, then move to Arizona.

My severance compensation from Cox lasted until October. I knew I had a long-term care insurance policy with John Hancock that I had paid for in premiums since 1994. Now, 10 years later, Jenny helped me find the policy information that I needed so that I could gain access and activate the benefit. It was a lifeline that helped me sustain my quality of life.

My first care provider under the plan was Jeff, who was qualified as a physical therapist. I paid him through the policy. This enabled me to find other caregivers and quickly learned to be cautious. In my case, some caregivers who believed my policy to be worth something pressured me about money. It wasn't fun. Blaire Crismond was one of the care providers who succeeded Jeff. She was good. Granted, at times Blaire and I would argue like husband and wife, but she was fun to be around. I even allowed her to bring her young daughter Avery when she came to help.

I tried to figure out a way to get off COBRA, which was an extremely expensive way to insure myself. I applied to the University of Utah, taking enough hours to qualify for student health insurance. This cut my premium from $515 a month to a $100-and-something a month.

As I said, I was coming to the end of my severance agreement. Fortunately for me, I had an agreement for six months. I then transitioned onto Social Security Disability, and had unemployment for a time, in which I had to show I was gainfully looking for work. In so doing, I economically secured myself well enough to sustain myself. Thank God, I also took out that John Hancock long-term care policy while I was still working for Cox which kicked in after my severance agreement had ended.

I matriculated as an undergraduate social work student, while pursuing my certification in mediation and disability studies. This undergraduate status and the courses I took would later help me when I would apply to the graduate program in social work at Arizona State University.

I was still not eligible for Medicare (until 2011), so I was also grateful that I got into the University of Utah and had coverage through student health. My faith was tested, as it had been numerous times. But this time was one of the greatest tests.

Jeff went with me to meet Dr. Kubiac to plan the surgery for my left hip. He gave us a 50% chance of success. Dr. Kubiac stated that if the hip would not remain stable, he would have to perform a girdlestone procedure instead of replacement, which means a cutting away of the femur bone, allowing it to float freely. It was up to me. With the odds being 50% and, in my opinion, an over-exaggeration on my rate of potential death, which was also placed at 50%, I was ready to go for it.

However, I was hopeful that Dr. Kubiac would not have to do the girdlestone procedure as an alternative. I remember asking him and Jeff, "The girdlestone procedure will limit my chances of further ambulation beyond limited standing ability, correct?"

Jeff and Dr. Kubiac said, "Yes, that would be the clinical result." I told Dr. Kubiac that as long as he gave it his best attempt to replace my hip, he had my consent, and, if all else failed, he could do the girdlestone procedure as a last resort.

Kubiac, a young desperado surgeon, agreed. So, in the coming days in October of 2009, I would again go under a surgeon's knife. As it turns out, my surgical wish was granted. The artificial hip was stabilized and placed in its socket, without the need of the alternative girdlestone procedure. This would mean that I would have a road ahead of rehabilitation at Health South Utah Rehabilitation Hospital, which would be my home for the next month.

I again bounced back into society with the help of physical rehabilitation, and the caring hands of the doctors and nurses who brought me back to normality (for a guy with the intersection of my disability and sexual orientation, what *is* normal, anyway?)

During my time in Salt Lake, I was blessed by the fact that Jeff was assistant director, and then director of Registered Physical Therapy, a group of clinics located primarily in the Salt Lake Valley.

Of course, this venture out to Utah was only going to be for six months, with the plan of moving to Arizona, but Jeff convinced me to stay in Salt Lake. I eventually found housing in Murray, a two bedroom/two bath condo in a four-story building. I utilized my 401k money to buy this condo. It was #206, on the second floor (there was an elevator), and I was right next to the Trax Station in north Murray. Trax is the light rail system of the Utah Transit Authority. I could see the station from my living room window.

My placement along the Trax line was very strategic. On a regular basis, three days a week a least, I was able to take myself to Registered Physical Therapy facilities in West Jordan, Utah. There I met a physical therapist by the name of Brett Cummings. Brett and I worked diligently to ensure that I maintained my physical strength, along with Jeff's supervision. I stretched, I lifted weights, and I ambulated on my four-arm walker.

Thanks to the guidance and care of Jeff and those at Registered Physical Therapy, I achieved the wanted outcome of increased mobility.

During my time in Salt Lake City, Jeff and I reconnected. I also developed a healthy friendship with Jenny. I have great respect for her. I spent a lot of time with Jeff and Jenny during my time in Salt Lake City, and I think our friendship overall reached a better equilibrium. I was also the godfather of their son Thor, who was born in 2008.

During this time, I was privileged to become very good friends with Jeff's dad Brian and his stepmom, Carrie. Most Sundays, I would take the light rail to Sandy to have dinner with them. I gave Brian the nickname "Muppethead". If you knew Brian and are familiar with Statler and Waldorf, the Muppet grouches, you would understand the connection.

In February 2010, my father's emphysema, heart issues, and issues related to his stroke back in 2001 caught up with him. Miraculously, he lived another nine years after that stroke, in large part due to, in my view, my mother's unselfish care for him while she herself was sick with multiple myeloma.

My father died February 23, 2010, in Pittsburgh. My brother Ed called me, and he also asked that I tell our Aunt Marguerite of our father's passing, since, in his words, he considered our Aunt Marguerite "a bitch" and did not want to have to deal with her. I said that I would be happy to let her know of her brother's passing. I was glad to connect with Aunt Marguerite and her son, John. The challenge for our family was the apparent disdain for either side, personally fueled by the wounded aspects of my parents' marriage. Regrettably, this disdain trickled down to our generation. In hindsight, I find it sad.

I actually had more feeling about my father's death than I thought I would. In the last few years of his life, we had gotten closer. My mother always said that my father would be the one to reach out to me because she felt that I would be the one to understand him, and I would be the one to give him comfort in his older years. And, in a way, I think that did happen. Apparently, he delighted in coming down with Arlene, his girlfriend whom he started dating six months after my mother's passing, to my home in Windermere, Florida. We were together for New Year's Eve 2009. I took him along with Arlene to our annual New Years' feast with Anne and Bill Sullivan and their family and friends. My father and Marge just hit it off so well; he had so much fun! I don't think Arlene thought much of it; that was my father. He was a ladies' man, even at 82.

That was the last time we were together. In the process of him becoming ill and not pulling out of it, it was more psychologically strenuous for me than I thought it would be. We've definitely had a . . . *conflicted* relationship. But he was still my dad. That last time he was in Florida, I managed to drag him to the mall so we could have a photo together. It is now the only picture I have left of him.

After telling my aunt of her brother's death, I went to Pittsburgh for the funeral.

Anne and Bill Sullivan sent one of their sons to represent their family at the funeral, which I felt was very classy and I appreciated it.

His passing also created a great economic upheaval in the family system. At the funeral, I sensed that something was awry from the very beginning, because Ed was very cold and distant, and so were some of the other relatives, who turned out to be key to the inheritance issue to come.

Kneeling beside me was Ed, or "Fast Buck", as he was known. He lived up to his nickname that I had given him back when he was 15 years old. He decided to usurp the resources of my father for his own personal gain and took 90% of my father's assets for himself. On paper, my father's assets totaled approximately $500,000, not counting properties and other unnamed assets. I decided that this was an egregious and unacceptable action on the part of Ed. So, I decided to sue him for, what I felt, was my rightful share.

As it turned out, this was easier said than done. An irrevocable trust fund was created back in December 2002, a month and a half after my mother's death. I was in charge of this trust fund. I had control over all my father's assets, as I've mentioned, from back in 2001. From my lens, my brother, knowing that my mother was no longer on this earth, could then create his own ill-gotten wealth by excluding both his brothers from the majority of this inheritance. It is extremely difficult to change a trust fund, no less an irrevocable one. Yet, during my father's funeral, my brother said, "I'm glad I got you off the documents." Referring to the fact that I was no longer was the main trustee of my father's assets.

I still question the validity of the documents, however. I believe that my brother was not honest in his pursuits, and I would put nothing past him. I now have a clearer understanding of why he was so aloof when he visited my home in Orlando in 2008 with his family.

I said to him, "I will attempt to correct this issue. And there is someone stronger than you, and more powerful."

His response was, "Who is that?"

"God, and Jesus."

His reply back was, "I don't believe in God."

"I will pray for you," I said.

When I returned from Pittsburgh to Salt Lake City, I began contemplating what I should do. The document that I did receive from Ed's attorney, who was in Pittsburgh, stated that I would receive $20,000, and my brother Frank would receive the same, and then Ed would receive the lion's share of the rest of the estate, and the heir would no longer be me, upon his signature, but Ed's eldest son. I acquired an attorney from Scranton, Pennsylvania, whom I had never met in person. He did what he could, I guess.

The result of the litigation was that the documents would stand, even though they were never checked for signature verification (because I'm sure that would cost more money), and that "This act was morally reprehensible," paraphrasing my attorney's words, *but*, it had to stand. So, I ended up with $18,000 after paying his fee. This case was not closed until 2016.

After my father's death, all contact with either of my brothers ceased. I don't even recall Frank being at the funeral. His relationship with our father was very strained. There was a conversation around the time of the case closure between Ed and me. He just said, "I'm sorry, you'll just have to rely on public programs. I have a family to support. Talk to you some time."

This period of my life, with Ed saying, basically, "See you later" has been one of the hardest for me to come to terms with, along with the loss of my job with Cox Enterprises. These two events shook my soul like a magnitude 10 earthquake. And, at times, it felt as though I was being buried alive.

This is where my faith came in, and where friends like Jeff and his father Brian and stepmother Carrie came not to the rescue but provided a safety net that permitted me to forge onward. These events are what marked the beginning of my time in Salt Lake City, Utah, the Land of Zion.

My inquisitive nature and desire to learn has always been a part of my being. After losing my job with Cox, due to—in my view—unsavory circumstances, it was important for me to regain a sense of myself. I applied and was accepted to the graduate certification programs of both Disability Studies and in Mediation. I became matriculated under the undergraduate program of Social Work. Thus began my educational adventure as a "Ute" at the University of Utah.

The University of Utah campus is located within the foothills of Salt Lake City. It is one of the most beautiful campuses I've had the honor of witnessing. To my knowledge, it is also one of the few campuses that has a suspension bridge crossing a major highway. The campus is designed on a three-tier approach, as it sits upon the side of an ascending mountain.

This time as well began my interest in the discipline and professional field of social work. I had the pleasure of taking various undergraduate courses that ignited my desire to become a practicing social worker.

I had already begun my exploration of other ideas of what it meant to believe in Jesus or God at the University of Arizona in the early and mid 1980s. Salt Lake City was a place of opportunity to further experience the quest for knowledge beyond myself. It is the home of the Mormon Church. It is also a place where faith is interwoven within the society of those who call Salt Lake City home. Catholicism, from my vantage point, is respected. However, it is almost a missionary field, where it takes a backseat to Mormonism.

One of the reasons I branched out from Catholicism during my time in Salt Lake City was because of how my curiosity manifested itself within the realm of my personal beliefs, ideology, and, quite frankly, my desire to be challenged. I thought, *This is my opportunity.* I would attend both the Unitarian Church of Salt Lake City and either the Newman Center and/or Blessed Sacrament Catholic Church on most Sundays and/or Saturday evenings. The drill would be Saturday evening Mass, Sunday morning Unitarian Church, with an occasional block service of LDS. This faith-hopping, if you will, was somewhat time-consuming, but very educational. In fact, Brian, who is Catholic, commented at one point, "You would be a good Mormon, because you're crazy enough to do so!"

Attending the University of Utah Newman Center showed this idea and its reality on more than one occasion. There were discussion groups in which the church had such topics as "the Ex-Mormon," introducing them to Catholicism almost as a self-help mantra, or a step program, to rid the Christian from the ugliness and destructiveness of being a Mormon, a recovery group, if you will. I witnessed a woman who had cried in a small group setting while she recounted her testimony of being ex-patriated from the Mormon Church and found the comfort and serenity of the Catholic Church. Being a cynical (but practicing) cradle Catholic and attending Mormon block services myself, I pondered: *What the hell is going on?*

I attended services at the Church of Latter Day Saints or LDS/Mormon (called Block) more than once. In fact, the Church even tried to recruit me for membership. Further still, Jeff's wife Jenny was a convert from Mormonism to Catholicism! My godchild's grandparents came to his baptism with frowns on their faces, realizing, with trepidation, that their beloved grandson would not be sealed in eternity, and from their eyes, would suffer the damnation of Catholicism.

This experience shook my faith foundation to the core. In that, I saw firsthand the humanity of faith. It almost seemed as though I was a missionary myself. I had friends who were Mormon (and still do, and whom I love) and I truly believe in Jesus, the same Jesus that they do. Many disagree with that assertion, stating that theirs is not the same Jesus. I will leave that interpretation up to the scholars and the philosophers. My experience taught me that those who are Mormon do believe in a Heavenly Father, even though they do not believe in the

Holy Trinity. My experience with the LDS Church has also made me a stronger Catholic, because I have grown to have a stronger empathy for all those who seek God.

As I mentioned, I attended the First Unitarian Universalist Church in Salt Lake City. I even became a member while still attending Catholic Mass. The Reverend Tom Goldsmith understood that, for me, being gay and Catholic was a bit of a challenge, but I still held on to and valued the sacramental and faith-oriented foundations of the Catholic Church. In fact, the term "catholic" means universal. So, from my vantage point, I was just living out the true meaning of my faith.

My time at the First Unitarian Church of Salt Lake was a time of enlightenment. I congregated both with those who believed in God and those who maybe didn't believe in God. Ironically, this strengthened my belief in God. It had been mentioned to me by Reverend Tom Goldsmith, on one occasion, that if the Catholic Church found out I was attending the Unitarian Church, that it could spell an issue. But, as it turns out, it didn't. Again, in fact, it strengthened my faith.

However, to be honest, I wasn't really that forthcoming with the clergy at the Catholic Church, specifically the Monsignor at Blessed Sacrament or at the Newman Center, that I was "moonlighting" as a Unitarian, or for that matter, attending the Mormon Block on occasion.

I was in my glory, experiencing what it meant for me to have faith in God, holding onto my Catholic practices and beliefs while stretching myself to others. In fact, one of my professors at the University of Utah found what I was doing to be quite interesting, she herself being a past-Catholic and now a Unitarian Universalist.

Sunday night dinners at Brian and Carrie's would become quite lively, because Brian would ask, "So what church did you attend today? And what did you learn?"

So, to recap. I attended the Newman Center at the University of Utah, the Church of the Blessed Sacrament in Sandy, and St. Joseph the Worker in West Jordan: three Catholic parishes; the Unitarian Church of Salt Lake; and, on occasion, various Mormon churches as well. As you can see, my faith calendar was pretty packed. Thank God I had a light rail system that whizzed by my condo!

It was a time of great faith-freedom for me. I felt very fortunate to be able to cross the lines of faith, while serving my omnipotent God. I even thought, *I wonder what God thinks about all of this, especially when I might be sitting beside an atheist at the first Unitarian Church of Salt Lake City! Or, for that matter, when I would be at a priesthood meeting at the Mormon Church, where they believe that Joseph Smith was given gold plates, and that Jesus walked the land of North America and met with the American Indians! Over a million people believe this steadfastly. The Mormon, like the Catholic, even has a secondary book. We, the Catholics have the Catechism; the Mormons have the Book of Mormon! Did Joseph Smith and the Apostle Peter meet?* That was my thought.

Well, if you believe that the Mormons go to the same Heaven, then, I suppose they could have met. For the sake of my understanding, I think they have met.

Interestingly, I had the great honor of meeting Thomas Monson, the then president of the Mormon Church at the opening of the St. Joseph the Worker Catholic Church. Jeff said, "Not everyone gets to meet the head of the Mormon Church. It's like meeting the pope!" Let alone have a private audience for over ten minutes, and then receive a signed letter from him, wishing me well with my studies at the University of Utah!

Honestly, I felt a sense of privilege, faith-privilege if you will, in meeting the head of the Mormon Church. Is that a sign from God? I think it was.

During this time as well, I became a little bolder about who I was sexually. I rolled in the gay pride parade. The Mormon Church, in fact, had a float in the gay pride parade, which I think was historic. I was cheered as I rolled down the streets of Salt Lake, asserting, in solidarity, with my brothers and sisters, that I was worthy in relation to my sexual orientation. I met a bisexual man there who said, and I paraphrase, "There aren't many of us in the parade that are in wheelchairs," and we both agreed that we needed to change that.

This was at the same time when Pope Benedict put out an edict from the Vatican that he wanted to hear about sexual orientation and how it affected Catholicism, and was the Catholic Church welcoming to those who, for years, had stayed silent, relating to their sexual attractions?

For me, this was a time of great discernment and soul-searching. In fact, Monsignor Servatius was the one who encouraged me to come out to the congregation of Blessed Sacrament, or at least the focus group that was discussing the survey. I thought about it and prayed about it, and that's exactly what I did.

"You know that I'm in a power wheelchair, but you can't tell as well that I am gay." This pronouncement seemed to lift a bit of weight from my faithful back, and everyone in attendance, at least publicly, was quite supportive. It was no Stonewall experience, but it was liberating. Finally, I felt like, at least at that particular parish, at that moment, I was accepted and belonged.

God and I had many conversations during my time in Salt Lake City. My friend Ken Harris, who was a parishioner at Blessed Sacrament Parish, tested the bounds of my faith even further. Every Wednesday, I would attend a Bible study, which numbered at least twenty members. I also became active with the juvenile justice system on behalf of the Diocese of Salt Lake City. Ken and I were chaplains for the Wasatch Youth Detention Center. I served in this role for approximately two years.

We had many boys come through our system, whose names are bound to confidentiality, but some of the stories humbled me. It was not always easy to get the boys to attend our service. In fact, after I left, Ken moved over to Decker Lake, which was another facility at the time, because they closed our facility. We did, through the efforts of a parish priest by the name of Father Silva, baptize one of the young men. Ken and I helped this individual become part of our faith family by utilizing the Catechism for Youth. This was an honor. And, out of all the boys that I have seen through the youth detention system, this is one example where I felt that Ken and I (and it was mostly Ken) made a difference.

I also had the opportunity to attend an adult incarceration facility. I only did that once or twice. It just was not the same for me as it was to work with the youth offenders. In fact, I even took the exam to become a juvenile corrections officer. This was interesting, since my disability was front and center. In fact, the proctor of the exam and the director met with me and said, "Even if you pass this exam, you will not be able to work in this capacity." I questioned why. The general response, "How will you be able to control the individual if there is a problem?"

Unbeknownst to them, I had an answer, and a practical one at that. They were not privy to the fact, at least at that time, that I already was volunteering with Wasatch detention—and no, we never had an incident, but I had built a good relationship with the residents who called Wasatch home. So, my answer was this, "Yes, you are right, that physically, I would be at a disadvantage. But you're incorrect in assuming that I would not be able to equalize the inherent disadvantage."

The director and the proctor asked, "How?"

I stopped for a moment and said, "Through brainpower and compassion."

Obviously, that's not a foolproof method. However, I then disclosed that I was currently a volunteer on the inside, and that it seemed to work just fine for almost two years. Both the director and the proctor had a little bit of crow to swallow and said, "We didn't realize that you were already part of our system."

I didn't take the juvenile correction officer position any further, primarily because, during my testing procedure, I was not given the proper academic support to complete the exam. This again was an issue of discrimination that seems to rear its ugly head when you are breaking new ground.

My recollections and reflections show that there are times when I had to pick my battles to win the overall war. The experience with Wasatch Detention Center ignited even more my desire to become a practicing social worker.

The faith of humanity, or the faith within humanity, was shown to me behind the gates of the Wasatch Detention facility. Many of those young men were so talented but did not see the talent that God had given them. It was up to Ken and me to stimulate the talent within so that it could be brought to the surface for all to see.

In this time, I became involved with the Utah Transit Authority Advisory Board and was serving as higher education chairman for the Coalition for people with Disabilities. I was also involved with the Board of Directors for the Center of Independent Living, and I ended up securing, for a short period, a position as a vocational rehabilitation counselor for the State of

Utah through my association with the then director, Russ Thelin.

Little did I know, however, that there would be such turmoil over budgetary issues. My outspoken nature, once again, got me in trouble. Russ Thelin was under the gun and eventually lost his job as director of the Utah State Office of Rehabilitation in March 2015. I, too, was attempting to learn the ins and outs of becoming a vocational rehabilitation counselor. My supervisor was a politician at best and found a way to oust me as well by saying that I yelled at him over a client issue. I was summarily discharged from my position as a vocational rehabilitation counselor under the heading of, "It was not a good fit." Little did I expect to be a political pawn in the agency that was supposed to assist those with disabilities.

I thoroughly enjoyed working with my colleagues, even for a short time. In fact, one of my fellow counselors whom I rode the high-speed train (the Frontrunner) with on an almost daily basis, came to my condo, stating how sorry he was relating to my dismissal and asked if I had considered taking legal action. I was only on the job for a month, so I didn't think I had a proverbial leg to stand on.

In hindsight, I probably should have spoken up. But, at times, I'm too much of a nice guy, and I let things pass, to my detriment. This is one such time. Now, though, I am writing for as many people as possible to see that the governmental agencies that are there to promote and defend those whom they serve are not always meeting those societal expectations. From that vantage point, I think you must be a servant leader, which, in our capitalistic system, is not always easy to accomplish.

I have great respect for vocational rehabilitation and its philosophical mission. I don't have much respect for what can happen on the ground when it comes to money and the way it is appropriated. Greed overshadows the philosophical nature of the program. The State of Utah's program was not the first that had problems.

Jeff and Jenny were living on the benches of the Wasatch Front (the foothills between Salt Lake and the higher peaks), so, on Sundays, traditionally, if I wasn't going to dinner with Brian and Carrie, who lived in Sandy, which is south of Salt Lake City, I would go to Jeff and Jenn on the benches, which was above the city.

Thor, probably three or four at the time, asked, "Uncle Louis, can you stay for dinner?"

How can you say "no" to a four-year-old?

We had a lovely dinner, and then I had to go home.

Everything in Utah is on a grid. I had to go west from the very eastern edge of 3300 South all the way down to State Street which was 39 blocks. I missed the last bus, which was at 6:15. So, I decided, since it wasn't snowing, that I would just roll all the way down, 39 blocks. Keep in mind, I say "roll down," because it's *all* downhill from the benches of the Wasatch Mountains toward downtown, where the Trax station was.

I got to 3300 South and 2300 East, and it was dark now. I didn't see a patch of ice, and my chair high-centered and flipped me over.

As luck would have it for me, there was a Salt Lake City police officer adjacent to me coming down. I think he was in a grocery store parking lot. He saw me flip over and off the sidewalk. He helped me get back into the chair, and he said that he had never seen a tuck and roll quite like that before.

I said, "Yes, I know. Thank you so much, Officer, for helping me."

He helped me get back up, and I made it to the Trax station. It was cold when I got there. I got off and I made it up to my condo. My personal care assistant was there and waiting (I had called and told her what was happening).

"I don't feel quite right. I think I broke something."

I called Jeff and he agreed to come over and go to the hospital with me. Sure enough, Jeff and I took the Trax to Intermountain Medical Center, which was the next stop to the South at 5200 South. We had X-Rays done, and the ER doc said, "You broke your left ankle."

In Utah, there's a big rivalry between BYU and U of U. He knew I was going to the University of Utah. He said he was going to put a blue cast on me, and I said, "Hell no, you're gonna put a *red* cast on me, Brother!" I was in the cast about 6 weeks until my ankle healed.

2014 was an interesting year. I was finishing my certification in Mediation. I also was finishing up my Disability Studies certification, and I was heavily involved with the Utah Legislative Coalition for People with Disabilities. But what almost derailed everything was a UTI that turned septic.

I took myself via Trax to the University of Utah hospital and was admitted. I almost did not come out alive. My UTI went into my bloodstream, causing me to be hospitalized as an inpatient. Unfortunately for me, the attending physician Christine Graves could not find the cause and could not find the antibiotic to kill it. She came to my room and said, "Louis, I have bad news. We can't find an antibiotic that will kill the infection. If we don't find one soon, there's not much more I can do. What do you want me to do?"

I said, "Dr. Graves, I trust you and I pray that you will do what you can to help me. Thank you for being honest with me."

A few more days passed. Dr. Graves came back to my hospital room and said, "I think we found something that will work: Meropenem."

I was staffed a lot by residents. One was quite cute. Remembering my sexual orientation for what it is (and they knew it), I would perk up whenever he showed up. So, I think they made sure he was part of the rounds.

Dr. Johnson always seemed to advocate for me, too. In fact, I overheard folks talking, including nursing, and they were thinking that I should be placed somewhere (such as acute rehab) so that I could get more help. And his response was, "No. Louis is doing just fine. He manages. Leave it alone."

Upon finding the Meropenem, I now had a choice: would I want the Meropenem to be done as an inpatient procedure or outpatient? Well, the decision was easy for me. I wanted to get back to my mediation and disability studies coursework. I told Dr. Graves, "I want to be an outpatient."

Dr. Graves said, "You know, Dr. Johnson and I don't want this to happen again. So, we're going to put a standing order in the system. If you ever have a problem, or if you ever feel like you have a UTI, come to us immediately." I said I appreciated it, and I was discharged from being inpatient.

The nurses were happy for me too because I had been there for *weeks*. When they now saw me as an outpatient, they would say, "Wow, it's great to see you! You were pretty sick." And I would say in response, "I know. And I appreciate your care very much."

So now it was infusions for a week. During the infusions, I had to ensure that I was on time for each of those seven days, without delay. I utilized the Trax system.

The same day I was discharged from the hospital, I recommenced my coursework, going to my night class. My professor Dr. Carolyn Camp said, "What are you doing here? We thought you were still in the hospital. We were told you were very sick."

"They found the drug that can help me! I told them that I was going back to my mediation class, and they know I'm stubborn, so they said, 'Oh well!' and here I am, ready to go!"

Professor Camp laughed and said, "We're glad to have you back."

The next Saturday, I arrived for my daily infusion and a male nurse appeared. I expected him to say something along the lines of "Glad to have ya." Instead, he said, "You know what I would do if I was in your shoes?"

I wasn't quite sure what he was getting at, so I said, "No, I don't."

He said, "I would kill myself."

It shocked me. That phrase. I said, "Excuse me—could you please repeat yourself?"

He did so. I then left after the infusion and was dumbstruck. What was I going to do? I knew it wasn't right.

When I went to my mediation class the next week, I told the story to a classmate who happened to be a doctor herself, a pediatrician. She said, "Louis. You have to report that person."

"I don't know if I want to, because he has a family. It's Christmastime. . . "

"I suggest you think about it."

I did. I pondered it for a week or two and then I finally notified the University of Utah Hospital. The only thing I asked was to not fire him, since he had a family, and to retrain him. They sent me a letter, saying that they would take care of the matter. And that's the last I heard.

It was a normal, lazy Sunday, a little chilly, as I recall. I was waiting at the Trax station to go to Harman's to pick up groceries for the coming week. I saw two individuals, a woman and a little boy, and the type of person that I am, of course, I had to be nosy and ask, "What are you doing today? And who is this little guy?" (Who was also interested in my wheels. The wheelchair can be like a dog: people are interested in it; it's usually little people, but sometimes adults are as well, so it's a good icebreaker).

The woman replied, "I am this little guy's grandmother, and his name is Michael."

Michael then got interested in the ticket machine and went off to investigate it down the platform, so his grandmother went to retrieve him. There isn't much room between the platform and the tracks below on either side. She unexpectedly and inexplicably fell onto the tracks, and she was unconscious.

"Oh crap" (that's exactly what I said). There weren't many people around. I had sense enough to call 9-1-1 (coming from Cox management, they train you with what to do in emergencies: we'd had bomb scares, etc).

When I called 9-1-1, I said where I was, and that a woman was down on the tracks, and to please get ahold of the Utah Transit Authority.

The 9-1-1 Operator from Salt Lake City said, "Can you look up and see when the next train is due?"

The next train was due in four minutes.

She suggested to get help.

I yelled to this group of women who were on the south side of the platform (there were no guys except for me).

The 9-1-1 operator said that I'd have to ask one of them to go down to the tracks and lift the woman. So, I went to the south side of the track, and I asked these women if one of them or all could go down onto the tracks to attend to this woman and remove her from the tracks.

They replied, "There's no way we can go down there. We can't lift her!"

So, we're down to three minutes before the northbound train comes into the station, heading toward downtown.

The 9-1-1 operator was like, "What about the buses?"

The buses connected with the light rail, so, I sent one of the women over to the bus area to get ahold of one of the bus drivers to call Dispatch, and that worked! So, at least, we thought we would get ahold of somebody with Dispatch to warn the driver of the light rail that there was someone down on the tracks.

Two minutes now.

Michael was crying. By this time, other people came and a first responder that was a nurse went down on the tracks and found she could not revive the woman; she had had a seizure. I relayed that info to the 9-1-1 operator.

She said that the police weren't going to make it in time before the train, so, I decided that I would clear everyone from the track (including the nurse). Only Michael's grandmother was left down there.

I can remember to this day, Michael said to me, "Please don't let the train hit my grandma."

I said, "I will do everything in my power to make sure that doesn't happen."

We cleared the track (minus the grandmother), Michael was crying, and the next thing I know, here comes the train. As God is my witness, I put my head down, and I prayed, and I looked up, and I saw the train, and I could tell that the driver was applying the brake . . . he had gotten our message, but there was no guarantee, because they come in fast. I prayed and prayed.

I said, "Please, God, if you are there, and I know you are, please stop the train."

Then, we waited.

As fate would dictate, the train stopped 100 to 200 feet shy of her. The Salt Lake City 9-1-1 operator was still on the line with me, and I told her what happened, and she said that EMS should be there shortly, if they were not there already.

The police arrived, and I'll never forget it, this one officer kept saying, "Who's in charge? Who's in charge?" and I kept saying, "I'm in charge, I'm in charge!" but he kept shouting, "Who's in charge?" and I kept shouting back, "I'm in charge!" until I finally shouted, "Look! I'm the one in charge, do you not believe me just because I'm in a wheelchair?!"

The officer's intonation changed, "Oh, sorry, sorry."

EMS arrived, and they learned of the woman's seizure; she had to be taken to Intermountain Hospital in an ambulance. Michael, however, was not allowed to ride in the ambulance. The police insisted that he ride in a police car to the hospital, all the while asking him who his parents were and what their phone number was. Michael was crying. I asked the officer in charge (the one who took a while to admit that I was in charge) if they could let him ride in the ambulance with his grandmother.

"We can't do that."

"Why not?"

"It's not protocol."

"I don't give a rat's ass if it's protocol or not. The boy is in shock and wants to ride with his grandmother in the ambulance!"

Sure enough, that's what he did. Just before the 9-1-1 operator hung up, she said this to me, "I must say something before I release the call. I want to say thank you, in case no one else does. You did a good job; you saved someone's life."

I have not heard what happened to Michael and his grandmother; I wonder to this day. I did hear from Michelle, who was on the Utah Transit Authority board with me, who sent a letter expressing appreciation for what I had done.

I said to Michelle, "I appreciated it. It wasn't a heroic action; it was just what anyone would do for a fellow human being."

Needless to say, after that, I did not go to the grocery store; I went home.

By 2015, I earned my certifications in Mediation and Disability Studies and was accepted into the Gerontology Master's Program at the University of Utah under Dr. Scott Wright. I had competing interests, however. I was honored to be considered, but I ultimately declined to enroll in the program. I thought of returning to the Southwestern Desert, where, as one of my advisors and director of the Tucson-based Disability Resource Center Dr. Kent Kloepping said, "Once Tucson is in your heart—and if it *is* in your heart— you will return." So, I found myself preparing to leave the city in which I had only planned to stay six months but ended up living in for five years!

My desire to return to Tucson was also eminently practical: being bound to a power wheelchair is not exactly ideal during harsh winter seasons like there are in Salt Lake. September 2015, I found myself leaving the City of Zion for the Southwestern Desert, returning to the Old Pueblo, the city of Tucson, Arizona.

return to the old pueblo

In September 2015, I landed in Tucson with my beloved cat, Lady Lou, who, as my certified "emotional support cat," had ridden in the seat beside me. The hot sun of that day revived a feeling of home, and I remembered the good ole days of my college years.

The gentleman who picked us up from the airport took us to The Place at Old Spanish Trail, which would be our home for the next year, where I had a one-bedroom apartment. That day I anticipated a care person from a local agency to arrive. Unfortunately, the wires got crossed and nobody was available to help me that first night. So, I asked a neighbor, who obliged. The other thing that didn't come until the very last minute was my bed. But fortunately for me, the mattress I had ordered ahead arrived at about 10 p.m.

Around midnight, I was in bed on my new mattress in my new apartment with Lady Lou. Unfortunately for us, around 3 a.m.—God does have a sense of humor—I slid off said mattress onto the floor. Then I was on the floor in my new apartment in Tucson, with Lady Lou meowing beside me, wondering, *What the heck are we going to do now?* Well, I'm stubborn (as some know), and I did not want to call for help.

I waited on the floor for about two hours; and, in the process, I felt the urge to relieve myself. The choices were to try to hold it or let it go. I chose the latter and peed on the carpet. I figured I could throw Lady Lou under the bus and say that she peed on the carpet.

At 5 a.m. I finally dialed 9-1-1, and the Tucson Fire department came to my rescue. I explained that no care would come until the following evening, so they were nice enough to dress me and ensure I was set until the evening. In fact, one of the firefighters came back with some groceries for my refrigerator since I had just gotten to Tucson. So, that's worth a big shoutout to the Tucson Fire Department. For those of you wondering, I didn't end up blaming Lady Lou but told them I couldn't hold my bladder at my age of 51.

The first few months back in Tucson were very nostalgic; it felt like being back home. The first order of business was to visit my friends from the DRC, including Carol Funckes, the assistant director who had connected me with an advocate and helped me find my apartment. I was proud to roll back into the DRC and to see Carol, who was gracious and said that I was always welcome. I think she sensed that I needed a place to call home. I was hoping that the University could once again be that home in Tucson.

However, being with friends and role models from the DRC made me feel like a failure because of my layoff from Cox. I thought to myself, *I'm glad I came back, but did I make the right decision? What am I going to do with myself?*

My next priority was my faith. I was trying to reclaim the happiness I'd had in Tucson, wondering, *Can we re-find happiness at a place that we've been?* I visited the Church of Christ on Mountain Avenue where my roommate Paul and I went as students. I also visited the Newman Center and met with Father Albert, who said, "We're glad to have you here. We need you." I thought to myself, *Why do they need me?* Ultimately, I decided the

Newman Center would be my spiritual home once again. I took it as a sign when Fr. Tom DeMan, the pastor from when I was a student back in the 1980s, arrived to be retired in residence. He might not have had as much piss and vinegar as he did in the 1980s, but he could still hold his own! Fr. Tom is a great delegator; if he sees a problem, he'll kindly tell you, "Here, come over here and move this," or something along those lines. And that's the way he was in the 1980s. Heck, he even had the altar moved during his tenure! So, he might not be like Moses, but he's close.

Each time I came to campus over the first few months of my return, I cried. Being back on the campus of my alma mater was cathartic. This began my internal process of healing, while still realizing that you can never truly go back in time. I was thankful that I had the opportunity to return. I was returning to a place that I loved, realizing that it may not be what I remembered, but it did resemble a place that I cherished once, and now I was able to be there again as an older man.

I had to decide what I was going to do back in the Old Pueblo. With the help of the Department of Economic Security Vocational Rehabilitation, which had previously started me on the trajectory of success and enabled me to have further self-confidence despite my limitation, I would pursue my master's in social work. I thought, *This is something I could do to make a difference, to make a living, that could help society.*

I applied to Arizona State University's School of Social Work. It took a while, but on my first attempt applying to Arizona State, I got in and was due to start that fall of 2016. However, I would have to delay my entry.

I had wanted to give myself a year to decide where I should move in Tucson. True to my word, I ended up buying a home in northwest Tucson. There were some concerns, however. The traffic on River Road went at a great speed, and I was moving from an apartment that had the benefit of the Old Spanish Trail pedestrian multi-use path.

Just prior to moving into my new home, I had my first car accident. I was on the multi-use path, and a lady not paying attention backed into me from her son's driveway as I was on the bike path.

Then after my move to the northwest side, right at Stone and River where the QT convenience store is, a white pick-up truck, not seeing me on the shoulder, hit me on the side. Needless to say, the summer of 2016 was memorable but painful. Unbelievably, *I* was cited. I tried to explain to the officer that there were no sidewalks, and the ones that were there were in such disrepair that I felt them unsafe to utilize. But he wasn't hearing it. I was sent to traffic school for the citation so that I wouldn't have to pay the fine. I never fit any molds, and this one certainly cracked.

When the instructor saw me roll into the defensive driving classroom, he did a sort of double-take, "You drive?"

I said, "No sir. And you wouldn't want me to drive; my reflexes aren't good enough."

"Then why are you in this class?"

I explained that, according to the Tucson police officer, the gentleman was cited for hitting me, but since I was on a wide shoulder which was not considered a bike path, he decided to cite me too. That was the honest truth.

So, after he stopped laughing, we proceeded with the class.

This experience caused me to wonder if I had made the right decision about returning to the Old Pueblo. I thought, *It is what it is*, as my general manager had said when I was getting laid off. I kind of like that philosophy, so I found an attorney and sued the driver for hitting me. The money I got from the suit paid for my traffic school, so I was happy.

The accidents threatened my independence and further delayed my entry into the social work program. They had triggered post-traumatic stress disorder (PTSD), which I quickly learned can dramatically change your life. I had been used to being out without concern on my power wheelchair, but then at intersections, especially the one where I'd been hit at Stone and River, I became paralyzed in fear. I underwent counseling, eye movement desensitization and reprocessing (EMDR), and physical therapy. I just didn't feel I was ready mentally, let alone physically, for the program. Fate and Jesus might have played a role in the delay, as at that time I would not have been able to fund school.

While I was hoping to recover the happiness of my college years, these first several years in Tucson were some of the darkest of my life. This was because of the care situation. While I had some good caregivers, I ended up with some awful ones. One caregiver I had live with me had an addiction to heroin (and denied it). Numerous other caregivers stole from me. Another caregiver manipulated me financially. Another was emotionally abusive and chronically arrived hours late to my house. I would sometimes feel like a prisoner in my own home, wondering whether or not the scheduled caregiver would actually show up. And what could I do? When I couldn't find other caregivers, I was stuck with the bad ones. I had been burned so many times; I needed a break. I asked God for a break. I've asked Him for that a lot.

I was also attempting to self-medicate through my sexual addiction. I needed to feel better, so the only way I knew how was to engage in unsafe sexual behavior.

A light reignited through the darkness. That light had to do with my time in Florida. I reconnected with my friend Teresa Romano. She had and still lived in the neighborhood directly across from mine in Ocoee. She was a Godsend. Speaking with Teresa connected me to this portion of my life. This was a portion where I was economically more stable—in fact, I was wealthy, materialistically.

I would call Teresa at all hours of the day and night just to talk. She would always pick up the phone. We spoke of the horrid care that I was receiving. She would call me to encourage me and to see how I was doing, mentally and physically. Teresa was battling health problems of her own and could relate with my personal care struggles because she had to fight to advocate for her mother's care. It usually falls on the family. But in my case, I had no family that cared. Words cannot express my gratitude for what Teresa did for me during this time period.

God sent me another light. In or around the end of 2016 or the beginning of 2017, I was riding the city bus which was no surprise, since that was my main form of transportation. As fate would have it, I met Bethany and Gwen. Bethany too has a physical disability and uses a powerchair just like me, and Gwen is her trusted, faithful companion, who also acts as her personal care assistant. Bethany and Gwen and I conversed, and eventually I began to see them quite often. So, finally, I said to Bethany, "Bethany, would you like to go to the mall sometime?" Plus, I would speak to Bethany when I would see her in various public places, and she knew I was having issues with my personal care. In fact, she later told me that she was concerned about me, more than once, because of what I was enduring in my own home.

Eventually, Bethany and Gwen and I began to interact on a more personal level. I would visit their church on occasion. Bethany was in her 30s, Gwen in her 40s. They are very loyal to their faith tradition. They didn't have a car at the time, but eventually Bethany, through her grandmother, received an accessible vehicle. That gave them some further freedom, along with me. We could go on trips together not limited to the Tucson public transit system. Gwen was happy to have the car as well. Gwen is a very intelligent individual. She is an environmental engineer. Bethany is also intelligent and is a very faithful person to God. We had that in common. And I think that's what brought us together to become friends.

God sent another light. Frequenting the Newman Center at this time allowed me to meet Kevin, who became one of my best friends in Tucson. We met at the 11 a.m. morning Mass in 2016 and just seemed to hit it off. He seemed lonely and in need of someone to talk to when I first met him. So I said to myself, *I'm going to go up and talk to that guy! After all, I'm kind of in a similar situation.* The rest is history. Borrowing from *Tuesdays with Morrie,*[3] our meetings became "Sundays with Louie", and for two years we met for lunch almost every Sunday, talked for hours, and then I would take the bus home.

Kevin was also very important from a practical standpoint because I would no longer need to hold my bladder going to church. Kevin graciously helped me go to the bathroom any time I needed before or after Mass. Literally and figuratively, this was such a relief. Kevin's actions allowed me to just concentrate on the beauty of the Mass.

Kevin is a smart dude; he's in quantum physics. I appreciated this because at the time I felt like my brain was on pause. He is a compassionate, intelligent, caring person who questions when there should be a question and is silent when he's not sure.

Eventually Kevin met a girl named Kelly, and of course relationships require time and attention. Unlike how I felt when Jeff met his now-wife Jenny, being older and more mature, I realized I didn't need to be jealous of Kelly. She wasn't taking Kevin away. In retrospect, I'd felt that Jenny took Jeff away.

I can confidently say that my growth since becoming friends with Jeff improved my friendship with Kevin. I was no longer jealous and self-oriented. I now see both women as helpers for both men. It's important for people with disabilities to come to an understanding of their own loneliness, and to know that just because someone is able-bodied doesn't mean they're not lonely. I sense that my friendship with Kevin began from mutual loneliness. I had also been lonely when I met Jeff, but I don't think he was. So, this friendship was different because with Jeff the mutuality of loneliness did not seem to exist.

After my experiences with Jeff, I knew I had to do something different in friendship so that I didn't hurt people I care about, or myself. I didn't want to go through a second "divorce". I asked my then-physician, Dr. William House, for advice, and he told me a very wise thing: "Louis, if you love someone, let them go. If they love you, they will come back."

A lot of times in my life, I have had to roll back and look at things objectively. Through my hurt of my perceived loss of the relationship with Jeff, I learned how to move forward and move on so that when Kelly came into the picture with Kevin, the adjustment was a bit easier for me.

My relationship with Kevin was a fun one, like when he had to dress up as an elf. It was a Christmas party with my next-door neighbors. They absolutely insisted upon Kevin putting on the elf costume—and he did it with grace. That's when I realized this guy was the real deal. Unbeknownst to Kevin, that showed me that he truly cared about me, that he loved me. Heck, anybody can help you go to the bathroom for money, but how many people will dress up as an elf for free?

The foundation of our friendship was based in large part around the St. Thomas More Catholic Newman Center. I met Kevin's parents, who were steadfast in their faith as well. Interestingly, Kevin was wrestling with agnosticism, whether there was a God or not, for some time. When Kevin and I met, he seemed to be on a journey to find the truth. This journey I was humbled and honored to be part of.

One of the aspects of finding the truth for Kevin was the Catholic Bible Institute of Southern Arizona, sponsored and administrated through the Diocese of Tucson. I applied to begin the course in 2018, and I asked Kevin if he would do so with me. As it turned out, Kevin's friend Fr. Felix Just, SJ, was the main facilitator of the course, along with Dr. Daniel Smith-Christopher from Loyola Marymount University, a Quaker who taught the Old Testament.

Kevin and I were on the journey together. One Saturday, a month, for three years, we participated in the class. Fr. Just opened the Bible for me, both practically and metaphorically. I was hungry for the Bible, but we were never encouraged to read the Bible when I was at college as an undergrad, even though we had fiery sermons from Fr. Tom DeMan. This is why I would stray, as I mentioned, with my roommate Paul Halinan, to the Mountain Avenue Church of Christ. The Bible Institute firmly solidified my belief system's alignment with the traditions and beliefs of the Church I was baptized into, the universal church, Catholicism.

The Bible Institute had different purposes for me and Kevin, for sure. But it brought us together. Kevin was exposed not only to the material that was being taught, but he was also exposed to my humanity, to my needs as a person. He had already begun to help me on a regular basis with the restroom. He then began to help me, when needed, with my care. That began a little earlier than the Bible Institute because of the poor care I was receiving. Kevin was there, and said at one point, "As long as I am in Tucson, you will never be left in the bed more than you need to be." This psychologically helped me, and I began to grow once again. The scars of the Mannion's substandard care and my biological family's abandonment were beginning to heal.

The Bible Institute further promoted the healing process by immersing us in the Bible, having us reflect on what we read, and us having to write term papers. As one priest at the Newman Center, Fr. Emmanuel Taylor, O.P., stated, "We used one of those texts in my seminary formation!" So, I knew it wasn't going to be easy. And it wasn't. But it was healing.

I truly appreciated having Kevin. We began renting accessible vehicles to go to Mt. Lemmon, to Phoenix, or to the aquarium. Can you believe there's an aquarium in the desert? I know for a fact that it wasn't always easy for Kevin. After our daytrips, usually, he would say, after putting me to bed, "I'm pretty tired. But I had fun." So, I was grateful. Still having to deal with lackluster care, it was a breath of fresh air.

Between reconnecting with Teresa and meeting Gwen, Bethany, and Kevin, this began the foundation for allowing me to feel better psychologically because, honestly, living with a heroin addict and some of the terrible care I was receiving just did not make me feel good. I understand addiction from a personal perspective because

I too was addicted and will always have to be mindful and cautious in relation to sex.

Now, being a social worker, I can see and have seen what addiction can do to the person, both exteriorly and interiorly. The foundation of Teresa, Bethany and Gwen, along with my friend Kevin and his girlfriend Kelly, helped me to begin escaping the cloud and haze of addiction.

As much as Kevin's backup supported me, I needed a new live-in caregiver. I needed a new care arrangement altogether. One solution proposed was what I'll call "the Mannion proposal". The Mannions are Jeff's mother and stepfather, Maureen and Mike. The "proposal" was for me to move into their middle-aged daughter's home in Florida with her husband. Her children were going to college at the time. I would pay to modify their guest bathroom to be wheelchair-accessible, $800 a month until the bathroom was paid off and then $600 a month for rent. The Mannions made it clear that they would not be doing any of my personal care; I would have to acquire care from outside sources and pay for it myself.

I got excited about the Mannion proposal because I would finally have my family. I thought the Mannions were my family; they had acted as such when I was in Ocoee. I would be a liar if I said there wasn't that connection. My newfound friend Kevin was even getting ready to say goodbye. However, there were warnings about the Mannions' intentions.

I was grateful for the opportunity with the Mannion family. But it just didn't feel right in the Spirit. I spoke with Teresa extensively about it: "Why would I pay to modify someone's bathroom and pay them rent when they're not doing any of my care?"

I had actually helped out the Mannion family a lot in the past. Teresa reminded me of this, "Are they helping you? Yes. But they are certainly helping themselves." Indeed, they would be making money off my needs. She asked me further, "How often do they call in and check on you?" I did recall that the Mannions remembered me on my birthday and Christmas. But beyond that, I was the one making the phone calls and reaching out to them.

Jeff's father Brian, who was Maureen's first husband, warned me. "Be careful Louis. This seems to be moving too quickly. What is their hurry?" In the Spirit, I was being told to listen to Brian and Teresa. I knew that the Mannions did want to help, and I really wanted to have a sense of family. But the Spirit was telling me this arrangement was not what God had planned. I needed to wait in faith for the hand of God to bring the person of His choosing and not my own.

While I waited, I still needed to find care. So, I asked a fellow parishioner at the Newman Center, Gerardo, if he knew anyone who would be interested in moving in with me. At first, he wasn't sure, but a few weeks passed and he said, "You know, I do know someone, my girlfriend, Monique!"

"Great!"

The main impetus of this connection was because, unfortunately, Monique was getting kicked out of her dorm and needed a place to go. I'm certain that she was uncertain of what this would be, but she took the leap and decided to move in.

Move-in day came, and Monique's self-proclaimed posse came along to move her in. The posse included Gerardo, Gerardo's roommate Cory, and their friend Matthias.

Interestingly, Matthias does not remember meeting me at that time, probably because he was busy in the role of mover. Knowing Matthias as I do now, if his mind isn't focused on you, he's probably going to forget you. Little did Matthias or I know that he was the spiritual gift that I'd been waiting for.

a scribe for school

Around my birthday in 2019, Monique moved in. In the beginning, Monique did my personal care. However, she had issues with handling me physically, due to her own physical situation. Gerardo ended up being the primary caregiver.

By the time Fall began, I was sufficiently recovered from the two cars hitting me and reapplied to ASU's School of Social Work. I was reaccepted and enrolled for Fall 2019. However, that same semester, I got cold feet and dropped all my classes. One of the professors, Dr. Mic Byers, strongly encouraged me to reconsider. In fact, she had me sit in one of her classes as a guest, and asked me afterward, "What do you think? Are you going to come back in?" I decided that I would. Each of my professors had to individually grant permission for me to re-enter their classes. Fortunately, they did.

I believe it was divine Providence that I couldn't start the Social Work Program until 2019. If I hadn't been hit by those two cars back in 2017, I would have started my graduate work without a very crucial gift from God. As fate would have it, my connection with Monique and Gerardo presented the opportunity for that gift to enter my life: Matthias—the man who didn't remember meeting me. Now he can't forget me because as you will learn, we are extremely close. I have called others "Bro," but Matthias has truly accepted the vocation of being my brother.

As you will see, this book will no longer just be my book. Matthias is a fellow traveler in my journey, telling the story and sharing in the sufferings and triumphs and carrying of our daily cross. I wanted to bring the reader a unique perspective, one that had not been written about as much in literature, and that is the relationship between a friend and caregiver and the intimacy that is shared, from both points of view. From here on out, the narration will alternate between Matthias and myself. I'll let him introduce himself.

Matthias

I was born in Austin, Texas in 1999. I am the middle of five kids. Cradle Catholics, my parents sent us all to Catholic schools and retreats. My siblings and parents would agree that I was (and still am) often off in my own world. I was generally a good kid and did well in school. Dad was a spaceflight instructor for Space Shuttle astronauts who is now teaching high school physics and engineering, and Mom is a doctor in family medicine. They're both very intelligent and raised us well.

In middle school and high school, I began cultivating my passions: playing trumpet, drums, and piano; running cross country and track; writing stories (with their own languages and maps); and learning as many languages as I could. I also began to make my faith my own. I became a youth leader at our home parish, St. Ignatius Martyr, and I was a small group leader more than once for "Cross Training", a retreat offered for rising high school freshmen.

As early as middle school I found myself attracted to religious life. In high school (St. Michael's Catholic Academy) I was the "Jesus friend" in my friend group. I went to daily Mass in our school's chapel and had a serious commitment to praying the Rosary. I prayed the

Divine Mercy Chaplet every time I learned of someone's passing. It was well established among my friends that the priesthood was a serious possibility for my future.

Little did I know that I would fall in love four times (five, depending on how you're counting). The first time was with one of my high school friends. We started dating toward the end of our senior year. She's a very good person, and I learned a lot from her. We were both in love and cared about each other, but we ultimately weren't compatible. One key disagreement was on Catholic sexual ethics: she thought gay marriage was okay; I took the traditional Catholic position: marriage is between a man and a woman. I was also not prepared to sustain a long-distance relationship while 1) going off to the University of Arizona while she stayed in Texas for college and 2) wrestling with the idea of being called to the priesthood.

You see, on our 3rd date, we went to Eucharistic Adoration together. I wanted to make sure we did good Catholic couple things. Then, as we were praying side by side, the Lord put three words into my mind: "Be a priest."

I would spend the next three years trying to get this call out of my head.

Fall 2018, on my third day of classes at the University of Arizona, we broke up. I was a mess. I was questioning the foundations of my beliefs (not just on sexual morality, but God's very existence) and trying to figure out how to respond to the very clear call that God put on my heart. He didn't mince words. However, I longed to experience a romantic relationship and the possibility of marriage with someone I could truly be compatible with—where we could be truly united in the pursuit of holiness together.

Such was the state of my heart when I entered my second semester of freshman year, Spring 2019. I had chosen linguistics for my major and was becoming heavily involved at the St. Thomas More Catholic Newman Center.

The first time I remember meeting Louis was Easter of that year, 2019. I was already friends with Gerardo and Monique (I sort of helped set them up with each other). They invited me over to Louis's. Monique's parents and Louis's next-door neighbors were also invited, along with my friend Tony, the sweetest Black blind Jewish guy you'll ever meet. It was a wonderful motley crew for an Easter feast.

I especially recall three things from this visit and encounter with Louis.

One: Louis led prayer before the meal and said something to this effect, "I have prayed to God that I could have a family, so I am so grateful . . ." Whatever the rest of the prayer was, I could hear the need and longing in his voice and saw the tear in his eye.

Two: I spent the night on the couch bed there, and by chance caught a glimpse through Louis's bedroom door. He was propped up on some sort of stand, buck naked, and Gerardo was wearing gloves and wiping up Louis's poop. I wondered, *Am I ever going to be doing something like that?* I have a generally compassionate nature, but I kind of hoped I wouldn't. I mean, I had experience changing my little cousin's diapers, but I had never wiped an adult's butt. No one was asking me, but I distinctly remember that thought crossing my mind.

Three: I was invited to pray with Louis after the others had left, and Gerardo and Monique had gotten him into his bed. He was in bed, naked except for his covers (I would learn later this is the most convenient and comfortable for him), with a CPAP mask on his face. Monique, Gerardo, and I were sort of huddled on the ground by Louis's bedside, the lights now off in the room. I think

Gerardo held Louis's hand as we prayed, and I'm pretty sure they exchanged an "I love you" afterward, too. Louis remembers giving me a hug, and I remember being very struck by the look in his eyes: he looked like a baby, smiling and totally dependent on us, happily trusting. As much as it caught me off guard, it moved my heart: *This is a very unique house.*

I didn't interact with Louis again until Fall 2019, the beginning of my sophomore year. We ran into each other at the Newman Center, and Louis asked me if I wanted a job. He was going back to school to get a master's in social work, and he needed a scribe to help him with academic support. He said he'd pay minimum wage ($11/hour at the time in Arizona was a pretty solid offer for a college student without a job yet). I said, "Sure. Why not?" All the while, I wondered, *Am I ever going to do that . . . personal care stuff? I hope not . . .*

We would meet every Tuesday at the Newman Center after one of my linguistics classes. We'd then spend the next four hours or so with him dictating emails, homework assignments, and me furiously typing away on my laptop. It was good work. Louis had a good work ethic, and this would likewise motivate me to be more consistent with my own homework. It was hard for me to imagine just taking four hours straight to get work done, but that's what we did every Tuesday.

Once or twice that year, I saw Louis and Kevin head to the restroom together, and I understood that Kevin was helping him pee (I had already met Kevin through the Newman Center). I think it was very important that I saw this, because it told me that this was an okay thing to do, and I wouldn't be the only person to do such a thing if I ever did. I mean, I knew that Louis would pee himself if no one helped him, but seeing Kevin help him made me feel less awkward when Louis finally *did* ask me to help him use the restroom.

We were working at the Newman Center, now halfway through the semester, when Louis asked for my help. We just went over to the bathroom and shut the door. He did all the touchy work, all I had to do was unzip his pants and hold the urinal bottle in place, all the while making sure I wasn't touching him AT ALL. I'd occasionally mess up, or be too slow, causing some leakage, but Louis was very gracious and took it all in stride. I'm amazed at how often he is so grateful whenever there's someone to help, even if they aren't very good at it.

This became a routine. We'd do homework or projects, and then we'd trundle over to the restroom, with me fervently hoping that we wouldn't see anyone along the way. (Of course, we did see people several times. It was fine.)

We'd occasionally get lunch together, and I eventually learned that Louis also wanted to write a memoir. So, we began working on that, too. Whenever we found time for the book, we'd write a section or chapter, and I slowly acquired a glimpse into this man's wild, sorrowful, and joyful life.

In February 2020, right when COVID was creeping up on the world, Louis had gotten very sick. Perhaps it was COVID, although it was too early in the pandemic for him to have been tested, and he was hospitalized. Though I was initially reluctant to set aside the time, I made sure to stop by the hospital to pay him a visit. We talked and organized his pick-up van to take him home, and before his discharge he asked me to shave him. I could see he needed it.

I was nervous about this; I'd never shaved anyone other than myself and worried about cutting him. I also had to use a wash basin that one of the nurses left there.

Was it supposed to be used for something else? Louis encouraged me to not worry about it. I finally agreed. It wasn't five-star barber quality, but it was a shave, and I knew Louis appreciated it.

During our academic support time, I learned so much about Louis as he dictated his autobiography or shared by way of anecdote. I had learned that he was gay after the Mass of the Holy Spirit in 2020, when in passing he said, "I don't think I'd become a priest, because of my sexual orientation. . . " I had put the rest together. I learned that the remaining members of his immediate family had walked out on him, and that he lost his career and major source of stability. I learned that he had been raped, that he had been literally saved by the hands of Jesus from an exploding van, and that he had an uncommon connection to the Spirit.

At the beginning of my junior year in fall 2020, I had already thought of taking the semester off; I really didn't want to do Zoom school during the pandemic. However, I never took the necessary steps to actually take a break from school. So, it looked like I was going to school anyway, and I flew back to Tucson from Austin. Before the beginning of the semester, Louis finally, for the first time, asked me to help him out once with his personal care.

The previous year and a half had prepared me greatly for that moment. I had become a close friend to Louis way before this point, and I was now accepting that I might be called upon to help meet his physical needs. We had even talked about the possibility of me doing his care the summer before. However, had he asked for this back in 2019, or in early 2020, I would have been extremely uncomfortable. Taking care of a man, including showering him and cleaning his privates, can be intimidating.

Now, by fall 2020, I wasn't so squeamish. At least, I was comfortable enough to try.

I thought of Fr. Emil Kapaun, the Czech-American Korean War chaplain. When he was imprisoned in a North Korean POW camp with his fellow soldiers, he would actually clean up their waste and steal food to feed them as best as he could. If Fr. Kapaun could do this sort of thing, so can I. As I was beginning to undertake some of Louis's personal care, he made it known to me that he would need to take the semester off from his graduate work because of some eight to 10 kidney stones that were found in his system. Seeing that his personal care situation was rather squirrely at the time (little did I realize it was almost *always* squirrely, and that's an understatement), and that I sort of wanted to take the semester off too, I decided I'd take the semester off with him and help out with a good chunk of his personal care. Oh, I didn't quite know what I was getting myself into!

Louis

In meeting Matthias, I was so happy. I thanked God and I cried right after we prayed all together that Easter night, Gerardo, Monique, and Matthias by my bedside. I knew that this was the person God had sent, the one I was waiting for, just like Simeon knew when he saw the child Jesus:

Now, Master, you may let your servant go in peace, according to your word, for my eyes have seen your salvation, which you prepared in sight of all the peoples, a light for revelation to the Gentiles, and glory for your people Israel. (Luke 2:29-32).

This was the reason the Spirit told me that I had to wait instead of opting for the "Mannion proposal". I finally felt like I was able to breathe, able to move, not having to worry about having to find someone to care for me. This deep chasm in my life would be filled by a young man whose name, Matthias, means "gift of God". Matthias is very humble, and I'm sure he doesn't like me talking about this, but I think he understands and appreciates that I must.

Matthias and I didn't know what the road would be like, but from my perspective, it's been a road of discovery. While we worked on my graduate assignments, we were also building a friendship that I know will endure.

When Matthias came to the hospital to visit me in February 2020, I was soon to be discharged. Little did he know when he came in that I had a bedpan underneath me that the nurse had placed there. I had taken a crap. At least an hour ago. Finally, the nursing staff came in to clean me from the rear, while Matthias stood by the window, gazing outward to allow for some privacy—and maybe to avoid the stench.

When Matthias agreed to shave me, it was one of the best shaves I had received in over a week since at that point I looked like Sasquatch going to the prom—and smelled that way, too. Such was Matthias's introduction to Personal Care 101.

After cleaning up and being discharged, Matthias and I ordered my non-emergency transportation to take me back to my home where Kevin and Kelly were waiting for my arrival. Matthias then had to go back to his apartment in the west desert of Tucson, which was not close. I was very grateful that he had helped me arrange for the transportation back home.

One would think this would be uneventful. Well, if you know anything about my life, the most uneventful things can turn into an event rather quickly. The non-emergency transportation ride home in the back of an ambulance was no exception. You see, the driver picked me up, placed me in the back on the stretcher, and began to drive north on Campbell Avenue toward my home in northwest Tucson. All of a sudden, I hear sirens behind us. We were going rather rapidly, and it was quite bumpy. The next thing I know, two Tucson police officers were peering in at me as the driver was requested to open the door. Said driver was speeding—not an emergency. So, he got a warning or a ticket. Of course, by this time, we are well delayed. When I did reach my home, Kevin and Kelly inquired, "What took you so long?" I explained.

Matthias is so caring. When the pandemic hit, it became harder to get people to care for me from United Cerebral Palsy. The case manager even said, "We're gonna have to let one of the caregivers go that takes care of you because he doesn't want to get the coronavirus shot, and our position is that he has to in order to retain him. Would you be willing to take him?" And I said "yes." I began to pay for that particular caregiver on a private basis.

Eventually, Matthias was front and center, my primary caregiver, and stayed with me for half the week each week. In fact, United Cerebral Palsy brought over provisions and PPE. I was also grateful for my long-term care insurance through John Hancock and my employer as an external benefit. At that time, it was so hard to find someone to care for you due to the pandemic. So, Matthias and I had to do whatever it took to take care of me. Fortunately, I was able to utilize the long-term care insurance to pay for my care.

This was a critical time, more than ever. Matthias became certified (which I paid for, with Academy on Demand, called Caregiver Academy of Excellence back then) so now he could officially work under my care policy. This was a trying time, and he was willing to do things that frankly only a family member would be willing to do. There are many caregivers that left the caregiving industry during the time of the pandemic. As we all have seen on the news, they just became burned out or disillusioned by the numbers who were dying.

The pandemic was extremely difficult for me and many like me who have severe physical disabilities. I believe it will be written that this was a time that changed the way we deliver healthcare. Now it is taken for granted that you can visit your doctor or mental health professional virtually.

This was also a time when great isolation occurred. The programs that supported the most vulnerable among us ceased. We must as a society remember the lessons we learned from the pandemic and grow from those lessons. In my view, our society is becoming more and more challenged to take care of those of us on the margins. We must remember that we are all connected in our humanity. My hope is that we all believe in God, because as you know, I do. But I also realize candidly that many do not. So let us remember that if you do not believe in God or Jesus, believe in humanity. Believe in our common humanity. That is what the pandemic taught us as a nation. What type of public policy will we create for those who live in the margins: our homeless, our hungry, our children, our elderly?

Whatever your political ideology, remember this: if we live long enough, we will all become disabled. I have come to realize that the resources that you have help you overcome many of the obstacles for humanity. If you have an abundance of resources, you have an abundance of opportunity. If you lack of resources, then you lack of opportunity. We as a collective must realize that those of us who have resources today may not have those resources tomorrow. This is what the coronavirus pandemic taught me. I lost many friends, as I'm sure many of you did, to the coronavirus. One thing I learned was that you can't take your resources with you when you travel to the other side. In my case, travel to the other side means traveling to the eternal side.

So, while we are on this earth, remember the resources, and I hope we all will share what we can.

Matthias

Even though I wasn't in school that year of 2020, it was my busiest semester ever. I was still working for the linguistics department online and was still an active student minister, helping run the Newman Center during all of this. Plus, I resumed my relationship with Nicole (the fourth time I have fallen in love), whom I had previously dated (the second time), just when the pandemic shut everything down. It was God's grace through many channels that enabled me to juggle it all in some sort of manageable rhythm. I would basically just stay at Louis's from Sunday evening until Wednesday morning, doing the majority of the personal care shifts in that whole span. Nicole would then pick me up from Louis's to take me to my house with my college roommates until Sunday evening and repeat the process.

Having taken a brunt of Louis's personal care upon myself, and realizing just how vulnerable he was and how great his needs were, I began to ask myself: *Why isn't our church community more invested in his needs? Is it not the call of the Church to care for the orphan and widow, to be attentive to the marginalized, and meet their needs? Is this not what the early church did?* "They had everything in common . . . and laid their money at the feet of the apostles, who distributed each according to their need"? (See Acts 4:32-35) Or how they appointed seven deacons to meet the needs of the Hellenistic widows? (See Acts 6:1-7) Where was our church, our Newman center, when this man, effectively an adult orphan and active member of the parish, had so many needs? I can see that Kevin and I, and a few others who were Newman Center members, happened to help Louis out. But the Church itself, as an institution, hadn't lifted too many fingers to help Louis in his need. Why did it feel like I was the only one who cared this much? This deeply troubled me.

I think of my friend Tony and the amazing amount of support he is able to receive from his Jewish community. "Need help paying rent? Talk to the rabbi!" For Catholics reading this, can you ever imagine asking a priest for help because you're short on your power bill? To me it's unheard of. To the Jewish community, it's standard fare. The rabbis are actually allotted a certain amount of money specifically for the purpose of helping congregants in need. Why doesn't our Church take greater responsibility for her children?

To be fair, I cannot neglect to mention the many members of the Newman community who have been incredibly supportive, even in small ways, of Louis and of me supporting Louis. I especially think of Nicole. It was quite providential that Nicole and I lived two blocks from each other *and* that her family's house (where she stayed for the weekends) was also in northwest Tucson, just a 10-minute drive from Louis's house. The stresses of Louis's and my relationship and of caregiving would be covered with joy as I looked forward to seeing her again. She is an incredible listener, and I continually thanked God for her. I think also of Ethan and Emma who had also given me countless rides from Louis's and back. I think of Fr. John Paul's spiritual direction, helping me navigate the boundaries and stresses of being a caregiver and close friend at the same time. I think of my roommates who supported me personally and emotionally.

Even still, when it came to Louis's direct material needs, it seemed like Kevin and I were the only Newman people who could or would lift a finger. This sometimes angered me. Sure, it's really personal stuff. Sure, it's time-consuming. Sure, Louis is just a needy guy in general. *But he's one of us, and what would Christ do for him? These are precisely the people He chose to identify with.*

I still don't have an answer to this tension within me, but I have accepted that I must be the change I wish to see in the world. I must be Christ's hands and feet on this earth.

Louis

Gerardo and Monique moved out of my home shortly before their child, Enzo, was born in February 2020. Prior to leaving my home, Gerardo said, "I'm sorry man, but I have my own family. I have to leave." I understood, and I was glad to help them and was happy for them when they later married.

Matthias and Kevin were still around, so I knew I had them for support. And Rich was still there doing the day-to-day personal care. Kevin would fill in voluntarily, and I was so grateful, because he always would say, "You never will have to worry about being left in bed, as long as I'm in Tucson." I must say as well that Rich never left me in bed either, as others had done.

February of 2020, when the country was in the beginning stages of the coronavirus pandemic, we had no idea of the changes that the pandemic would make and cause. During that time, as a nation, we knew very little about virtual platforms or virtual visits. In fact, just in December of 2019, I was in the midst of my graduate work and one of my professors had centered one of our big assignments around the use of Zoom, and how she felt Zoom would be such an important tool for us to utilize as practitioners. That prophecy, if you will, could have not been more timely. My professor took much heat from the administration, but she pursued and persisted. I am so glad that she did. It was only four months later that Dr. Michelle Beyer's prophecy came to reality. We were now living on virtual platforms. Zoom was the way. In fact, we switched rather abruptly from in-person to Zoom.

I had another professor, who is now since retired, Dr. Holschuh, who struggled gallantly to continue our statistics class via Zoom, never thinking, in her words, that she would have to use this form of media to teach her craft. We as a class and a collective encouraged Dr. Holschuh as we all struggled in the beginning of the pandemic. Life would never be the same; especially when I took the semester off to take care of my kidney stones.

Matthias

Louis and my father have a lot in common. They are both "professional patients", as my father likes to call himself. Louis readily adopted the phrase and now uses it for himself. Like my father, he is no stranger to the ins and outs of medical procedures, hospitals, being an inpatient and outpatient. I know it is my father's experiences with his immunodeficiency (Wiskott-Aldrich Syndrome) *and* my mother's tireless, devoted care and advocacy for him that helped prepare me to be a caregiver for Louis. Further, my mother, herself a doctor, extended this kind of care to anyone who found themselves in her circle.

I particularly remember when my mother would take us with her when she was helping her best friend's aging father with wound treatment. She had no qualms taking my younger brothers and me to the assisted living facility with her to visit Mr. Buxkemper. I was deeply affected, seeing this 90-year-old man, missing limbs and fingers to recent amputations, with his frail wife beside him, reminiscing of how he had been the quarterback for

UT Austin and was doing backflips when she met him. But even more poignant than these was my mother's dedicated service to him, his wife, and her friend (their daughter). I was in high school at the time and altar-served at Mr. Buxkemper's funeral when the time came.

Like Fr. Kapaun's tireless service for his fellow soldiers in the U.S. Army in the Korean War, my mother's example and my father's experience gave me much of the crucial formation needed to be a caregiver for Louis. And he knew it. He never tires of expressing his deep love for me on account of this. The days leading up to the first kidney stone procedure were an ample opportunity for Louis to reflect on his mortality and my presence in his life.

I thought he was being a little dramatic. All he had to do was an ultrasonic shockwave lithotripsy, a non-invasive procedure wherein he would be immersed in a bath as ultrasonic waves propagated through the fluid would hopefully break up the stones in his kidneys. He would need to go under anesthesia, but the procedure seemed fairly low-risk to me. Louis was more nervous about the anesthesia and going unconscious—they've had trouble waking him up before. But I was not aware of this at the time.

It was some day between the 5th and 7th of September 2020. What happened that day I recorded as soon as I possibly could after it happened. This is what I wrote, with some additional words for clarity's sake in brackets.

[September 2020, a few days before the first lithotripsy. Transcribed from the green notebook.]

Louis appears to have had a vision.

We were just talking, and he was expressing just how deeply he loved me, making sure I knew before he went into surgery. [We were in the alcove of his house.]

He removed his glasses, was crying a little, then he mentioned that there was a tingling in his leg and his hands, just after he expressed his deep, complete love for me.

[He started looking away, as if looking into the distance.] Then he said he saw the garden, that he was going to it. He was walking, and there were many purple violets . . . and lots of orange and purple chrysanthemums, and he saw his grandfather, his grandmother, AND his mom's dad. (So, both grandfathers.)

He had never seen Grandfather Vujevich's face before. But he was very convinced it was him. He said he had a darker complexion, wasn't very tall, and had black hair. Said he looks like Uncle John.

But this whole time, I was filled with not the idea that he might start walking, but that *I*, faith completely in Christ, would remove the crossbar, put up his footplates, grab his hand, another hand on his stomach, and say "Rise and walk!" and he would get up, and his stomach would come to normal size.

But I recognized that I hadn't had enough faith, and that I just needed a little more, that Christ WOULD use me to work a miracle, and have Louis walk, right then and there. He would use me, an instrument of His, to make him rise, because I, *we* believe in Him.

This is what filled my heart and mind; filled me with awe. I was terrified.

The Lord has big plans.

"If you have faith the size of a mustard seed, you would say to this mulberry tree, 'be uprooted and planted in the sea,' and it would obey you." (Luke 17:6)

[Later that day, Louis told me, speaking of when he passes on.] "My brothers won't recognize me, but I'll recognize them. Matthias, when I go, you'll be praying for me, and I'll be praying for you. And when you come, I'll be there to greet you."

[While he was in the field, he explained that] "There was no pain, no pain in my body."

Afterward he said, "I feel my left hip again."

This wasn't the first time Louis had crossed the veil. He told me that he had visited this field numerous times, usually while unconscious. Beyond the flowers and people, he mentioned that there is no pain. No hunger. And he walks, even runs, feeling the grass under his feet. Other times, he stated that the atmosphere was of love. Only on that September day before the procedure did I witness him go there.

Since that day, I began to nurture a serious hope and expectation that a miraculous healing was not only possible, but highly likely. When? No clue. But we began to discuss the idea of a pilgrimage to Lourdes, France, where the Blessed Virgin Mary appeared to St. Bernadette in 1858. Some 70 or so miraculous healings have been *officially* verified to have occurred there because of Our Lady's intercession. This isn't counting the many other miracles that have not been officially investigated, such as my friend from the Newman Center being cured of celiac. She said, "I didn't know how to feel. People come to Lourdes wanting to be cured of cancer, and I came back able to eat cookies."

There we would seek the healing that could end so many of Louis's physical and care issues. Such a potential healing seemed to be hinted at by the tingling in Louis's legs, a phenomenon that he would report at other key, spiritually charged moments.

Louis ended up needing three kidney stone procedures, and I was able to accompany him to the hospital for all three of them. This was in spite of the COVID restrictions, which were prohibiting all visitors at the time, but we made sure to call Northwest Medical Center ahead of time for each procedure, requesting that I be allowed in because I was Louis's PCA (personal care assistant). They even put my name on Louis's whiteboard!

The first shockwave lithotripsy wasn't too rough. Louis just had to deal with the after-effects of the anesthetic (almost throwing up, being groggy the rest of the day). The second lithotripsy was even less eventful; neither Louis nor I remember there being any symptoms whatsoever. All well and good. The third lithotripsy, however, was a nightmare.

Before this third procedure, we met with Dr. Page. He explained that the shockwave procedures had broken up some of the stones pretty well, but the stone fragments were all still stuck in Louis's kidneys. His solution was a ureteroscopy. He'd use a scope with a camera, laser, and basket attached to it to break up the final stones and fragments and scoop them up. Dr. Page made sure that we understood that this was a risky procedure, especially with Louis's very twisted back. Louis agreed.

You see, I had put two and two together and recognized that Louis was in for a really fun surgery: ureteroscopy = ureter + scope. There's only one entry point to reach the ureters. I knew what that meant. However, when Louis was dictating an email to me, I had to ask him. . . "Uh, Louis, you do realize that this isn't another shockwave lithotripsy, right?"

"What?"

"It's a ureteroscopy. They stick the tube up your, you know . . ."

"Really? Are you sure?"

"I brought home the pamphlet; it says it all right here."

And Louis had to agree that I was right. All he said was, "Okay."

I couldn't believe it. "You signed up for a ureteroscopy, and you didn't even know what it was?!"

Louis just laughed.

It was sort of funny at the time, but not in the aftermath of the procedure. Dr. Page said it was one of the most difficult surgeries he had ever performed, owing particularly to the curvature of Louis's spine. But he managed to get every last stone.

After a ureteroscopy, the ureters are very swollen, and stents (thin plastic tubes) must be left in there to keep them open so that the kidneys don't back up and fail. To keep the stents in there and be able to get them out, they are tied to a catheter running outside of the urethra. Dr. Page's orders were that it would stay in for a week before we could pull them out. As you can imagine, Louis was *not* a happy camper when he awoke from anesthesia.

His first words, uttered several times thereafter, were, "Take it out!" The nurse Luc and I told him again and again, "No, Louis, we can't take it out." He kept demanding (and sometimes asking) anyway.

After several minutes, Louis accepted his post-op fate, and we went home, exhausted. I had the instructions on how to clean the catheter and empty the catheter bag to prevent a UTI, and life would continue.

It only took a day for Louis to be back to his usual self. His urine was still fairly bloody owing to the surgery. I'd be emptying the catheter bag of said bloody urine, and he would say things like, "Red wine anyone? Hot off the grapes!"

Despite our efforts, Louis did end up getting an infection. A nasty one. Just five days or so after the procedure, he developed a very high fever and just wanted to stay in bed for most of the day. I was back and forth between calling my mother (who is a doctor), AZ Urology (to reach Dr. Page, if at all possible), and Kevin.

It was Monday. At some point in the afternoon, Dr. Page scheduled Louis to go to the lab for a urine sample which would take place Wednesday. At best, he could prescribe a specific antibiotic by Wednesday afternoon or Thursday morning to target whatever Louis had. Until then, we just had to sit tight.

Louis recommended we check his temperature again: 103.9 F. I called my mother (who's an hour ahead of us over in Texas), and she said that was really bad. I then called the AZ Urology emergency number, and thank God, it was Dr. Page who was on call.

"A 103.9?" he asked.

"Yes," I said.

"Screw the urine sample. I'm going to prescribe a general antibiotic *now*, and you're going to pick it up *tonight*. Louis isn't going to make it to Wednesday."

My eyes widened. I understood. Dr. Page and I agreed on a pharmacy that was near Louis's house, and I slipped on a backpack and my running shoes and ran out of the house. I wasn't going to wait for an Uber if the pharmacy was that close.

Several minutes into my frantic run, I received a phone call from Dr. Page. He said I had to go to a different pharmacy (the other CVS was closed, it turns out), a little farther away. I thanked him for the call. I hailed an Uber.

I explained the dire situation to the Uber driver, and he was kind enough to wait outside the pharmacy until I came back with the emergency prescription so that he would be my ride back to Louis's house and I wouldn't have to wait.

I arrived at the house and rushed inside to have a semi-conscious Louis take the heavy-duty amoxicillin. Time felt blurred, and when I wasn't thinking about what I was doing, I was praying, *God, keep him safe. I don't think it's his time yet.* Yes, I was very worried, but I honestly felt pretty sure that Louis would make it out at the end of this one. Something told me that God wasn't done with him or me.

Sure enough, his fever began lowering the next day, and he was more or less back to normal by Thursday.

Louis always tells me that he thinks it brought us closer together when I saved his life. He's probably right, but there's one crucial element to the story I must not leave out. It wasn't until much later that Louis told me *his* side of the story.

"You remember Matthias, while you were out and about, calling Dr. Page, and I was totally unconscious and about to potentially die?"

"You think I'd forget?"

"I left my body again. I went to the field."

My ears perked up.

"I went to the field again, and there was this one part of the field that I've never gone to before. There were these big golden gates. No words were spoken, but, in the spirit, I knew, 'Louis, if you go past these gates, you will have to stay. But if you stay on this side of the gates, you can choose to go back. The choice is yours.' Well, I decided to stay because of you. And Kevin."

I have had to pray about this a lot. It is difficult to express how this makes me feel, how it humbles me. The man turned down early entry into eternal *bliss,* final rest from this difficult life of his with his broken body, so that he could be here *for me.* And Kevin. I still cannot adequately put this to words.

Louis

I personally have a vague recollection of Matthias's return from the pharmacy run, but I do know that I was glad to see him. I had the sense that he was taking care of me, and I felt safe. I didn't really think about my independence at that time or whether or not I had a physical disability. All I knew was that I was glad to have a friend who cared for me.

My relationship with Matthias has been interesting for me, because he is a gift. However, at times, I'm not sure he likes being a gift because I think he thinks it objectifies him. I hope that he truly realizes that he is a gift, not an objectifying one, but I can understand his concern. We have had many discussions about boundaries, and we both have grown—and are still growing— a lot. This is where our relationship is fairly deep. We can talk about just about anything very openly. The expanse of our age difference doesn't seem to matter. I enjoy having him by my side.

I can say this for sure: I love him. We have had many discussions about love and intimacy and what they mean. I have gone through counseling for this because my sexuality is such a part of me. The incident with Cox, my relationship with a subordinate, wasn't the first one, and it wasn't the last where I had feelings for a person and really didn't know how to manage them. Up until very, very recently I even had feelings for a person that took care of me who was toxic and abusive in financial and emotional ways. But at the same time, I felt responsible, because we did have sexual encounters. This is something that isn't often talked about openly. Although in both situations the other party was a willing participant, I learned that you must have boundaries.

Since I am trying to be as candid as possible, I know for certain that Matthias loves me, and I am learning how to love more appropriately. And for this, I thank him.

The idea of hurting Matthias is one that I think about often because I've not always been good with boundaries. As I've mentioned earlier in the book, I have been raped more than once. I've had indiscriminate sex with anybody that would. Sex was an addiction for me. As of late, I've gotten much better through counseling, and I've decided that if I'm going to be an effective social worker, I have to figure *me* out. Having sex was a way of escaping many pains: the pain of having a father, who at best, was conflicted about my existence; the pain of the loss of my mother; the pain of being institutionalized as a child at the Home of the Merciful Savior; the pain of being taken from the home and the family to the Home of the Merciful Savior, not knowing where I was going; the physical pain of surgeries as a child; the physical, emotional, and psychological pain of watching the abuse of my mother and brothers; the pain of knowing, in fact *meeting*, one of my father's girlfriends, and never telling my mother. The pain of looking like a Norman Rockwell painting on the outside, but with the cracks beginning to show as domestic violence reared its ugly head. One of the basic tenants of that endemic disease is of silence: Do not tell. I felt as though I was a captive witness.

On the positive side, that pain began to turn into advocacy. On the negative side, it turned into sexual addiction.

The one thing that Matthias has taught me is that he loves me unconditionally. Honestly, I don't always trust that because I think there must be a motive. Matthias is teaching me to take into account the person, and at times, the pain of the person. I think I've learned that I was trying to cover up the pain, but I was using the wrong medicine.

I wonder if I can stay on this tight rope without falling off. There is no net beneath me. Having Matthias in my life has provided some sense of a safety net. I believe this is all interconnected in a psychosocial way to having a disability. I have come from a family of privilege in which my brothers biblically did what Cain did to his brother, Abel: stripped him of his privilege. I honestly have been angry. I am still learning how to forget. I fear being on the street. It's not very rational, but the way the world's going and anything is possible. I am grateful for Matthias and his care, but I just don't want to overwhelm him with the weight of caring for me.

Recently, I've been thinking a lot about my animal companions during my early years back in Tucson: Lady Lou the cat, Lily the Shih Tzu, and Toby the pit bull mix. Those three beings also taught me how to love and how to receive unconditional love. The question is, have we learned from the animals that love us unconditionally, that see no disability, physical, mental, or emotionally?

I think the main thing I have learned from my furry friends is that unconditional love derives from love itself. I hope and pray that to those (and you know who you are) that I have had sex with who may read this book, I apologize for objectifying you, and I hope that you can forgive me, unconditionally.

beginning to see the light once again

In Spring 2021, the academic counselor for Arizona State University and I decided I should resume my studies in the Fall, after my sabbatical, to ensure course alignment. I believe this was a good decision. The extra semester gave me further time to heal, and it also allowed me to engage with other events surrounding my life.

Kevin and I were in our final year for the Catholic Bible Institute of Southern Arizona. It was the practicum period of the course and so we had to design a program that we would deliver on the parish level, which was quite extensive. Again, the stars seemed to align to allow me the flexibility to concentrate on my faith while healing from the ureteroscopy, which was more than I thought it would be. As Matthias mentioned, I underestimated the toll the surgery would have on my body. Bessel van der Kolk is correct: The body does keep the score.[4]

One thing I've witnessed in Matthias is his strong sense of social justice, particularly in regard to one of my overarching issues, that of personal care. How did the Church, specifically the Newman Center at the University of Arizona, view my situation from a social justice perspective? He was determined to find out. He wrote an email to Sr. Angélica, one of the sisters at the

Newman Center, who was responsible for the Social Justice Committee, which he served on.

Matthias Jeffery Mahoney
Feb 10, 2021 5:13 PM
to: Kerst J Kingsbury, Sr. Angelica Velez, O.P.

Hello!

I have been considering composing an email like this for some time. Since I was at least a high-schooler, I have nurtured a vague dream within me, one whereby the Church effectively and generously provides support for those most in need.

I do not see this at the Newman Center. My perception that "something is missing" is certainly fueled by very particular circumstances, but, re-gardless of my bias and the particularities which drive me to write this, I think as a Social Justice Committee, we have the opportunity to become something amazing.

What I see lacking is the fact that Louis, as far as I have seen, has received only nominal sup-port in his needs from the Newman Center *per se*. Never has he seriously imagined that substantial support was to be found in the Newman Center it-self, or any Catholic Church for that matter. I can't help but reel back at this perception. I compare this with my Jewish friend Tony, who largely hesitates to join Catholicism (which he has seriously consid-ered) because there isn't the same system of social support like from his synagogue community. ("Oh yeah, we need help with my housing payment? Call the rabbi!") Jews take care of their own, and (at least so I've heard) so do the Mormons, in ways more substantial than Catholic communities tend to in our modern culture.[5] I sense (and so do others) a weaker commitment to social justice among our very own communities than that which is found amongst other religious groups.

In the short-term, I desire that the Newman Center community be committed to Louis's care in such a way that he would never have to worry about his stability of care again. The most stable care he ever had in Tucson was with Gerardo and Monique because they were living right there with him and picking up all the care shifts (getting him out of and into bed, cooking, etc) that others couldn't. Even with things being sort of stablish now, there is still great insecurity in that there is no guarantee of sustained care in future years, especially his older age. To behold such a state of life of one of the members of the Body of Christ and let him *remain* in such insecurity is unacceptable. I recall the Hellenistic Jews, who complain to the Apostles about their widows who were being neglected (Acts 6:1-7). Their response was to appoint the seven deacons to minister to their needs. What are we doing?

Secondly, in the long-term, I desire that the Newman Center community be a community that can effectively meet the particular needs of its members, especially the most vulnerable, be it from disability, lack of family support, aging, loneliness, etc. As the Social Justice Committee, this very type of need ought to fall right under our purview! My dream is not merely a desire to help Louis out, but to grow something in this Newman Center that enables us to care effectively for many people throughout the years and generations to come, whether these be caregiving needs, disability needs, food needs, etc. We must be a Church that cares for her members, especially the most vulnerable. Can we provide for every physical need that our community experiences? Of course not. But we can certainly do more. Could we provide for Louis's every physical need? Of course not. But we can certainly do more. And this "more" requires a well-planned structure and base. It requires time, commitment, people, and lots of love.

I confess that my dream is vague, and that it demands a lot. But I believe that we are capable, and that we can foster something very beautiful with the Social Justice Committee and the Newman Center—something that would give us a very concrete and powerful sense of purpose. I feel that our Social Justice Committee lacks this strong sense of purpose, and I want that to change. I am in no way disappointed with the many things we have done over the last two semesters; I think our last Newman Night was pretty fantastic and that our plans for the next one are awesome. But I fervently believe that we can be more.

Yours sincerely,
Matthias Mahoney

Sr. Angelica Velez, O.P.
Feb 11, 2021, 4:56 PM
to Matthias Mahoney, Kerst J Kingsbury
Thank you, Matthias,

You are correct in challenging what social justice looks like in our midst. This is a question that tugs deeply in my heart as a person, as a woman religious, and as a member of the Church. It is what Pope

Francis continually challenges us as Catholics! You have started the conversation of what I believe is truly at the heart of being a Church for the poor and vulnerable!

As you describe your encounter with your Jewish friend and how his community takes care of their own, it resonates with what I often witness and know about other Christians who take the gospel of feeding the hungry, visiting the sick to heart. When I see the way other faiths live the call to be merciful, and companion the vulnerable, I know individuals do respond. I also know that some parishes do more because individuals take the lead in their faith communities. It isn't that the Church does not take care of its own, it is however, a call to ask ourselves how we do justice! The Catholic Church and for that matter parishes are generous in feeding the hungry, visiting the sick/imprisoned but we do not always comfort/support one on one as you speak about in Louis' life. The mission of the Church is to protect the dignity of the human person and to take responsibility for the common good. Justice is not an option yet as you point out, individuals act generously, are moved by compassion, and have a sense of being merciful.

Rather than go on, I want to affirm your deep reflection which raises the question of what it is to do social justice! I want us to have this conversation and to begin a way of talking about what matters in our faith by asking deep questions! You have pushed the button towards moving beyond just doing service, you have asked for theological reflection! We will begin!
Thank you, See you later.
Sister Angelica Velez, OP
Pastoral Associate

Louis

Matthias's compassion for folks who face some type of vulnerability is omnipresent, just like Jesus. I asked Matthias as we were writing this section, "Did we do anything?" His response, "We had a discussion once. Myself, Sr. Angélica, and Kerst. Nothing really came of it."

To be fair, Sr. Angélica, like many positions in the Newman community, is transitory. That's the challenge for most Newman Centers. The Social Justice Committee did eventually create a resource board that they posted on the bulletin board downstairs (directing students to resources such as Campus Pantry, which offers free food for students, etc). Matthias speculated to me that his email and subsequent conversation with Kerst and Sr. Angélica helped prompt this posting. I believe he had an impact.

It seems to me that the question of church and state comes into play. The Church, and in this case, I am referring to my Church, the U.S. Catholic Church, had a rich history, and then sadly, has scaled back its efforts.

The Catholic Church built many hospitals and children's homes. Now, the Church, due to, in my view, the sexual abuse scandals that rocked the Church in the '90s, and, quite honestly, the litigious nature of our American society, keeps itself at arm's length, where once there was embrace. This is not entirely the fault of the Church. There are about 70 million Catholics in the United States, as of 2020. The challenge is, how many are practicing? Of the number practicing, how many think they have the time to do such initiatives?

Matthias's fervor is youthful fervor. When I was in my youth, I too had great fervor. As I am now in the latter portion of my existence, the fervor seems to dissipate slightly. But I still have the drive to make a difference and facilitate change. I think the answer to the question is what Jesus did when he saw the Samaritan woman. That's what Matthias does, or attempts to do, hopefully with care. Like Sr. Angélica stated, she has a passion for helping and understands the need. As she also stated, however, you have to have the structure and resource. You have to have the *want* to. If we want to, we can do anything we want to do. But if we see, in my view, obstacles and let them dictate our response, then we will not move forward. We will only be entangled in our own obstacle, no matter our verbiage.

I believe that in my friendships with Matthias and Kevin I was given two gifts. Prior to them, I was dealing with so much transactional care and being taken advantage of. I say "transactional care" because the majority of paid caregivers are there to do a job: they are there to get paid. This is not to say that all transactional caregivers are bad. Some are professional and ethical. But you can feel the difference between someone who cares to make money and someone who cares to care.

And the page turned to a new era of Kevin and Matthias, surrounded by people who tended not to look at the care as transactional, but as purposeful. As my friend Maryanne Schiavone stated when she herself needed care, it is a very tough position to be in. She had a care agency take care of her. Some of them weren't so good, some were good. Bottom line, it was all about the dollar. And that's what a lot of folks with disabilities face.

There was a recent study done by the University of Minnesota which I took part in. One of the questions asked was, "How many people around you are not paid to be there?" It was done on a Likert scale. Quite telling. Because most of the people, I'm certain, were paid to be around the individual. That's the way our system is set up. If the family is not the bedrock of the care, even just to be there, then in my view, a lot of abuse can take place: psychological, financial, and for that matter, physical and/or sexual.

Research from a 2018 NPR report shows that individuals with intellectual and/or developmental disabilities (IDD) are seven to 10 times more likely to be victims of sexual abuse.[11] Better screening of individuals that care for us needs to occur. You can't correct everything, and I am the first to say that I had my own issues with boundaries and sexual behavior.

My sexual behavior of the time that I speak of stemmed from when I was a young man, just starting college. As a teenager I did not feel comfortable in my own skin because I don't believe my parents were comfortable with having a gay son.

I experimented with women when I was in college and at Cox (I have spoken of one of them). I had a relationship with a woman who was a 9-1-1 operator for a little while. It was after my mother's death. In fact, my father's girlfriend at the time met her. So, I had two relationships with women. Most of my other relationships were with men. I never had to pay for sex with women, but indirectly or directly, I paid for it with men.

I'm ashamed to say that I was ill. I was trying to fill a hole, especially after my mother's death. But this was going on even before her death. Why do I think this was a problem even before then? For a couple of reasons. One, when I was nine years old, as I mentioned previously, my father took me to a female strip bar on our way home from discharging me from the Home of the Merciful Savior. Just looking at it objectively, how many people do you know take their son, who happens to be *nine* years old, to a female topless bar after being discharged from an institution that he stayed in against his will for three years? Well, I know one. My father.

The night my father took me to the topless bar changed how I looked at sex. First and foremost, how the heck was I allowed into that bar? God only knows, but my father knew a lot of questionable individuals. That experience changed me. It took away my innocence. It also taught me some bad lessons. One: it was okay to objectify. Two: you could give money to people, and they will do sexual things: shake their boobs, their rear ends, or whatever. To me, that translated later in life to *Well, if you give someone some money, you can have sex with them as an adult.* That isn't cool. I am so ashamed of that part of me.

It is only quite recently that I have begun to heal. ASU's social work program required me to participate in two internships. Prior to starting my second internship, which would be with Southern Arizona Center Against Sexual Assault (SACASA), my first internship supervisor, Dr. Lynne Tomasa, suggested I seek counseling for myself because of my sexual abuse experiences. Thank God I did, because it also uncovered other experiences from my childhood. It took me a lot of years to face these experiences and be able to speak about them.

In my social work master's program, I reflected a lot because that's what we had to do in the program. This also helped me directly and indirectly with my own personal growth and development. I pray with great fervor to my God that I will never have to endure or go back to the person that I was prior to the social work program. I was exiting, in my view, this dark period. Matthias officially entered my life on Easter Sunday 2019; the day we celebrated Jesus' resurrection. It was also the day for me personally that I celebrated *my* resurrection from the Good Fridays I experienced almost on a daily basis.

Matthias is much younger than I am. I think at first many were concerned what my motives were, not the least being Matthias's older brother James. I believe that James was concerned because he knew me only from Matthias's eyes. I was older, had trouble with boundaries, especially when it came to sexual boundaries, and Matthias, I believe, reported such. So, if I were James, I'd have been concerned, too.

Matthias was 20 when he started the personal care. I also told him about my long-term care policy and asked if he would like to get certified. He said he would, so he did. I paid $600, and that got him certified under my long-term care policy, *thank God*. He is extremely intelligent, so it didn't take much for him to pass and do the clinicals at a local assisted living place. They seemed to like him there. He always was on time. He was always very respectful, and it was just a joy to have him around me.

One of the conversations that we would have from very early on in our friendship and relationship was, "What is the difference between sex and intimacy?" Matthias and I are extremely intimate with each other. We might hold each other or hug each other. We've slept in the same room and the same bed a few times, but we respect each other. I have cried in Matthias's arms. We discuss boundaries. I have crossed boundaries. But we have never had sex. And it's the best intimacy I've ever had. And since I've known Matthias, that chasm of loneliness has gone away.

Matthias

As Louis hinted and I'm sure you can imagine, being an intimate instrument of brotherly healing can be a very rocky road. Week after week I would come back to his house because his care needs dictated it. I loved the idea of being a scribe, the humility that is required to give your hands over to transcribe another person's voice and the dexterity required to keep up with the typing (which I thoroughly enjoy; any Dvorak keyboarders out there?), not to mention the simple gratification received in helping someone out with the kinds of physical needs that Louis has. It feels good to help.

Nevertheless, as the weeks went on, I began to dread coming back to Louis's house. A sense of anxiety would slowly creep in. I had begun a routine of mental preparation to steel myself for what might come up in our time together. *Why?* I honestly didn't understand it myself for a long time.

Entering into the deep relationship with Louis, I was keenly aware of his sexual wounds. By this time, he had already dictated the first half of this autobiography to me. He shared openly. I was also keenly aware of my own wounded sexuality. It was in high school that I finally began the arduous battle of seeking sexual sobriety from masturbation and "soft" porn. Only after several years, midway into college, did I finally reach a point, by the grace of God, that I could say I was sober; I was free. Recalling particular moments of that healing journey still brings me to tears to this day.

I experienced Christ's redemption of my sexuality. For too long, the experience of feminine beauty was a source of anxiety, a temptation to avoid, overstimulation to fear. But as I grew into greater freedom and self-control, *beauty commanded respect.* I can now peacefully protect myself from overstimulation (that's by much prayer and practice) *and* I can rejoice simultaneously in the powerful goodness of my sexuality and feminine beauty, recognizing them as icons of God's love. It's energy; if rightly channeled, it is a source of intimacy and life with my potential spouse.

That being said, another question weighed heavily on my heart, ever since high school. *What can that healing redemption be like for people attracted to the same sex?* The disagreement with my first girlfriend intensified my interest in this matter. Intuitively, at least, I know that my desires have a natural orientation and fulfilment. That very idea is crucial for healing and acceptance: God made us good, and our sexualities, though broken in this world, are inherently good—*and thus redeemable.* But if I were gay, then there isn't an obvious natural way to direct my desires . . . is there? I'm sexually attracted to the sex I'm not supposed to be attracted to! As a devout Catholic, what can I expect myself to tell people, how can I expect myself to encourage others, especially those of us who are attracted to the same sex, on the journey of sexual redemption in Christ Jesus?

I read Eve Tushnet's *Gay and Catholic,*[6] and following her recommendation, Wesley Hill's *Washed and Waiting,*[7] as well as his more recent *Spiritual Friendship.*[8] I highly recommend all three of these raw, heart-wrenching (and sometimes spunky) testimonies on the topic. They are incredibly insightful, and I believe very valuable for anyone: gay, straight, or otherwise.

But little did I know that God had been preparing for me to learn what that sort of healing could look like, on a very personal level. This is no academic theological reflection (you bet I've reflected on it theologically though, don't get me wrong). I was given a window into that healing process in the most direct way possible (as much as possible for this straight guy, anyway) and that is on the journey of me learning how to love Louis and Louis learning how to love me.

evolving fraternal intimacy

I, Matthias, have never truly dealt with abandonment issues before. They are very real and not trivial at all. Consider Louis's position and his needs. His brothers walked out, his parents are gone from this earth, he lost his one job that really supported him, and his needs are all the same—more actually, as he's aged. Spending a lot of time with him, I saw how all these things cut to his soul and left very deep marks. Many times, he would just break down, crying, and tell me, "Don't leave me!" Or he would tell me, "Hold me!" and I would hold him, and I would tell him, "I'm not leaving you, Louis."

During one of these episodes, Louis was crying, "Don't abandon me!" and I think it just came from my gut when I told him, "Stop. You're in *my* family now." I meant it then, and I still do today. I wasn't quite sure what I was getting myself into, but I didn't want to see Louis in this pain anymore, so I decided that I would be part of the answer. You could say this was the third time I fell in love. Not a romantic love like the other times, but a significant moving of my heart and soul nonetheless, a very emotionally invested and serious commitment.

Now you don't just say things like that and expect no consequence. I said this before him and before God, and I will be held to it. And I could tell that Louis took it very seriously.

Louis

When Matthias uttered, "You are in my family now," at first, I was taken aback with emotion. Then, in my style of reflection, I wondered, *What did he really mean?* During this time, I was not very trusting of most people. Matthias seemed to be different. Teresa Romano would always say, "Do they call you or are you calling them?" Matthias's words were ones that indicated he was calling me. Matthias is a soul beyond his years. He's also human. So, I proceeded with caution.

Matthias

Very often, when I was caught up in uncertainty about my vocation in life, especially about whether or not I would continue dating Nicole or pursue religious life, Louis would go into big brother mode. "Matthias. This!" (pointing at my heart), "Not this!" (pointing at my head). These are the moments I can appreciate more easily, and when I am overwhelmed with his physical affection and outpourings of love, I would turn to these moments as a refuge. These are the moments he felt to me more like a father or big brother figure, rather than like a lover. Those moments when he's pouring out his affection, desiring to hold me, or talking to me the way I would only talk to a woman, are the moments when I wish he weren't gay.

Louis

Matthias isn't the only one who's felt this way. My sexuality has been a source of internal struggle for me as long as I can remember.

One day, I was talking to God, "You must think I'm pretty strong. You have me gay AND disabled. Man made me this way, not you, and I know this, because my brother who was also born a preemie escaped the clutches of disability. Well, I'm not that strong, God. Either you gotta take my disability, or the LGBTQ issues . . . on second thought, you can leave the disability, I can't handle being gay."

So, God asked me in the Spirit, "You don't want to be gay, but you can handle being disabled?"

I said, "Yes. Because the faith practice says, 'You can't do that.'" *Or does it say that?*

God said to me, "No it doesn't say that. It says, 'You are my son.'"

"Who is it that says that?" I asked.

"The Bible. Romans, Chapter 11."

Romans Chapter 11 basically teaches this: The Church started out of Judaism. Then the Gentiles listened to Jesus' teachings. So, bringing it back to my situation, being gay and a practicing Catholic, and one who has not always followed the exact letter of the teaching, but one who loves God, wants to please God, appreciates God's gifts, I was somewhat concerned. As Paul was discerning, "Who's the outcast and who's in?"

We are all part of the body. Each of us make up a different part of that body. So, my question to God was, "Being gay: is that part of the body of Christ?"

I tend to think the answer is yes. Thanks to Pope Francis, we're in a period of greater inclusion. Paraphrasing Fr. Mike Schmitz, "We are *us*. The Church doesn't *tolerate* you. You *belong* to the Church."[10] So, in my opinion, there is something to be learned.

Regardless, I kept asking God to take away my sexual orientation.

God said, "No, I'm not taking that away from you. You are going to learn from this. You are going to bring people to Me with your being gay and being physically disabled. Your disability and sexual orientation are vehicles that will bring people to me."

I said, "Okay, could you give this assignment to someone else?"

He quickly said, "Nope. It's your assignment, customized and custom-made for you."

My experience of being on the margins, of being not understood, of BEING is an act of grace. Even though God pointed this out to me, it's not always easy.

Matthias

While I was still wrestling with the potential call to the priesthood, Louis told me: "You know, if you don't get married, I feel like I'm the closest thing to a spouse you're gonna get. Now if you were to get married, that's a little different, and my role would be a little more drawn back. But the way I see it, if you were to become a priest, I feel I would have a little more latitude. Sure, you have the congregation and the parish. But versus being with a woman, who has a claim on you for many reasons . . . financial support, procreation, taking the kids to Little League, making sure you're home for dinner . . . There's a definite line there. But even if you were to marry Nicole, we have a mutual understanding."

Louis would say that about Nicole and me many times. It really bothered me because every time I heard him say that, it meant to me that Nicole would have to just "understand" how Louis was occupying emotional and physical intimacy space that should be reserved for her. In fact, the very idea of crossing over that space is one that can make me very angry. If you know me, I'm terrible at getting angry. I sort of gave up getting mad at people around nine years old when I gave up fighting with my younger brother. But when it felt like Louis was crossing over into this territory, claiming some kind of *rights* to this intimacy space I had no intention of including him in, that struck a chord which made me *very angry.* Incensed is a good word. Most of the time, though, I would say nothing.

As time has gone on, though, he compares this imagined outcome to Kelly's understanding of his relationship with Kevin. From what I can see of Louis's dynamic with them (and that's a lot), their example is much healthier than what I feared would exist in that potential future with Nicole, myself, and Louis. However, that reassurance hardly quelled my concern, considering how Louis would still blur that line, the line between friendship intimacy and what felt like lover-intimacy with me.

One of these line-blurrings was his suspicion of my conversations with others about us. I remember us talking about this. I was often stressed out and anxious about our interactions and thus needed to confide in people frequently. Louis was always curious (read, *suspicious*) of what others had to say about us. Not to say that I'm not concerned about what others think; I definitely am, but Louis would always ask me. One time, I built up the courage to ask him, "Do you need to know what other people say?"

"Yes. If I ask you, I do."

"No, you don't."

"Look. Your mom, James, Nicole, Kevin, Michael. These are the only people I trust. Anyone else, you need to tell me about them."

"No, I don't."

"Yes, you do."

"Do you trust me?"

Louis paused at that one. "That's a really good point. . . . point taken."

This was not the only time we had had conversations like this. To be fair, while Louis has a responsibility to let me have my own conversations about him, I have come to recognize that I also have the responsibility to be discerning about what I share and with whom I share it. In this close relationship, especially with the level of dependence Louis has on me, I have to recognize the extent to which my openness to other people's thoughts impacts my own thoughts and thus has a direct impact on Louis. Sometimes people contribute sobering, constructive criticism (such as reminding me to set clear boundaries and that Louis needs to respect them) and sometimes people sow destructive seeds of fear ("You need to exit being with Louis ASAP, no matter what.").

Another of these line-blurrings was Louis's desire for a ring to express the commitment of our relationship. We would call this our friendship, our brotherhood, our fraternal covenant; we had a hard time pinning down a consistent term for it. Louis wanted a ring that would tell him that I was truly committed to him and that would be his commitment to me. As he was growing in chastity, he would say things like, "The ring, Bro, would be the symbol of my commitment to you. That I will be chaste to you."

It wouldn't necessarily always be a ring. Sometimes, the idea would be for a ceremony, something analogous to a marriage or an adoption, something to ratify the mutual commitment between each other. When I shared this idea with my spiritual director, Fr. John Paul, he observed, "It sounds like this is more for Louis than it is for you." That was true. When I shared that with Nicole, she agreed. Fr. John Paul also asked me, "Is that going to be enough for Louis? You have shown him that family level of commitment time and time again. I'm not convinced that any ceremony, symbol, or sign will be enough if what you have done is not enough."

When I shared the ring idea with my vocation director at the time, Fr. John Marie, I also explained how

Louis saw it as his way of being "chaste to me". Fr. John Marie said, "Matthias, that's for Jesus. Not for you."

All difficulties of Louis's and my friendship aside, I need to also state how supportive Louis was for my relationship with Nicole. He would calmly listen to me and offer brotherly advice (like the heart-over-head admonishment) as I navigated my relationship with her and my vocation discernment. He strongly encouraged me to enjoy the relationship; Nicole was very good for me, and Louis thought I was good for her. He would often remind me of how I would light up, smiling more and laughing more just talking (or thinking) about her.

Nevertheless, the time came for me to stop dating Nicole. I have felt the pull toward religious life since 7th grade and was agonizing over the question since graduating high school. I finally accepted that I could not die without trying religious life. Even though I was very much in love with Nicole and was delighted beyond belief at the very thought of giving my entire life to her, I could never convince myself that I was called to be a husband. I *tried* to convince myself that out of my love for Nicole, but I just couldn't do it. In fact, the notion of having my own wife and kids felt like a constraint on my heart.

I greatly respect the freeing exclusivity of giving yourself completely to your spouse (and to no one else in that same way), but my heart felt a greater love—and in a different direction. There is something alluring, beautiful, and intoxicating about belonging exclusively to Love Himself. I knew in my heart that I would not be loving in my most authentic way if I were not celibate. As much as the joyful redemption of my sexuality pointed me toward a happy marriage with Nicole, I feel a deeper fulfilment even with respect to my sexuality with the prospect of vowing myself to God.

Further, I knew that I needed to be freer to give myself for people like Louis, for people like Tony. God has given me a heart for His people, especially the poor, and having my own family would be too great a material and spiritual conflict with that wider calling. So, as much as I was infuriated by the idea of Louis's needs encroaching upon my theoretical marriage, my commitment to him testified to the reasons I could no longer date Nicole in good conscience.

Nicole and I were going to have a day trip up Mt. Lemmon. It was May of 2021. We had been dating consistently for an entire year. Louis encouraged me, "Wait 'til you get to the top of the mountain." So, I did. This was the best possible relationship I could have ever asked for; it was one of the hardest conversations I had to start in a long time. She took it very well, and our continued friendship to this day (though a rocky road, too) is a source of great gratitude to God.

I can't thank God enough for the grace of her presence in my life when we were dating and after. I called the Dominican Friars of the Western Province, the same province that ministers our Newman Center. I would not be able to visit them until November. I went back home to Texas that summer and drove up to Dallas to visit the Southern Province Dominicans for a day. I liked them but did not feel called to their community. I stayed the night with Nick Stavitsky, my roommate from 2020-2021 and a very good friend.

When I described my relationship with Louis, the idea about us "being brothers", and Louis's strong desire to have it ceremonially ratified in some way, Nick said, "Matthias, you put your life on hold for this man. If that doesn't make you brothers, I don't know what does."

Months later, early November 2021, I flew out to Oakland, California to stay for a weekend at St. Albert's, the homebase priory of the Western Dominican Province.

It was now time for me to fall in love the fifth time. To explain what happened during my visit to St. Albert's and why I want to be a Dominican now, I *could* talk about the deep resonance in my heart with the Dominican way of life (to praise, to bless, and to preach; sharing the fruits of contemplation. . .), how my fascination with language so delightfully lines up with this, and my desire to be a confessor; but those are just ancillary details. When the day comes and you ask me, "Matthias, why did you become a Dominican priest?" the truest and most succinct reason is this: Mary smiled.

At St. Albert's, there's a beautiful statue of Mary in the courtyard. One night during my visit, I prayed there, and in my heart, I told her: *I want to be a part of your family.* Boy did she respond. The next night, I was praying by the statue of Mary again. Suddenly, I received a flash of an intuition, a glimpse of her sheer beauty in her identity as the Mother of God. It is nothing less than falling in love.

That love that I knew about, that love that demanded exclusivity to God, that love that felt constrained by nothing less than celibacy, came flooding into my heart in full force through the Immaculate Heart of Our Blessed Lady herself. In love with a woman, I see her beauty and she delights me, moves me to want nothing else than to give my entire life to her. Well, raise the beauty, magnify the divine love involved, what follows? Delight in being pure self-gift, back to One who Is Love, at the behest of His Mother. I so very much wanted to go and start religious life.

This great joy was tinged with a sadness though. What if Louis's needs are too great, and he would need me to not go enter the Dominican Order so that he can have the quality of life he has a right to? One of the novices there was in a similar situation with respect to his older brother with severe autism. He understood, but he was happy, nonetheless.

My Dearest Mother, Our Blessed Mother, gave me this answer in the Spirit: *Do not be afraid to take Louis on.* As vague and mysterious as her encouragement was, there was peace. I also understood that she was encouraging me to receive Louis as family as she had received me. From that point forward, my conviction to pursue religious life has been rock solid. There was no turning back. And, one way or another, Louis was going to be a part of that journey.

While I was there, Fr. John Marie also invited us discerners to join the Angelic Warfare Confraternity for chastity. Under the patronage of the great Dominican theologian and saint, Thomas Aquinas, it is a prayer-confraternity, meaning that members who are enrolled commit to praying 15 Hail Marys a day for chastity. This commitment is not binding under pain of sin, but the graces come a lot more readily if you actually pray it. I initially thought to myself, *I've already mastered chastity, I'm good.* But then I thought better of it, knowing that arrogance, especially when it comes to this arena, would not be helpful. Fr. John Marie enrolled us, and as a sign of membership, I put on the white cord (under my shirt) with 15 knots for the fifteen Hail Marys. You could alternatively wear a small medal, but I opted for the more traditional cord, which hearkens back to the cincture with which St. Thomas Aquinas was girded by two angels for the protection of his purity.

Novitiate is the first year of formation in religious life for many religious orders in the Catholic Church. It is a year reserved for prayer and spiritual formation in addition to deep discernment on the vows of poverty, chastity, and obedience. When you profess final vows to religious life, it is on the level of marriage vows. You are professing yourself to God and His Church. Nuns are brides of Christ, and a priest is bridegroom to the Church.

As a Dominican novice, I would be very removed from the rest of the world. There is quite a bit of removal from the rest of the world that also continues throughout religious life. As you can imagine, the prospect of me effectively dropping off the face of the planet was no small area of concern for Louis and myself. Now, try to enter my head. There is a great growing tension as I not only navigate boundaries with Louis in our day-to-day life, but also as we navigate and plan for my entry into religious life. I couldn't stay with him for much longer. I tend to keep a lid on things, that is to say, I don't express much anger. Ever. But these two things were pulling at my mind and heart with greater and greater tension.

Two big things would bring me back to center to help relieve these tensions. One was divine reassurance. One time in prayer, up on Mt. Lemmon, Our Lady encouraged me at a particularly stressful moment in my heart; She told me in the Spirit, *Do you want to enter religious life? I will bring you there.* Whenever I doubt that I won't be able to make it (i.e., never be able to leave from caring for Louis), I return to her reassurance. Further, in spite of the boundary blurriness and frustrations that could arise between Louis and myself, I knew that he had a fierce love for me, the kind that Scripture talks about, "Love is as stern as death" (Song of Songs, 8:6).

I composed the following little poem about Louis's care for me:

How important it is to know this:

the amount of people you can really count
who would beyond the shadow of a doubt
die for you, at a moment's notice.

So often when I am stressed or feel discouraged about continuing forward helping Louis in all his needs, I repeatedly come back to this insight about Louis and our friendship: I know he's willing to suffer the worst for me. He would die for me if the opportunity presented itself to him. One summer we went up to the Grand Canyon together, just him and me. There was one point where Louis thought I fell off the side of the canyon. I had run a bit farther ahead on the rim trail, and evening was approaching. At one point, I heard Louis's call, looking for me. I heard the heartbreak in the tremor of his voice. You could have pulled his soul out for all I knew. Part of me was put off by that kind of response to me. I said to myself, *He doesn't need to be that attached to me.* But another part of me could not help but be impressed. There's a kind of love there that is rare in this world, and I know I have that kind of love for him, even if I am often afraid of that love within me.

This is the kind of connection that Louis and I have. He would die for me; he *knows* some secret part of my soul because he is one of the few people that I know that has that kind of love, the love that is truly willing to suffer for another. He turned down early entry into eternal life (and freedom from life with disability!) to remain here longer on this earth for my sake and for Kevin's! That's a love I cannot forget. That's a love I cannot afford to spurn.

Louis

I'm sure the reader has put a lot of the dots together and is asking, "Is Louis in love with Matthias?" The answer to this question is unequivocally *yes*.

Beginning in Easter of 2019, a spark ignited in my soul. Matthias was whom I was waiting for. In my view, Jesus, God, and the Holy Spirit, along with the Blessed Mother, brought me a gift. In 2019, I fell in love. A love that is deep. It is not a sexual love. Have I ever had the image in my mind of having sex with Matthias? I have. However, I place them in God's merciful hands, then say, "Stay away from me, Satan and demons!" You see, my crossing of sexual boundaries has caused me great pain.

Matthias is one of the first individuals in my life whom I have pledged to my God that I will not cross that boundary. My chastity is too important. It does not mean, however, that I am not in deep love with Matthias. I love him fraternally; I love him for the person that he is. I will not objectify him. I will care for him if he is sick; I will bathe him if I need to. I will clean his excrement, and as he has said, I would die for him. If you think about it, a lot of these qualities are what our veterans say about their fellow brothers in arms. I was never a veteran, but I serve veterans at the VA Hospital in Tucson. I have been doing so since the Fall of 2015. Many of the stories that veterans tell me are about their brothers in arms and the love for their brother after being together on the battlefield.

Prior to meeting Matthias, I was on a battlefield. Beginning in 2001, when I first thought about this book, my life began to become more and more conflicted. After my father's stroke and learning that my mother had multiple myeloma, a form of bone cancer, I offered to do a bone marrow transplant if I was a match, but my mother refused because she did not want me to go through the pain. As the reader knows by now as well, my mother and I had conflict over the money that my father set aside and that she wanted to give a portion of it to my brothers, which I finally conceded to do. But it was very contentious and calling my mother a bitch was one of the worst things I ever did for my soul and in my life because the person who helped me so selflessly was the one whom I so selfishly treated.

How does this relate to me and Matthias? I learned from my experiences that when you have someone who loves you, you treat that person with dignity and respect. Quite honestly, I saw that from my mother, and although he softened in his older years, I never witnessed it from my father. My father treated my mother with great disrespect. Being the oldest child, I was witness to more than my two younger brothers were. They were too young.

With all this being said, when Matthias came along, I knew he was a gift. I wasn't going to screw this gift up. Matthias is the first person to really not have any misgiving of showing his love. Maybe it's because he was discerning religious life. Maybe it's because it's just the type of person he has become through his parents' childrearing and example. Matthias has great parents, Marjorie and Bob, along with his siblings. Maybe that's the family whom I was looking for. So certainly when God, the Holy Spirit, and Jesus, along with the Blessed Mother, placed Matthias in my life, I fell in love, just like Matthias fell in love with Jesus and the Blessed Mother. Our love is based in and around our faith. I can tell you with certainty that if we did not have common faith, we would not have common love.

Ours is a love story, just like John Cappelletti and his brother Joey's story in *Something for Joey*. This film chronicles John Cappelletti's love for his brother as he wins the Heisman Trophy for Penn State in 1973. This love is the type of love that Matthias and I have. It doesn't come around all the time. It's a love given by God and through God. Our love has never been objectifying.

He has never stolen from me, physically, emotionally, or spiritually. He has only heightened those opportunities.

You know, Matthias never questioned me or asked me about the monetary resource he was being given to take care of me. I was paying him through my John Hancock Long-Term Care Policy, but he never pressured me. Most individuals would demand their due. Matthias, from the beginning, has not wanted his due, but only to ensure that, in love, the man he calls his brother was taken care of. Hence, he has chosen to be his brother's keeper.

Matthias

As much as I would feel uncomfortable with the idea of Louis "being in love with me", another aspect which he frequently emphasized was that he never loved anyone like me, except for his mother. This perspective helped put me at ease—but I would question it, too. One Sunday night I was telling myself, *Louis's love is a selfish love. He's just satisfying his own needs by pouring out his affection onto me. All of this is a dreadful, impure SOMETHING that's way out of proportion for love between friends, between "chosen brothers". He just loves me for what I can do for him . . .* This kind of distorted thinking is what demons love to feed on.

The next day we watched *A Beautiful Mind*. I was struck by a singular grace, a special insight about Louis and me. As he reached out for my embrace (reflecting on how Nash's wife's love for him paralleled our own dynamic), we prayed, and I was filled with a unique calm peace.

My soul was at ease before Mary, and I saw that Louis's and my relationship—in all the emotions, all the intensity—and my care was something distinct from everything I feared it to be. This wasn't the exclusive, romanticized/romantic love I was so skittish about.

This was something different. It's not that my fears were without validity. Inasmuch as Louis may try to use our relationship to fill his need for exclusive love (that need we feel so keenly in our sexuality), it will hamper the ability for our friendship and brotherly love to authentically flourish. It's not that a very deep intimacy cannot exist in the context of a friendship like ours. But we do not often see that level of intensity except in exclusive, romantic love.

It's also understandable that I may feel Louis just loves me for what I can do for him. Louis, being physically disabled and emotionally needy, makes it such that he is often benefitting at my effort, and, physically, I receive little in return (that I could easily receive elsewhere, namely money and food). So, yeah, he loves me for everything I can do for him. But that is not all he loves me for. This is proven by the fact that he turned down early entry into Heaven to be with me and Kevin.

purposeful suffering

What is meant by purposeful suffering? I, Louis, have wrestled with this question since birth. You think God allowed my disability to occur? Or did God send me down to the place we call Earth whole? NICUs for preemies in the '60s were not what they are today. But, even with all the advances in technology of the 21st Century, the incidence of cerebral palsy as a birth injury is still statistically prevalent within the United States today.[12] In my case, it was because of mistakes made by man in my first days on Earth. For others, they are simply born with it. Does God allow—no matter the technology—imperfections of His creations?

In order to give this a bit more clarity, I need to go back to my brother Edward who was also born premature; his birth weight was even less than mine. I have often wondered why he was spared the clutches of a physical disability, while I was not. I think it has something to do with purposeful suffering. When our father died in 2010, Ed said he didn't believe in God. I had to ponder this. If you know and believe in your God, that He died for you on the Cross, you know and believe that He also suffered with a purpose, the ultimate purpose: the forgiveness of man's sins. If one does not believe in God, like my brother at that time, can he experience purposeful suffering? When he does suffer, does his suffering go unrewarded?

In my case, my faith in Jesus has allowed me to see meaning in my suffering. I think suffering is not always easy, but it has great rewards. Man does not necessarily know how to react to someone's suffering. I know I certainly don't. It is very much an individual journey; it's unique like your DNA; we all handle it differently. It doesn't make it right or wrong. I do believe, however, that if you don't have your faith, you won't have purposeful suffering. I question whether or not you could look at suffering objectively. Without objectivity, you can only see suffering from a one-dimensional view, and that one-dimensional view blinds you from experiencing the joy and totality of suffering.

Recently, I was at a mall in Tucson, and a blind man walked by. I have great respect for individuals who are blind and perform activities of daily life like it's no big deal. This was one such person. I could not currently handle such an existence. It doesn't mean, however, that I couldn't learn—through faith—how to handle the next challenge. I think that's the key: faith.

Joni Eareckson Tada is one of my heroines. She is disabled due to a diving accident in the Chesapeake Bay back in the late 1960s. She acquired her disability adventitiously. I acquired my disability congenitally. Both of us, I believe, understand the value of suffering. An interesting research question would be, "Does someone who has a congenital condition like me versus someone like Joni, who has an acquired condition, have a greater understanding of the meaning of suffering?" Or does that not matter? I don't think it matters whether you have a disability from birth or from an accident. In my view, these are gifts, unwrapped at different times in purposeful suffering. I have said that my disability is like an unwrapped gift underneath the Christmas tree on Christmas Day. Sometimes, I prefer to leave it that way. Other times, I accept it, and when I do, I tend to learn something about my humanity that I didn't think about before.

Sometimes the present under the proverbial tree is connected to my sexuality. Even today, people don't think of people with disabilities wanting to express their sexuality. They tend to only see the surface which is the device they're in and what type of physical needs they have, but not their sexual or intimacy needs.

One of my professors at Arizona State University, Dr. Lela Williams, has done some groundbreaking work, along with other colleagues, on intimacy and ability status. Well, as a budding social worker myself, I hope to continue in that vein, to bring intimacy and ability status to the forefront.

The majority of the times that I have had sex, I've had to pay for it. It's been very transactional. It doesn't make the other person bad, but that's just been my experience. I would also say that that's part of purposeful suffering and my self-image as a person. Honestly, I have only recently been willing to admit that I struggle with pornography. I'm sure I'm not the only one, even though sometimes it's felt that way. It doesn't matter whether it's straight pornography or gay pornography—it's pornography. For me, it's gay pornography.

I think of my friend Liberace, whose lap I sat on when I was nine with his big white mink coat. Little did I know that the guy's knee that I was sitting on was a gay man. But he was. Sort of ironic, because I later found out that Liberace not only struggled with sexual addiction, but also struggled with, or tried to justify, the idea of faith and being addicted to pornography, let alone being a closeted gay man at the time.

Supposedly Liberace stated, in later years, that God gave him a pass, basically. He died of AIDS in the mid

'80s. I've since wondered, since we are both Catholic, if God really did give Liberace a pass. I kind of hope so, since I too struggled with that same addiction.

Faith is not a Disney ride. It is a roller coaster. It has its twists, its turns, its ups, its downs. Just like the roller coaster, it's all about how you enjoy the ride. Well, we should enjoy our faith. It's a gift from God. Going back to my heroine, Joni Eareckson Tada (whom I've never had the pleasure of meeting by the way) seems to truly enjoy her faith. Is that not what we all should do? Take one's faith into one's heart, like one takes their lover on their marriage day? Should we not be lovers of faith, which means we are lovers of Christ? Just like a marriage, it's not always easy. But in the end, is it not worth it? I think so.

Connecting an experience like rape to purposeful suffering is not easy either, as, quite frankly, I realized that this did *not* have to happen. I've asked God numerous times in my prayer what I should have done differently so that I wouldn't have been a male rape victim. A male rape victim with a disability is not an anomaly; there are more than just me. This is another area in which I think God is guiding me. Perhaps when I become a social worker, this experience will allow me to better help others.

Sexuality and intimacy have been a challenge for me. I no longer hide behind my past and present. I only hope for the future that my faith can heal. It's kind of interesting because I hope to find someone whom I can share with, where I don't have to rely on friends with benefits, and I can find someone who truly loves me and I love them. Is that what we all want? Whether you have a disability or not, that isn't the point, I think. The point is, we're relational people. We are made by Jesus, and Jesus does not make junk. Life and its challenges tend to make us feel like objective junk. Or, at least, it can.

As you all know, from the pages of this book, my family looked like Ozzie and Harriet from the outside with the well-manicured grass and the immaculately kept home. But inside that home, there was lots of pain and suffering, which still today, causes estrangement for my two brothers and me. My hope is that my story, as I am telling it as candidly and honestly as I can, will help bring you joy in your purposeful suffering.

When God told me he had taken my mother because, "She needed to rest", it made a lot of sense. My mother was the epitome of suffering to me. She had three children with some type of complication or death. Her first was my older brother, unnamed, buried in Mt. Carmel Cemetery in Pittsburgh; her second was me, who had an issue of cerebral palsy; and her third was my brother Edward, who had heart problems and was not expected to live.

My mother was the one who shared her faith with all of her boys; but for me, it was a faith that was intertwined with suffering. My mother lost her father when she was about 18 years of age. She, along with my uncle Steve, had to raise their younger siblings to ensure that they had educational benefits and opportunity. Their mother, my grandmother Eva, was an immigrant from Croatia, who, to the day she died, did not truly speak English clearly. In fact, at one point, she said to my mother, "Why did you not teach me more English?" I found that to be an interesting comment. She was asking her eldest daughter the question in such a way that it almost seemed as though, in my view, she was really saying, "Why did you cause me to suffer?"

In my life journey, as I progress, now entering the later years of my existence, I value suffering even more. I think I am to learn, with each passing day, that suffering is a learning tool, not from this Earth, but from the Divine. Some of the happiest people I have ever met were those in hospice and palliative care, people who are suffering from our societal vantage point. Those individuals are on the other side of suffering in many cases.

For instance, I remember Dr. Costanza, whom I met at a hospice house I volunteered for in Orlando. He was "suffering" from Lou Gehrig's disease. When I met Dr. Costanza, the first thing he asked me was not my name, but what time it was. I said it was 3 p.m. He quickly responded back and said, "No, it's not. It's 2:59 and so many seconds to 3 p.m. In the future, when I ask you what time it is, young man, that's how I would like you to tell the time."

"OK, yessir." So, ever thereafter, whenever I would talk with Dr. Costanza, I would make sure I told him the time to the second.

What I learned from that time experience relates to purposeful suffering. We only have so much time. Dr. Costanza, who was 'suffering' from Lou Gehrig's disease, wanted to know the *exact time* so that he didn't waste any of it. That gave me some things to think about: *What did it mean to waste time?*

At that point in my life I was a 30-something young man, working for Cox Automotive and doing hospice volunteer work on the weekends. Time to me always seemed to be in a rush; it wasn't precious. When I was with Dr. Costanza, in our weekly conversations, time took on a whole new meaning. It was a time of reflection, a time of storytelling, and quite frankly, when Dr. Costanza fell asleep, it was a time for me to sleep, because I was tired at times, and I felt comfortable, I suppose, and so I would fall asleep with him as I was listening to him breathe.

When Dr. Costanza passed on, it was a beautiful experience. He told me that he appreciated me and not to worry about it, that he would be okay. His friend came from the Bahamas and laid beside him, staying in his room for the final days of his earthly existence, which I felt was an awesome thing to do.

If you talked to my friend Kevin, he would tell you that one of my fears is of dying alone. This too relates to purposeful suffering. I know I won't die alone because I know Jesus; but the human part of me, just like Dr. Costanza, wanted to have, in his final moments of earthly existence, human touch. I am grateful because, as of the last few years, I have met individuals like my friend Kevin, or Matthias, or Steven, who, in my view, assist in the journey of purposeful suffering. Matthias, in the way that he helped me achieve my Master's degree and in the writing of this book; Kevin, in the way that he gives of himself like a brother to ensure that I don't feel alone; and Steven, who had a brother with autism whom he so desperately loved and cared for but did not have the opportunity to continue to show his brotherly love. Of course, obviously, there are others who have impacted my interwoven purposeful suffering throughout the tapestry of my life. These gentlemen that I have mentioned here are the most acute, currently, at understanding my suffering—just like Mother Teresa suffered. She suffered with dignity and joy; but there was still pain.

I am hopeful that my joyful, purposeful suffering will not be in vain but will be a learning tool for those who come after me who face disability. Disability is not about the "dis", it's about the ability of the individual. We will all suffer, but do we realize and recognize the value of our suffering?

the anatomy of care

For those of you who have enjoyed the journey thus far, we wanted to take this time to talk about something that's just as much a public policy issue as it is a personal and social one: personal care, and what does that look like on a daily basis?

Matthias

The Routine

To help give you a good idea of what the caregiver must do for Louis, this is the routine as I learned it. Granted, I started doing personal care for him when he was 56; his needs had increased much since his childhood; diabetes, hip surgeries, and other medical adventures had taken their tolls.

First, Louis is lying in his hospital bed from last night's sleep. I don a pair of latex gloves before anything else. I have to take off his CPAP mask (if he hasn't taken it off himself already) and shift his over-the-bed table to the side.

Now I need to get Louis out of bed. Only since the summer of 2025 did Louis finally get a ceiling lift installed in his bedroom. This has significantly expanded the potential caregiver pool. Without that ceiling lift, strength was needed (Louis has a pretty big belly) to rotate him, sit him up, and then use a different device to transfer him from the bed. With the ceiling lift, I only need to be strong enough to roll him while he's in bed. I roll him to one side to slip the lift sling under his back. I roll him to the other side to pull the sling further down his back, about halfway down his torso. Next, I use the lift remote to bring the ceiling motor over to Louis. It rests on an overhead track. Now that the motor has slid over to be above the bed, I use the remote to lower the swivel bar. Next, the sling under Louis is connected to the swivel bar. Once the sling has been fastened, I press "up" on the remote, and Louis is lifted from his bed. I keep one hand on his back so he doesn't swivel too much as I slide him along the track to now be above bare ground. I grab the shower chair (which is on wheels), which doubles as a commode. I have to land Louis properly in the shower chair. It often requires multiple tries to make sure that Louis is centered on the shower chair when I lower him into it.

There's a big hole in the center of the shower chair's seat so that the bowel movement can go through. However, between the shape of Louis's body, the shape of the shower chair, and the shape of the toilet bowl I'm about to put him over, if Louis pees while he's doing his business, it will get all over the bathroom floor.

After trying several other methods, I finally crafted a unique "pee guard" out of a used deli meat container, cut in carefully marked locations. I place it on the front side of the hole in the shower chair. Now, should Louis need to pee, it will go into the container and out the hole I cut on its backside, directly into the toilet bowl. This saves Louis from having to pee onto the floor or needing me to hold the urinal bottle for him while he's over the toilet. This saves me precious time during this routine to get other chores done.

With Louis in the shower chair and the pee guard placed, it's time to use the enema and roll him over the toilet. If, like Louis, you cannot easily make use of the toilet during the day to go #2, it's very handy to be able to schedule your quality time on the john yourself.

The first time I did this, I was very worried about how sensitive Louis might be (and if I was aiming properly), but he was very patient with me and explained it very calmly. It is so helpful that Louis is an effusively grateful man and constantly reassuring me whenever I'd mess up this, that, or the other thing: "Don't worry, it's all right– I'm glad you're helping me."

Once I've applied the enema and removed the bottle tip from his anus, it's a race to get Louis over the toilet as reasonably fast as I can. If I'm too slow, I might find some saline—and some other stuff—on the floor . . . that's happened more than a couple of times.

Louis can take anywhere from 20 minutes to an hour to do his business. Once he's done, I roll him from the toilet and then use wipes to clean him up. Then I roll him into the shower.

It's a sacred moment. We are isolated from the rest of the world with the calm of steam and running water, and we engage in an act of service. I give and he receives. I use body wash and a loofah sponge to clean from chest to toe. Last is his perineal care.

Note: you can't have too many qualms regarding cleaning someone's private area, especially when they can't do it themselves *and* they have a sedentary lifestyle. Otherwise, you will let them get stinky and gross. I was hesitant at first. Sure, I'd helped him pee before, but I'd do my darndest not to touch him. Well, there's no way to not touch him when he needs to be cleaned. It took me a bit of time to get used to it and give him a proper, thorough scrubbing there. Louis has turned down potential caregivers because they wouldn't be comfortable doing that. When I share shifts with other caregivers who don't clean Louis's groin as well, I have to take extra time during my shift with Louis to make sure he gets cleaned.

Sometimes, Louis also really itches on his scrotum or in his bottom with hemorrhoids* (a common symptom of the sedentary lifestyle) and this can be irritating. He'll often ask me to scratch his itches. This is one of those things that Louis doesn't ask anyone else to do. There is a profound trust; when I'm providing the most personal care for Louis, I feel as though I have a sacred part of his life in my hands. As Louis tells me again and again, "It's a sacred trust."

Now the sanctity of the shower need not always be solemn. A sacred trust is one way of describing it, but Louis has given others. "It's a rite of passage, scratching my butthole" and "You know Bro, it's kinda funny. We'll just be talking when you're cleaning my balls. That's a special friendship right there."

*Louis's doctor actually advised us not to scratch his hemorrhoids, so we have since relied on the application of hemorrhoid cream. It is generally advisable not to scratch hemorrhoids in order to avoid aggravating the already swollen blood vessels.

Sometimes I call out commentary for the Caregiving Olympics, imagining us racing through the routine to beat competing caregiver-recipient teams. "Louis and Matthias are ahead of Janet and Julie; they've already got the laundry running while in the shower; what fantastically coordinated parallel tasking!" Louis enjoys it.

During the shower, I also hand Louis his toothbrush, tongue scraper, flosser, and mouthwash. I started trying to mark the record of how high on the shower wall he could spew the mouthwash. So far, he hasn't managed to spit it above the shower handle; Janet and Julie have us beat there.

Done with the shower, I give him his towel, let him dry some of his head, then I dry the rest of him. When I reach Louis's feet, I take a special moment to bless them. I wear a Miraculous Medal with the image of the Blessed Virgin Mary. Right after drying, I place the medal on Louis's feet and pray for a blessing that he may one day walk and that I may love him well. I make the Sign of the Cross, then hold his feet in my hands for a moment. Often, Louis would tell me as I was kneeling before him, "Matthias, you have the face of Jesus." Knowing that Louis is privileged to see things that many of us don't get to see, it would give me great pause.

Blessing complete, I roll him back into his bedroom and grab his socks. I put on his socks (which takes longer than you'd think) and then put on his pants (I'll pull them all the way up in a minute). Next, we use the sit-to-stand lift, which is easier to use for the post-shower steps than the ceiling lift. I roll the sit-to-stand over, place Louis's feet on its bottom platform (remember, he's diabetic, so his feet are sensitive), and wrap the blue sling around his back and fasten it to the sit-to-stand's lift arms. I then pump the handle and up Louis goes. The sling, being hoisted up, supports Louis's back and shoulders while he holds on to the lift bar with his hands. With Louis now "standing," it's time to dry his rear end. Then I apply a lidocaine patch to his very-often-pained left hip, and I apply hemorrhoid cream directly to his anus. Next I apply some antifungal cream to the back of Louis's privates, and I apply a generous coating of Desitin over the affected skin on Louis's left leg. His left thigh takes the severest beating of his whole body. Owing to his severe scoliosis and his asymmetrical obesity, Louis's left thigh takes the most pressure and thus is the most prone to pressure sores. The Desitin provides a very effective shield. Finally, Desitin applied, I pull up his pants, paying very close attention to make sure that they are lined up correctly. Alignment is crucial for comfort, and doubly crucial so that he can use a urinal later.

I then move the shower chair back to the restroom and turn on his powerchair. I roll it over to Louis, currently propped up in the sit-to-stand, and Louis tells me whether or not he feels sufficiently close to the powerchair's seat to be able to "land" in it. I lower him down, undo the sling, and grab the antifungal cream again to apply it to his underarms and sometimes under his pecs. I apply deodorant and grab Louis a shirt. I haven't uncoupled Louis from the sit-to-stand yet, so he can grab onto it to pull himself forward which enables me to pull the shirt down his back as I put it on him.

Now that he is dressed, I untangle Louis's feet from the base of the sit-to-stand and roll it out of the way. Louis leans himself back in the chair, (that powerchair has so many nifty features!), so that I can turn him and align his back properly. Next—and I'm the only caregiver whom Louis allows to do this part—I gently grab and pull up Louis's scrotum so he doesn't have to sit on it all day. I fasten his seat belt to keep him in place, then grab his watch, glasses, and crucifix. (I've developed the habit of saying "Good morning, Jesus!" each time, and Louis will join in). Finally, I put on Louis's shoes.

After that it's breakfast. But before I can let Louis eat, I can't forget the bib; Louis is not the neatest eater. Some in the profession will insist that we call such things "protective covers" so as not to infantilize the recipient of care. Louis doesn't care; it's a bib.

The first time I did this all for Louis, it took us almost three hours. We've gotten much quicker with practice, and it now typically takes about two and a half hours or a little less . . . assuming Louis doesn't ask me to rub his sore legs, itch something (which can take some time to find and sufficiently relieve) or something else happens, which often does. The routine as I've described it here has also varied in certain ways in the five years I've been caring for Louis, but I wanted to give a good window into what meeting his needs on a daily basis looks like.

Louis
The Personal Level

I've had long-term care or personal care since I was 15 years old. Prior to that, my mother performed my care. My last bubble bath from Mom was before I entered the Home of the Merciful Savior at the age of six. When I was nine, when I returned home from The Home of the Merciful Savior, my mother would *never* give me a bath or shower. The shower was left to my father, which he would do twice a week. That being said, my mom would get me up, feed me, and take me to the store, with all the extra work required getting me in and out of the car and into my chair. There were times when someone might stop and say, "Can I help you?" but those were few and far between.

Around the age of 15, my mother said to me, "Louis, I think it's time for you to get some other folks to help you." I was getting too big in stature, and I was becoming a man.

So, as fate would have it, my caregivers shifted in many respects from my mother to my friends, who would help me take a shower (when my father couldn't), and, even at times, helping me go to bed when night fell.

My mother, for a large extent, continued the morning care. My friend Derrick in high school, whom I cared about quite a bit, helped me from about the age of 16 until around 18. It was kind of fun; he would drag me up the stairs in the house that we were renting, and we would have guy time. So, being a guy attracted to guys, sometimes it became more than guy time . . . sometimes it became downright fun! This, for me, was the first time I got to experience my own sexuality. I truly cared about this particular friend of mine, who today, I have reconnected with on a minimal level, and I've always appreciated the fact that he took the time to help a fellow classmate with the most intimate of care.

During this time around the age of 15, there began to be a paradigm shift. Derrick and I enjoyed our time together in the shower. However, as I progressed in high school and then in college at the University of Arizona, showering became less fun from the eyes of a teenager and more like scheduling an event. It wasn't as spontaneous as it had been with Derrick and me.

When I went to college at the University of Arizona, my first personal care assistant was John Jennings, whom I paid $100 a month. That was the going rate back in 1982 for a student caregiver position, which was coordinated through the Disability Resource Center. As I progressed in the college years, I had some paid caregivers and others that were a barter-type situation of some type or another. I did what I needed to do to get by, and my mother always made sure that I had the funds to do so.

When I was a student orientation host and then RA, I had personal care assistants in the morning. In the evening, I could take care of my own needs, so it really wasn't that big a deal. The last year of my work as an orientation host and RA during the summer I stayed at Kaibab-Huachuca and had a personal care assistant who was also my roommate. So, care during the college years was just part of the process.

As I moved away from college and worked for Cox Enterprises / Manheim Auctions, the first year I hired people independently like Mrs. Giles. Beginning in 1988 when I met Jeff, Joe Greco paid Jeff extra to care for my personal needs per hour (I think he gave him about $1 more an hour). Once Jeff had left in 1993, I again had help from the Auction where I could. In 1994, Robert Mowers came aboard as general manager. I had been writing to the president of Manheim at the time, Darryll Ceccoli, explaining my situation. After numerous explanations, he and Bob Gardner authorized the coverage of my personal care as part of my benefits. This stayed in effect until my departure in 2009.

The advocacy component was extremely important, especially since I had a "severe" disability that required assistance daily. Through the grace of God and those on the ground, I was successful in securing adequate personal care that allowed me to perform my job functions at a high level.

My father always attempted to shine a light on future challenges. There was one moment when he stated, "You know as you age, Lou, it's not going to be quite as easy as it is now." I think he was referring to the aging process, which in reality, is harder for everyone, disability or not. As I have said to many of my friends in my circle, if you live long enough, everyone is going to belong to the disability club. There are no dues, no fees. The perk of the club is longevity of life, which, as my grandmother Jenny Fazio said, "It's a great life if you don't weaken."

When I was working in Orlando, I was among those with influence and connection. Interestingly, I chose to distance myself from those, except for maybe a few, that had signs of outward disability. I did serve on boards relating to disability, but with reluctance. I did not want to pigeonhole myself into that category.

In keeping fidelity to my experience of my early childhood, I did finally agree to serve on a group focused on disability with Orange County, Florida.

Sammy Ripley (now retired, I'm sure) headed up the group. She was the ADA coordinator for the county. I do believe they asked me more than once to serve in the group until I finally agreed.

Sammy and I became good friends, and she understood, to a certain level, my reluctance. She told me once, at Faller Groves Mall, "When you work with people with disabilities, you yourself can suffer some of the same societal stigma." That is the stigma I was so ardently trying to escape. I don't think this is a new phenomenon; it still exists today, but many don't talk about it. I am choosing to talk about it because I think it needs to be brought out into the light.

Individuals with disabilities are as numerous and diverse as any persons living in this country or on this Earth. My book primarily is concerned with folks with disabilities who call the United States of America home. My lens does not really shed light on any other country or culture besides the one I grew up in.

There weren't many like me at the table. My peers saw me as a trailblazer. Yet even though I was concentrating on helping, in the name of Cox, the less fortunate, I honestly wasn't thinking much about the rights of the disabled. Sure, individuals like Jim Hukill would come to my office, asking for money for his nonprofit Lift Disability Network, Florida, where he serves as founder and executive director, still to this day. He himself also happens to be in a power wheelchair, requiring the assistance of numerous individuals to make his day a success in the most basic but meaningful way. Sure, I served on a diversity board which focused on disabilities (after they asked me several times). But I chose to distance myself from that population in the sense that I did not see myself in that same lens. I saw myself in the lens of the privileged. I was reluctant to completely accept that I too had these needs.

What does it mean to need the help of another human being? What does it mean to need someone else to perform the most basic necessities of one's daily life? Well, I think we have to go to Jesus for the answer. Jesus washed his disciples' feet. My friends washed mine and continue to do so.

I am no longer a high school kid of 15; I am now a man of 61 at the time of this writing. In those intermittent years, what have I learned? I've learned that caregiving is not easy for the person that is caring for you, nor is it easy for the person being cared for. I had a caregiver friend say to me, "You always want your caregivers to be friends." Is that really the right way? From his lens, he didn't think so. From my lens, I think it's the only way because you don't want your caregiver to be this robotic, systematic individual who is just going through every motion to get the job done. This is why I've stayed in my own home for a number of years, even though it can be quite stressful and inconsistent getting care.

The Americans with Disabilities Act in 1990, as I have mentioned previously, gave us with disabilities our civil rights. This act is not an end but a beginning. Many within our society, whether you have a disability or not, from my view, look at the Act as an end: "We've made it." I say, "No we have not, we have much further to go." This was a starting point. I challenge my fellow Americans to enact policies relating to personal care that emphasize the dignity of the individual. Can we do this? I think we can. How can we do this? We are interdependent. When you have a disability, in my view, that interdependence is part of your mantra. If it were not for friends of mine that helped me, beginning in my high school years, I might not have graduated from high school. If it wasn't for my mother, I know I wouldn't have gone as far as I have.

In my case, my mother was very supportive, whereas my father was conflicted, so it is not a surprise to me, really, that my brothers (in the nuclear family sense) opted for the money instead of caring for their brother. Hence, the subtitle *My Brother's Keeper.* What does that really mean? Well, it means, from my view, that we help and take care of each other. This sentiment is more relevant today than ever before. We are one of the richest nations in the world, yet we have one in 5 children facing hunger. We are one of the richest nations in the world, yet, we have homelessness. We are one of the richest nations in the world, yet we choose to not traditionally share all our resources all the time; we choose to hoard them for ourselves.

The National Level

In our society, the sacredness of money tends to blind—or at least diminish—our sight in this regard. Though we have come a long way since the 1960s and the models of the Home of the Merciful Savior and the D.T. Watson home, back then it wasn't about the money. It was about compassion and care. I wonder: Do the models of today do justice for the models of yesterday? In the community-based model, I would hasten to say that most of the individuals that have worked for me, if it were not for some type of economic remuneration, would say, "I like ya, but I need to go on." In fact, that has happened multiple times. As I age, it is becoming increasingly important to find a solution that embodies the principles of compassion and care, allowing an individual to gracefully age with dignity, yet without going bankrupt.

However, the phenomenon of the economics of compassion is not just limited to individuals, it is also structurally ingrained within our American society. In January 2011, the first Baby Boomer reached the age of 65. This was a milestone, because there are twenty million of us yet to follow. Supply and demand now play a role in the long-term care of our Baby Boomer generation which I am at the tail end of. Never before has our system been so stressed. Now, some 14 years out, I see the results of the ever-increasing needs of our Baby Boomer generation. Our states are dealing on an individual basis with the concept of long-term care—long-term care with dignity. I've known long-term care without so much dignity. I was removed from my family as a child and institutionalized. That day still brings back memories that I don't always wish to remember.

On the one hand, I am grateful that I have made it to the age of 61. Many with my level of spastic cerebral palsy do not. Science has helped, but it has also caused this societal dilemma of what do you do with a person who happens to have a physical developmental disability who has worked but is neither wealthy nor poor. The safety-net programs won't catch the person because the person does not qualify, so the person is forced to pay for his own way.

How does this relate to my long-term care? Well, it directly relates, because Cox, in their actions, took away my economic security. I am fortunate, as I've mentioned previously. I worked in a management position for 22 years. As many have said, there weren't many like me at the table of decision. But, due to unfortunate circumstances, I find myself struggling to find a pathway to maintain personal autonomy while still gaining the care that I need on a daily basis. There are many within the disability community aging who are not as fortunate or privileged, and this is one reason the book title includes the phrase "privilege interrupted".

I am determined to advocate for myself and others as best I can. The costs of care, as an example, can range from \$68,000~\$70,000 a year (such as at the Delaney at Southshore, League City, Texas), or ~\$54,000 a year, such as at the Heritage Oaks care home in Tucson, Arizona. Most of the care provided to disabled individuals is by the family. What happens if you don't have a family to provide said care? What happens if you haven't worked, and you don't have long-term care insurance on yourself? Those individuals have to become impoverished for the safety net programs to kick in.

In the state of Arizona, for example, ALTCS (Arizona Long Term Care System) is our safety net program, but, as Tess Mew with Southern Arizona Placement Agency (SAPA) recently told me, "Sadly, the cost and overhead of the care homes or facilities and the reimbursement amount of the state (in this case, Arizona) don't match up." So, it's very difficult to place individuals that need care but can't afford it and rely on ALTCS for help.

Being in Tucson, we are close to the Mexican border to our south. An observation that I have made personally and through my academic studies is that the Mexican American takes care of their own and does not put them in a home as readily as the Anglo American. A research article in 2008 addressed the issue of Mexican elders and the use of Skilled Nursing services, compared to their Anglo counterparts.[13] The study showed that there is a cultural propensity for the lack of use of skilled nursing and/or its facilities, based on seven key factors among Mexican American elders. These factors are "expectations of discrimination, lack of knowledge about services, expectations embedded in familism, lack of sense of prevention, lack of health insurance, preference for traditional remedies, and neglect/abuse."[13] Familism indicates the belief that the family takes first responsibility for the family, including when it is difficult; the family has the first responsibility to its own, not the government.

Our system in the United States is less about family, and we have what are called "Assisted Living" or "care-homes" where people that don't know each other are placed because they need some type of care, whether it be physical or cognitive or both. Or, we have agencies that come in to assist you, but they're quite costly because they have to cover overhead expenses, pay their employees, and make a profit.

I bring this to the reader's attention with a solution in mind. I was told by many bosses at Cox, "If you are to be a good manager, don't bring me a problem, bring me a solution." So here is my solution: We must not rely on the government, state or federal. We must, in all humility, go back to the system of non-profit intervention, partnering possibly with the government to make up the economic shortfall. How can we do that? We need to re-invent our social safety network infrastructure. For those that can work, as I myself have done, we should. For those that cannot through no fault of their own, there needs to be a cooperative of care so that when you reach a point where you need care and your resources are only so much, the cooperative will help defray some of the costs.

Is this perfect? No. But it's a start. We have to get away from the idea of spending down so that the frayed safety net can hopefully catch you. We have to come up with proactive solutions, like the Able Trust, which is a fairly new concept that allows a disabled individual or their family member or a friend to place money in a trust, in their name, for care, up to $500,000, without counting as an additional asset that would disqualify you from programs such as Medicaid.

We are one of the wealthiest nations on Earth, but we struggle with some of the most basic needs of our society. Organizations such as Easter Seals or United Cerebral Palsy, depending on the state and jurisdiction, have programs maintaining a person in their own home. The question is, what if this model is no longer sustainable as more and more individuals from the Baby Boomer generation usurp the resources of certified nursing assistants and/or direct caregivers? To help meet the growing demand for caregivers, could we provide another path for those that are seeking citizenship? Would they be willing to help or live with someone with a disability once their background is checked? Or how about a nonviolent offender, that was put in jail for marijuana use? How about putting them in a position of opportunity to assist a person with a disability or a person that is aging? The question remains, are we willing, as a society, to think outside of the proverbial box?

Of course, nothing is perfect. But if we don't try, we don't know. In my personal experience, I have lived with a heroin addict that tried to help. Not a good idea in hindsight. Once I found out about the problem, I had to dismiss him. But how about the person that wants a second chance? We are incarcerating so many people within our country. As of February 2025, the United States has 541 prisoners per 100,000 citizens.[14] Could we not look at some of these individuals, scrutinize why they are behind bars, and give them a chance to redeem themselves with a share-the-care model?

To make this an on-the-ground reality, it will take action. One thing I've noted about our upcoming generation from some of the stories I have seen through our media outlets is that our upcoming generation seems to have compassion for social justice.[15] This is a promising aspect for our ever-evolving society. As has been mentioned by greater minds than I, the test of a great society is how it treats its most vulnerable. If we live long enough, all of us—all 360 million of us—could eventually become part of that category. Is it not proactively prudent to address solutions ahead of the issue? That's what I'm trying to do on a personal basis. Sixty-one seems fairly young when the average life expectancy for men is 76 in the United States. I potentially have another 15 years to live to meet that expectancy. Things could meet me along the way that might cut that short or prolong it. The point being, folks with disabilities like me are living longer in general. It places a further burden on our society economically, so we must come up with innovative solutions as humanity ages.

The other issue is intersectionality of disability, aging, and long-term care. What if you are a person of color? What if you are LGBTQ? What does the experience look like? We must, as a society, be willing to talk about the issue. There is no one-size-fits-all, but I feel if we work together, we can make a change.

In light of the recent coronavirus pandemic, our United States' society has faced its mortality head-on. At one point in the pandemic, we were losing over 3,100 people per day. I personally experienced loss through individuals whom I'd known or had individuals whom I knew who were sick. John Faillace's mother, Meff, was taken by COVID. The pandemic has shown us that all are vulnerable. I hope we as a society take up the call to help arrive at sustainable solutions when it comes to the aging process, disability, and long-term care.

When I think about it critically, at least from my experience, people tend to say that I have admirable qualities, or that they admire me. However, very few people, unless they're getting paid for it quite handsomely, want to clean my ass. As my friend Matthias will say, quoting

Dorothy Day, "Everyone wants to save the world, but no one wants to clean the toilets." People see the injustice, but don't want to clean the toilets.

I say that people see the injustice but don't want to face it. But that's not to say that my life is an injustice because whether we want to admit it or not, is life really fair? One could have a privileged life, as the title of my book indicates, but it can be interrupted. That's my point. And really, again, what is privilege? I think we're pretty privileged in the USA. When we go to a grocery store, even during the pandemic of 2020, we have pretty much anything we want at our fingertips, versus other parts of the globe that struggle just for water.

I always chuckle when individuals say "society" or "the government", like the government is this far-off entity. Well, who is society or the government? The people are, *we* are. We are the government. More than ever, we the people need to stand up, or for that matter, sit down and take note, that it is *we* the people. In fact, we are at a tipping point in our society. Do we want our democratic republic to survive? Or do we want something different? I hope we want it to survive.

"Everyone wants to save the world, but no one wants to clean the toilets." They choose, in many cases, to hire someone else to clean said toilet. What they fail to realize is, someday, *they* might be that dirty toilet. If we as a nation don't have the infrastructure or the desire, then I wonder where that dirty toilet may end up. They may end up in even worse conditions than they imagined because it was all about *the,* and not about *we.* The Preamble says, "We, the people". As Justice Ruth Bader Ginsberg showed us, "we, the people" means *all,* not just a few.

christmas in austin

Thanksgiving week 2021 was one of joy. We hosted our friend Tony, who took the train from Milwaukee to spend the week with us. In addition, we were planning to travel to Austin for Christmas with Matthias's family, Margie and Bob Mahoney, and their extended family and children. But as the day approached, I was getting cold feet and said to Matthias, "Y'know Bro, I don't think I should go, because of COVID-19."

Matthias was like, "I don't think that's an issue we should be concerned with. We've been planning this; we need to go."

I still resisted a bit. I didn't want to impose on Matthias enjoying his time because I knew we were going to be on "disability time". For those of you who don't know disability time, it's a unique time zone where the able-bodied loved one (in this case, Matthias) is constantly taking care of me and my physical and emotional needs. Quite honestly, I figured that he had already been through the ringer when we had Tony (at my recommendation) come visit, which added to the stress between Tony's disability needs and my own. So, I did not want Matthias to be in the disability time zone once again for Christmas.

I finally said to myself, "Oh well, what the heck, I'll go." Plus, Kevin was willing to drive both of us to Phoenix Sky Harbor so that we would have a nonstop flight. Also,

I was wrapping up the semester for my graduate work, and my internship was coming to its end for the semester at the Sonoran University Center for Excellence in Disabilities with Dr. Lynne Tomasa. From my view, I had everything covered. And, if I didn't go, I had the sense that I would be missing out on a gift that Matthias and his family were presenting me. In fact, the family had an online spreadsheet for gift-giving, which I was also a part of.

Interestingly, one of the things that I was working on with Dr. Tomasa was "belonging". What does it mean to belong for someone with a developmental or intellectual disability, or autism? So, the Mahoney Christmas was definitely part of the spiritual equation.

As the day approached, another interesting thing was that Matthias's mom Margie usually has a video done by her children for her birthday. Margie and I were born the same year, but she was a New Year's Eve baby at the end of our birth year. The video, which was shot in multiple states and locations, is a long-standing tradition of Matthias's siblings, produced, directed, and filmed by the Mahoney children with some help from Bob, their father. I was part of this year's film; my role was the *Saguaro Sniper* (one of my live-in caregivers at the time even played a part!). Our friend Tony was mentioned in the film credits due to his artistic suggestions, so he was included as well.

As God would have it, we proceeded with our trip, and the day came where we were on our way to Austin, December 23, 2021. We flew Southwest; and when we got to the gate, I explained to the agent that we needed an aisle chair to help me through the process of boarding. Matthias and I boarded first, and then at the end of the jetway, they transferred me onto the aisle chair while Matthias took apart my wheelchair, removing the joystick so that the control device would not be damaged by aircraft loading—which, from my numerous years of experience in flying, can happen. It is certainly not fun when you get to the other end, and your chair doesn't work. So, I was grateful to have Matthias, my brother, there. I felt privileged.

We arrived in Austin in early evening and now began, from my view, our Christmas vacation. The first person I met from the Mahoney clan was Bob. I don't know if many of you remember, but there was a show called *Eight is Enough* that aired in the '70s and '80s. That was the first thing I thought of when I saw Bob Mahoney. *Eight is Enough* was a sitcom that chronicled the lives of this huge family, and Matthias comes from a pretty sizable one himself, so maybe that's the connection.

Soon thereafter, I met the rest of the family, after we stopped at our Extended Stay Hotel and dropped off our luggage. We weren't sleeping at Matthias's home, but we certainly planned on being there.

The next folks I met were Matthias's grandmother Nonit, cousins, aunts, Mom (whom I met before in Tucson), brothers James, Nathaniel, and Nicholas, and sister Cella and her husband, Mike.

We visited various spots around Austin, like UT, and saw the statue of Barbara Jordan, which, for me, was significant. She was a trailblazer for both voting rights and human rights, was the first Black person elected to the Texas Senate, and was the first woman elected to represent Texas in the House of Representatives. Matthias's mom, Margie, is a graduate of the University of Texas at Austin (so is Bob). We were there due to her Great Uncle Chris's interest in college campuses. He was visiting the family and is a Jesuit priest.

I was glad to be included with the family, but I was also nervous. For me, this was something I had not experienced for many years. During my college years, I very rarely went back home to Pittsburgh for Thanksgiving, Christmas, or New Year's. When I completed my degree and moved to Orlando in 1987, I went back to Arizona for Christmas during that first year of my employment. I felt closer to my friends than my nuclear family, with the exception of my beloved mother. So, I felt blessed and had a tentative sense of belonging here with Matthias's family.

We had to finish our video—my role as *Saguaro Sniper* was only partially complete—knowing that the unveiling of this 2021 video would be New Year's Eve, since Margie's birthday is on New Year's Eve. We finished our video shoot at St. Edward's University.

We also met my long-time friends Donna and John and their grandchildren and family, who came up from the Houston Area (League City, just outside of Houston). John is the friend of mine whom I've known now for 40+ years and is one of the only two friends I still keep in contact with from high school. We met them at Hopdoddy's Burger Bar, which is an Austin go-to, and had an enjoyable afternoon of reminiscence. I had not seen John and Donna once since their wedding in 2010. Again, I felt privileged to have such a long friendship.

The theme of that Christmas trip was gratitude, privilege, and belonging. Matthias said to me, *I want you to belong.* So meaningful when my brothers—my biological brothers, Edward and Frank—tore up that invitation. That was on my mind as well.

James, Matthias's eldest brother, gave me a large wood rosary which he had been given by a fellow Boy Scout years prior. He preferred not to pray with an extra-large rosary and figured I could use it more easily with my dexterity and hand-eye coordination limitations. James has a deep faith, and this gift showed that he had my particular needs in mind. I was really touched by that. This wasn't carpentry's only role that Christmas; both Bob and James were the ones instrumental in making sure that I interacted with family by building the ramp (that is very sturdy, I must say) to the front door. I thought, *That's what Jesus would do.* And that's what James and Bob did.

Then we have Nathaniel, Nicholas, and Mike. I got to bond with them over drying the dishes on a nightly basis. Everyone took their turn drying the dishes. I seemed to be there as often as I could because I wanted to make sure that I was part of the ritual. This again made me think of *Eight is Enough* because that's what they would do as a family: they would dry the dishes. I said to myself, *Man, I'm a part of a family, and a family I want to be part of.*

There was one night when we were there late into the early morning because Tony had called from Milwaukee and expressed his dismay and hurt that he wasn't part of this Christmas. At first, I was like, "He should've known that he wasn't part of this Christmas; that's why we had him over for Thanksgiving in Arizona." However, I became aware of something: it doesn't matter, he still feels the way he feels. Matthias did what Matthias would do, and that was create a stocking to mail to Tony. I was proud of him, and I thought, *I would expect nothing less.*

In fact, Cella (Matthias's sister born the same month as me: February) taught Matthias how to embroider in a matter of hours. Still, it took a long time for him to do the stocking, and we were there *way* into the early morning. I knew that this was a labor of love and that I needed to be there to support him, and indirectly, acknowledge my love for Tony in his loneliness.

The stocking was finished, and Matthias said, "Do you want to split it together?" (as far as the cost of stuffing it), and I was like, "Yes, of course." Again, I felt like I was privileged, and that I needed to give back. Sidenote: that was how I felt working with Cox because I was so privileged, having a job—a good job—I had to give back. I think that's the sense I have with getting my master's in social work. I have to give back.

Matthias's family has a large backyard. As I mentioned earlier in the book, at times I am given the privilege to go beyond the veil to a field where I walk or run. In my dreams, Matthias and I even walk there and run together. When we were in Austin, on our Christmas vacation, Matthias and I were in the backyard, and I said to him, "This reminds me of the field that I go to when I cross through the veil, and when I'm running with you in my dreams." Now, we were in that similar spot that seemed to be in my heavenly dreams where I was at home. Now, that home was shown to me in real time, in the Mahoneys' backyard. I was home.

the letter of appeal

Matthias

Not long after our Christmas in Austin together, I felt the need to ask my family directly how they felt about calling Louis "family". I was anxious to help establish Louis's stability in my prospective absence whenever I would depart for religious life, so I wanted to know how much my family could do or would do. I wanted to know how much they were willing to invest in Louis whom I had invested so much in myself. I typed the letter and sent individual copies to my parents and each of my siblings. Could my declaration to Louis (*you're in my family now*) have more concrete continuity after I leave?

3.7.2022

Dearest Family,

I write this letter to begin a conversation that I've been needing to start for some time. Finally, today, I think I can find the words, and the best way for me is to put them on paper. Dad, I think you're responsible for this trait. :)

As I've told many (if not all) of y'all, there was a point where I told Louis, "You're in <u>my</u> family now," and I meant that very sincerely. I saw his suffering, his catastrophic loss of family, his desperate need and desire for family, and the very real, direct consequences this has for his wellbeing. And I wanted to somehow be part of the answer to his need.

I did something very odd, and not good when I told him that he was in my family. It was not wrong that I said so. Not at all. However, somehow, I meant it in some way such that there was a very significant difference between "my" family, and all of you guys . . . my family; as if "my" family was something I could do all on my own, that this "Louis-project" is something that no one else could (or should) be involved in, as if "my" family was something that did not include you all.

Of course, such a distinction is absurd, and y'all have clearly shown that to be so, for which I am so, so, so grateful. Y'all's support for me, the care and graciousness you have shown Louis while he was in town, Dad's work on the book, Mom's caring for Louis from afar (especially during his bout with COVID), building the ramp, the personalized gifts that y'all gave to him, every act of helping me do the straps in the rental van to secure Louis's wheelchair . . . I could go on.

Louis felt very welcomed this Christmas and does not stop telling me how much he thinks of you guys, prays for you guys, and wishes y'all's wellbeing.

One thing that Louis has also brought up with me a lot is the desire to become my brother. What does this mean? I think simply this: to be chosen family. To have me care for him and receive care from him as one would expect from any of us to do for each other, and to share life in the way that a family does: eating together, praying together, going on vacations together, putting up with each other's difficulties together.

I'm still fairly confident that such a thing is not (currently) legally possible*, and because we are not Eastern Catholics, we don't have a liturgical way of declaring or recognizing such a chosen relationship. I confess I'm not always so sure of the idea myself; sometimes I'm on board, other times it feels more like something for him than it is for me.

*Technically, the only way to legally create non-biological siblinghood in this case would be for the parents to adopt the person in question . . . which seems a bit odd in our situation.

My friend Ethan pointed out something very relevant when I shared this with him. "So, is he going to become Cella's brother, James's brother, Nathaniel's brother and Nicholas's brother?" I have concluded that the answer must be yes. *If such a chosen relationship is to be declared and recognized (or just lived *de facto* and not *de jure*), it is not completely up to me; it rests upon all of us. In us, Louis feels he has potentially found a new family, having been abandoned by the majority of his own biological family.

As our school years come closer to their conclusions (Fall 2022 for me, Spring 2023 for him) I wonder how I am going to *both* apply for entrance into religious life *and* make sure that Louis is better off than how I found him when I first met him. I can't move forward unless he's in a better place.

What do I mean? Before I met Louis, he had been living some 10 years after both of his parents had passed away and had lived about five years in Tucson. In that time, he has been exposed to some of the worst care I've ever heard of, owing to his vulnerability: one caregiver was a heroin addict, another emotionally abused him, another financially abused him, and many—too many—have stolen from him. Why does this happen? Simply because Louis needs people, and it's hard to find good people.

Louis needs stable care, and the answer cannot simply be in the form of "find the right assisted living home, drop Louis off, and you'll be okay!" I cannot treat Louis that way. He needs more than that. He needs a stable, committed group of people around him that are willing to sacrifice for him, go out of their way to make sure his needs are met, to love him. In other words, he needs a family. All too often, the kinds of care models that are available in a facility-type setting are very transactional; the real personal connection lacks—and as a consequence, the care is all too often inadequate. This isn't to say there are no good places, but it is to say that they are few and far between, especially considering the unique needs of Louis's care. We've been told by several assisted-living places that they simply couldn't handle Louis's care: he needed too much.

Finally, let's not forget the financial aspect: care costs *a lot.* And Louis is running out of money. The only way, either for governmental supports, or for certain institutions to offer care for him is if he spends practically all of his money so that he's eligible for "financial aid." Louis doesn't want to become a ward of the state. And I cannot let that happen either.

As we search for answers and pray about our respective futures, Louis has mentioned more than once the idea of going to Texas. "What if I was close to the family? I feel that they would actually care and be able to do so." I honestly agree because I know y'all are trustworthy, and as I mentioned before, you have extended that care to him already. Louis has received this sort of offer, actually from two other families before, but this is the only time he's considered a group of people and truly felt comfortable about it. He feels he can trust y'all. And I think he has good reason to feel that way (if such an offer is extended to him).

This does not mean "Ask the Mahoneys to cover all of Louis's personal care needs and maintain every aspect of his wellbeing so that Matthias can go to the novitiate." Absolutely not. But it would entail him being nearby and part of the extended family dynamic, I suppose in a way like David is, along with Alexa and Chris, as well as Nadja. To be honest, I believe that seeing how Mom cared for Alexa's parents is part of the reason I do what I do for Louis.

Louis, like Ethan, very quickly pointed out to me that this is something that would require *all of us* to be on board about, if such a thing were to come about. Louis and I both realize it is wrong to expect something like this of anyone without them being okay with it.

Dearest family, at this moment, I ask only two things from each of you: I ask for your ardent prayers that God will show us the right path forward, and I ask for each of y'all's sincere and candid thoughts about this.

Love,

Teo

"Teo" (pronounced "TAY-oh") is my nickname in the family. Matthias is a Greek variant of "Matthew", which is "Matteo" in Italian. Hence, "Teo."

Louis

When Matthias informed me about this letter to the Mahoney family, I was filled with grace. The grace of someone giving himself to another. Matthias has given himself in so many ways to me. I was not in total surprise that he would write such a letter, nor was I surprised by the family response. Some responses were in writing; some responses were verbal. Really, he was saying to his family, "I have this friend that is an adult orphan. Do you think we can help provide him a family?"

One of the first responses to Matthias's letter came from his eldest sibling, Cella, and her husband, Mike. They said, "Yes, we would love to have Louis as part of the family. However, there's not much we can do in actuality, because we live in New Jersey." I appreciated this response. It made me feel good. Next there was Nathaniel's response. Nathaniel said (paraphrasing), "I don't say this out of malice, but rather out of love. I don't know Louis very well; I've only met him once. I am open to the possibility of him becoming a 'dear friend', but I don't think I would be able to call him family." I also appreciated Nathaniel's response because it came from his heart.

Marjorie and Bob, Matthias's parents, stated that there was only so much that they could do, but that they were open to helping where they could. I remember Nicholas saying at one point, not necessarily connected to this letter, "Louis isn't going to live with us, is he? Where would he sleep?" Marjorie did actually mention the idea of building an extension on to the house to accommodate me but regretted that it was well beyond their means. Still, it meant a lot that she did bring it forward.

While I had been considering moving to Houston to be close to John and Donna, I was now seriously considering moving to Austin to be close to Matthias's family and have that sense of belonging. This became a real option that Matthias and I (along with Marjorie, especially) would investigate for several years.

CHAPTER 21

UCEDD

y first internship for my master's degree was with Sonoran UCEDD. The acronym UCEDD stands for "University Center for Excellence in Disabilities." Little did I know at that time, when I started my internship in August of 2021, how important a role the internship at UCEDD would play, not only in my pursuit of my master's degree, but in healing.

My clinical supervisor was Dr. Lynne Tomasa. Dr. Tomasa was a very knowledgeable individual in the study of disability. One of her research projects which had started the year before, in 2020, was on sexual violence against those with intellectual and developmental disabilities (I/DD). I was tasked with being part of the research team, collaborating with Dr. Tomasa; Dr. Phil Johnson, PhD CRC; and my fellow interns. My disability had given me some insight anecdotally because I had been a victim of sexual assault. However, at that point, I still didn't really see it as such.

The research team's work would finally be published in May 2024.[16] The team's work further supports the original NPR story which shocked the nation in relation to sexual assault and those with disabilities. The story revealed that people with intellectual and developmental disabilities are 7 to 10 times more likely to be victims of sexual assault.[11] I was honored to be on the University of Arizona research team as part of my internship with the Sonoran UCEDD. Their collaboration and the work of my fellow research team brought forward a hidden secret—unimaginable to many—that now was brought to light by the brave individuals who shared our story.

I blamed myself for my lack of discretion when it came to finding love. It was all about finding love. And it made me feel good. So, I let things happen that I should never have, and I did things that I should never have done. In hindsight and retrospect, I had been doing some pretty risky things. These behaviors went unchecked for many years. Then, I finally realized what I had been doing to myself and what I had done to my soul when I'd lost my job with Cox Enterprises. I questioned myself: Had I caused my rape, when I was raped by the individual who helped me and put me to bed that evening, when I had just arrived in Orlando in 1987? Had I caused my rape when I was raped by a married man who I had a relationship with for a number of years, even before he was married?

I began to talk with Dr. Tomasa and Dr. Johnson about my experiences of sexual assault. This is when I began to realize that what had happened to me in the guest room of my home was indeed rape at the hands of someone I cared about, a gentleman who worked in my department at Cox Enterprises, Manheim Auctions. He will be left unnamed, to protect his anonymity, but his story will be told in full.

He was a young man when he began to work in my area at the Auto Auction. He had a troubled beginning. He was no stranger to the justice system. He had assaulted a person—I believe at a bar. So, he was trying to get his record expunged, which he ultimately did.

One night, he was driving my company vehicle and reached over to grab my hand. We went into my home, he put me into bed, but there was more to come. This was the beginning, before he had a son, before he was married, this was the beginning of a clandestine relationship. No one was to be the wiser, except us, and for that matter, God. We began a sexual relationship. He was 19 and I was 31.

We had a relationship for over five years. Eventually, he got married. We would watch straight porn (not gay porn) so that he would get aroused sexually and then he would have sex with me.

Unfortunately, this was just continuing my need to fill a void. I thought he loved me. Common theme. I was looking for love, but in all the wrong places. This relationship even continued after he got married. I'm not proud about that. I even knew his wife. So, I was the mistress. But I have a feeling that she'd known and was actually accepting of it, at least from an economic perspective. He would always ask, "Can you loan me some money?" Again, I thought he loved me. So, I did, sometimes large sums of money because they were struggling and he would say that both he and his wife appreciated it.

At one point in the early 2000s, it was different. He came over, but this time it was on his terms and less on mine. We went into the guest bedroom at my home, which was not usual. He took me out of my chair, bent me over the bed of the guestroom, pulled my trousers down to expose my back side, and anally penetrated me.

At the end of the act, he said, "You are my bitch now. I'm young, dumb, and full of cum."

That incident from the early 2000s was finally coming to the surface.

After hearing me share, Dr. Johnson and Dr. Tomasa felt that it would be a good idea for me to seek further counseling.

I recommend this for any social worker. If you think you have it all together, think again. Even the most balanced should have someone to talk to. That was part of my fear. I didn't want to appear to be "off my rocker" or unregulated. *How can you be a social worker,* I thought, *if you yourself need a social worker?* I found out that a lot of great social workers, a good percentage of them—at least the ones whom I had as professors—had engaged in some type of therapy! The stigma evaporated for me—slowly—but it did, because I said to myself, *if I'm going to help someone else, I need to make sure that I have the help that I need.* I was also dealing with a perception that many people with disabilities wrestle with: you don't want to seem unsure of yourself, and we often feel over-scrutinized anyway due to our circumstances. I was struggling with this feeling as well.

I agreed to seek counseling. During the latter part of my last semester at UCEDD, March 2022, I asked Dr. Johnson for recommendations. Dr. Johnson was gracious and connected me with Clayton Black.

Clayton worked with the Southern Arizona Center Against Sexual Assault (SACASA). We met virtually for weeks, once a week, discussing the topic of my sexual assaults. The SACASA approach is based on trauma-informed care and solution-focused intervention. This is what I needed. I have been traumatized both by domestic violence and sexual assault. I've had multiple counseling interventions in the past, but my sessions with Clayton were the most helpful. That's what brought out most pronouncedly the incident with the person that I worked with at Cox, Manheim Orlando.

The work of healing with Clayton began a process of hurt and discovery, along with an acknowledgement to myself that I was of value. Through my personal enlightenment, I further realized that my sexual experience was mine alone. In order for me to heal, I had to honestly process what had happened to me. The challenge was to process my experience in its totality. How did my early development become affected by the toxic relationship of my parents? Then, by being institutionalized at a critical time in my development at the age of six? Then, by realizing that not only was I different physically but psychosexually? I was a boy who was attracted to other boys. As I progressed through life, I was a man attracted to other men, all the while knowing that I believed in God and Jesus, and His mother, our Blessed Mother.

Through the eyes of my faith, I believe that Dr. Tomasa and Dr. Johnson were angelic messengers that brought me to face the truth of my struggle with my humanity. My internship with UCEDD provided a pathway for initial healing that will last for the remainder of my earthly journey.

While I was an intern at UCEDD, I had a live-in caregiver, Zane, who was on the autism spectrum. On account of this, Dr. Tomasa allowed me to count two hours a week that I spent working with Zane toward the internship requirements. Unfortunately for us, I had to kick him out in April of 2022 after he threatened to kill me and another caregiver. He stated to us, "RIP," with the fire of the devil emanating from his eyeballs. We were aghast, but Joshua (the other caregiver) kept his composure, and we both asked him to repeat what he had said. He said, "Rest in peace." He said he would burn the house down. Joshua took rapid action. He asked Zane to come out of his room and guided him toward the front door.

Zane was bare-footed, shirtless, wearing a pair of jockey shorts; Joshua opened the front door, swung him out and closed the door. Zane was then crying, "Let me in, let me in!" Joshua and I both said, "No, you will have to wait until the sheriff comes."

Upon the deputy sheriff's arrival, we were questioned related to the disturbance. Joshua and I gave a verbal report, and then they spoke to Zane. Upon speaking to

Zane, corroborating the report that Joshua and I had given, they arrested Zane on the driveway.

Maybe I was not such a good observer of character and behavior in that case when we hired Zane. He did classify himself as "crazy", and that he was on the autism spectrum. In humility, it led me to wonder, as a student of social work, *Do we always catch everything that we should?*

I was hopeful that I could learn something from Zane while he helped with my personal care. I was giving him a chance. I thought I could've given him some stability.

In the end, there was some sense of justice. A year and a half after Zane was arrested, I ended up being subpoenaed by the court to go to one of Zane's last court appearances for a restitution hearing. Zane had successfully completed his program, which included an anger management course.

The restitution, in my view, was not economical, but he did complete the program. I hope that he will now be on a positive path of recovery. In fact, as he walked out of the courtroom on that Fall day in September of 2023, Zane turned to me and said, "I hope you have a nice day," with a smile—a normal smile, as opposed to the wild look of glee he had as I watched his arraignment back in the Spring of 2022.

Now, being a social worker looking back at Zane and others, I realized that I can't help everyone, or, at least, I can only help some people to a certain level. I always bring up this analogy with Matthias, as any good flight attendant will tell you: *In case of emergency, place your oxygen mask on first, then assist small children and others who may need assistance.* This phrase rings so true with me. One of my professors put it in practical terms. When I first started the social work program back in 2019, my professor for social policy said, "Take it easy Louis.

You're just starting the program. There'll be plenty to help. That will never go away. Trust me."

Unlike Zane, Joshua never lived with me and was very self-sufficient. I enjoyed Joshua. He was a member of *The Wailers*, founded by Bob Marley. He is a man of deep faith. We had very profound conversations together, along with Matthias. Joshua saved our lives when he had to throw Zane out of the house. He provided a pillar of stability amid the currents of unhealthy dependence surrounding Zane.

Joshua, too, however, would eventually go the way of the bricks. We had a sharp disagreement, and I had to fire him. He did reach out to me a year or so later to apologize, and I apologized for my side of things. I'm grateful for the reconciliation, and we keep up with each other to this day.

During this time of my life, so many caregivers were coming and going. But in the end, the one that remained was Matthias.

A few years back I made this commitment to myself: I will place myself, rather than be placed. I've looked at various care homes for myself to begin this process. Well, I'll give you a recent example. A care finding agency in Austin TX said, "Oh, you should put yourself in a nursing home, because your level of care and the way the system is. It's no fault of your own; it's just the way the system is. The cost of care in Austin TX can be upward of $10,000 a month. And if we find something, we have to do it quickly."

I thought to myself, *This is disgusting.* That's $120,000 a year. And what type of care do you get? "We put you in front of the TV." I thought, *What an existence and what a waste.*

That's something, my friends, that needs to change. In this process of finding care, and from the brief little excerpts of my caregivers, I have noted that the United States needs to do a lot of work. We need to recognize the dignity of the person. It all starts with the family.

In my case, after my parents' death, my brothers threw me to the wolves. I'm not too amazed by that. Look what they did with Joseph in Genesis. But in the end, who won out? Read Genesis. I only pray that my brothers don't need help, like Joseph's brothers did. As I mentioned, my brother Edward was in worse shape than I when he was born, but due to the advancement of technology from 1964 to 1970, he was spared.

In my internship with Sonoran UCEDD, the concept of belonging was a key focus. We wanted to develop a program that would open a pathway to belonging for those with developmental and intellectual disabilities. So, through collaboration with Dr. Tomasa and Vanessa Zuber (with United Cerebral Palsy), we decided to create "Peer-to-Peer on Wheels, A Summer Retreat on Belonging." The sessions were four in total over the summer of 2022. Matthias, Dr. Tomasa, and I collaborated to formulate this program over the Zoom platform.

Matthias was there at the beginning, and then he left to go to Austin for the summer. So, I lost my scribe and cheerleader, so to speak. I was fortunate that I had technology support through UCEDD. They handled technical aspects of the Peer-to-Peer on Wheels sessions.

I must say I was nervous. I never quite had the experience of leading a therapeutic group like that. I was grateful to have the presence of Dr. Tomasa. But this summer, we planned to have four sessions, each an hour long: Session 1 was "Introduction and Belonging".

In our first session, we talked about belonging. What did it mean? I brought up the well-known researcher,

Dr. Erik Carter, of Baylor University. In that session, we discussed what it meant to belong. Each individual had a different take. Some were married; some were single. Some worked and some did not. Some were in care homes or group homes. Bottom line, it was interesting for me, because I was like, "Yep. I hear ya. And I feel your pain."

Afterward, I thought to myself, *What does this mean to me professionally?* I hearkened back to what Cheryl at the VA had said to me, back in the Recreation Department, prior to entering the social work program. I think it was the summer before. She said, "You know, Louis, you can go to many places where we cannot." Cheryl herself was a veteran. I got that same feeling when I was leading the group. Sure, anybody could lead this group, but does my life experience add something to this group? I thought it did. We moved on the Session 2, "Moving to the Beat". This was the best of all of them, the most attended. And it was *awesome*.

People were happy. People were smiling. We didn't really see a disability then, whether it was physical or intellectual or otherwise. We had the music. I picked the songs that we would groove to, the first being Sheena Easton's "My Baby Takes the Morning Train". I picked that one because more and more of us are taking that train to get to work. The next was "Sir Duke" by Stevie Wonder. I picked that one because Stevie is part of our team (he is blind). And then "Footloose" by Kenny Loggins. We were just having a great old time, meta-phorically moving those feet, and where we could we'd move the arms, too. By the end of that session, I was pretty exhausted but had a lot of fun. I think Dr. Tomasa also thought that was the best out of the four. Needless to say: What does it truly mean to belong?

Sessions 3 and 4 had to be combined because holiday (July 4th) got in the way and nobody showed up for one of them.

boundaries

Matthias

May 2022, Louis was pretty rattled, particularly with his life having been threatened by another personal caregiver, Zane, in his own home (I trained this caregiver, by the way, and was with Louis when we interviewed him). I was living on Elm Street a few blocks north of the University of Arizona in my second to last semester. Because I had deferred the Fall 2020 semester when Louis had the kidney stone procedures, I was slated to graduate in December 2022.

Our lease was up with the house I was living in with my friends, so I needed a new place to live for my final semester of school when August would come around. The Newman Center has three apartments which they lease to Newman students on a case-by-case basis. I was very eager to be one of those cases. I love the Newman Center community; they are my home-away-from-home in Tucson. I loved being part of the Student Ministry Team under Fr. John Paul's leadership—I basically lived at Newman and slept at my Elm Street apartment (when I wasn't doing care for Louis).

By this time, I would come over to Louis's on Tuesdays and Thursdays to do academic support and occasionally the Thursday evening shift of care. I would stay with him over the weekend to do his weekend care, go to Church with him, and then take the bus back to school Monday morning (if Nicole couldn't drive me).

As you can imagine, Louis was understandably unsettled by the incident with Zane. He asked me to move in with him for the Fall 2022 semester. We had spoken about me moving in, potentially at the beginning of 2023 after I'd be finished with my undergraduate degree. I knew quite well that it would be very difficult for me to live with Louis while trying to finish my coursework. No matter how many care shifts could be covered by others, simply living with Louis would demand a lot of attention to help meet everyday needs ("Bro, I need to pee. Bro, can you wash my glasses? Bro, so-and-so can't make it until 8 p.m., can you cook dinner?") I was confident that it would not be wise for finishing my degree. Nevertheless, Louis was very uncomfortable relying on others' care, namely, people who weren't as trustworthy as myself. I knew full well that I was the best and most trustworthy caregiver he had available, but I knew I just couldn't be that available during that upcoming semester.

That being said, I was not immediately settled on a decision. My heart ached knowing what Louis had suffered (I was very grateful that Joshua was there, when Zane threatened Louis), and I also deeply felt his concerns about the vulnerability he was so keenly feeling. I honestly was not sure what God's will was. I needed extra help.

I've prayed novenas to St. Thérèse of the Child Jesus (St. Thérèse of Lisieux) a few times before. If you are not familiar with this dear Catholic devotion, I will briefly explain. St. Thérèse promised to "let down a shower of roses from Heaven" upon her death. She has fulfilled that promise countless times in the lives of many, many people. One prays a novena, that is, a series of prayers over nine days, asking for St. Thérèse to send roses. I had actually done one once before in regard to Louis, and she didn't send me any roses that time which, with my spiritual director's counsel, helped me to understand that I would not leave Tucson and still help Louis for the year of 2023.

I got a strong sense that it was time to ask her for a favor again. I prayed the novena, with this request, "St. Thérèse, if it is God's will that I should move in with Louis early, for the Fall 2022 semester, please send me three yellow roses." (Yellow is Louis's favorite color). "But if it is not God's will that I should move in with him for the Fall 2022 semester, please send me three white roses." I was thinking of the white habits of the Dominicans.

I prayed the novena: day one, two, three . . . all the way to nine. I forgot if I was on day nine or if it was day 10, so, at the Newman Center chapel, I went to the wonderful image of Our Lady of Guadalupe and prayed the novena prayer again. "God, I have faith that you have heard my prayer anyway, but I'm going to pray this again today in case it's day nine or if I skipped a day." I prayed the prayer and then exited the chapel to the lobby.

Lo and behold, smack dab on the lobby table where various announcements, prayer cards, and rosaries may be found, was a new flyer that I hadn't seen before. The design featured a large picture of three, big, white roses. Clear as day. I felt my soul immediately at peace and thanked God.

That very night, I was supposed to meet with Louis at Culver's for dinner. I was convinced beyond a shadow of a doubt. St. Thérèse came through for me!

I found Louis at the Culver's, and soon after we ordered our food, I simply stated, "Louis, it is not God's will that I move in with you for this coming Fall semester."

In classic Louis fashion, he challenged me. He questioned the authenticity of this "spiritual experience". I then explained that this was the same means by which I had discerned that I was to stay with him through the year of 2023. He was mollified—still concerned, but he accepted my resolution.

This was one of the grace-filled moments where divine intervention had to reveal to me the difference between extending myself in charity and recognizing when and where I am not called to extend that charity in a given time. It's not like I wasn't going to be helping out with Louis's academic support or personal care on the weekends, but I was going to have the space necessary to finish my undergraduate work—and live at the Newman Center no less. I was very excited for that opportunity.

Louis

During this time, Matthias was not living with me directly until the beginning of the year 2023. Toward the latter part of 2022, I too became a member of the Angelic Warfare Confraternity. Father JP initiated me into the Confraternity, which is a Dominican rite, on a Sunday, after the 11 a.m. Mass at Newman. We were in the cry-room. I said, "I'm sure people are wondering what we are doing." Fr. JP chuckled. We continued with the initiation.

After the completion of the initiation, Fr. JP said, "Remember Louis, this is not magic. You will still struggle with chastity." I would still struggle, but I was finally beginning to face my chastity head-on after so many years of impulsive sexual behavior that put me in grave danger at times. I was determined, with God's help, as He had in the past, to make this solemn vow to myself: I am going to be celibate. I was going to think more of myself because I knew, more fervently, that I now was in a war for my own chastity—and ultimately, my own soul.

Matthias

There are times when I am proud of Louis. At the same time, it feels odd to me to have a sense of pride in a man who is clearly my elder. But it's true. Being on the journey with Louis as he was fighting for his chastity and sexual sobriety, I count one of my greatest privileges. To be of any support to anyone in the healing process as regards their sexuality is a great privilege, indeed, one I cherish very deeply in my heart. When Louis wanted to join the Angelic Warfare Confraternity, I was made even happier in prayer with the Blessed Mother who let me know in the Spirit, *Thank you for bringing him to me.* The virtue of chastity is so important, and it is very dear to her, too. "Blessed are the pure of heart, for they will see God." (Matthew 5:8, New Catholic Bible translation) I was also extremely grateful because it signaled to me the hope for further progress in our "evolving fraternal intimacy" as Louis has termed it.

Nearing May 2022, after I had made my decision to move into Newman and not move in early with Louis, I had a busy summer ahead of me. I would be visiting St. Anselm's Abbey in Washington, D.C. after attending the Thomistic Institute Student Leadership Conference and staying with my cousin Tommy. Next, I would be flying to Milwaukee to visit Tony, take Amtrak back to Austin, and a short week later, fly out to Albuquerque to wind my way up to the very remote Monastery of Christ in the Desert.

Though I was (and still am) not convinced I am called to be a monk, I greatly desired to spend an extended period of time with a monastic community to help my discernment of religious life in general. The abbot granted permission for me to stay for two weeks.

After that stay, I would return to Tucson to move into the Newman apartment and begin my final semester as an undergrad.

Louis earnestly desired for us to have a foot washing, as we had done several times, in imitation of Jesus and the example he sets for his disciples at the Last Supper (John 13:1-17). Louis particularly wanted us to do this as a final special prayer together before I left for my summer's adventures.

The way it ended up happening though was particularly providential. . . and unexpected (as most particularly providential things are). The moment after it happened, I recorded my reflection of the event with my smartphone. This event also sheds some light on the "evolving fraternal intimacy" dynamic at the time. This is the story of the foot washing on May 30, 2022.

I had finally decided, at the counsel of my spiritual director Fr. John Paul, to restate certain boundaries with Louis and to be very clear with them and to make sure that we practice them. We had this conversation while I was giving him a shower.

The boundary was about Louis touching me. Louis would often reach out and place his hand on my chest or on my shoulder, say like when I'm working on the computer beside him or when I'm shaving him in the shower. He would just reach his hand out to me and put it there. Often, he would pray a blessing over me, too. I recognized that for Louis this was an expression of love and also helped give him a sense of security, but I also recognized that I didn't always like it and would become really anxious about it. I started worrying whenever Louis was nearby or whenever he approached me. I would start thinking, *Oh no, do I need to avoid him now so he doesn't touch me? Is this time to state a boundary even if it bothers him?* I also worried that I was too reluctant to accept Louis's love, but as Fr. John Paul had counseled me, I needed to be authentic and respect my own sensitivity because it's not loving to let Louis ignore that and never bring it up. I asked Louis to stop the hand-reaching-out altogether.

Louis said, "Yeahhh, we're gonna have to compromise on that one, Matthias. You have to be patient with me. I'm human. I'm not perfect. But I try. I'm going to try. But ehhh . . ."

Louis's hesitant recognition of the boundaries seemed good enough.

The shower continued. Out of deference to the boundary that I had asked for, Louis didn't touch me once while I was shaving him. I felt a huge relief. I said, "Oh my goodness, I feel such a lightness in my heart, and I feel loved because I am being respected and I have that space that you give me."

Louis said, "Whoa. Normally, when you tell me not to touch you, Matthias, I think, 'Oh, it's because you don't want to accept my love.' That's how I hear it. But when you tell me that you feel loved by my *not* doing that, it helps me, because you're telling me, 'No, that's not what it's about.'"

This was progress. Fr. John Paul taught me that love, *charity*, is both in the reaching out and the holding back, the grasping and the letting go. In the right contexts, all of these can be love. I felt so often overwhelmed by Louis's affection I couldn't keep peace in my heart. It's not that I was rejecting Louis's love. But because I know that he loves me, I could (and should) ask him to respect my sensitivity, my love language, and my capacity to receive his love well. That shower left me feeling greater peace. However, the peace was short-lived.

It was May 29th. There were three times throughout the day that Louis reached out and touched me, on the shoulder or the side. They were very brief, almost taps. What happened to the boundary we had just established? I did not speak up though. It would be too much energy and time to have that conversation all over again while we were trying to get other tasks done. We needed to get to bed early; Joshua would be coming for the morning shift at 6 a.m. the next day.

However, recalling the recommendation of a friend from the Newman Center, Louis wanted to watch *A Man for All Seasons*. It's a two-hour long film, so I said, "No, we need to finish our Rosary for today after dinner. If we watch the movie, there won't be enough time before we need to get to bed."

"Oh, we can just have Joshua come at 8 a.m. instead of 6 a.m.!"

"Okay . . ." I never like it when Louis suddenly shifts the schedule, but little did I know how providential this shift would be.

We prayed the Rosary after dinner and ended up not being able to watch the movie anyway; the internet crapped out. But the schedule was still changed for Joshua to arrive at 8 a.m. rather than 6 a.m. the next day. I helped Louis get to bed, which went unusually quick.

Finally, it was time for my own night routine. I had silently held onto the trespasses of my recently-established boundary all day. They returned to mind as I was examining my conscience before the Divine Mercy image. "You know, Jesus, I think I should bring this up with Louis because it will disturb my peace if I just hold it in. But I'm not sure when I'm going to do it!" Although I was spending the night, Louis was already in bed. Joshua was going to come in for the morning shift at 8 a.m. Maybe I could have the conversation with Louis after Joshua's gotten him up? Keep in mind, that's a three-hour process.

It wasn't so much that I was deeply hurt or offended by the fact that "Oh, Louis reached out and touched me." But it was more so that I had established that boundary and had asked him to respect it, and he did not in those moments, even if only in tiny ways.

As I was examining my conscience, I also realized, "You know, Jesus, I promised you this weekend I was going to work on Louis's book. But I didn't get to do it." Now I was faced with two problems: (1) I needed to have this conversation with Louis which would be awkward and hard for me to bring up; and (2) I needed to work on the book, which I hadn't done over the weekend. So, unsure how to resolve these two problems, I went to bed.

In the middle of the night, I suddenly heard a metallic *clang!* I immediately jumped out of bed; I knew exactly what that was. Louis's ventilator machine had fallen over. I rushed over there. Thank God, nothing had been broken, but apparently some water got into the mask. The mask was still connected to Louis's face. Amazingly, none of the piping was torn; the machine was intact. It was just all over the floor. I collected everything and put the bedstand back up. Seems that Louis had inadvertently raised the head of the bed and accidently pushed the table, causing it to fall over.

Louis took the mask off. I was putting everything back together—and then he had to pee. *Bam!* I had the urinal ready like clockwork. It was beautiful caregiver-care receiver teamwork.

After helping Louis pee, I had to use the restroom myself. As I was sitting on the toilet, I was trying to think, *Okay, God, what are you up to? What's your purpose here? I know you're up to something. I wonder what it is.* Maybe it would be some kind of sacrifice that I would have to offer; maybe Louis had an itch really bad and I would just have to scratch it? Maybe he's gonna need his leg muscles rubbed a lot, which would push me when I would want to go to sleep? Maybe not.

Then I remembered. I needed to have that conversation with Louis. I needed to talk about the boundaries thing because it was pushed. I needed to talk about it or else I wouldn't have peace. Still, I stalled on the toilet trying to convince myself I needed to go #2.

I finally gave it up. It was around 3:40 a.m. I emerged from the bathroom, and Louis and I began to talk. I finally said, "We need to talk about the boundaries that you pushed yesterday." Louis wasn't aware of what I was talking about. So, I explained.

"Oh. I don't think that was really significant, Matthias. You know, I wasn't even thinking about that. That was a different thing; I was just reaching out. That's the kind of thing like when you brush up against people at the Newman Center or in a crowd or something."

I replied, "But that's not intentional; this is intentional."

"Okay, yeah." Then, Louis said, "I think you're being hypersensitive. That boundary seems too stringent. I want to love you Matthias. I'm human, you know."

I accepted that my boundary (no reaching out and touching me unexpectedly) was perhaps too strict, but I wasn't able to quite get out there that it bothered me that my explicit will was contradicted. Even if the stated boundary needed to be modified, I wasn't respected. I didn't think that was Louis's intention at all. There was no malice or anything like that. Nevertheless, I had not been respected by his actions.

I finally said, "Yeah, I'm human, too." I forgave him, not for wanting to love me but for going against what my intentions were, for trespassing the boundary.

Louis also pointed out, "This just came out of nowhere for me man; you're bringing this up at like 4 in the morning, like what's the deal?" Louis is very patient with me in that respect, and I am very grateful for that.

After we had come to that resolution and forgiveness, Louis reached his hand out, and I took his hand, so we were holding hands there, and I asked, "Uh, what are we doing?" I was trying to ask, "Uh, are we going in for a hug, or is this a hand hold?"

And he said, "We're being friends."

He then asked if he could reach out to me and touch me, and I said, "yes." So, he placed his hand on my chest, and he prayed very quickly. I did likewise with my hand on his shoulder. He asked me for a hug, so I held him there in the bed which is always a very interesting position because I have to keep my feet on the floor at a funny angle.

Louis apologized again, saying, "I'm sorry Bro, you know, I didn't want to hurt you, and I'm sorry for crossing that boundary. I'm sorry for that."

That's when I fully received his contrition. That was when I realized he fully acknowledged, "I'm sorry it went against your will in that matter you had asked me." And I was able to say again, "I forgive you."

After I had gotten up from the embrace, I said, "Yeah, the boundary's too stringent, and I think there's a difference between when you reach out your hand and you hold it there, in moments like when we're working on the computer or I'm giving you a shower, and when you just kinda give me that tap. Those are different things, I agree."

By this time, it was 4:34 a.m. I was ready to go back to bed and just sleep for the rest of the morning. But I noticed that the sun was starting to rise. In Arizona in the summer, the sun's coming up at 4:30; you can see the blue light dawning.

Louis asked, "Hey, you wanna get me up? We can go watch the sunrise!"

After a bit of deliberation, I agreed.

So, up we got. We skipped most of the normal morning routine. We just got him out of bed, put some pants and a shirt on him, stuck him in his wheelchair, and out we came. It was beautiful. The birds were all singing; we could see the blue light start to change to yellow. Louis quipped, "Hey, it's too bad we don't have a basin out here; I could wash your feet out here; it would be awesome!"

I responded, "There's an easy solution to your problem." I walked inside, procured a basin, filled it with warm water, got a soap bar, and came out with a towel. I recognized that this would be the last time Louis and I could wash each other's feet before I headed to Texas for the summer. It was also the best time, in a glorious morning, beholding the sun rise.

I sat in the chair outside, gave Louis my right foot, and held up the basin for him. He put his hands in the water, soaped them up, and took my foot and began to wash it and rub it. We wouldn't do just a simple washing of feet. Louis would rub my feet, go in between the toes, very thorough, very loving. When I would feel that I was being overwhelmed by the intensity, I would close my eyes. I would still trust in the moment, but I'd close my eyes so that I could receive it without feeling pushed too much.

He washed my feet. He asked if he could kiss them, and I said, "One time." He did so. Then it was my turn. I lifted his left leg, and began to wash his foot, soap in my hands and kneeling on the ground, with the towel on my chest. Louis would tell me, "Matthias, every time you touch my feet, they tingle! They come alive! You have healing hands." This morning was no exception.

Whenever Louis would say that, I would pray, *Blessed Mother, if now's the time, you can heal Louis.* Or maybe it would be at Lourdes or some other time. Father John Paul had told me not to worry about knowing whether I was being called to facilitate a spontaneous, miraculous healing. If I was, rest assured, "It will be very obvious."

There was no physical miraculous healing that day, but that was okay. There were other miracles. As I was washing Louis's feet, he was praying, "Jesus, I submit my will to you and to Matthias. I submit to your will and to Matthias's will." I was very moved by that. It was a very humble submission.

After I'd washed his feet, as per tradition, I placed my Miraculous Medal on top of his foot and prayed that he might be healed. Not only that he might walk physically, but that we might walk uprightly and be perfected in our love in Christ. I made the sign of the Cross on his foot, and I kissed it. I did so with the other foot.

After I got up, Louis asked for me to hold him, so I did. It was a very long embrace. Louis and were prone to those. There's no such thing as a short hug with Louis if you're close to him. Holding him there, I began to pray, "Jesus, as you give Yourself in the Eucharist, so I give myself to Louis." He gives Himself to us, even knowing that we'll sin again. "Jesus, as you give Yourself in the Eucharist, so I give myself to him." I was giving him my body, holding him right there.

To indicate that I was about to finish, I held him a bit tighter, and he responded back, tighter. I gave him a kiss on the cheek, and he did likewise. I stood up. Louis's first word was, "Whoooa. Bro, we merged! We were one! We were like one body! That was intimate!" Then we prayed the Rosary together outside—or at least, I prayed it while Louis snored in his powerchair.

I couldn't help but be amazed and grateful for the incredibly delicate work of Providence in these events. If our friend hadn't recommended watching *A Man for All Seasons*, we wouldn't have tried to watch it. If we hadn't tried to watch the movie, we wouldn't have told Joshua to come later at 8 a.m. rather than 6 a.m. and we would have gone to bed earlier. *And,* if that hadn't happened, the over-the-bed table likely wouldn't have fallen over. And if the over-the-bed table hadn't fallen over, we wouldn't have woken up in the middle of the night at 3:15 a.m., and I wouldn't have had the opportunity to have the discussion about boundaries. If we hadn't had that discussion, we wouldn't have stayed up even later after 3:15 a.m., we would have gone right back to sleep. Instead, we went outside, noticing the morning sun coming up and shared a beautiful foot-washing moment that neither of us had planned at all. All of these things conspired to help bring about that holy moment.

If it weren't for obedience to my spiritual director, teaching me to maintain my boundaries, we wouldn't have had the readiness to have such an intimate moment. Without the boundary in place, I wouldn't have felt free to have such an intensely intimate experience. To top it all off, if we hadn't had the movie prompt us to delay Joshua's coming, we wouldn't have had enough time in the morning to have all this conversation and then pray the Rosary afterward because Joshua would have already arrived. Everything was arranged to be able to have this moment. And this moment provided everything I needed to contribute to the book.

God, You are a good God, and You orchestrate everything so well! Thank You God, for teaching me how much boundaries, in their proper place, and the process of learning them, actually facilitates our oneness.

When I look back at that foot washing experience from May 2022, I have mixed feelings. I am certainly appreciative of the graces that clearly came in that moment. Reconciliation, learning how to discuss these things openly, yet I am also ashamed of myself. Timidity is one of my principal weaknesses. I am ashamed of how easily I would often dismiss, minimize, or ignore violations of my boundaries in times past. Looking back, I see how easily I folded into agreeing that my boundary was too stringent and accepting that I needed to accommodate Louis's desire rather than maintain a healthy and *reasonable* boundary that I needed for myself.

Why would I do this? If we take a step back and examine Louis's situation and personality, alongside my own, we can recognize the risky recipe. Louis has had great insecurity, stemming from his wound of abandonment. He has a long history of dangerously trying to fill that hole through sexual promiscuity—trying to grab intimacy that is not freely, truly given (*dysphoric intimacy* is a term he coined for it). The insecurity and need for a sense of safety is only exacerbated by his physical vulnerability. Plus, Louis is very forward about expressing what he wants or needs. Now, I'm a young guy (20 when I first started doing Louis's personal care) who is extremely compassionate, very emotionally driven (I'm a 4 on the Enneagram, the "Artist/Helpless Romantic/Individualist"), *AND* very timid/reluctant about advocating for my own wants and needs. Do you see the ingredients for an unhealthy relationship down the road? Nevertheless, God's mercy infinitely exceeds our misery. And by grace, we have experienced that.

Why did I so often compromise my own spiritual, psychological, and bodily integrity? It was in the name of love and self-denial. For instance, early in our relationship, Louis had a great desire to do personal care activities for me like I do for him. One would be to shower me ("*You can keep your shorts on . . .*"). I did let Louis shampoo and wash my hair two times or so, and once or twice I let him apply my shaving cream (it wouldn't be a good idea to let him handle a razor on me. Shaky hands + razor = bad news). And of course, we had many foot washings.

I need to thank God again and again for my spiritual director, Fr. John Paul. As Louis said, coining another classic Louisism, "It's no accident that we both know Fr. JP, he's sort of like the traffic cop, making sure we don't get into an eternal accident." Fr. JP and I had begun meeting monthly since I was a freshman at the U of A. He had journeyed with me in the aftermath of my breakup with my high school girlfriend and wrestling with/trying to avoid the call to religious life. He encouraged me to date; he was with me when I broke up with Nicole; and he accompanies me still pursuing religious life while taking care of Louis and doing his academic support, in addition to being on the Student Ministry Team under his direction all the while finishing my own undergraduate work. He was the perfect spiritual director that I needed to help me navigate the dual relationship (caregiver and friend) with Louis.

Obedience saved me. I needed Fr. JP's hard *no* to be at peace telling Louis, "No, I won't have you shower me."

Fr. JP told me, "Where is the self? You seem to be losing sense of self in this relationship with Louis."

I asked, "But isn't self-denial the goal of the Christian life? Deny yourself, take up your cross? Isn't that what charity requires?"

"I'm talking about the healthy self, the self integrated with God, not the unhealthy ego that tries to be without God. If you can't maintain healthy boundaries, you're going to be continually overwhelmed and frustrated— then charity begins to wane."

I knew Fr. JP was right because each time I emerged from our spiritual direction meetings having discussed this, I would have to cry (or at least I wanted to). I needed the objective (and wise) third party to make me recognize the cloud looming over me. Though unintentionally (unintentional on both Louis's part and mine) I was letting myself be abused.

Let me be clear. This kind of non-aggressive abuse is nowhere near the level of abuse that, for instance, Louis witnessed and experienced at the hands of his father. Many people in situations of violent abuse need to leave as soon as they can, if they can (it's very complicated; I'm no expert in this field). In Louis's and my case though, what kept me from saying, "This is unhealthy and I need to leave" was the fact that Louis *genuinely* apologized every time I'd bring this up *and* sought to amend himself and respect my boundaries. He was genuinely crushed when I would reveal to him how badly these violations affected me. How did I know his contrition was genuine? Because he would try to do better. Now, sometimes he failed.

But Louis would eventually apologize (not just "I'm sorry you feel that way," but "I'm sorry I did that"), and I would apologize whenever I was too harsh or insensitive with respect to his feelings. But I never apologized for articulating and maintaining my needed boundaries again.

There have been other boundaries, and we've had multiple versions of this conversation throughout the years. There's been real progress, though it is often slow and requires many candid, loving (and tough-love) conversations; lots of apologizing and forgiving, messing up and starting again.

Fr. JP needed to tell me time and time again, "Work on loving, caring, boundaries." That very concept, "loving, caring, boundary" was very difficult for me to accept, but it is incredibly freeing. I was so afraid of spurning Louis's love or not being loving enough in return. But, as Fr. Mike Schmitz taught me through YouTube,[17] articulating your boundaries with someone is a very necessary and generous act of love because you are telling the other person how they can love you; how they can take care of you.

I also had to learn the difference between a boundary and a wall. Fr. JP had to teach me that over the course of many months. As I learn to articulate and maintain loving boundaries, I've also had to learn how to not weaponize boundaries by turning them into antiseptic walls. Loving friendships, not-spousal or spousal, need to be alive; they need to have warmth. But sometimes it's tempting to run away from the challenge of loving the other by cutting off contact and being cold. Louis would call me out on this (though the line between him calling me out on this and him minimizing my need for space has been blurry at times, too). Louis has learned to respect my need for space, and if he wants a hug, he'll ask me. Sometimes I say, "no," and we're both cool. Sometimes I say, "yes." My heart remains free, but that freedom requires a tricky balance of affection and space, and that takes energy to sustain. *Does it have to be this much energy?*

I took this to Our Lord and Lady with the Rosary, and the Spirit directed me to a very helpful image: *This is a treasure surrounded by thorns.* If I am to hold this treasure, this rose, there is suffering that is unavoidable. Some thorns must be avoided, and so you learn how to hold the rose very carefully while still being able to enjoy its fragrance. When Louis's affection pierces my heart uncomfortably, I try to remember the rose that I am holding onto.

matthias's summer adventures, 2022

The time came for me to move into the Newman apartment in anticipation of the Fall semester, my final semester of undergrad, before flying home to Texas. The Siml brothers, Joseph and John Paul (who moved into a different Newman apartment), along with Nicole helped me move my stuff from my house on Elm Street to the Newman Center apartment.

I was only spending one night there before flying back to Texas the next morning. The Siml brothers had somewhere else to be, so I asked Nicole if she would stay for dinner (a comical invitation given my sparse and hardly unpacked supplies). She did. She had just graduated; I would have graduated with her and our class had I not taken the semester off with Louis, hence Fall 2022 being my final semester. So, I took the opportunity for both of us to reflect on the whole of our undergraduate experiences: life lessons, challenges, greatest joys, and so on. I will share two special things that she shared with me that evening.

First, she said, "It gives me exceeding joy to see your zeal for pursuing religious life." This was such a grace. You see, the very knot at the center of my heart (until the Blessed Mother stepped in in 2021) was that I had to give up loving Nicole in order to pursue the radical love of God I felt called to. In an abstract, intellectual way, I understood that I ultimately love Nicole more by fulfilling my love for God. Now I saw it in her eyes and heard it in her voice. Here she was, made exceedingly *joyful* by my desire for religious life. Before I went to sleep that night, I was just pouring out my thanksgiving to God.

Second, she said, "I am very grateful for what you do for Louis. You show an example of real Christian love and sacrifice, one that challenges me and many others. I thank you for that." It was that grace again. I had feared that my love for Louis (and Tony, and others on the margins) was a conflict with my love for Nicole when we were dating. Yet, as it was now, what seemed like it was pulling away from my love for Nicole was actually building her up. I could only thank God.

I went home to Texas, spent a short few days there, and flew off to D.C. for the Thomistic Institute Student Leadership Conference. After the conference was completed, I spent a few nights at my cousin's. My cousin Tommy is not super religious, but toward the end of our time together, I screwed up the courage to ask him something, something I had asked Mom and a few other people to do.

"Can I ask you a favor?"

"Sure, anything."

"Louis and I are making plans to eventually go to Lourdes for a pilgrimage. Could you pray for us, for Louis's healing and for our pilgrimage, in a particular way every day?"

"I guess. You know I don't do much prayer, though."

"That's okay. It goes like this: you just say three Hail Marys every day, one in honor of each of the persons of the Trinity. 'In honor of God the Father, *Hail Mary*... In honor of God the Son, *Hail Mary*... in honor of God the Holy Spirit, *Hail Mary*...' That's it."

Tommy said, "Sure." I have no idea how faithfully he kept to it, and I'm ashamed to say I never kept him updated when we finally did make the pilgrimage.

I share this little part of my Summer 2022 adventures because it highlights the kind of preparation I was beginning to make for the Lourdes pilgrimage. I knew that such an endeavor would likely require some serious fundraising, but I'm not much of a money guy. So, I figured I could do the prayer-fundraising. We'll need the graces; plus, it's a nice little way I can evangelize. I didn't think I could appeal to Tommy on religious grounds, like I could with fellow devout Catholics, but I realized that I could count on his care for me as my cousin. I wasn't trying to teach or preach (preach as I may have wanted to, prospective Dominican that I am); I was asking for help. And people generally like to help. Tommy did. He at least said so, and I was very grateful for that.

Tommy dropped me off at St. Anselm's Abbey where I would be staying for a few nights. Br. (now Fr.) Ignacio, "monkle" to my friend from Pre-K (He's her uncle, and he's a monk; so . . . monkle!) welcomed me with full, warm, Benedictine hospitality.

I loved being at the Abbey very much: the silence, the prayers, and the monks. Memory eternal to Fr. Christopher and Fr. Joseph; Fr. Christopher was a very sweet guestmaster who led us visitors in the Rosary. Fr. Joseph preached a sermon on St. Kateri Tekakwitha that greatly edified and moved me. It was comical and intimidating at the same time to behold Fr. Joseph charging down the hall with his walker toward breakfast after morning prayer.

A clear recognition resounded in me: *I love it here, but I'm not called to be here.* That being said, my chance meeting with a certain Fr. Andrew Fisher, a priest of the

Diocese of Arlington who was making his personal retreat at the Abbey, proved to be crucial.

Fr. Fisher and I were chatting, and I opened up about my vocation discernment and work with Louis. I further explained that we were looking at going to Lourdes, probably in 2023. Fr. Fisher highly recommended that I reach out to the Order of Malta. I had never heard of them. He explained that they were a lay religious order that sponsored large groups of pilgrims going to Lourdes each year. Fr. Fisher had worked with the Eastern Province of the Order of Malta in his own diocese. He highly recommended that I reach out to the Western Province.

Before I could do that though, it was time to fly to Milwaukee. I was very grateful to be able to see Tony, and I was also very grateful to have the permission to stay with our friend Michael Janczakowski (from here on out, Michael J) at the St. Francis de Sales seminary of the Archdiocese of Milwaukee. Michael J was a senior at the Newman Center at the University of Arizona when I was a freshman. He is an upstanding man whose example I admire and from whom I learned a lot as a young Newmanite. He preceded me in making the journey from dating to discerning priesthood. There were a couple of times that Michael J actually went with Louis to the Edith Ball Recreation Center therapy pool in Tucson, along with Steven. They would help him walk in the water.

Now, Michael J was a seminarian for the Diocese of Green Bay (his hometown), studying at the seminary in Milwaukee. So, what does this have to do with Tony . . . or Louis, for that matter?

Tony, as I like to introduce him, is the sweetest big Black blind Jewish guy you'll ever meet. He has faced many struggles on account of his race, religion, disability, and poverty, not to mention his own particularly complicated family circumstances. His dream is to complete his undergraduate degree; but, as of yet, he has not been able to do so. Money is usually the nail that gets driven in that coffin. He has spent many disjointed semesters (or chunks of semesters) at various schools across the Midwest and the country. He is incredibly resilient. One of those semesters was the Spring of 2019, studying at the University of Arizona. He just so happened to be a fellow resident at Kaibab-Huachuca dorm when I was a freshman.

However, once again, the exorbitant costs of schooling (out-of-state schooling no less) sent Tony back home to Milwaukee. However, we were never long without hearing from him. He would call many times a week, and it's taken Louis and I a while to learn how to keep up with him while maintaining a loving, healthy boundary. At the same time, Tony is often short on money and asks us for food help. So, I'll go through GrubHub or UberEats to get something delivered to him every now and then. Louis often splits the bill with me.

It is very providential that Michael J happened to be sent to Milwaukee for his seminary education. We got Michael J and Tony connected and have been very grateful for the support that Michael has been able to offer Tony. Michael is also grateful for the experience that Tony can share with him and the lessons he is able to learn through spending time with him.

We were spending time with Tony, but Michael also took the opportunity to show me the amazing shrines, basilicas, and pilgrimage sites of the Milwaukee area (St. Jehoshaphat's Basilica—wow). Not the least of these was Holy Hill. Administered by the Discalced Carmelites, Holy Hill is a beautiful church atop a rural mount outside of Milwaukee. Several wooded trails crisscross the hill, one of them being a poignant Stations of The Cross trail. Inside the church, there is a pile of crutches and other assistive devices sitting before one of the altars, left there in thanksgiving for miraculous healings over the years.

My trail hikes and prayers with Michael J prompted an unexpected conversation. I don't remember who asked first; I think it was Michael.

"Matthias, what if there was a religious order that took care of people like Louis and Tony? What if we started it?"

"You know, I've thought about that a lot, actually."

We began opening a whole world of possibilities. It was an idea that Louis and I had mentioned once or twice but never got off the ground. I never imagined Louis being a professed religious, so the idea of that particular care mechanism faded from our discussions. But it was a whole other thing to discuss such a thing with Michael J, a man seriously contemplating religious life himself.

We decided to pray a novena to St. Thérèse for guidance. I don't entirely remember what we specifically asked, but we at least asked for this sign: if we are to investigate this path further, of beginning a new religious order in the Church that would specialize in the care of people like Louis and Tony, please send us a *blue rose*. "Let it be unusual, that'll make it really jump out for us," Michael said. "God's involved. He can do what He wants."

On a completely unrelated note, Louis had a mission for me in Milwaukee. You see, Louis loves cheese, and I was in the cheese capital of the world. With Tony's direction, we located a good cheese shop in downtown Milwaukee. I purchased blocks of Basil Mozzarella and Hatch Chile Havarti. With Tony tutoring me in blind practice, we made our way to the bus stop to get back to Tony's place where Michael J would eventually pick me up. I had my sunglasses on, eyes tightly shut. It really was the blind leading the blind. Tony really enjoyed the opportunity to share a little bit of his world with me.

With cheese properly stored (as best as I could keep it away from warmth as possible), I boarded the Amtrak Texas Eagle bound for Austin. This was another one of Tony's ideas to share his world with me. I usually fly for interstate travel, but as Tony asserted, "Poor people take the trains or bus." The costs are not really that different a lot of the time, but I took Tony's invitation.

I only spent a few days back home before getting on the road again (well, up in the air). While at home, the nine days were completed for Michael J's and my novena to St. Thérèse regarding the potential religious order with the charism of care. I called Michael. We both got nothing. Michael offered a sage reflection. "You know Matthias, I think we both really care a lot about our friends Louis and Tony and are trying to think of something to help improve their situations. But it seems that at this time, we're not really in a position to start a new congregation." I believe he was right. Otherwise, St. Thérèse would have sent us a bright blue rose, just as obvious as the three white roses she sent me just a few months before.

It was time to fly to Albuquerque. After landing at the Albuquerque Sunport, I walked with my luggage (cheese carefully stored in one backpack which I did my best to keep under my shadow as I walked) all the way to a Catholic church to attend Mass. I was (a little unrealistically) hoping to meet someone who might be able to drive me to the train station where I needed to catch the Roadrunner to get to Santa Fe. After the Mass—said and prayed in Spanish—I did not muster the courage to ask anyone for a ride. I did ask the priest for a blessing for my journey to the Monastery, which he cheerfully gave.

I walked the mile or two that remained to the train station and soon boarded the Roadrunner. It meep-meeps, just like the cartoon. It's cute for a couple times, but after an hour and a half of hearing it every time the train stops, it gets old.

I made it to Santa Fe where I was picked up by my mom's friend from medical school, Dr. Johnson (not to be confused with Louis's mentor, Dr. Phil Johnson). She is a wise lady, a devout member of the Renewal movement in Judaism (this is the movement of Judaism born from the leadership of Reb Zalman, who had done significant work with Dr. Martin Luther King, Jr.) She kindly allowed me to store the Wisconsin cheese in her fridge.

Dr. Johnson and I got along swimmingly. We talked about prayer, religion, expiation, and our own respective journeys. I told her the whole story of my vocation discernment and my personal care/academic support role with Louis. Especially prominent was the challenge of leaving in the future for religious life while Louis was still on the search for quality care.

She counseled me thus: "It sounds like you're in a hurry. You don't need to be." I haven't forgotten that, and after I shared that with Louis, he made sure to remind me of this wisdom many a time.

Dr. Johnson dropped me off at the station for the Santa Fe Blue Bus. It's a small shuttle bus that is fare-free. We bid our farewells and promised to pray, one for the other.

I transferred to the Taos-bound Blue Bus at Española and went up toward Ghost Ranch. There, I would be picked up by Kevin Spitzer in his van; he owns and operates the White Buffalo Shuttle Service. The fare-free Blue Bus, unfortunately, does not travel up the 13-mile dirt road to the Monastery (Forest Road 151, if you're curious).

Mr. Spitzer dropped me off, and I was greeted warmly by the Abbot himself in front of the Monastery church. He directed me to my living space for my two-week stay, and I was situated. I was designated as a "prospective vocation", though I had clearly told the guestmaster that I was fairly convinced of my call to the Dominicans. I am very grateful they afforded this privilege to me as a discerner of religious life in general. I did explain that I very much wanted to experience the monastic way of life. This was the best way to do it. The Abbot directed me to the ranch house (where another guest was staying) to make use of the fridge to store the cheese.

During my time there, it was not so clear as it was at St. Anselm's Abbey in D.C. I *really* loved it there. The silence, the prayers, the monks . . . Sure, that sounds a lot like St. Anselm's Abbey, but it was *more* silence, more prayers, and more monks. The notion that I *wasn't* called here was not so obvious. I am very grateful for the kindness of Br. David who showed me many of the inner workings of the monastery and the various kinds of manual and technical work required for its upkeep (psalters, electrical equipment, electronics, wool-cleaning, weaving . . . the list goes on). I am also grateful for Br. Benedict's loving admonition my second day there. You see, I had neglected to inform my mother and father that I had made it. I was planning to, but all cell service dropped off somewhere along that 13-mile dirt road. While I was out pulling weeds during the work period, Br. André came up to me, "Matthias, there's someone on the phone for you." It became known among the monks that my mother had called. Br. Benedict said, "You had your mother worried about you? Shame on you!" It was a loving (and slightly humorous) admonition, so I hope you hear that tone as you read his words.

Memory eternal to Br. Leander and Fr. Bernard. By the end of my two weeks, Br. Leander, then 95, had likened me to a "familiar piece of furniture" in the choir of the church. "I'm going to miss that piece of furniture," he said, in his posh English accent. "I'm going to miss you guys, too," I said.

Fr. Bernard was 89 or so at the time, and very frail. He required a lot of personal care, including being spoon-fed. Fr. Caedmon and Fr. Zachary would faithfully wheel him into the church for most of the prayers and for Mass, and would dutifully bring him to meals and help feed him. During the Mass, all of the priests, not just the main celebrant, raise their hands during the invocation of the Holy Spirit and the words of consecration where the priest repeats Jesus' command at the Last Supper: "Take this, all of you, and eat of it. This is my body, given up for you . . ." There was Fr. Bernard, uncomfortably crooked in his manual wheelchair, his stole over his shoulders, and hands lifted up as high as he could manage, mouthing the words in concert with his brother priests.

I also caught a glimpse of Fr. Zachary feeding him one time, a little later after the rest of the monks had left from the dinner meal. I don't know how else to say it: I saw the face of God. Fr. Zachary is a very intelligent and eloquent preacher whose brilliance you would never suspect from his faithful monastic silence, and I could see (maybe it takes a caregiver to see sometimes) the love that he had, simply feeding Fr. Bernard his dinner that evening. I will never forget that.

There is a beautiful icon of the Theotokos (the God-bearer, that is, Mary, the Mother of God) with the child Jesus in the Monastery church, flanked by impressive icons of St. John the Baptist and St. Benedict. I came specifically before this icon to pray with my Dearest Mother many a time. Examining the way of life of these monks and this expression of the vows of poverty, chastity, and obedience, I wondered off and on about how Louis might be able to be cared for in such an environment. At one point, I asked Mary in prayer, "When will Louis be healed?" The answer I received in the Spirit was the following: *When he is ready to be sent.*

Vague as this is (the Blessed Mother usually gives me some berth for receiving her wishes) I took it to mean two things: 1) Louis needs to be ready before healing may occur, and it's not just about his care being solved. He has a mission. 2) It's also about when *I* am ready to be sent. I wondered whether this "being sent" was something for this life, or a veiled allusion to Louis's death, his final sending to his eternal mission in Heaven. I still don't really know. But, for the sake of practicality (and God is very practical), I lean on the interpretation of "sent" as a mission in this life. This began my change of attitude regarding his care. It's not just about finding who/what/where/how is Louis going to be cared for. It's about where and *to whom* he belongs, for the particular mission that God has for him. I cannot say I have always faithfully operated by this new attitude, an attitude driven by faith rather than worldly concern. But it was here, by my Dearest Mother's inspiring, that the seed of this notion was planted.

Fr. Abbot Christian invited me to have a conversation with him about my vocation. We had a great talk in front of the chickens he dutifully cares for (with the cloister courtyard behind us). I enquired about the possibility of Louis coming over to visit in the future. Fr. Abbot Christian explained that they indeed do have a "drive-in shower," as he liked to call it. This was good news.

Sort of like my arrival in Albuquerque, I had not yet figured out how I was getting to Tucson. The Abbot very graciously allowed me to make use of his personal computer (in his office next to a private mini-adoration chapel—that's awesome!) to search for bus and/or train tickets. To no avail. This would be solved further down the road.

As my two weeks at the Monastery were drawing to a close, though I would have liked to stay for much longer (or maybe forever), I had the peaceful conviction that it was time for me to go. It was time to return to Tucson to my schoolwork and to Louis, with his personal care and academic support.

In the early morning of August 15th, the Feast of the Assumption, I attended the first prayer, Vigils, at 4 a.m., procured my breakfast, and recovered the cheese from the ranch house fridge. Br. Bede kindly drove me down the 13-mile dirt road to the stop for the Blue Bus (I had cancelled my return trip with Mr. Spitzer; the Monastery understood that his was not a very affordable service for me). I went down to Española, transferred to the Santa Fe Blue Bus, and caught the Roadrunner down to Albuquerque. I still hadn't figured out how I was getting to Tucson.

Thankfully my older brother James came to my rescue. During our phone call, we arranged for a flight (which he paid for) to get me from the Albuquerque Sunport to Tucson International. A Newmanite friend picked me up that evening, and I was soon back at the apartment at Newman. I was so happy to be there. I stopped by the adoration chapel to tell Jesus thank you. In spite of the great peace and soaring of spirit that I could experience in all my two weeks at the Monastery, the pure joy I had that night, in that one moment, simply living here at the Newman Center, the heart of ministry and Dominican life as I knew it there, out-shone all of my time at the Monastery. And I knew it. That was clear. Every single time I entered my room, I touched the threshold of the door and thanked God that I got to live there.

a surprise for matthias

Matthias

Early in my time at the Newman apartment, I finally made contact with the Order of Malta about our intention to make a pilgrimage to Lourdes. I had sent an email during the summer, but that didn't go too far. So, in August at my apartment at Newman, I did some looking online. On one newsletter (or something similar) the contact info was posted for Mr. Mark Tiernan, the pilgrimage director. I dialed the phone number.

Mr. Tiernan was surprised I found his number. He was the director of the pilgrimage, after all. He was very warm and encouraging. After describing Louis's situation and our hopes to make a pilgrimage, Mr. Tiernan said, "Oh, yeah, Louis would be a shoe-in." The Order of Malta, if they accept a pilgrim's application to travel with them, would cover all the expenses of the "malade" (the term they use for the sick or disabled individual they are sponsoring). I would be allowed to accompany Louis as his personal care companion, but my $3,700 fee would still need to be paid.

Mark directed me to contact a certain Tony Pescatore, who would then connect me with the Local Lourdes Representative for our area. Recording Mr. Pescatore's phone number, I said, "goodbye."

Early that semester was also the Newman undergraduate retreat. This was to be my final retreat as an undergraduate with the Newman Center. I was excited. Four years ago, as an undergraduate freshman hardly introduced to the Newman Center, I went on my first retreat. It was in the tiny town of Hereford, near Sierra Vista, right down on the border, at La Purisima Retreat Center. When I was there for that first time, back in 2018, Kerst, who became a fast friend, actually invited me to give a talk. I spoke about my recently ended high school relationship and my conflicted discernment of the priesthood. I unpacked how I was confused and heartbroken but walking forward with faith.

Now, for Fall 2022, my final retreat as an undergrad was here at La Purisima again. I wasn't invited to give a talk this time, but I ended up sort of giving one unofficially. It began as an answer to a question from someone about my past relationship with Nicole and current discernment of religious life (basically, "How did you get from A to B?"). Her older brother joined, and soon enough I had mustered up a little posse for story time.

What unfolded was the best story I have ever told. God had written it; I was just telling it. The day before leaving for the retreat, I had actually written a letter to a good friend who was also discerning religious life. I told this story, the ups and downs and forwards and backwards of my journey from my high school relationship to discerning priesthood, dating Nicole, then the culmination and healing of the Blessed Mother's love washing over my heart, setting me on fire for total consecration to God. What made the story so good was the sheer volume of fulfillments. So many loose ends were tied up by the Blessed Mother; so many moments that seemed so painful or confusing in the past were repeated but in ways that were healing and clarifying. I saw that God had made my life rhyme; there was a harmony that could be drawn out from the confusion. There is no loose end, no wound, no question, no strife, that the Lord does not (in His time) tie, bind up, answer, and heal. And through the Blessed Mother, I had experienced that in a dramatic and beautiful way. I was blessed. Incredibly blessed. It was the single most fulfilling moment of my life to date. I didn't just get to tell the good news of the story of Jesus. I got to tell the good news of the story of Jesus *in my life.*

After recounting the story at that retreat, I poured out my thanksgiving to the Blessed Mother. Then she charged me, regarding the book I was working on with Louis: *See how amazing this story was that you told? The book must be like that.*

Louis

The semester was proceeding. Matthias was helping with my academic support and staying with me on the weekends. For Thanksgiving that year, we were with Bethany and Gwen, and we termed it "Friendsgiving", which was a nice event. Thanksgiving is one of my favorite times of year. Matthias was in great anticipation for his graduation, to take place in early December. The Mahoneys would be coming to visit, and I wanted to do something special for Matthias. So, this is when I really got to know Marjorie, Matthias's mother. We were in cahoots planning a surprise for Matthias—including Nicole and other friends from the Newman Center. Joseph Siml was a key individual in the execution of the surprise. It was to be kept under wraps as best as possible. So, we had clandestine meetings, sometimes in close proximity to Matthias. Matthias will act like he's not in the know, but in reality, he likes to be in the know. This was no exception.

Matthias

I like to be in the know, sure. But I don't go out of my way to try to uncover these sorts of things. One time at Sunday Mass, before or after, at the Newman Center, I happened upon Joseph, Nicole, and Louis having an unusually quiet conversation together. A word escaped Louis's mouth: "Oops." I simply walked away and pretended like nothing happened. But from then on, I knew Louis was planning something with Nicole and Joseph, and presumably other close Newman folk.

Louis

So, as gently as I could, I thought I was metaphorically tiptoeing around the idea of the graduation surprise. However, in the midst of planning the surprise for Matthias, I got an unwelcome surprise of my own. The power wheelchair, my Permobil, broke down when nobody was around. I had no live-in caregiver since Zane's departure; and Kevin, by this time, was in Denver starting his new career and life with his wife Kelly. So, the only one I really could count on with any degree of certainty was Matthias. I had to use my ADT Medicalert™ that called the 24-hour call center. I asked them to call Matthias. He was the only one on the list that was still active. She did so. She got ahold of Matthias, and I talked to him and told him that he needed to come because I was stuck in the bathroom. The chair wasn't moving. He was reluctant. He said, "Do I *really* need to come?" I said, "Yes, you really do. I wouldn't call you if you didn't, and I wouldn't have gone through such effort." He finally said, "Okay, I will take an Uber and be there shortly."

I heard the garage open, and I was so relieved that he was there. He then found me in the bathroom jammed up against the sink in a forward tilt position. The tilt had stopped working. I always say, "It's great when the electronics work, but when they don't, *boy* do you realize your vulnerability." I said, "I'm sorry, but I didn't have any other choice but to call"—in the relay fashion that it was. I was so grateful for the Medicalert™ and Matthias. It was well worth the $30 a month that I spend on this device.

Back to the surprise—the more welcome one. Matthias, for his part, was diligently working to stay on course to graduate. I was so happy for him. I was honored to be his fraternal friend. I was also feeling free. Matthias always gives me a feeling of freedom, and he actually gives me freedom. I wanted to give him something in return. Something to show him that I authentically cared for him. That I respected him. That I cherished him. I was excited to show him in the form of a surprise party. I wanted to have it at a place that he loved; so, no other place came to mind, upon consultation with Nicole and Joseph, than the Newman Center Curry Classroom. It was the perfect spot.

Manny, the business manager for the Newman Center, was quite helpful. He was used to these things coming from us. Matthias had requested the use of the Curry Classroom for Gerardo and Monique's baby shower a few years prior. Now it was a surprise party for Matthias, the Newman Center's man of faith to the Newman Community at large. Young and old alike would listen as Matthias exclaimed with enthusiasm about our faith in Jesus, the Blessed Mother, and the saints. This was going to be a celebration of faith, while honoring a man of faith.

There was much work to be done, and I had a great team to help me pull this off. We invited many more than Matthias would ever imagine. We just had a good ole time celebrating Matthias, after his great accomplishments in academia. It was a joyous time.

Matthias

Being privy to an upcoming surprise, I was concerned that Nonit (my mom's mom) might not necessarily be in the loop. Of course, I wouldn't tell Louis anything because that would spoil it. I let Nonit know that I knew a surprise party of some kind would be happening, but I was not sure of the details. I'm not really sure Nonit was much informed either until she came to Tucson with Mom. Even then, I wondered if Nonit didn't even know until she was brought to the Curry Classroom.

Anyway, we had the Baccalaureate Mass at Newman. The last Baccalaureate was when Nicole and many of my other friends of my cohort graduated. That was a bittersweet moment; I was so happy for them, but also sad to see them go, and sad not to be up there with them. Still, it was good; I had no regrets.

This time around, I was the *only* student present being commemorated for that Baccalaureate. I can't pretend I didn't enjoy the attention, but man I was praying for humility, too, because I would need it. Wearing the shiny Honors College Medal on my chest and the cap and gown with a cord for good grades filled me with a sense of gratitude and duty. These symbols of honor conferred upon me signaled their concomitant responsibilities. Years of upbringing by my parents, countless teachers and mentors, tens of thousands of dollars of education have been invested in me (Yes, a lot was scholarship money from the U of A, but that only adds to the sense of pure gift received). All this investment for my learning and formation. It's an awesome feeling, and I feel the great responsibility to go forward as a citizen with such education.

After the conclusion of the Baccalaureate mass, Monique pulled me aside. She was very anxious to have a private conversation with me at the side of the church.

How pointedly uncharacteristic, I thought. I knew what was up. Given how the weekend would be, it made perfect sense that Louis's scheme was scheduled for that very evening. I can't remember what Monique found so important to talk about, but I guess it didn't matter much. To her credit, it was a believable topic of interest, but I knew she was only keeping me in position, away from the surprise. She was stalling me.

She invited me to come with her to the lobby, then the classroom. I had caught a glimpse through the classroom door window earlier that day. I gleaned that streamers were involved. All my suspicions were adding up.

When I was finally brought through the door, I was actually surprised. Not by the surprise, but by its magnitude. There was Nicole, the Siml brothers, many Newman friends, and my parents and siblings along with Nonit. It was a sizeable crowd; I was not expecting Louis to have pulled together this many people. It was the greatest crossover episode of my life.

There were speakers. Gerardo gave a very moving reflection on the role I had (and continue to) played in his and his family's life. Martin Lamb recalled how I started the Newman Center Groupchat (originally named the "Shawn Mendez Fan Club." If you know, you know). Monique recounted how we first met each other; I apparently came on a little strong at first. Everyone laughed, while little Enzo toddled around or was carried by his father Gerardo. Nathan Payne, now the music director at Newman, also spoke. Louis spoke briefly. I think he was a little shy about expressing more of his feelings with everyone (and my family) around. All of the speakers had me blushing and everyone laughing. I was even made to recite some Polish poetry, which was also a wonderful opportunity to share some of the saintly wisdom of St. Faustyna.

I was very touched. I could not have imagined a better sendoff for the end of my undergraduate time at the Newman Center and the University of Arizona. I have put so much love and effort into the Newman Center, and I love the people there very much. It was so humbling and deeply gratifying. I was witnessing some of the fruits of my four and half years of being a member of the Newman community whom I so loved serving and being a part of. I will always cherish that moment. Louis, together with my family and our friends, in those couple hours, indeed gave me a treasure beyond compare.

Louis

Matthias's mom, dad, and brothers, as mentioned earlier, came and spent some time in the Old Pueblo. James cooked at the stove, which reminded me of 2021 in Austin. Nonit was there, whom I love. My heart was filled with joy because these people, many people, were at my home—*our* home, as I like to call it for Matthias and me. They weren't paid to be there; they were there because they loved Matthias. That was great to see and be witness to.

Marjorie and I grew closer in our relationship because we had to work undercover. We're not even sure that Bob knew about it. But as Bob will tell you, that's nothing new. We had a great time. Nathaniel and Nicholas stayed at my home which I was grateful for. I was feeling love. And that is a great feeling. I hope everyone that reads this book has that experience: to feel true love. There's nothing like it.

After the party, it was time for Matthias and other members of the Mahoney family to go to bed. The next morning, we all got up and had breakfast at my home. Bob and the Mahoney men went to Albertson's to get some bread and other items. James cooked breakfast for everyone. Then it was time to pack, for everyone to leave. They were on their way to the Grand Canyon to celebrate as a family.

Cella and Mike weren't able to be there for Matthias's graduation. I had met them in 2021, and they were the ones that responded to the letter, saying, "Sure, we'd love to have Louis in the family," so I was disappointed that they weren't there.

Everybody loaded the car, said their goodbyes and it was time to go. Marjorie and I were on the driveway, and before Marjorie shut the door of the car, she said, "Don't worry. He'll be back."

matthias moves in

"*My heart suffered with the hearts of Jesus and Mary. Mine was a silent suffering, for it was my special vocation to hide and shield, as long as God willed, the Virgin Mother and Son from the malice and hatred of men. The most painful of my sorrows was that I knew beforehand of their passion yet would not be there to console them. Their future suffering was ever present to me and became my daily cross. Through compassion for the sufferings of Jesus and Mary I co-operated as no other, in the salvation of the world.*" –St. Joseph's words in 1958 to Sister Mary Ephrem, during alleged apparitions from Our Lady of America and Saint Joseph.[18]

My family and I (Matthias) had a great time in the Grand Canyon. It was cold, but we enjoyed hiking in the snow. We road-tripped back to Austin, stopping by Santa Fe to stay a night with Mom's med school friend, Dr. Johnson. It was good to see her again, and even *more* interesting to behold her philosophical-religious conversations with my father. He was tactfully silent on certain matters and cheerfully reflective while speaking about others.

Two days after Christmas, Louis called me.

"Bro, I gotta tell you something. You won't believe it."

"I've seen about everything with you, Louis. It's hard to tell me something that crazy when it's coming from you."

"I saw the gates."

My curiosity was piqued. "Yeah . . . Wait. You went to the field again?"

"No. I saw the gates. In person."

"What?"

Louis proceeded to explain that he had gone on a little Christmas trip with Bethany and Gwen to see an alpaca farm in Sierra Vista. There would be no vistas of alpacas, to Bethany's disappointment; they were closed for Christmas. Go figure. Louis proposed that they go to Tombstone. Tombstone is a sort of touristy town that features a famous wild-west live action show. On their way back from Tombstone, they elected to drive through St. David, a small (mostly Mormon) town near Benson, which is about an hour southeast of Tucson.

"Yeah, Bro, on our way to St. David's, we passed by this monastery."

I knew the place.

Louis continued, "Oh, so you know the gates, right? The gates to the monastery? Those were the same gates. The same gates I saw when I moved further in the field."

I think I stopped talking at that point for a good 10 seconds. If that wasn't a sign of *something,* I don't know what was.

"We need to go there, Bro," said Louis.

I agreed. We speculated about the possibility of spending Holy Week there, or at least Good Friday through Easter.

After I hung up, I reflected for a good moment. *God, what* are *you up to?*

Louis

As previously told, in 2020 I had an out-of-body experience, and I moved from the field further, on the other side of the veil, to gates. Golden gates. This is where I was given the choice. Gwen, Bethany, and I went by, in

St. David, Holy Trinity Monastery, which once was a cloistered community of monks. Now, the monks have left and gone back to their motherhouse (or were released from their vows), leaving the monastery in the hands of the oblate community. No longer was Mass said because the bishop had received reports of not following the Magisterium.

When we went by, those gates that I had seen in my near-death experience were those same gates that were attached to the Trinity monastery. I had never gone by there before. I was amazed. I said to myself and to Gwen and Bethany, "The Gates! I have to tell Matthias!" I'm sure they, being Methodist, thought I was nuts, but they were gracious and said, "Oh."

I was looking so forward to the beginning of 2023 because that is when Matthias would finally move in. In my view, he would be home. At least his Arizona home.

Matthias

I had some trepidation about moving in with Louis. It made a lot of sense, given my position as his primary caregiver and helping him finish his graduate work, especially with his internship coming up with the Southern Arizona Center Against Sexual Assault. That being said, some concerns remained, not the least of which was, "How much sleep am I going to get?"

In the many weeks and weekends that I had already spent at Louis's house, anywhere between 15 to 50 percent of the time, he will wake up in the middle of the night, needing help to pee, usually. Sometimes he needs water, in which case I have to undo his mask, get the water, then get the mask back on . . . assuming Louis has stopped talking. If he keeps talking with the mask on, his mouth will dry out, and he will want water again.

Also, I knew it would make things stickier. Fr. John Marie, when he was still the vocations director for the Western Dominican Province, counseled against such a move. "From many other similar situations that I know of, Matthias, it just makes moving out that much harder. It makes it *very* difficult, actually." I knew he was right, but at the same time, I knew I was on a mission: to help Louis finish his graduate work, to help him finish the book, and *somehow* leave him in a better place than I found him.

Of course, I was also concerned about our intimacy dynamic and how sane I would remain. I was grateful for the progress that we had made up to that point, but I also recognized that it would be taxing. Louis will frequently emphasize, "This is *our* home," even well before I moved in. Maybe it felt that way for him, but it didn't feel that way for me. It has never really felt like home with Louis in his home. It feels like a mission post—or boot camp, depending on the day. But Louis's heartfelt declarations of "our home" always left a funny feeling in my heart. Call it "our home" as much as he might, it did not make it completely *feel* that way.

Perhaps the true greatest challenge of this move in would be the work-life balance. The boundary between care-labor and rest would be a very blurry one. I was already familiar with Louis's habit of dictating emails and other correspondence while he's on the toilet (or even when he's in the shower) and that mealtimes could also be shifted around, depending on what he wanted to accomplish. I wouldn't just be the live-in caregiver. I was to be the caregiver, the secretary, and the housekeeper, all at once (I can only imagine what it was like for my parents raising me and my four siblings . . . I think I've gotten a smattering of what these noble domestic vocations require . . . there's no such thing as "just" a stay-at-home mom or stay-at-home dad). I knew I would be continual-ly struggling to carve out time for myself, whatever that might be (time at Newman, time with friends, time to read, time to exercise . . .). In other words, my job would be to facilitate Louis's life. He later conferred upon me the title of "scribe in residence". It would be a more de-manding sacrifice than before. I wasn't always confident I was up for it, but I suppose I was confident enough and had enough faith that God was supporting me.

I also recognized some plusses that would help keep me going when I would move in. I deeply appreciate the fact that Louis and I can pray together whenever we want, and it's completely normal. I don't enjoy that freedom with many people. Prayer is interwoven into our conversations and meals, the care routine and when we're out and about. It's often an atmosphere of prayer, poured often as simple thanksgiving to God. Louis's go-to phrase is, "Thank you Jesus!" If you haven't heard Louis say, "Thank you Jesus" or "Thank you Blessed Mother" 50 times by evening, you haven't been paying attention.

In fact, shortly after Christmas, I composed a poem for Louis. I knew I needed to focus on the brighter side of things. This was one of the ways that I did. I was work-ing on it while I was on the plane to Tucson.

[a belated Christmas gift]

Emmanuel and God with me in you

This season we celebrate Emmanuel—God with us.
Today I wish to commemorate God with me in you.
Sometimes I take a while to recognize this God with us,
But the briefest moment's reflection and I realize He's not far from view.

The way you strive to accommodate anything that
I may need,
Or that you do not hesitate to abandon all around
To assist me in any way, no matter how difficult
the deed,
And heed every word I say, as if cherishing every
sound.

God with me through you you also show
In sharing how the Spirit moves, to th'eternal goal,
Or in speaking freely, with your eyes aglow
Of your love for me, with all your soul.

Yet perhaps most of all is in your lack
I see God glorified—my greatest privilege to have
your back
And share our common life, consumed as bread
and wine,
To share in your redemption, and you in mine.

Louis

January 2023 came. Matthias came back from Austin to live with me. What would this mean? Well, I knew the room would be clean. So, I was glad about that. That was the first thought that came to my mind.

I also would not have to worry about getting up in the morning and going to bed at night. Matthias was very faithful. It took a load off my mind. I was also concerned about finishing graduate school, and I knew this as well would make things easier. If I had to stay up later, no problem. If I had to get up earlier, no problem. I was on my own schedule thanks to Matthias being in the guest room across the way. I felt a sense of freedom.

Ironically, from what some other people told Matthias, like Fr. John Marie, etc., it seemed to me as though they were trying to tell him he was losing his freedom. They're missing a point, in my view. If you care about someone, your freedom isn't lost. Your freedom is actually expanded. They were looking at it from probably past situations and their own self-centeredness, which I despise—but accept.

As Matthias has mentioned earlier in this book, we have female inverse counterparts, Gwen and Bethany. Gwen knows as well that people will naysay it out of their own fears. She speaks of her parents and how they tried to dissuade her from caring for Bethany, but now they've just accepted it because Gwen has told them, "It ain't gonna change."

Matthias is more timid than Gwen, but he as well has told them, "It ain't gonna change." In our case, we struggle with his call to the priesthood or religious life because he knows eventually that he must be called. Many have told him, including Dr. Johnson, (Marjorie's friend, not Dr. Phil Johnson) that he's moving too fast. I figure God will slow him down. I'm just along for the ride. That is one of Matthias's shortcomings; he moves too fast. I think that's the issue with youth. I did the same thing, so I don't hold it against him.

A few days after Matthias moved in, he read the poem to me that he had composed. My immediate response was, "Whoa. When you were reading that, I was thinking of how I want us to have a ceremony for our brotherhood covenant. That was your covenant."

It was a beautiful moment. However, that covenant would be tested.

Matthias

The night Monique was induced into labor for her second son was the night I yelled at Louis. I finally let out how I would feel at his every show of abundant affection, joy, and effusive gratitude for me and every desire of his to hold me. There had been a lot of progress up to that point, but things were far from perfect. It didn't help that the tensions and stressors I was holding on to were exacerbated by my own lack of faith and pride. Lack of trust in God ignites anxiety and pride enflames stress like gasoline poured onto fire.

I explained to Louis how I saw our time together as both the Visitation and Exodus. In the Visitation, (Luke 1:39-56), Mary has just received the news that she is to bear the Savior. Instead of thinking herself so important that she had to be aloof from everyone else, she goes in haste to greet her cousin Elizabeth, who also received a calling to be the mother of John the Baptist. Mary stays with her three months, to be with her and help her give birth.

I see myself like Mary, in that I have heard the call to religious life, but I also hear Louis's call (to Social Work, his future employment, to write the book . . .) and am now remaining with him for a while.

I also see us like Exodus. I am like Moses, helping lead Louis out of the slavery of abandonment, unemployment, and loneliness, to the Promised Land of stable care, friendship, and gainful employment, while I await *my* Promised Land of religious life.

There is a marked emphasis on *transition* in my vision of Louis's and my time together. Not to mention something of an overemphasis on myself as a kind of savior.

Louis was straightforward: "That's not how I see it, Bro. I just like our isolation. I don't like many people coming in and out of the home. I love our quiet. It's our time, *our* time to be together, to learn in our faith from each other, and to just relax. I know you're young and full of plans about the future; I was there too when I was 23. Believe me. But as I've gotten older, I just want a more monastic rhythm; I like the quiet. Bro, I just want to enjoy you."

He's told me that many times. But now, weeks—months—of tension finally burst. "I don't want to be enjoyed!"

Louis jumped at this. His arms went up.

"Your love hurts me!" I continued, "Every time you look at me all starry-eyed, 'I love you so much Bro', or 'I wanna hold you', it drives me insane!"

He jumped every time I yelled, which gave me the impression that I was scaring him.

"I'm not going to change, Bro. I love you. What do you want me to do, stop wanting to hold you? Stop saying 'I'm so grateful for you, Bro?'"

I paused. "YES! I wish you could just be less intense, or . . . not so focused on *me!* I *despise* having so much of your affection directed toward me. It drives me NUTS! Your exuberant joy hurts me."

"Bro, that's the last thing I want . . . I don't want my love to hurt you."

"But it does!" My voice shot up again. "You don't get it, OK? It infuriates me!"

"I'm sorry my love hurts you; I love you Bro, that's not what I want. I will never hurt you, not intentionally."

"I know," I said out loud, but inside I grumbled, *you already have.*

In spite of my outbursts, Louis was very level-headed, and my own temper was punctuated with moments of calm: many were the moments I was sincerely fighting the desire to slap him in the face. I've felt that many times when we have these conversations. This time that desire was that much stronger; I thank God I restrained myself. I'd snapped at him once about a much smaller thing, and one time yelled some, venting to him about something else. However, this was the first time I was really yelling at Louis about Louis. This was the first time I was really yelling at *him*, multiple times, in my exasperated attempts to express my frustration concerning our relationship.

I calmed down some. "Look, every time you pour out your affection onto me, I feel more rooted here. But I ultimately long to go to the Order; I have to pursue religious life. And so our moments here are like a microcosm of my life, but I want my life to be elsewhere."

"Ahh. You're afraid of being stuck. I see what's going on. You wanna be over there in the Order, but right now you're here. And you're like 'ooooh! But how am I going to get there and not be stuck with this guy and all his disability needs?' You don't wanna be stuck in the disability time zone."

"Yes, I hate it! When I was at the Monastery in New Mexico, everything was on a regimented schedule. I *loved* it. Here, yeah, you can't really do that, because of your needs. I can't predict when you're going to have to poop or pee or need me to rub your legs... And, and you *hate* being on a tight schedule! You don't like everything overmedicalized."

"Yes, I don't; that's true."

"Yeah. It drives me nuts."

"You are really controlling. My dad was like that; he had to control everything. I told him that before he died."

The slap instinct welled up within me. I was angry, but there was more sadness underneath that anger; Louis had struck a chord. I harbor a fear of responding to Louis's needs like his father: every ambivalence and inability to accept him. I would question myself whenever

I was feeling selfish toward Louis and his needs. *How am I any different than his father?*

Louis was right; I had become very controlling. I anxiously harped on his diet (need to promote weight loss! and grumbling internally whenever he requested more cheese or carby foods) and I squirmed every time his needs upset a planned-out schedule. I tried to control him, and I was trying to control the future. I wanted certainty. I wanted a guarantee that Louis's needs would be met so I could feel free to move on. No one else was lining up to provide the level of care that I provided. Who would take better care of Louis than I do?

But Louis began to challenge me. It was a toned-down version of his manager mode; the faith-oriented version. "You say you believe in God."

"I do."

"And who called you here? Who brought you here?"

I pointed up, "He did."

"Alright. And who's calling you to the Order? God, right?"

I nodded.

"And what did the Blessed Mother tell you? I didn't tell you this, you told me this. What did she tell you?"

"To not be afraid to take you on."

"Right. Do you have faith in God? You say you do. Yet you're over here all worried about yourself. You have become really selfish around me and my needs. Do you know that? You weren't always that way. You say you have faith in God. Did He make a mistake? Do you think He made a mistake in putting us together?"

I was pausing, twinging at the "putting us together" bit, but also angered by the challenge to my faith. But at the same time, I recognized it was a worthy charge: I was giving plenty of reason to be questioned. "No. God doesn't make mistakes."

"Alright. You say you believe in God. Then have faith! I tell you this all the time. We are not promised tomorrow. I don't know what two years down the road is going to look like. I just don't know. If I'm blessed to get my MSW and to get a job, I'll be very grateful. But we can't decide about that. We only have today. Can you just relax and focus on today? Can you just let me love you?"

"No! Your love hurts; its intensity just reinforces how much I've changed things for you; your exuberant joy just makes this all SO good that I feel like I shouldn't leave."

"Bro. You need to go to the religious order. If you really want to go, and I felt like I was holding you back . . . That wouldn't be good. I would feel really bad. And you know Bro, even if you weren't going into the priesthood, I don't think you'd stick around here your whole life. Yeah, we'd be connected, but realistically, I don't think so."

This would have relieved me, had I trusted him about this. Instead, I thought to myself, *but no one's going to take care of you better than I do.*

As if reading my mind, Louis said, "Wait . . . I get it. You think that before I met you, my life was all rain puddles and hum-dum, but now, since you've come along, I'm all happy hoo hoo, and that when you leave, I'm going to be all in the dumps and besotted of what to do with myself." He had a smirk on his face. Manager mode up 12%.

I said nothing. There was an extent to which I thought that way. I thought of how many times he'd told me, with utmost sincerity, "You make my life so much better, Bro," or "I'm so grateful, I couldn't do it without you," or crying in fear of abandonment, "Don't leave me!"

He wasn't finished. Grin still on his face, "You know what? What if I call Kevin and we ask him? Why don't we call Kevin and ask him if he thinks I'm going to be all dismayed when you go forward?"

At first, I thought he was just being rhetorical, but as he pulled out his phone, I remembered that Louis is never "Just rhetorical".

He activated Siri. "Call Kevin Kuper."

I was ready to yell again, or just say, "Wow, you can be a real jerk." I couldn't believe he was just going to bring someone else into this very private conversation ...well, actually, I could believe it. This was Louis.

Kevin's voice came on, calm and cheerful, completely unaware of the mess he was being invited into. "Hey, Louis, how's it going?"

"Kevin! Matthias and I have a question, he's with me here now."

"Okay. What's up?"

"Do you think that before I met Matthias, I was always sad and in the dumps? Matthias seems to think that when he goes off to novitiate, I am going to be so sad and won't be able to be happy in my life. I wanted to call you so that Matthias could hear what you think."

I felt like I was being humiliated like Jesus up on the Cross . . . a purifying humiliation. Except much unlike Jesus, I recognized I deserved to be up here, exposed as such to Kevin.

If your brother sins against you, go and tell him his fault between you and him alone. If he listens to you, you have won over your brother. If he does not listen, take one or two others along with you, so that "every fact may be established on the testimony of two or three witnesses." (Matthew, 18:15-16)

Louis wisely saw that we needed another witness. Perhaps he could have waited to see if I was listening or not; I guess he figured I needed the additional voice anyway. Embarrassed as I was, Kevin was the best choice for that.

"Matthias is saying that he doesn't want me to love him, that he wants me to stop loving him."

That's not what I said, but I kept my mouth shut.

Kevin immediately recognized the awkwardness of the situation and was very gracious. "You know, I feel like there's a bigger conversation that's going on here, and I'm just being brought in without having the full context."

I nodded. I didn't want to speak.

"Yes, Kevin, Matthias is shaking his head in agreement."

"Okay. I will say, you know, I've known Louis since 2016, before either of us met you, Matthias, and Louis just has this ability to kind of pull everything together when he needs it. I mean things were pretty good when you had Vincent."

"Yeah, Vincent was pretty good."

"And, you know, God provides. It hasn't always been easy of course, but Louis always found a way to make it work. I wouldn't say he was 'all in the dumps.' Some days were better than others, and Louis, you would always get back up whenever life would throw you something that would knock you down."

"I understand, Matthias, that you've done more for Louis than any of us have, and that makes it hard to move on, knowing that you're not going to be there to do his care or help out with things like that. But that's where we just have to trust that the Lord provides and then let the Spirit guide you. I mean, just using myself as an example, I wasn't sure where I was going to work for a long time, and it really only all came together at the last minute, and now we're up here in Denver."

"And Kelly and I have talked about this; we're both willing to help out in whatever ways we can, whether it's financially, or if Louis decides to move up to Denver close to us, you know, we'll be able to stay more in touch."

"So, whenever you go to the Order, I'm not worried: Louis is going to be okay. There will be challenges of course, but there's always challenges. Maybe some of those things will be harder after you're not there immediately with Louis, but we have yet to see what the Lord will provide."

Louis looked at me, "You see, Matthias?"

I remained silent.

Kevin piped back up, "You know, I think I'm not really getting both sides of this conversation. Matthias, would it be a good idea for us to talk sometime soon, just the two of us?"

I finally spoke up, "Yes, I think so."

Kevin and I arranged to speak two nights later.

All during this conversation, I realized that Louis was quite right. I was losing my trust in God's goodness, and His promises to provide (for both Louis and myself) and as a result, became much more self-centered and irritable, especially with Louis's emotional and physical needs, and his desire to give me love. Though I didn't say exactly "I don't want your love," I might as well have. Because, at least in appearance, to let Louis love me so much invited me to reciprocate. And, because I don't want to plant my tent here, I fear reciprocating too much.

I recognized my error, or at least the gist of it, and resolved to get to confession the next day. I said to Louis, "I have sinned against Heaven and against you. So many times, God has shown me His goodness, and how He can resolve the seeming impossibilities in wonderful ways. I have been shown that *abundantly* in my life and have been given every reason to trust Him. I know better. But I have failed in trust anyway. And I'm sorry that I've taken that out on you."

"Well, I'm glad you've let it out. You needed to express yourself."

"Yes, but I'm sorry I yelled at you, too, especially seeing how that would make you jump."

"Oh, that's just the cerebral palsy. I forgive you. I love you!"

It was that easy. His readiness to forgive me always amazes me.

He quipped, "You can be a real spitfire Irish-Italian, you know that?"

He laughed. And so did I.

That night I turned in prayer to the Blessed Mother. I was ashamed of myself for my fault of faith. Truly, I was Moses on this Exodus, hitting the rock twice not trusting God's word. Moses was barred the privilege of entering the Promised Land for that. Was I only delaying my departure further into the future because of my anxiety and lack of trust? At the Visitation, Elizabeth greets Mary, "Blessed are you who believed that what was spoken to you by the Lord would be fulfilled" (Luke 1:45). I was Elizabeth's husband Zechariah, who was made mute for his fault of faith. I wasn't Mary. I needed mercy and I needed her reassurance.

While I don't typically hear audible voices of Jesus or the Blessed Mother in my prayers, I allow my imagination and knowledge of true things to facilitate their messages to me in my heart, and sometimes these come across as distinct words or ideas. This especially happens in times of need. I was alone in my room, having already put Louis to bed.

Our Lady addressed me in the Spirit, *"My son."*

"I am your son?"

"Yes."

"I am your son!" I cried. Simply being reminded that she is my mother brings me to tears.

"Trust. Do not be afraid to take Louis on. You will enter the religious life when you are ready. Louis will walk when he is ready. Have a strategy, as Fr. John Paul counseled. Leave the rest to me. Remember Juan Diego—am I not your mother?"

"You are . . . you are!"

"Why are you afraid?"

"Because the fulfilment of claiming Louis as my family seems impossible alongside the fulfilment of religious life."

"Remember what the angel told me? 'Nothing shall be impossible for God.'"

"How can I strengthen my faith?"

"Let go; surrender control. Keep praying the Rosary. Talk to your spiritual director."

When Mary appeared as Our Lady of Guadalupe to the Aztec peasant Juan Diego in the 16th century on Tepeyac Hill, he was worried about his uncle, Juan Bernardino, who had fallen mortally ill. She asked him, "Am I not here, who am your Mother? Do not fear the present illness. Do not let your face be downcast." Later, Juan Diego missed his appointment with her because he was trying to find a priest to give his uncle last rites, but she appeared to him on the way and gently chastised him for his lack of faith. She had already come to his uncle and healed him.

Was she going to heal Louis like she healed Juan Bernardino? Would that be soon? How much longer would I be in this difficult position? I wasn't sure. But in this moment of prayer, I made the resolution to let go of needing to know how it will all work out and to discuss with Fr. John Paul other ways I can remove obstacles to a solid faith. As Fr. JP had said, we would need a strategy for preparing for my departure, and I just had to entrust the rest to Our Lady. Let go, keep praying the Rosary, talk to Fr. JP. I could do those things.

I spoke with Kevin two days later. Most of the things he told me I already knew, but I needed to hear them from him. Chief among his counsels was this: "Yes, you've called Louis family. But that doesn't mean he isn't family anymore when you move away. I mean, you have brothers and a sister, and they never stopped being your siblings when you moved to Arizona."

I was put at peace by my conversation with Kevin, with a simple conviction: Louis will be okay when you go. Another time when I was really worried about this, The Father spoke forcefully to my heart: *I'm taking care of Louis. Stop worrying about it.* I knew it was from God because I was suddenly filled with an indescribable peace of a caliber that I certainly can't produce myself. He also promised me, *I will vindicate you, son.* God cares and provides. I confess I was not always steadfast in this conviction, but it was a promise I would keep coming back to. Yes, there will be struggle for Louis, and likely struggle that will be harder without me, but God nonetheless cares and provides.

my "internship" at SACASA

Louis: A lot of the younger people here, this is their first time seeing all this stuff. I've been around a longer time. This isn't the first round for me.

Matthias: That's a gift you bring.

Louis: It's kind of like Cox where people would come to me, and they're the most important person to me in that moment. Here it's much more. You're not dealing with a car title. You're dealing with a person's life.

January 2023 also marked the beginning of my internship with the Southern Arizona Center Against Sexual Assault (SACASA), under the direction of Katlyn Monje. I had already gone through the extensive training required for onboarding with them in July of 2022. But as fate would have it, I would not officially start as an advocate intern until the Spring of 2023, due to cluster headaches associated with the personal care struggles. That training was invaluable and quite extensive!

In a way, those cluster headaches were a Godsend because it gave me time to work on my internal self with my counselor, Clayton. My supervisor for my first internship with UCEDD, Dr. Lynne Tomasa, along with Dr. Phil Johnson, were both concerned about me taking the role of an advocate intern with SACASA. They recognized that I needed to process my own trauma before assisting others facing sexual trauma. Further, it wouldn't be appropriate for me to take an internship at SACASA while I was a client of one of their counselors. So, God intervened and caused me to delay due to the cluster headaches, and my primary care physician strongly recommended I delay the SACASA internship until January 2023.

My position at SACASA was one that I would come to enjoy, even though there were a lot of painful situations to discuss, witness, and listen to.

Matthias and I just had a discussion about the phrase, "It will be OK." What I saw at SACASA and listened to was not always OK. I think the phrase, "It will be OK," is an anesthetic that we all use to numb ourselves to the truth. In many ways, working at SACASA, I too had to say, when I left, at the end of the day, "It will be OK," but I rejected that phrase and replaced it with, "This isn't OK, but I have to put it aside for now so that I can come back tomorrow." There were many times at SACASA that I had to leave my office and walk away. There were many times at SACASA that I shed a tear.

Matthias was there as my personal assistant, similar to the position that someone would have at Cox Manheim. My time at SACASA brought me back to a time when I took Warren Young, Jr., my then-supervisor at Manheim Orlando, to the Russell Home. The Russell Home for Atypical Children served children and adults with severe disabilities, and Cox supported them financially. I spearheaded this event every Christmas. Warren said to me, "I'm glad you have this job because I couldn't do it." I had to reflect on his words when I was at SACASA. No, this isn't OK. Nor was the issue with the severe disability that I, along with my boss, witnessed at the Russel Home in Orlando.

What makes it OK? It is made OK by those who give of their time, talents, and treasure to ensure that their fellow human being is cared for as best as possible.

The first challenge I had with my internship was when I went through training. This was the result of me falling asleep through part of the training. Not a large portion, but I did fall asleep. I felt very bad about this. Katlyn was gracious. She didn't know me very well, but I knew that she knew I fell asleep. My sleep apnea had kicked in, so I thought, *Is this going to happen when I'm interning?* In fact, I think it happened twice. This was confirmed by Matthias, who was by my computer. I had to face this, but I also knew I wanted to do a great job.

The internship was enriching. I enjoyed helping; I especially had an affinity for male survivors. We would do tabling events at the University of Arizona. There was one gentleman who gravitated toward me when I first started. Elena, one of the advocates I worked with, even mentioned to Katlyn how well I handled the situation. I was appreciative of those accolades because inside I thought, *I want to do a great job, but I have these issues . . . like falling asleep . . . and needing help with the bathroom.*

In my monthly reports to my vocational rehabilitation counselor, I spoke about the need to be more independent with the bathroom, as much as I could be. I told him I came up with this idea of Velcro trousers. This did work fairly well. Matthias had to help less, which was good. However, I still needed support just like I did in my Cox positions. Katlyn was understanding and willing.

Then it came to the documentation portion, which is so important for social workers. I'm honestly much more comfortable just dictating to someone rather than using software like Dragon Dictate. There were times when I had to ask Matthias to do some of the documentation, so again I needed support.

I've always needed some type of supportive assistance while working competitively. That's just being honest. Technology is getting better. Dragon Dictate is getting somewhat better; I am hopeful. There is always hope. Eleos was a program that was being tried at SACASA by one of the individuals that also had a disability.

Interestingly though, if I wanted to get a job with SACASA, I would be precluded because, according to their application process, you must have a driver's license. I think that practice is a bit discriminatory and should be changed. That would make it more open to employment possibilities for individuals with disabilities. I hope they proactively do something. Their parent company is CODAC, which is the acronym for Community Organization for Drug Abuse Control, founded in 1969. During the spring and summer semesters, I think I did a good job, and I was told by Katlyn that I was a hard worker and did an excellent job.

Being part of these internships at UCEDD and then at SACASA showed me that I wasn't the only one who was healing through this work. These internships, along with counseling with Clayton Black, helped me bring my own sexual assault to the surface. They also showed me that individuals who have been assaulted are not responsible for their assault. I struggled with that idea because, in my case anyway, I put myself in some risky positions. I realize that at many points in my development I was addicted to sex. Now, I am currently living a chaste life.

I must say, however, I struggle from time to time. Find someone to talk to if you are facing the situations that I faced. Maybe they won't be exactly the same, but there will be similarity. And if you have an addiction to sex, find someone who can help you.

My time at UCEDD and SACASA, I realized that I was placed here at this moment in time for a reason beyond my comprehension. My position was frontline; fielding calls for those who had either questions or had been assaulted.

One of my calls was from a mother whose little girl had been assaulted. After fielding that call, I said to Matthias, "Matthias, I need to go out for a moment because I need to take a break." That call made me think, it made me angry. That call changed me.

During the call, I had to remove my headset that allowed me to use Dragon Dictate. The call was so egregious in detail that the only thing I wanted to do was be present and actively listen as best as possible, not worrying about documentation, not worrying about anything but the other person on the line: a mother who was distressed over the fact that her four-year-old child had been sexually assaulted. It was imperative to me that I use every skill I had been taught in my master's program. In that moment, I was the one whom the mother was asking to help her, so that she might help her child.

SACASA does everything to help an individual. We also have partners. In this case, it was coordinated through one of my fellow advocates through the Children's Advocacy Center of Southern Arizona. This was the agency that handled children of sexual assault up to the age of 18.

I learned a lot about resources and agencies. You can never learn too much as a social worker. This was a time for me that made me reflect. That's what a lot of the program is about at Arizona State University. Reflect on how you feel, how your internal person feels. This was one of those moments. There were many, but this is one that is quite memorable and has lodged into the cerebral cortex of my brain. It will not be forgotten.

The cases I witnessed at SACASA were unsettling, but I also saw the resilience of healing. Through the experience of being a survivor of sexual assault, you can help others heal and empower others to come forward. I can't answer why you were assaulted. But I do know, through your healing process, you make the world a better place.

triduum at trinity monastery

In April 2023, to celebrate Holy Week, Matthias and I made good on our idea to spend it at Holy Trinity Monastery in St. David, Arizona. You may recall that I had a near-death experience back in 2020 that the Benedictine Monastery of Holy Trinity played a part in. The front gates of the monastery were the same gates in my near-death experience where I had to make the choice of either staying on one side of the golden gates; or, if I entered the gates it meant I must stay on that side of the veil. I chose the former and came back to my body, in the Spirit.

Matthias and I spent Holy Thursday, Good Friday, Holy Saturday, and Easter Sunday morning (the Triduum) at the monastery. We were the only overnight guests for the weekend. There is a beautiful statue of the Blessed Mother in the middle of a pond just outside the cloister where we stayed. We prayed there with her multiple times. That was a highlight of our stay.

We went to Easter Vigil Mass at Our Lady of Lourdes parish in Benson. For us, this was a sign because we knew that we were going to go to Lourdes. *How interesting,* we thought, that we were attending Easter Vigil Mass at Our Lady of Lourdes parish. From my view, it wasn't the most vibrant of parishes, but the folks were friendly, and we were with the Blessed Mother. The connection was there. We would be going to Lourdes.

They also passed out a free copy of Brant Pitre's book, *Jesus and the Jewish Roots of the Eucharist: Unlocking the Secrets of the Last Supper*, which Matthias would read aloud at home with me during breakfast after we returned to Tucson. We haven't finished it yet. A monk most recently asked me, "Do you read all the books that are in your extensive library?" My response was (remembering I did not want to lie to a monk), "I have skimmed all the books, or at least most of the books in my extensive library. But by no means have I read them all. I pay closer attention to those that are faith-based."

After we attended vigil Mass, which lasted well into the wee hours of the morning, we headed back to St. David, which was about a 20-minute ride from Benson. As fate would have it, we got to those same gates I saw in my near-death experience. Remember how I'd said that if I went through those gates, I would have to remain on the other side of the veil? Well, I guess God wanted me to remain on earth, because my brother Matthias, as he often does, misremembered the code.

Matthias contacted Jay, the oblate responsible for guest interactions. It took a moment because we were calling well after midnight. During our waiting period, I came up with the brilliant idea to have Matthias squeeze through the gates of the monastery—he can do this because he is rather skinny in stature—he did it with ease. Once on the other side, I told him to jump and furl his arms around to see if that would open the gate. My idea didn't work. Matthias wasn't as big as a car or even a linebacker for the Pittsburgh Steelers.

Eventually, Jay called Matthias back and we got into the monastery.

It is unfortunate that such a beautiful monastery was ordered to be closed by their Abbot General and his council in Italy.

Matthias

Our time at Trinity Monastery provided us a much-needed opportunity to further renew and refine our relationship. I wanted to love Louis freely, but was so often filled with frustrations and confusion, trying to establish (and maintain) boundaries, decide what boundaries were appropriate, all the while being in some way detached so as to not become too rooted here with him. Could not my love be simpler?

I poured out my concerns to Jesus in the Tabernacle, and He listened to me so kindly. He pointed me to the Way of the Cross, specifically the 4th and 5th station, Jesus Meets His Mother and Simon of Cyrene Helps Jesus Carry His Cross. There's a hymn of rhyming triplets, sung to the tune of "Stabat Mater", which sometimes accompanies the devotion of the Stations of the Cross. I remembered the words that are sung to the 5th station: "Simon stopped in hesitation / not foreseeing his proud station / called to bear the Cross of Christ."

Jesus told me, from His very heart, that I was Simon with Him, helping carry His cross. This gave me great reassurance. Helping Louis carry his cross isn't easy, and not just the cross of his physical care needs. The healing of Louis's soul, through him learning how to love me and me learning how to love him, is often an arduous, confusing, and frustrating journey. I often stop in hesitation, not foreseeing my proud station with Louis. However, I trust that dignity is indeed there, and that it somehow all fits together. I praised God, rejoicing in Jesus' reassurance: I am helping Him carry His Cross.

Before we went to the Easter Vigil Mass at Our Lady of Lourdes parish, Louis and I washed each other's feet, facing the statue of Our Lady in the pond. However, before this, I told him, "Bro, I don't like it when you linger rubbing my feet; it just feels like you're rubbing my foot to rub it, which feels weird."

I was glad to get that off my chest. Many of our foot washings between the big one in 2022 and now had left me feeling uncomfortable. Louis said, "Okay."

Granted, there's no hard and fast rule for determining what constitutes "lingering" and "acceptably rubbing the foot in the washing process". It's a bit fuzzy. I held up my foot for Louis, and he asked me, "Do you trust me?"

I said, "I am entrusting my feet to you." I couldn't say "I trust you" as a blanket statement because, to some extent, I *didn't* trust Louis. But to some extent, I could trust him.

It was a good foot washing, I didn't feel uncomfortable—except for one moment, a gray-area moment (Was that lingering; was it not? Was it worth bringing up?). Perhaps I should have mentioned it. Either way, we laughed a lot. I experienced much peace, the most peace I had experienced around Louis in a long time.

We were outside the cloister; the sun was beginning to set. As I noticed how diligently Louis gave his all to scrub my foot and even in between my toes, I began to better understand his intention. "Louis, you're trying to give back to me all the care I give to you, aren't you?"

"Yep."

I'd hit it on the money. It was also fitting that I had to help Louis to help me in this way. I had to hold the water basin up for him, and it is challenging for him to clean my feet as he washes them, given the limitations to his dexterity. Caring for Louis as a caregiver isn't always easy, so I came to better appreciate the value of Louis offering this service to me.

Sure, I can wash my own feet, but Jesus insisted that He wash His disciples' feet, or else "You will have no inheritance with me." (John 13:8) It is an example of love, a model to follow, and an incredibly practical one at that. Even though it is a "concession" of sorts to Louis (I'm perfectly capable), the requirements of successfully doing the job prevent this ritual from becoming mere "do-this-to-do-it", from becoming fetishized. In other words, this is not a purely symbolic ritual nor simply an activity that I can give Louis to do to satisfy his desire to serve me in an intimate, tactile way. No, the goal is to wash my feet; stinky feet need cleaning! Yes, I needed to give Louis a gentle reminder ("please don't linger") but when I thought of the foot washing this way, I could accept the discomfort that often accompanied it.

The peace gained during this particular foot washing held the foreground of my mind that Paschal weekend. Mass was awesome; I was all smiles. Fr. Martin gave a very spirited homily; he was genuinely filled with joy. He focused on the following question: Why did the newly resurrected Jesus have his disciples meet him in Galilee?

The reason was to remind the disciples that they had run away, thus showing Jesus' great mercy toward them, AND Galilee is the place where they first came to know Jesus. It was a new beginning. In a way, I had gotten a new beginning for myself and with Louis that weekend. I opened up to Louis in greater detail than before about my own struggles with my sexuality. I cried in front of him. Jesus reminded me of how He had rescued me, taking me back to where I received His mercy and saving power in my life. This helped me to grow closer to Louis in a non-frustrated, purer way. It was free from the stickiness and weirdness that accompanied our tactile intimacy. It also brought us to be more two-sided. In terms of sharing our interior selves, I tended to know a lot more about Louis than he knew about me. It was uneven. This moment brought us to greater parity.

Triduum at Trinity Monastery effected real progress. In the foot washing, I had the courage to tell Louis how I was feeling, and Louis gave no resistance trying to accommodate my request. I opened up a little more to Louis. The Lord encouraged me, reminding me why I was there with Louis in the first place, and how important it was to Him. There was greater freedom, respect, and peace than there had been before. But deeper underneath, I didn't realize that things still weren't quite right.

Upon our return to Tucson, we were reinvigorated to plan our pilgrimage to Lourdes with greater resolve. While we were originally hoping to go on the 2023 pilgrimage with the Order of Malta, with Louis's graduate work extending into the summer of 2024, this did not appear feasible. We never submitted the application (due March 2023) and decided to shoot our shot for 2024.

Jane Lacovara, the Local Lourdes Representative (whom Tony Pescatore sent me to) informed us that we would need our applications submitted no later than December 15, 2023. The pilgrimage was to begin on April 30th, 2024. This is a special date for me. I have a strong devotion to the Divine Mercy and St. Faustyna and have experienced many great graces in my journey of vocation discernment particularly associated with the Feast of Divine Mercy, celebrated the Sunday after Easter.

St. Faustyna was the Polish nun who received revelations from Jesus in the '30s and '40s, directing her to write a diary and prepare the world for devotion to the Divine Mercy. April 30, 2000, was the *first* official Divine Mercy Sunday feast, instituted by Pope John Paul II the same day he canonized St. Faustyna. If you have ever seen the image of Jesus with the red and bluish (pale) rays streaming from his heart, with the signature, "Jesus, I trust in You," that's the Divine Mercy Image which Jesus requested St. Faustyna to have painted. To top it all off, April 30th was the day I first asked out my high school girlfriend.

All that said, this made me more certain that it was the Lord's will for us to go with the Order of Malta to Lourdes. We would not have had such a coinciding of dates of such personal significance had we gone in 2023. So, I was happy with the delay.

That summer, just a couple of weeks after Louis officially completed his graduate work in late July, I flew out to the Bay Area to visit the Dominicans in Oakland. This was now my second visit with them. Fr. John Winkowitsch was the new vocations director. Fr. John is a fantastic, jolly Montana man of a friar. He cuts an imposing figure, being well over 6'5", but has all the disposition of a joyful teddy bear—with a keen memory for powerful stories and theology. I did miss working with Fr. John Marie, but I was also very grateful to now be working with Fr. John. He was well disposed to have great compassion and understanding for my relationship with Louis. (In case you haven't noticed, the Dominican Western Province is replete with Fathers John: my spiritual director Fr. John Paul Forté, vocation directors Fr. John Marie Bingham and then Fr. John Winkowitsch.)

My second visit to the priory only reinforced my desire to continue on the road toward religious life. All the same, the uncertainties in Louis's personal care situation still loomed overhead. How attached could I remain to Louis's situation in light of this call from God? What responsibility did I have in his particular case—where I perceive the Church needs to step up—while at the same time, I feel called to step away from his particular situation or from being there immediately, anyway.

Fr. John shared a very powerful story with me during my time there. It went something like this, "I knew a diocesan priest by the name of Fr. Michael. Fr. Michael had a brother who had a debilitating accident that damaged his brain and severely paralyzed him. He was a brilliant man, a mathematician, but the brain damage left him susceptible to severe psychotic breaks. He needed to be spoon-fed and cared for constantly. They tried valiantly to keep him in his home, but after he stabbed his mother with a knife (just one of those episodes) they had to send him to an institution. And Matthias, there's something mysterious and powerful, the graces of which we will only understand in Heaven, about these special relationships where one person goes through so much suffering and the other cares for them. . . For instance, when Fr. Michael would go to visit his brother, he would be begging him for his prayers, 'Patrick, you need to pray for me, I haven't been keeping up with the Divine Office, I've been slacking here and there . . . Patrick, you need to pray for such-and-such, I need your prayers.' I tell you this Matthias because I firmly believe that you and Louis's relationship will only continue to enrich your lives, you in religious life, and he in his life."

This perspective was new to me. It was a fresh, positive, and deeply faith-filled take on what so often felt like an insoluble problem. It gave me hope.

The plan was for me to apply to the Dominicans and join the following year, 2024. However, in addition to the personal care situation and his graduate work, there was another issue that Louis was not keen on facing without me. Kidney stones. Dr. Page had informed us that Louis potentially had a 9mm stone (or cluster of stones) in his kidney, which had formed at some point after the grueling 2020 ureteroscopy. Dr. Page was fine with leaving it alone until after Louis completed his graduate work. Fine by Louis, fine by me. We didn't have to worry about such a risky procedure for a while yet. Either way, Dr.

Page was confident that such a stone was not going to pass any time soon.

As Louis's graduate work was coming closer to completion (graduation to take place in December 2023), the potential kidney stone procedure could likely conflict with my departure. I doubted we would schedule any surgeries before our pilgrimage (April/May 2024) and if I were accepted to the Dominicans, I would start in August 2024. I didn't believe it was my duty to stay longer with Louis for such a procedure, as much as Louis would have hoped that I would. However, we didn't talk too much about it. Cross that bridge when we get there.

the disability time zone

Louis

What is the disability time zone? It's a time zone like no other. It relates to having a disability and how you, as the disabled individual, manage the 24-hour cycle. For many able-bodied individuals, this time zone is very foreign. However, for those of us with disabilities (and again, I can't speak for all of us), it is a time zone that is part of our being from the time we are disabled, for whatever reason. It not only affects the disabled person themselves, it also affects those within the disabled person's orbit. They too must adjust to the disability time zone. When a family says, "Let's go to the beach," for most families, if they are all "able-bodied", that process seems seamless. For families that have members that happen to have a disability, that process can be challenging, especially prior to the Americans with Disabilities Act of July 1990.

Prior to the Americans with Disabilities Act, restaurant accessibility, curb cuts, bathrooms, hotels, and many other public facilities did not accommodate families who happened to have a member with a disability. So, it was up to the family member, or the family as a unit, to make the accommodations for themselves.

Case in point: my childhood home on Tall Timber Dr, to the able-bodied observer, was terrific. It had a huge game room with shuffleboard, pool tables, trains that ran on tracks that my father had built . . . this was no accident. My parents had the means to create amusement down in the basement which covered the full length of our home. Why did they do so? Why did my grandparents or aunts and uncles come to our home as opposed to us going to theirs on a regular basis? The answer lay, in my case, in the disability time zone.

It also lay in the fact that our American society, from 1964, the year of my birth, to 2000, did not have access. While the Americans with Disabilities Act was signed in 1990, it did not really take full effect until the year 2000. That's the length of time that was given to states and municipalities to make the necessary societal changes to be in compliance with the new law. So, for 36 years of my life, many in our society did not really see their fellow citizen with a disability. Nor were they aware of the disability time zone.

I am certain many families grew closer because of their member with a disability. I am just as certain that many families, such as my own nuclear and extended family, grew further apart, to a lesser and greater degree, depending on the individual member. You, as the individual with a disability, must learn how to operate within the time zone, and the family members and/or friends must be willing to operate in that time zone with you. Most of my inner circle, to a lesser or greater degree, have entered the time zone. Some find it exhausting, some accept the inevitability, and some do not remain friends. In my view, I've come to realize that's okay with me. Some just don't have the fortitude or energy to hang within the zone.

It was difficult on my parents' marriage, and the disability time zone did not always match with what my parents needed or wanted to do. For the most part, they struggled to maintain a peaceful equilibrium, which in my view caused great distress for my biological brothers, Edward and Frank. In Edward's case, he escaped the jaws of disability due to the advancement in technology at the time of his birth in 1970, versus 1964.

Moving the clock forward, accommodation is now more prevalent. Does that accommodation make it easier to live within the time zone? From my observation, the answer is yes. I caution, however, that we must continue to move forward. Parents and families still struggle on a daily basis. Public policy administrators and legislators must realize that the Americans with Disabilities Act is only a beginning—it is not an end. Individuals with disabilities such as myself must strongly advocate for social inclusion versus social isolation. The person with a disability must be at the forefront. Their allies can be there, but the individuals with disabilities must be the voice, unless they are unable. It is up to us, allies or those with disabilities who can advocate, to advocate for those who cannot.

It was October 2023. The time came for our road trip with our female inverse counterparts to Tuacahn, outside of St. George, Utah. We went to St. George, along with a stop in Salt Lake City, where, as you know, I lived for five years. We had a great time, but the disability time zone was in full force. Now it was *two* individuals with varying levels of severity of disability that needed to be considered with their companions in tow. It took us about 1.5 times as long to travel between the three destinations and intermediate stops: Tucson to Flagstaff (4 hours 45 minutes per Google maps = about 7 hours for us in the disability time zone (DBT)), Flagstaff to St. George (4 hours 36 minutes per Google maps, another 7 hours in DBT), St. George to Salt Lake City (4 hours 9 minutes per Google = about 6.5 hours DBT), and then Salt Lake City all the way back to our home in the Old

Pueblo, Tucson (11 hours 59 minutes per Google Maps, about 18 hours DBT). Why did we make an 18-hour shot? That will be explained as the story is told.

It was quite interesting because while we were in Salt Lake City, I had an unexpected movement. Salt Lake *is* on the San Andreas fault line, but it was no earthquake. I'll leave it to the reader's imagination. This particular event slowed us considerably, but we made it through and continued on to Las Vegas on our way back to Tucson.

Matthias

In case you didn't imagine it accurately, Louis pooped himself. We were scheduled to leave around 10 a.m. that day so that we could drive all the way to Flagstaff to stop for a night before continuing on to Tucson. However, as often happens in the disability time zone, we didn't manage to check out until around noon. Then, after the car was all packed, Gwen and Bethany awaiting our entry into van, Louis had his accident. This meant that we would need to re-shower. In order to re-shower him, we had to get the sit-to-stand and shower chair back out of the van, lift Louis up with the sit-to-stand, undress him, clean him, transfer him to the shower chair, roll him into the shower, and . . . oh, by the way, we had already checked out of the hotel. Thankfully, Louis was able to ask the hotel manager if we could still use the room with the roll-in shower to handle the situation. The manager was gracious and allowed us to do so.

Louis felt really embarrassed, and I was grateful to be able to be someone in that moment who did not yell at him or blame him or make him feel any worse than he already did while I re-showered him. Sure, I would have liked to have left Salt Lake City at the time we initially intended, but I knew that this was one of those special moments when God's mercy must be shown. I can only imagine the vulnerability of being in Louis's position and how that can make him feel.

This whole process took about three hours. That's the time zone. During this interruption, Gwen, Louis, Bethany, and I were discussing all sorts of ways we might pivot: do the ladies just drive home without us and we go home on a plane? Do we still drive to Flagstaff? Or do we just make a single shot for Tucson? (Normally, a 12-hour drive . . . which meant an 18-hour drive in this time zone. Having *two* friends in powerchairs makes restroom trips all the more frequent and lengthier. Oh, and don't forget just needing to stop because riding in the car is too un-comfortable for extended periods of time, especially if you're in a wheelchair).

We opted for the one-shot to Tucson. Instead of going through Flagstaff, we altered our course to go through Las Vegas. Gwen and I would trade turns at the wheel, and I would drink a lot of tea. Coffee is too strong for me. Perhaps this was not the most prudent of paths, but we made it safe and sound—after the flat tire at 3 a.m., of course.

Louis

It was 3 in the morning, and we ended up with a flat tire on I-15, just outside of Las Vegas. Fortunately for us, Gwen handled the car well and pulled over onto a median so that cars could see us at this early hour. We were fortunate as well that two individuals stopped to assist. Then, we went to a 24-hour tire place. Fortunately, we were in Las Vegas; these places do exist. We replaced the back tires, and we were on our way back to Tucson.

Matthias

Next to Louis's love for cheese is his love for Cracker Barrel. He made sure (and the three of us agreed) to eat dinner there one of our first nights in St. George. Now, between Gwen and I trading shifts at the wheel, dawn had broken as we made our way to the Phoenix metro area. Bethany was even sleepier than I was (Gwen was driving this portion), and I was hardly conscious in the back seat. I awoke to find us in a familiar style of parking lot. I asked, "Cracker Barrel again?"

Gwen explained, "Well, this is what happens when Louis is the only one making meal decisions!" Louis snickered his characteristic "gotcha" snicker, I chuckled, and Bethany woke up. It was a good meal; all were satisfied. We needed the driving break and we were tired.

Louis

After our trip to Tuacahn in St. George, Salt Lake City, and Sin City, we had to atone for our sin. Part of our atonement came by Matthias's next trip to the Dominicans he was discerning with. On a secular note, this brought me to my mother's death on October 30, 2002, which I commemorate every year. She had now been passed over for 21 years. Amazing. I warn everyone who's around me to tread lightly during this time because it is a time of mourning, but also of celebration, celebrating her life and her devotion, similar to the devotion that the Blessed Mother had to her son, Jesus.

Once October was over with Halloween at its end, we moved into the Thanksgiving season. I was also volunteering at the time with the VA, and one of my individuals was 106 years old. She was a feisty one. Such a super person to talk to. This November would be her send-off, though she didn't know it. A local politician had found out that she was in the VA Hospital. So, as most politicians want to do, they wanted to have a photo op with constituents, especially those who are 106. Well, he didn't know what he was in for.

I, of course, bowed out of the photo, along with other staff members, and allowed the politician and our friend of 106 to take a picture together. Well, in spending a lot of time with her, I realized that she was a character. I was *wondering* what she was going to do. In this age of political correctness, a 106-year-old might not get the memo—or the email, for that matter.

Sure enough, she hadn't gotten it. They were posed, ready to take that photo. Our friend of 106 reached around the Congressman's back, but went a little lower, and gave him a nice squeeze on the butt. The staff and I and his staff gasped but underneath I was chuckling because I knew she would do such a thing, and the front-line personal care assistants knew it, too.

They said, "You got a little feel on his rear!"

"Yeah, I'm 106. Why not?"

On our way back to the unit (we used to term it our "walk-and-rolls"), she told me, because she was still pretty sharp at the time, "What are they gonna do? Get me for sexual harassment?" I didn't say much because I wanted to stay fairly neutral. But again, I was like, "okay!"

She was such a joy to be around. Sadly, we lost her later in 2024. She will be missed. She was the ambassador for the Southern Arizona VA Hospital. She was one of the first female Navy Corpsmen the country ever had. She voted for Franklin Roosevelt, but she didn't think much of him. I think later on she became a Republican.

She told me one day in the dining room at the CLC (community living center) that she needed to vote. So, I got with my supervisor, and we contacted voluntary services. They took it from there. The charge nurse/nurse manager had told the story of helping her vote in a previous election. It was heartwarming to see that she still wanted to be engaged. And she certainly was engaged with that Congressman.

After the congressional pat down by my friend at the VA, we had to get ready for our next friend, Tony, for Thanksgiving. And he ain't no turkey. You see, he's Jewish. So, everything must be kosher.

Tony is also, shall we say, a handful. Matthias and I both enjoy having him, but Matthias tends to always put a week time frame in the mix. I think it has something to do with the disability time zone, but more, shall we say, of a hyper nature. Tony's time zone is a zone of its own. Bethany doesn't much care for him. I think Gwen likes him, and the rest of us enjoy his humor. I think Bethany just doesn't get the punch lines. That's okay, not everybody likes me either. Sidenote: if you think everybody likes you, you're fooling yourself.

Tony enjoys the couch in the great room. Once he's on that couch, he doesn't move much. This Thanksgiving I wasn't having it. So, just like Andrew Jackson did the March of the Indians, I did the March of Tony. I said, "C'mon, Tony, we need to exercise." He came up with every excuse not to, but eventually, we went around the block. I was going to make him go twice, but he was like, "I'm tired, I'm tired." I said, "OK."

We also invited a person from Africa to join us for Thanksgiving. She has two sons attending the University of Arizona. Both graduated since this time period, and she was very proud of their accomplishments. My interaction with her reminds me that we are all a type of immigrant. Except for the Native Americans, we all came from somewhere else. That dream is still being sought. She is a personification of that dream.

Unfortunately, according to Matthias, due to his blindness, Tony fell off a bus and injured himself. He used to go all over Milwaukee but now restricts himself to very short distances. Honestly, I understand, but I just want him to keep going.

He lives in Milwaukee by himself. He says he won the lotto because he got into housing that was much better than what he was in, so we are all grateful. It's interesting having fellow friends that are physically or visually or hearing challenged. Not one is the same. I hope and pray that we are there so we can support and help each other, along with our friends who have no physical or mental or intellectual challenges, to achieve the American Dream, whatever that may be.

Matthias

I don't know how much sin I was atoning for in my third visit with the Dominican friars, but I hoped my prayers for Louis, Gwen, Bethany, and others while I was there were of some benefit. This was the most serious visit yet. I was scheduled for six one-hour-long interviews with different friars. I had to write up a 10-page spiritual autobiography (most people balk at having to write so much . . . I had the most trouble whittling my first draft down from 19 pages). The friars talked with me about what I had written about myself.

The primary challenge that arose during these examinations of my vocation was my situation with Louis. The friars had their own respective nuanced takes on the matter, but one general takeaway landed harder than the rest: if you want to come, you need to get going. Soon. The deadline proposed for me to move out was June 1, 2024. Br Michael James OP strongly encouraged having some down time, with few responsibilities, before making the transition into novitiate. He was an only child and said that one month wasn't even enough for him. The Dominicans (of the Western Province) have their potential novices enter on August 15th each year, the Feast of the Assumption of the Blessed Virgin Mary. Two and a half months seemed like a good amount of time, but also so soon . . . especially with the pilgrimage to Lourdes we had upcoming, from April 30th to May 8th.

I prayed with this deadline, contemplated potential scenarios that Louis was working with (like selling his house, among others), and concluded that I would hold myself to this date. Fr. Stephen Maria OP counseled, "Set a deadline and stick to it. You can't leave wiggle room." Fr. John Marie, now having become the novice master (and thus my potential next superior) observed, "You still have disentangling to do before moving forward." He also asked me, "Religious life is filled with the mundane, and you will be mostly with middle class guys with middle class problems. Will you be okay with that?"

This was a poignant question for me because of the great sense of duty I feel to the poor and the marginalized. "If you want this, you need to step on the accelerator and start gunning it toward the deadline," he added.

My final interview was with Fr. John. His insights were the most helpful and grace-filled for me, as far as I am aware. That very day he interviewed me, November 30th, was the anniversary of his father's death, nine years prior. Fr. John described how he had to surrender his own father to the will of God while he was pursuing priestly studies. At one key moment of surrender, Fr. John recounted, "I gained a better understanding of sacrifice that night. It's weird, but when we are completely detached, we are free to love most purely (and passionately). Your heart belongs completely to God now; your love is now infinite. You let go of the temporal to embrace the eternal. You know you're on this path that God has placed you on to make you available for countless souls. For this, you must sacrifice and trust."

I still struggle with this concept of detaching from the temporal to embrace the eternal, but I did make a resolute act of trust in prayer to Our Lady during my time there. In fact, I felt like I got a spiritual resuscitation during my prayer. So much anxiety and worry had been clouding over my ardent desire for religious life; I hadn't felt that powerful joy and longing like I had experienced in 2021 for a long time. I was zapped back into order with a resolute act of trust. "Blessed Mother, I surrender myself to you under the Lord God. I entrust myself completely to you. I surrender everything to you. I surrender Louis's kidney stones. I surrender Louis's care needs. I surrender Louis's care options. I surrender the book. I surrender all." I went to bed peacefully. It is all in her Immaculate and Merciful hands, in the power of God.

This was my journal entry from the following day.

12.1.23 Reflections from last night's prayer
Oh, thank you Righteous Father for Fr. John your servant! For he was able to synthesize and show me the harmony of these difficult and paradoxical truths in the way I needed to hear, and especially when he revealed his heart with the story about his father... For this I bless you and ask that you bless him.

Oh, I can see how my desires to extend and join family are to be united and fulfilled! For but one year after I declared Louis to be my family, I begged the Blessed Mother to allow me to be a part of hers—and boy did she respond! Initially, I saw this regarding Louis as an invitation to a challenge: Are you willing, Matthias, to extend to Louis what I have extended to you?

Now, I see that there is a deeper invitation. This moment with my Dearest Mother was much the fruit of my Marian Consecration, in large part inspired and prepared for by my relationship with Nicole.

Now, in many ways inspired by me, I help Louis to prepare for Marian Consecration (many thanks also to Louis's mother and Maryanne Schiavone . . .)

I was truly called to that relationship with Nicole, and that love found its deeper fulfillment in the heart of Our Lady, from love I passed to love.

Now, being truly called to this relationship with Louis, and he with me, I am to consecrate him to Our Blessed Mother, from love he shall pass to love.

Indeed, brothers we have become, in a deeper way with both of us radically given to Our Lady, to Jesus, in her Maternity, which is also her Motherhood of Christ, and this shall be on the feast of Our Lady of Lourdes [Louis was scheduled to complete his 33-day preparation for Marian Consecration that upcoming February 11th 2024, the Feast of Our Lady of Lourdes] . . . so that we may prepare to ratify this covenant, and give one another completely to the Lord in the hands of Our Lady, at Lourdes, at the waters of Lourdes. This is our preparation to be sent, I to religious life and he to the establishment of his mission. There we will give each other to the maternal protection and commission of Our Lady Immaculate, and so enter the next phase of our lives, as brothers, brothers given to God.

My brotherhood toward Louis is not defined by how I have cared for him or what we have done together. Yes, these experiences confirm our love and exemplify it, but it is not what makes us brothers. At the end of the day, our brotherhood is in and because of the Fatherhood of God and the motherhood of Our Blessed Mother. One is a brother in virtue of a common parentage.

My siblings and I have the same parents; therefore, we are brothers and sisters. Fellow citizens have a common "mother" in their motherland and are thus brothers and sisters. We have common parents in Adam and Eve and are thus all brothers and sisters on that wider level. As baptized Christians, we are adopted brothers and sisters in the Fatherhood of God, and Christ Jesus, the Only Begotten Son, is our Brother.

Now, as baptized Christians, we are little Christs. And so that makes Mary, the Mother of Christ, our mother. This was a ceremony and declaration of covenantal relationship that I felt more inclined to participating in with Louis than anything discussed before. It was also right in line with my desires for religious life and relationship with My Dearest Mother.

reaching the educational summit

This next time period was pretty exciting, busy, and life-affirming. I was set to graduate. I hadn't been part of any type of graduation ceremony since I graduated from Arizona in December 1986. Now, December 2023, I would ceremonially graduate. My degree was conferred in August, but I still wanted and had the desire to go through the ceremony. It was 37 years later that I received my Master's in social work.

There is a thing called imposter syndrome. Many graduates experience it. It's the feeling of *is it really true? Am I ready?* I had this syndrome. I couldn't believe, at the age of 59, I had my master's. I greatly appreciated Matthias's help beyond mention. I greatly appreciated John Hancock Long Term Care Insurance company, which enabled me to pay for care since my dismissal from Cox. I appreciated Cox for offering it as an external benefit.

I wrote to my professors, each and every one of them, and those who supported me throughout this interesting journey. The email's subject line was "Tree of Knowledge, Leaves of Gratitude". This mighty tree stands not for me alone. My hope is that it will stand and weather the storm of any political or social movement that threatens the opportunity of education for those of us that live on the margins of American society, now and in the future.

Stemming from the roots cultivated by my mother's tireless advocacy, Ms. Laughlin teaching me to read, and Ms. Pascarelli's firm resolve, I desired to give due acknowledgement and respect to all who had made my master's degree possible. The email I sent presented many parts of my story which we've already shared, to me, each of these persons and situations are leaves that shaded the pathway from underprivilege to the top of the mighty oak of educational inclusion.

Now, Matthias and I could take a break, being provided with some shade from the Tree of Knowledge. It was time to celebrate. It was time to relax. It was time for a miracle. In order for the miracle to occur, we had to travel to Phoenix, to Arizona State University's main campus so that I would be able to attend my graduation.

Matthias and I checked into our hotel in Scottsdale, the Hampton Inn (which is one of our favorites, because of the pool). Bethany and Gwen drove us up, along with our friend from Nigeria. Kevin flew in from Denver. Monique and Gerardo also came up with their children; I was grateful that they took the time to do so.

It was a great event. I was glad to be part of it. The pinnacle for me was when I rolled across the stage to accept my master's degree. Our friend from Nigeria took many. We had a celebratory dinner at a Teppan steakhouse. My long-time friend Tom and his significant other Peter attended the dinner along with their friend whom we affectionately refer to as "John Candy".

I had some time of personal reflection as well. What was my mother thinking? I was grateful. Without my mother's foundational commitment, I knew this day would have never happened. I knew as well that Matthias's commitment was at a similar level to my mother's. It was like Matthias and my mother were meeting through my educational success.

I also had time to reflect about my relationship with God and Jesus and the Blessed Mother. I knew as well that my faith in Jesus, God, and the Blessed Mother, and the Holy Spirit provided a pathway for me to succeed. Matthias was placed at just the right spot and time. I reflected back to the many challenges in getting to this point and had a vivid understanding that it was no accident that those circumstances which precluded me from graduating earlier were divinely placed.

I was very excited to get into the pool at our hotel. I hadn't done so for a long time. It would also be the first time for Matthias to assist me in the pool.

Matthias

Louis was determined to make as much use of that pool as possible. It was beach entry, and the jacuzzi had a lift. Gwen and Bethany enjoyed the jacuzzi as well; they were staying at the same hotel with our friend from Nigeria.

The first day, Louis was very excited, and I was too. I had never helped anybody walk in the water like this before. It was fantastic. I would hold Louis's arms or hands, and he would propel himself forward, step by step, able to lift his legs with the buoyancy afforded by the water. It's a rather curious kind of walking. Because of the misalignment of Louis's legs and feet, I had to carefully course correct as we went.

Louis

Matthias and I enjoyed the water with Kevin as well. It was coming to the end of our time for swimming. The two men whom I trusted and loved were with me. I decided to be a little brave and to start swimming, not just walking in the water. The challenge is that the person that is with me needs to know that I need to come up out of the water because once my face is in the water, I can't turn my head enough to either side to get a breath.

I thought I had told Matthias and Kevin to remember to pick me up when I squeezed their hand. I had Matthias to my right, and I was getting closer to the wall, but I had to come up. So, I squeezed his hand, but he didn't pull me up! *Wait a moment!* I said to myself. I squeezed again. Both Kevin and he thought I wanted to stay swimming.

Not a good time for miscommunication. They finally figured out that I needed to come up because my face had been under the water for some time. Everything turned out okay, no problems. However, unbeknownst to Kevin and Matthias, this caused me to flashback to when I was nine years old, when I almost drowned due to the lack of action on the part of my father. This event with Kevin and Matthias felt like that to me. I had to think about it for a minute and realize that the connection that I was making was not a rational one. The intention is what makes the difference to me.

Unfortunately for me and my mother, we knew that my father's intentions were not good. They in fact were sinister—almost fatal. Thank God the better angels prevailed. Matthias and Kevin's intentions were benign.

Matthias

Louis's eagerness had not abated in the slightest the next day, in spite of the miscommunication and delayed resurfacing. "We gotta go into the water again, Bro!" I was also excited. I enjoy spending time in the water, and after the water feels too cold, it's nice getting into the jacuzzi.

The third day, Louis was as eager as ever. "Bro, we gotta go in the water again!"

"I'm tired." Truth be told, I was being a little lazy.

Louis said, "Bro. It's like a precursor for when we go to Lourdes."

That got me. The prospect of healing, of spiritual renewal, and other kinds of graces at Lourdes, where pilgrims are invited to drink and bathe in the waters from the miraculously discovered spring, was pretty prominent in my mind. I had my timeline in mind for leaving to join the Dominicans, and I greatly desired to see that healing for Louis. So, I started getting ready to go downstairs to the pool.

Both previous times, I had removed my Miraculous Medal and left it upstairs. The Miraculous Medal I wear is a sign of my Marian Consecration. This is the same medal I would bless Louis's feet with. It is a powerful devotion to the Blessed Mother, given to us through St. Catherine Labouré in 1830. Our Lady appeared to her in a vision, standing atop a globe, with rings on her fingers and graces streaming forth from these rings as rays of light. St. Catherine noted there were gaps between the grace-rays, and she asked Our Lady what that was about. Our Lady explained: "Those are the graces that people forget to ask for."

However, this time, as I was about to remove my Miraculous Medal for going into the pool downstairs, something nudged me in the Spirit: *Keep it with you.*

"Uh, are you sure?"

I'm sure. Take it with you.

Not certain if I was just imagining things or really cuing in to the prompting of the Holy Spirit, I went along with it and kept my medal on.

When we got down to the pool, I didn't wear the medal in the water, I left it on the pool bench with our belongings. Louis and I spent some time in the main pool but didn't do as much walking as the previous days. We needed to have some bro talk, and we prayed the Angelic Warfare Confraternity Prayers together. It was a good little reconciliation and spiritual renewal.

We hopped into the jacuzzi, and after maxing out our time warming up, we got ready to go back upstairs. "Bro, I'm gonna need to use the toilet when we get up there."

"Okay."

I started moving us a *little* faster up the elevator and into our room. I promptly rolled Louis in his shower chair to be over the toilet. As he was doing his number 2 business, he called out, "Bro, I need to pee."

"Okay."

I got into position to hold the urinal for him.

"Bro, it feels *weird*."

I was puzzled. Louis never mentions his peeing feeling "weird". Sometimes it burns, sometimes it's a little tickle, sometimes it's pressure. But never just "weird".

He peed. I wasn't going to dump the urinal yet because Louis was still over the toilet in the shower chair, but I had to do a double-take after glancing at it. I kid you not, it looked like there was a bunch of peppercorns in his pee. I didn't know *what* to think. I was wondering what leafy debris might have gotten onto his swim trunks while I was wheeling him from the pool outside, and then subsequently fallen into the urinal. But that seemed rather . . . convoluted. Louis had an alternative (and simpler) explanation.

"Bro, I think those are stones."

"Kidney stones? Bro. You would have been *screaming*."

Louis replied, "No, I know they're stones. It didn't hurt. But it just felt weird."

Louis

This led me to think that the Blessed Mother had intervened. About 13 stones came out, which Matthias dutifully collected. Unfortunately for us, Dr. Page informed us that he would be moving to Salt Lake City, and that I would have to be referred to another physician, Dr.

David Tzou. We took the stones to Dr. Tzou at our first appointment. I don't think he was really that impressed. But we certainly were, considering all the struggles we had gone through with various kidney procedures and the fact that on the last one, the ureteroscopy, I had a near-death experience. This was a gift from the Blessed Mother, in my view, and it foretold of our upcoming journey to Lourdes, France.

Matthias

The amazing (and more amazingly painless) passing of Louis's stones left a deep impression on me. I was supposed to bring that Miraculous Medal, the sign of Our Lady, down to that pool for a reason. And just like the three days of waiting to find Jesus in the Temple, and the three days of waiting for Jesus to re-emerge, resurrected, from the tomb, we had received this grace, this miracle. Miracles need not be naturally inexplicable; even naturally explainable events of extraordinary consequence and significance can be miracles.

A miracle is simply a mighty act of God. Sometimes these exceed our ability to explain by science. But not always. I finished this trip with the following conviction: great graces are in store for us when we'd go to Lourdes, the Sanctuary of Healing, the Sanctuary of Our Lady. Great graces were in store, and we must go to the waters of Lourdes for three days, following the pattern of the three sets of three days aforementioned (searching for the boy Jesus in Jerusalem, three days of Jesus in the tomb, and three times for Louis and I going to the water at this hotel pool in Scottsdale, Arizona).

Louis

We returned to Tucson Thursday, December 14th. We had one day left to complete our application for the pilgrimage with the Order of Malta. The due date was December 15th. Back in November, I mentioned to Matthias that we needed to pick up the pace on the acquisition of passports. We'd had over a year and a half to do so, and in November we were down to a month and half. This wasn't good.

He agreed, and we began filling out the passport applications. This was really going to create a need for divine intervention. I voiced to Matthias that this was going to be highly unlikely to achieve, including the acquisition of the passport, which we hadn't even lifted a finger to do.

Now, mind you, we were busy with my graduate work and Matthias's undergrad graduation during that extended time period. But from our view, we dropped the proverbial ball.

We were blessed by the fact that Jane Lacovara said, "As long as you both have the majority of the paperwork in, I will extend until February/March the need for the passport." We were appreciative of her extension and willingness to help in that regard.

We then had to go to Cherrybell Post Office, which is a little south of downtown Tucson. We paid for our passports, submitted our photos, and hoped for the best.

Matthias

The passport agent assured us that our passports would likely arrive in the mail by March, maybe even February. That worked for Jane's requirements, so we were happy.

When Louis and I had our long discussion about this at the house, he flat out told me, "Bro, this is embarrassing. We don't deserve to go on this pilgrimage. We had a year and half to apply for passports and did nothing."

"Yeah . . ." I felt that he was right. "We probably don't deserve it. But I believe in Divine Mercy. And I believe that Our Lady wants us to go with the Order of Malta. There are too many reasons and little things that have lined up *just so* that point us in this direction. We need to pray."

When we went outside to pray our Confraternity prayers, I got down on my knees on the tarmac and begged the Lord for mercy and Our Lady for her clemency.

Fridays are my day of reflection and focus on prayer. The Lord had requested this of me in the Spirit several months before I first moved in with Louis. It was a strategic directive from the Lord I had not expected. It functionally became my day off from personal care. So, most Fridays while I have been living with Louis, another person of the care team would cover Louis's a.m. and p.m. care shifts. I would go off to Mass, say my Rosary, perhaps go for a hike, and other times make some prayerful study. Fridays had become my unplug and recharge day, providing the quality time apart from Louis that I needed to relax and renew.

December 15th happened to be a Friday, but it was a little bit of an exception. Before I left for my Friday prayer/break/Matthias time, Louis and I were frantically finishing our application for the pilgrimage with the Order of Malta. We submitted it, and I finally caught the bus to head my way out. That evening, I returned. Normally, I try to spend very little time with Louis and the p.m. caregiver (unless I feel called to pray with them) on Fridays, to hopefully snag some time to myself in my room. This time however, before I could disappear into my room, Louis called out, "Bro, I left some mail for you on your bed."

"Thanks."

It was from the government. To my delight and surprise, there was my fresh new passport. Louis's was in the mail stack. On the very day that we were *supposed* to have these by . . . in spite of our ridiculously delayed application in *November*, here they were. Blessed Mother wanted us to know.

I emerged from my room, holding my passport proudly in the air, and declared one word to Louis and the evening caregiver: "Miracles."

christmas in austin 2023

Louis

Soon after Matthias and I returned from Scottsdale to celebrate my graduation, we once again traveled to Austin to spend time with Matthias's family during the Christmas season. The last time I was there was in December 2021, and I enjoyed my time immensely with the Mahoney family and the extended family, which included the Viscardi-Bieter family and Matthias's aunts and uncles and cousins. This time the grace of familiarity was present. I was more a part of the activities. Matthias and I were also so appreciative of everyone's care.

Our time in Austin was one of warmth of heart. We didn't do anything spectacular; we were just together. Christmas Day was great fun, unwrapping Christmas gifts. We created the annual film again in celebration of Marjorie's birthday. I was so thankful to be part of the chosen family. And of course, we had the Mahoney-Viscardi tradition of ravioli on Christmas Eve. Everyone celebrated lovingly.

Nonit, Matthias's grandmother, holds a special spot in my heart for her kindness, similar to Marjorie and Bob. The other brothers, James, Nathaniel, and Nicholas also got to interact with me a little more. I actually got to play goalie in the backyard during a soccer game. Matthias isn't much for sports, but he was still out there. It was just a great time of camaraderie.

Nathaniel, the sibling who is just after Matthias in birth order, had an awesome announcement. He not only announced but showed his proposal to his fiancée, Camila. Camila is a very compassionate person, beautiful of heart, mind, and appearance—and soul, for that matter. The video chronicled Nathaniel proposing and how Camila's family, who live in Mexico south of Tijuana, were all in on the operation to engage Nathaniel and Camila in the future sacrament of marriage. Not to hold you in suspense, Camila said yes. I'm so happy for them both.

Being part of the Mahoney family is a gift for many reasons. However, the main one that sticks out is the care they show for each other, especially their mother and father, Marjorie and Bob. Bob and I have a common connection in our struggle with disability and illness. Bob battled Wiskott-Aldrich Syndrome, which is an immune deficiency disease, and he was given the grace of a bone marrow transplant that eradicated the Wiskott disease from his body. He no longer has to contend with immunodeficiency on the same level. He does still have to contend with it on a smaller scale daily. He taught me the word "professional patient", which I now borrow, lovingly, from his vocabulary.

Bob worked for NASA during the days of the Space Shuttle in Houston. So, we have a great connection in that regard because I have always wanted to go up into space. I would like to be the first "seriously disabled" individual to do so.

At one point I even wrote the director of NASA back in the '90s, Dan Goldin, stating my desire. They sent me information directing me to Space Camp in Huntsville, Alabama. I was working for Cox, and I didn't know if they were going to let me off for Space Camp. So, I didn't take it very far. I'm sure some of my folks in my department would've loved to have sent me to space, especially some that I sent to the woodshed!

Marjorie is a caring individual. This is where Matthias gets a lot of his compassion. Not that Bob isn't compassionate, but Marjorie has a sense about her that you can just trust her. In my interactions with Marjorie, I have learned to appreciate more and more the care that she shows, not only to her family, but also her extended family and the community around her.

I got to coordinate a lot of Matthias's graduation surprise with his mother. This is not one of Marjorie's greatest strengths. What I mean by that is communicating with her husband Bob about what's happening. Bob will tell you himself, or his children will, that he's "only the dad," and he'll go along basically with whatever Marjorie has to say. The funny thing is to witness (which I have more than once now) when Marjorie will say, "I told you that," and Bob will say, "I don't think you did, Dear." But it is truly a family who cares about each other.

The brothers James, Nathaniel, and Nicholas, and Cella and Mike, are outstanding individuals in their own right. James is now working as an engineer in Houston, following in his father's footsteps. Nathaniel graduated in sports analytics, Cella is a thriving and upcoming artist, and her husband Mike is an acoustics engineer. Last but certainly not least is Nicholas, aka Nichol, who at time of writing, just began his sophomore year at Texas A&M University down in College Station. That's a big deal on a couple of fronts. The main one for the Mahoney clan is because most of them had an affiliation or went to University of Texas at Austin. There's a big rivalry between Texas A&M and UT Austin. So, Marjorie, being the gracious mother she is, even though she graduated from UT Austin, now has a son who is an Aggie. That son, in his own right, is very astute and keeps up with politics. He's innovative. Nicholas keeps a journal where he writes his thoughts at the end of the day. He's very entrepreneurial, and he just began a position as a resident assistant for A&M.

So, as you can see, my chosen family has many gifts, and they are gifts to be had.

One of the other notable moments during our Christmas trip of 2023 was our trip to San Marcos where Nonit and part of the extended family live for a New Year's party. Bob, who is an engineer-minded individual, both in practice and in theory, said that we would need a ramp. We were all deciding how we should handle the ramp because Carolyn, Marjorie's sister, had just finished her home recently that was on Nonit's homestead.

It rained quite a bit that day as we were going down I-35 toward San Marcos—which can be a parking lot, especially in the city of Austin. Fortunately for Matthias and me, it wasn't an ice-skating rink. Just as in Arizona, or in Florida, if you get rain, they don't know how to drive in it. If you get snow, you might as well call out the National Guard because the whole city will shut down. This coming from a born native of Pittsburgh, Pennsylvania, where wind chills can be 60 below and the snow blows.

We had no snow, but we had rain. We got down to San Marcos. We had the ramp but had to get the rental car from Wheelchair Accessible Transportation alongside Carolyn's house. Bob had said that he probably should have gone down to survey the situation instead of relying on secondhand reporting, but it was too late now. The event was taking place. Matthias and I arrived at his Aunt Carolyn's.

We got as close to the house as we could, but unfortunately, the ground was just too soggy. We started to sink into the ground.

We sank far enough that the mud was up to the car's fenders. This posed a dilemma. What were we going to do? How were we going to get me out of the car? You know when you have more than one person in the crowd, and you have an issue, and how everybody has their own thoughts on the best way is to alleviate the situation? That's the situation we were in.

Bob took the wheel; Matthias got in the backseat. Bob tried to rock it out. Well, I know he likes to listen to hard rock, but that ground was too soft and we just kept sinking. Next came the push. Everyone was in the front of the vehicle pushing while Matthias gallantly put it in reverse and tried to back it out of the hole. If you had bet on us getting out with that one, you would have lost your money. We were now even deeper in the hole.

By this time, Matthias and I were getting hungry, and everyone was pretty sorry about us not being able to get into the house. So, Marjorie brought us plates of food, with the traditional ravioli for the evening. So, we had drive-thru service, but we were stuck at the window.

Next, we tried calling for a tow truck. The dispatcher on the line said, "I don't think so. How close are you to pavement?"

The answer wasn't too good. Nonit's homestead is accessed by a long gravel driveway. However, we weren't close to the driveway. The only spot we thought accessible for me to enter the house was on the backside, all dirt ground now turned into mud.

"Mmm, I need asphalt. Sorry. We cannot help you."

So, this left us with the Hays County Emergency Services. As we should have before, we should have listened to the women. Men don't like to follow directions, and we especially don't like to listen to the women. Aunt May, originally from Pittsburgh said, "Y'all need to call 9-1-1."

So, we took Aunt May's advice and called 9-1-1, The first on the scene was the county sheriff. Fortunately for us, Nonit had paid her taxes because we were certainly gonna use them tonight. The Hays County Sheriff then promptly called the fire department.

By this time, Matthias and I had finished our drive-thru meal, and others were engaging in conversation, both in and out, until the fire department arrived on the scene. They didn't have any sirens going, so that was good. We didn't want to alert the neighborhood.

The fire department attached the ropes and told everyone to get inside because it was probably going to get a little messy. So, Matthias and I were in the rental car, and Operation Pull-Out began. Everyone waited with bated breath as I looked toward the dining room window. Were they going to get Matthias and I out of this holey situation? We needed divine intervention and a few angels on the ground.

On the first attempt, the rope broke. After a short consultation, the first responders decided to apply straps. I wasn't quite sure, but I think it was the way they attached the straps this time; they also used chains.

Alexa, Marjorie's best friend from grade school, prayed aloud to God the Father, and Matthias and I prayed to the Blessed Mother, so we had the Father and Mother going. The Son was on the rope, trying to help pull us out!

Well, this time it worked. We were extricated from the hole. By that time—it took about an hour at least—everyone had eaten, but they were glad to see that Matthias and I had come through the ordeal without a scratch. We can't say that for the van, though.

What does it mean to belong? The Mahoney family has come to epitomize belonging. I'm not the only one who is shown that courtesy by the family. We have grown in a friendship that extends into not only the immediate family of the Mahoneys, but the extended family. For those of us with disabilities, and those of us who are on the latter end of their human journey on Earth, belonging is key.

I want to speak for one more moment about belonging in the Mahoney clan. Their mother Marjorie is about my age. The Mahoney children love their mother dearly, along with their father. That is quite evident. The annual film in celebration of Marjorie's birthday was a beautiful way of showing that. This time it was even more grand than 2021, because all 10 of the films were combined together in one huge presentation. We again had to do our parts for the film. Cella and Mike were there for Christmas; I was so happy to see them. But they weren't there for the filming and/or the presentation of the last film. So, James ensured that their portion was done ahead of time, and their friends from Pittsburgh also acted in their portion of the film. I was honored to be featured again as the "Saguaro Sniper".

This 2023 presentation was slated to be the last because the children were all moving on and the nest was emptying, but that sense of gratitude and belonging is omnipresent in the films they create. On the day of presentation, they blindfolded Marjorie and took her to an undisclosed location. She thought they were taking her into a sewer. You gotta know Marjorie; she has a vivid imagination.

It was no sewer; it was St. Michael's Catholic Preparatory School's auditorium where all five Mahoney children had attended. Bob, being on faculty there, had secured the auditorium for his family. You could tell that Marjorie was so overwhelmed by the love shown. This sense of belonging in the Mahoney family is the type that we need as a nation.

There was potential that I might move to Austin. If I did live in Austin, I would be around the Mahoney family. Mostly the parents, because the children were older and sprouting their own wings and paths. But that aside, I still belonged, and you can bet your sweet bippy that I would be a docent at the LBJ Library.

Lyndon Baines Johnson was one of the presidents who, in my view, did much, after the assassination of John F. Kennedy. In his public policy agenda, he worked tirelessly for the 1965 Voting Rights Act and civil rights. Through Medicare and Medicaid, I believe he was remembering his days of being impoverished.

Unfortunately, these days, we as a nation, through the individuals whom we elect to certain positions, do not value those programs. If we did, we would ensure that they are sustainable, not taking from the trust funds in some form or fashion, but making sure that they are secure and not utilizing them as political footballs.

We tend to forget that today we may be young and virile, but tomorrow, if we live to see it, we may be on the other side of the spectrum. We are growing older. We must remember that all of us are human, with human frailty and original sin. It is a sin to not treat others as you wish to be treated. If you violate that rule, look what can happen. I need not review human history, but only remind readers that if we do not stand together, we will fall.

the paschal lamb, spring 2024

Matthias

The opening of the new year had me fraught with a tough decision. It was only six months until my move-out deadline for leaving and preparing to join the Order that August, on the Feast of the Assumption. Through discussion with Louis and my spiritual director Fr. JP, we had modified my cutoff date to June 15th. However, here's what was on the docket: Louis had an LMSW exam to still schedule, the Order of Malta pilgrimage would take place from April 30th to May 8th, and we still had to finish this book. That's barely six and one-half months. And, we still had no real certainty about where Louis would move or how he would be situated for personal care after my departure.

After a week or so of concentrated prayer and discernment, I concluded that it was the will of God that I should not enter the Dominicans in 2024. It was just too much that I also felt called to do what needed to be done first. In one of our conversations, Louis threatened to cancel the pilgrimage because there wouldn't be enough time to prepare for my move-out. That helped seal the deal, frankly.

I was heartbroken, but I knew I was also on a mission, and that God would provide. Our Lady has her hands all over this mission of Louis's and mine, so that helped me to trust that this was indeed the right decision despite many people's concerns that I was only making my future departure that much harder. I agree. It has. It does only get harder the longer you stay. Louis has admitted this, too. However, when you have a concrete purpose and are not just kicking the can down the road because you're too afraid to jump, it's a reasonable, though difficult, decision. By grace, it's one that I've been able to stand behind.

I took comfort in the example of St. Faustyna. She too received the call to religious life, but for reasons she doesn't even explain in her diary, she had to remain in the world for another year and some months. She says that time was filled with trials, but that God was lavish with His graces. He certainly has been lavish with graces for me in this "extension" as well.

When I finally let Louis know of my decision of my own free will, one of the phrases of his response has remained with me: "You are an unselfish man." A lot of pressure was released from trying to figure everything out much more quickly than would have been possible. And we both felt a lot more comfortable about going on the pilgrimage.

The time was coming for our Marian Consecration. I had already done Marian Consecration back in February of 2021, but now Louis was finally making Marian Consecration, too. We used Michael Gaitley's *33 Days to Morning Glory.*[19] Our ending date: February 11th, the Feast of Our Lady of Lourdes.

Traditionally, the Diocese of Tucson Healing Mass is celebrated on or near that day. This year was no exception; it was scheduled for Saturday, February 10th—right after Louis's birthday! It should also be noted that this is sponsored by the Order of Malta. Our application had been submitted the December prior; we were still awaiting their decision.

We attended the Healing Mass at St. Thomas the Apostle in the foothills of Tucson. Bishop emeritus Kicanas celebrated and preached. A beautiful church with a beautiful liturgy. After the Mass, we saw Jane. She hadn't really waved at us or acknowledged us the previous times we passed by her. Yes, the liturgy was going on, but it seemed a little odd.

When we approached her after the Mass, she broke it to us straight. "I'm really sorry you guys, but the medical team didn't clear you to go. The doctors and nurses of the medical team did not feel comfortable with Louis having to sit for 12 hours in an economy airline seat on the way to Lourdes from LA. I'm really sorry guys; I really wanted you to go."

I was sad at first, but I retained peace in my heart. *If not this way, then that way wasn't what the Blessed Mother wanted for us.*

Louis

Once we got the definitive response from Jane with the Order of Malta, my wheels were kicked into a steady drive mode. I told Matthias that we shouldn't depend on anybody taking us; we needed to carve our own way of getting there. So, I figured, *heck, if the Order of Malta doesn't want me to fly*—which I get—*it's their deal. So, we'll make our own. Let's go by boat.*

We started the process that February by making an appointment with Bon Voyage Travel, a highly respected travel agency in the city of Tucson. They were right adjacent to my physical therapy, Body Central River Rd, where I was undergoing therapy for being in an accident while on Sun Tran, our mass transit bus service for the city of Tucson.

Matthias

One of the reasons I was reluctant to *not* go with a pilgrimage group to sponsor us was the cost. Paying $3,700 or so for me was reasonable enough, with Louis's costs covered. But at a *minimum*, sailing to England and then traveling to France on our own would not cost less than $6,000. In fact, it was much more likely to be $8,000-10,000. So, our initial stab at carving our own path looked unfeasible. We closed our case, so to speak, with Bon Voyage. Perhaps we would fly on our own.

The day after the Healing Mass, we went to 11 a.m. Sunday Mass at the Newman Center. We had 10 visitors: Fr. John Marie and all nine novices for the newest upcoming class of prospective Dominicans. Br. Alphonsus Vu was at the same discernment retreat where I fell in love with the Blessed Mother back in 2021. Br. Norbert (the name he received when he was vested, I knew him by a different name) was a fellow leader from the Thomistic Institute. There was great temptation for me to be very sad or angry in this moment. This was the class I *could* have joined. But didn't. I knew such rumination would be harmful for my soul, so I prayed a lot. But God sent a special little favor.

It was the day for Louis and I to make/renew our Marian Consecration before the image of Our Lady of Guadalupe in the Newman Center chapel. Louis and I were chatting with Br. Norbert about our Marian Consecration, and he offered, "Can we join you guys? We'll chant the *Salve* and everything" (The Dominicans have their own elaborate and beautiful version of chanting the *Salve Regina*, the *Hail Holy Queen*). "Sure!" I said.

Lo and behold, Brother Norbert gathered six of his fellow novices and Nathan Payne, now the music director, and we all knelt (Louis metaphorically kneeling, as he likes to say) before Our Lady. I read through the consecration prayer with Louis and the novices and Nathan repeating after me. Then, the brothers chanted the *Salve* to lift our consecration prayer to Our Mother. Br. Hyacinthe-Marie offered some Lourdes water of his own that he had with him; Louis and I blessed one another; and Nathan and the brothers blessed themselves in turn.

I poured out my thanksgiving to God in that moment because what could have been simply a sad reminder of what I had to sacrifice was actually a healing, bridging, moment. Here, the family I wished to join and the family I had claimed were all together before the Lady who is our Mother. The worlds are not so divided as they may appear. This was one of those lavish graces.

I wasn't done with Marian Consecration (you never are, it's a lifelong commitment). What I mean to say though, is that I finally learned how I wanted to concretely ask people to join us in prayer in preparation for the pilgrimage. Of course, we still had to figure out how we were going to get there, but that would come. It would come. I was at a wedding for two good friends up in Phoenix (Ethan Tang and Erynn Labut. . . I had a small, small part in helping set them up). While at Mass, Our Lady simply invited me, in the Spirit: *Invite as many people as possible to Marian Consecration.*

Sweet! I prayed. *Sounds good to me!* I promptly ordered 150 copies of Michael Gaitley's consecration magazine from the Marian Fathers of the Immaculate Conception to begin the mission.

When one does a Marian Consecration, it is traditional to complete it on a special Marian feast day (such as Our Lady of Lourdes). This year, I decided to have us do the Annunciation. The Annunciation, celebrating the moment the Angel Gabriel announced to Mary that she would conceive the Son of God and would call him Jesus, almost always falls on March 25th, exactly nine months before Christmas. Something in me told me to double check that the Annunciation was indeed on March 25th this year. That did seem awfully close to Holy Week.

Scrolling through the United States Conference of Catholic Bishops' official liturgical calendar on my smartphone, I was surprised to find the Annunciation on April 8th! Doing some more digging, I found (and I paraphrase) "When the Feast of the Annunciation falls during Holy Week, the feast is moved to the first suitable day of Eastertide." Easter Sunday 2024 would be March 31st. The whole week after is a big, eight-day-long Easter Sunday (liturgically speaking), and for this reason it is called "the Octave of Easter," following the tradition of week-long Jewish celebrations of feasts. That octave is book-ended by Easter Sunday and *Divine Mercy Sunday.* (April 7th). The unusually dated Annunciation was the following Monday, April 8th.

Oh, also, there just so happened to be a total solar eclipse in parts of the United States that same day.

I was thrilled. It was a special Marian Year of Mercy. This fueled my desire to spread the devotion to Our Lady and promote our pilgrimage all the more. I was only *more* convinced that Our Lady and Our Lord indeed wanted us to make this pilgrimage, and this way of doing it would not have been possible without my decision to delay my entry with the Dominicans. I got to work.

Louis

We had looked at Bon Voyage Travel, and their price tags were a bit far out of reach.

I had originally planned on going back to my native hometown of Pittsburgh. I hadn't been there since 2010 when my father passed. I felt a need to go to see people, to see my relatives, extended family, and nuclear family if possible; my brother Edward, his wife and four children currently live in the Cranberry area of Pittsburgh. I also wanted to see my friend Pat and my friend Tom's mother, Mimi, who knew my mother very well. We were to go to Pittsburgh prior to the pilgrimage.

Matthias

Normally, given the timelines (extended or not) that I was working with, I would not be so amenable to making a trip to Pittsburgh. However, Louis had been talking about this trip for years now (he really wanted to show me around, among other things); plus, I saw it as essential for the pilgrimage. If we were going to pursue healing at Lourdes, Louis needed to make some journey of spiritual healing, especially regarding his brother Ed. Louis and I both recognized that it would be a crucial part of the healing journey.

We scheduled our week in Pittsburgh with Southwest Airlines and found a van rental company. We would be there from May 15th to May 22nd. We were still not decided about how we would go to Lourdes. We were wondering if we might fly ourselves, or if we would try to go with the North American Lourdes Volunteers in October (we were too late to apply for their summer pilgrimage). However, we had at least pinned down the where, how, and when for Pittsburgh.

Louis

My managerial experience kicked in and I thought, *Hmmm . . . we're already on the East Coast.* So, I said to

Matthias, "Let's check with Cunard shipping line and see what happens."

Matthias

Cunard is the shipping line that operates the *Queen Mary 2*, the last remaining ocean liner that makes regular transatlantic voyages between New York and Southampton, outside of London, England. I looked on their website. My jaw dropped. The next voyage (after our planned time in Pittsburgh) began on May 23rd, disembarking in England May 30th.

We got down to pray. I prayed aloud, "Blessed Mother, if the tickets are available, we're taking that as your sign. We're going for it."

Louis

As Matthias says, the Blessed Mother had her hand in it. I couldn't believe it. When I spoke to the reservationist, she said availability was there for May 23rd. I asked, "Do you have a wheelchair-accessible cabin?" She said, "They're hard to get. Let me check." She came back and said, "We do, but you need to book it right away." I said, "OK. But we need to get back. When do you have something returning?" She said, "Let me check."

"Well, we have something on June 9th, landing in New York on June 15th." I said, "How much are they?", holding my breath. She said, in total, it would be a little over $4,000, for both Matthias and me, both directions. I said, "We'll take it!" That price was a gift.

When I say "We'll take it" sometimes, I'm not certain if Matthias hears me. In most cases, I'm glad he doesn't because then he can't stop me. Just like Bob will say about Marjorie, "I'm just the dad," Matthias will say something similar when I cook up some of my plans. He won't shoot down my ideas, but he will offer resistance.

This case was an exception because we both wanted to go. He is about as stubborn as I am but extremely loving.

Matthias

Louis is right. I would often likely want to stop him when he wants to jump on a purchase—especially an expensive one, and especially an expensive one that requires my labor-intensive cooperation and significant scheduling. He makes a lot of those. This time though, I believed Our Lady was guiding us on the path forward.

Louis

We booked the tickets. We were going to England—at least Southampton. The question was, how were we going to pay for it? Well, our friend Tony came up with some suggestions. He told Matthias, "You're not gonna get much unless you ask people straight up. That's what you gotta do. And ask them more than once." He said, "That's what I do, and eventually it will come through."

Well, Tony's methodology worked, in large part due to friends and chosen family and even one or two of my relatives, which I greatly appreciated. I was so thankful. Even one of my supervisors, Warren Young Jr. donated. So, I felt like people really were helping us. Matthias's future sister-in-law, Camila, donated multiple times. Kevin and Kelly donated multiple times. In the end, we raised our goal of $15,000. I couldn't believe it. It was a gift, not only from God, but the Blessed Mother herself.

Matthias

April 8th finally came. I succeeded in marshalling many Newmanites and folks in a few other places to participate (or at least consider participating in) Marian Consecration. However, it also just so happened that we had to reschedule Louis's CT scan appointment for his upcoming stone clinic with the new urologist, Dr. Tzou, for that same day.

We were on the bus going toward Banner Medical Center. We got off, and you could tell the sky was eerily darker than normal. It wasn't *dark*, but it wasn't as bright as it should be. It had an ominous quality to it, but so had the Lord marked this year's Feast of the Annunciation.

Louis and I were privileged (with the appropriate eclipse glasses) to behold the maximum coverage of the moon blocking the sun, just outside the hospital. His appointment was scheduled for 10 minutes from then. God lined it up nice for us. This CT scan would reveal whether or not the astonishingly painless passage of Louis's 13 stones last December had cleared his kidney or not. That is, whether or not Louis was spared from the need for another highly risky stone removal procedure.

After the CT scan, we went to Newman, and with nine fellow Newmanites or so, we made our consecration prayer, like we did with the Dominican novices a few months earlier. This time though, we prayed outside before the statue of Mary by the Newman lawn. I intentionally took the opportunity to vocally renew the fraternal aspect of this for Louis and myself before the Newman crew. Our fraternity is in Our Lady's maternity.

Louis

It was now April 2024. Matthias and I created our itinerary. We had spoken about going to Milwaukee to see Tony instead of going immediately back to Tucson from New York after our return voyage across the Atlantic. We checked flights and hotels for Milwaukee. The flights were fine, but Matthias was pensive about it. I was still encouraging it. We were able to secure a hotel; that wasn't an issue. However, given Matthias's conflicted attitude combined with my conviction that I should go see my Aunt Betty, we decided that it would be best to go to South Carolina instead. So, we booked flights and the itinerary was set.

The itinerary as of April 2024:
  May 15: Fly to Pittsburgh
  May 15 – 22: Stay in Pittsburgh
  May 22ⁿ Fly to New York City, La Guardia, check into Holiday Inn, Brooklyn Downtown
  May 23: Embark on *Queen Mary 2* from Brooklyn Cruise Terminal
  May 23 – May 30: Eastbound Transatlantic Voyage
  May 30: Disembark in Southampton, England, ride in Cunard shuttle to London Heathrow Airport, fly to Toulouse, take train to Lourdes, check into Hôtel Roissy.
  May 30 – June 6: Stay in Lourdes
  June 7: Take train to Toulouse, fly to London Heathrow, check into Hilton Garden Inn London Heathrow Airport
  June 8: Enjoy London, recuperate
  June 9: Shuttle to Southampton, embark on *Queen Mary 2* from Mayflower Cruise Terminal.
  June 9 – June 15: Westbound Transatlantic Voyage
  June 15: Disembark in Brooklyn, check into Holiday Inn Brooklyn Downtown
  June 16 – June 18: Spend time with Mike and Cella touring New York City
  June 19: Fly to Myrtle Beach, South Carolina
  June 19 – June 24: Spend time with Aunt Betty in Little River, South Carolina
  June 25: Return flight to Tucson.

Such was our original itinerary.

I was very concerned about going back to my hometown. I wanted to go, like Matthias said, for years, and I was finally going to go, so there was a level of excitement. I was going to see some of my extended family and hopefully see my nieces and my nephew, Teo (pronounced "TEE-oh", unlike Matthias's family nickname, pronounced "TAY-oh").

I made initial contact with my cousin Mark whom I was going to see when I visited Mt. Lebanon, an upscale area of Pittsburgh. The reason I contacted Mark was to get my brother Edward's cell phone number. We had not spoken at any length since my father's death in February 2010. It was now late April 2024; some 14 years had passed.

Mark contacted Ed, and then Ed reached out to me in group text with Mark. Ed used profanity that is inappropriate to publish. I will leave those portions blank, but I think the reader should get the idea.

First Exchange, Friday April 26, 2024.

Ed

Louis, I have Mark attached. You're not visiting me. So get it out of your mind. I will come see you at some point. Don't even bother giving me your ******** back I could care less.
Maybe later down the road. But not now. Reality.
God bless us all!
Save the number though.

Louis

Ed, we have a lot of things that I am asking you to forgive, and that's why I want to see you. The phone lines do work both ways, I have reached out before. I am your brother. I

> appreciate the fact that you want me to save your number; please save mine, it's a new one.
>
> My concern is if we don't reconcile, it's both our losses. I know you're angry. Like I said, I will be in town. I am going to Mom's grave. I rented a car so I will be able to get around. If you don't want to see me, I understand. But we're both getting older, I am 60 years old now. We don't know when our last day on this earth will be. I am in town from the 16th to the 22nd. And then I am going to New York and then on to Lourdes via ocean passage, in honor of our mother. Healing for myself both spiritually and physically, hopefully. I don't hate you, never have. In fact, I love you. But if you don't like me, I understand. I will always love you and Frank. Love to Christine.
>
> Thank you again Mark for connecting us, it is greatly appreciated. Again, I hope to see the rest of the extended family that are in the Burg.

During this first exchange with Edward, I was not surprised. In fact, I was grateful that we communicated over text. Being estranged for fourteen years is a long time. So, I thought, *at least I opened the door.*

In this busy time leading up to our pilgrimage, there were a few things going through my mind beyond the circumstances around Ed.

One: I was 60 years old, and this was the only time I believed I would be going to Europe.

Two: I was grateful for all the benefactors who contributed to our pilgrimage. I couldn't believe that we raised $15,000. What a gift.

I was also thankful to have Matthias accompany me to Pittsburgh. I knew I wanted to and needed to go to Pittsburgh, but I was still apprehensive. I hadn't seen some of these relatives in quite some time: 2010 to be exact. I'd written them and I'd gotten a few Christmas cards, but the Pittsburgh clan, once my mother died, seemed to fade away like old photos.

At the same time, I was studying for my LMSW exam, which is the licensed Master of Social Work exam for the state of Arizona (this is the associate license, as opposed to the independent licensure). Matthias and I had done practice tests and flash card review. Like most things in life, once you've studied, *you gotta do it*. When I actually took the exam, Matthias would be allowed to sit there in the waiting area in case I needed to go to the bathroom or have a drink or something related to my diabetes type II situation. Otherwise, I would be in the exam room with the scribe.

However, Matthias got sick.

Matthias

Louis often wonders if I have irritable bowel syndrome. Mom wonders if I have a mild gluten intolerance. I know I'm lactose "sensitive" (if not lactose intolerant outright), and I know I can be somewhat prone to diarrhea.

The Friday before we were to leave, May 10th, it was particularly bad. It was fairly mild and manageable at first, but by Friday, I couldn't stop losing fluids. I spent Friday as my day off, with Amoz (who was living with us at the time) covering the care. However, that evening at the Newman Center, I almost passed out. I reached out to Cher who was able to pick up some anti-diarrhea caplets. Another friend, a fellow Newmanite (and part-time Uber driver), was able to drive me home.

Things did not improve on Saturday. I was concerned, knowing that Louis's LMSW exam was the following Monday and our flight to Pittsburgh two days after! What condition would I be in? As Saturday evening approached, I was shivering under the covers. I called Mom again, and we agreed it was time to go to the ER.

Louis

After Marjorie told Matthias to Not Pass Go and go directly to the hospital, she called my cell phone and asked what I would be doing. I told her I was on my way to the hospital; I was in the driveway right after Cher had taken Matthias to take the city bus to Banner University Medical Center. Marjorie was concerned how I would get back home, considering the late hour. After a moment's reflection, I contacted Gwen, who offered to drive me along with Bethany and Amoz. Marjorie said, "Okay . . ."

We rendezvoused with Cher and Matthias in the ER waiting room. It looked like a MASH unit: people coughing, sneezing. Amoz eventually said, "How long are we going to be here?" By this time, Matthias had gotten a room, and the nurse told us only one person could go in with him. I let his friend Cher go with him.

In retrospect, I wish we had switched off, but Matthias was happy with the way it turned out. The only issue was that Marjorie would be calling wanting to know how he was doing, and all I could say was, "I don't know; Cher is there with him." So, Marjorie told me at one point, "Just smile a lot; they'll let you in."

Well, I tried it. I must be losing it because it didn't work. Eventually, Amoz was getting antsy because people were ferociously coughing and sneezing, so he said, "Can we go?" Gwen told him it was up to me. I eventually said OK because I didn't want to cause any issue, and I knew Matthias was being cared for by Cher.

It was about 1:30 a.m., Sunday morning. Fortunately, Matthias came home at 9 a.m., so he live-streamed the Mass from the Newman Center at 11 a.m. while I went to Mass in person. I brought him Communion, which I was happy to do. I was so glad that he was safe and on the mend because, we had planned this trip, but if we had to, I would have cancelled. However, we didn't have to, thank God. The Blessed Mother, again, was watching out for us.

Matthias

I was very grateful Cher could get me there, and that Louis, Amoz, Gwen, Bethany, and our friends of the Champagne family were able to show up.

I didn't want Louis to be allowed into my patient room that evening for two reasons:

1) I had become very sensitive to when Louis wanted to show great concern and/or affection for me. What do I mean? Through the years of our friendship, his shows of affection and concern had become very difficult to not associate with his propensity to cross over boundaries (like with reaching out to me in the shower, needing to know what I was telling other people about him . . . in a word, what felt like excessive clinginess and insecurity). I was incredibly grateful for the progress we had made thus far. We had grown in our ability to manage these tendencies. However, one of the consequences of these patterns was that I gained a dislike for situations where I was particularly vulnerable, and thus Louis would especially want to be there, to be close, to comfort me. I didn't want any "big deal" about me from Louis's concern for me because what had caused me so much

pain over a period of a few years was how hard it felt to breathe.

I didn't trust him to be the best support in that moment. I admit I feel somewhat guilty for feeling this way, but at the same time, I had to acknowledge how I was feeling. It wouldn't make sense to ignore that, particularly in my dehydrated state of vulnerability.

2) I hadn't seen Cher in a long time. It was a providential moment to catch up and express our care for one another.

We spent the whole night there. I quickly drained two IV bottles of saline and was put on the BRAT diet (bananas, rice, apple sauce, toast). I was finally discharged, and Cher brought me home, 9:00 a.m. Sunday. I hoped Louis hadn't lost too much sleep for his upcoming exam.

Amoz was particularly helpful that week, not only covering my shifts that Friday and Saturday while I was incapacitated, but also volunteering to cover the rest of the care shifts until Louis and I departed for Pittsburgh. That helped a lot (especially with the packing I had to do), and I am very grateful to him for that.

Louis

For my part, I was just glad that Matthias was feeling better. And actually, Cher and I mutually agreed to let her go in, so I am glad that's what Matthias wanted because both of us were none the wiser. So, it was divinely interventional.

Monday morning came, May 13, 2023, the day of my licensure exam. Matthias and I borrowed Gwen and Bethany's van, which they so graciously allowed us to do on many an occasion. We got to the testing center. I had extra time through the Americans with Disabilities Act, which I was grateful for. I took my exam. It was 170 multiple-choice questions. It wasn't easy.

Matthias

Neither Louis nor I had planned this, but his friend Maryanne Schiavone pointed out that May 13th was the Feast of Our Lady of Fátima. The litany of lineups corresponding to the Blessed Mother was only encouraging us more and more.

While Louis took his exam, I got to pray the Rosary outside in the testing center courtyard. With my saltines and bananas, I was able to eat; it was a good time. I knew Louis would be brain-fried and ready to go eat something, but I made sure to record a short video to post on our pilgrimage Instagram. I'm not much of a social media person, but I created this account for the purposes of spreading the invitation to Marian Consecration, spreading word about the pilgrimage to garner funds, getting people to journey with us in spirit, and spreading word about this book.

Louis

I passed the exam on my first attempt! I was like "yippie ai yay!" In today's testing environment, you know right away whether you passed it or failed it; there's no guess work. So, now my title, in the state of Arizona anyway, was LMSW. I sent out an email letting people whom I cared about know that I passed.

That hurdle crossed, we prepared to go to Pittsburgh on that Wednesday, May 15th.

coming home

may 15–may 23, 2024

I finally was going back to the Steel City. I hadn't been back there since my father's passing in February 2010. Now that I think about it, my grandfather Pap-pap, my father's father Frank, died February 8, 1983, and his son, my father, passed February 23, 2010. It made me think. My birthday's on February 9th. My grandfather and father died right around my birthday. I think there's something to that, but I'm not quite sure what it was telling me.

Now back home, I had hopes of meeting my brother, but as our group text eluded, that was not going to materialize, and I truly felt sorry for him. I won't really trust him, and that is sad. I wanted to meet with my nephew and nieces as well. I hadn't seen them since they were small. My nephew Teo, for instance, I hadn't seen since he was eight years old when he visited my home in Orlando and we went to Discovery Cove and swam with the dolphins. I'm sure he remembers me, but he was fairly young. The nieces were even younger, so I'm not certain they would remember me at all.

Thursday, the day after we arrived, I was chomping at the bit to go to Rico's. Matthias must have heard about Rico's 10 times. I remembered going there as a teenager and later on as an adult.

It was a nice thing to hear when I came through the door, "Sir Fazio!" from David Lorenzini, the current proprietor of Rico's. His father Rico was the original founder in 1979. While eating there, it brought back memories with every bite, along with some comfort. It was a great beginning to our time in Pittsburgh.

Matthias

Rico's is *fancy*. I have never seen a Caesar salad prepared with so much love and style before my very eyes. I didn't grow up eating at restaurants like this, so I always feel a little strange when Louis takes me to places for dinner that can cost $100 to feed two people. Yet, I appreciated, as Louis explained the family's weekly tradition of eating there, that his was a background with some privilege.

I can't deny, I was extremely grateful that this was my first day back to being able to eat regular food, no longer constrained to the BRAT diet. I really enjoyed that fancy Caesar salad and the spinach pinwheel pasta. It was well worth it. (Easy for me to say, Louis was the one paying!) I was happy to see the memories and joy associated with Rico's in Louis's face.

As we were on our way out, David very warmly told Louis, "If you ever need anything, just let us know—well, you have Ed."

Louis and I sort of looked at each other, and Louis responded with gentle tact.

Louis

I didn't say word one against Ed. David didn't know. David only remembered when my dad would drive up under the canopy with his (usually black) Cadillac Seville. That was one of his perks from the Auto Auction; he would get a new car every other year. Had to be new. And then, the parking attendant would help him take my manual chair out of the car and bring me into the restaurant.

Those were the days when Dad would talk to the waitresses and give them a pinch on the rear; you couldn't do that these days, but back then that was normal behavior. Then they'd ask, "What do you want to eat, Lou?" and the meal would go from there. And my mother, in her elegant attire, would be giving her order as well to the waitress. We usually sat in a similar spot every Saturday night.

There were some Saturdays when Frank, Ed, and I would not go, and we would be home watching the CBS lineup of *All in the Family, MASH, The Mary Tyler Moore Show, The Bob Newhart Show*, and *The Carol Burnett Show*. The boys would usually be in bed before me, so I usually watched the *The Carol Burnett Show* with the babysitter.

Matthias

The next morning, Louis and I had a frank shower discussion (a lot of our best conversations are in the shower) about the healing that *we* needed in our own relationship. This was the first time I ever described some of the unhealthy aspects of Louis's and my relationship as abuse, using the words "abuse" and "codependency". The latter was a recent addition to my vocabulary. Originally coined to describe toxic relationship patterns with alcoholics, such as a partner enabling the spouse to continue in addiction, codependency is a broad term now used to refer to any kind of unhealthy level of dependence in a relationship. It is sometimes also referred to as "relationship addiction". Every time I would look up "codependency" on the internet, I couldn't help seeing Louis and me all over it.

People to whom God has given very caring hearts and a strong sense of compassion must steward well the gifts they have. This requires learning to recognize what is truly beneficial for your soul—and what isn't. When people have trouble establishing boundaries for themselves and do not temper their "need to be needed", they are especially susceptible to this type of relationship dysfunction. They become the "giver" often sacrificing themselves for the "taker" in an imbalanced way. This often leads to burnout, and a loving, caring heart runs the risk of losing that deep love and sense of compassion with which a relationship was entered in the first place. This is contrasted with healthy interdependence, where mutual reliance, care, and loving sacrifice exist together in equilibrium.

By this point in our relationship, there had been a lot of progress; and I had come to accept and articulate more boundaries that I needed, especially physical ones. I accepted that I could no longer handle Louis kissing me (it would usually be on the cheek or my feet for a foot washing); holding each other for extended periods (there were a couple of times where we got up to 30 minutes), or letting him see me with my shirt off (there were a couple of times when Louis did see me, and it was this huge deal for him, "Whoa, Bro, you let me see you . . ." That's just too much. I can be shirtless around my brothers and we don't say anything because it's no big deal. But it's a big deal for Louis, allegedly because I make it a big deal to *not* let him see me and so I just don't bother anymore on this one. It makes me uncomfortable, so it's a "no". End of story.).

We don't even do foot washing anymore. I really appreciate the power of foot washing in certain contexts and highly encourage people to practice it when appropriate. But I have finally come to accept that in the context of Louis's and my relationship, it's just too much for me; it's overstimulating, and with the history

Louis and I have, I just can't receive it as a gesture of love without being uncomfortable. This weighed more on my mind while we were in Pittsburgh anticipating our arrival in Lourdes. Our foot washings had been special precursors for encountering the healing waters of Lourdes, but I knew that allowing Louis to wash my feet was no longer good for my spirit.

That being said, we will still hug each other and sometimes lay hands on the other's head to pray a blessing. We both express our feelings. Louis verbalizes his love for me on a daily basis. I'm much less expressive of my love verbally, but that's fine. If Louis wants a hug, he'll ask me. Sometimes I say, "no," and we're both cool. Sometimes I say, "yes."

With all that growth, our conversation in our Pittsburgh hotel shower reminded us that there was still a lot of work to do. We mutually recognized the need for acknowledgement, contrition, and repentance for having caused, participated in, or been complicit for patterns of abuse; and we committed to addressing root causes of this through professional help and spiritual direction. Louis also expressed his need to feel safe from Ed and Frank, from abusive caregivers, and from "robotic caregivers" (that is, purely transactional care).

Louis

The next day, Saturday, we went to the North Hills to visit my mother's grave in Allegheny County Cemetery. This is the third time I've been to my mother's grave since her passing in 2002. I was glad to be back. There was one aspect that I'm very thankful for: Ed did a splendid job honoring our mother. She is in a mausoleum with a statue of the Blessed Mother on top.

Another interesting aspect that I found a bit humorous was the fact that you could see the beauty shop she went to weekly, from her grave. This brings me joy. I always talk to her when I'm there and say, "You know, you picked a great spot for your final resting place." When I'm leaving, I end it with, "Love you, Mom."

Matthias

I was greatly honored to pay respect to the great woman who gave Louis life, defended that life, and self-sacrificially advocated for his life with every fiber of her being. I wasn't sure what to expect as I witnessed Louis speaking aloud with his "Momma". It was very blunt, especially when he spoke about "Ed and Frank and the rest". Not that I hadn't heard that all before, but Louis is just as candid around his mom's grave as he is anywhere else.

We prayed the Rosary together. Louis even sent Ed a text, complimenting him for the placement of the mausoleum. There was indeed a line of sight to Calaizzi's beauty shop.

On another note, Louis said, "I want someone whom I can pour my love onto. I pray to the Blessed Mother and God and Jesus for that person . . . that person I can love."

I replied, "I can never be that person in its totality. Even if I weren't going to be a priest, or not get married, I just never could be. And I think how you have tried to have me be that person is what colors a lot of our strife and tension."

Louis said, "I know that now; you're not that."

"But you didn't always. And even now that you do, I think it's not always easy to actualize that understanding."

We both felt a great peace in this moment. We then prayed the Divine Mercy Chaplet together there before his mother and our Blessed Mother. I noted in the pilgrimage log, *I need to feel secure that we are respecting my role properly. We're getting there.*

Louis

After visiting Mom's gravesite, we went down Duncan Avenue to Mt. Royal Boulevard and went up to Tall Timber Drive, Allison Park, Pennsylvania. This was where I grew up. I showed Matthias the house from the exterior.

"Let's go knock on Joanne's door and see if she's there." Sure enough, Joanne was there. Joanne Scotty-Greer (or Joanne Scotty, as we knew her when I was living on Tall Timber Dr) was the daughter of Dr. Lou and Regina Scotty. If you recall, Dr. Lou Scotty was the one that came running when I had been plunged into nine feet of water. Joanne came from a rather large family and was over at our house quite often because she got along very well with my mother. As Joanne puts it, my mother felt that she was the daughter she never had.

Joanne was, by her own description, afraid of my father. She truly saw him in his element, his domestic abuse element. I am certain she heard yelling, not only on the night that I fell into the pool, but at other times as well. She was with us quite often. I was grateful to have her there because it seemed to temper the environment.

Joanne and I reminisced about old times. Her husband, Dan, whom I hadn't met until this visit, got to hear us trading stories relating to our families, including when I fell into the pool.

Matthias

It was delightful to see Joanne and Louis meet. It was one thing to be with Louis and Tom when he visits from Phoenix (or we visit from Tucson) since they've known each other since Louis was 18. It's another thing to meet Joanne, who's known Louis since he was six. I got to hear some of the details that Louis either leaves out . . . or just doesn't emphasize.

"Oh my god! His laugh never changed!" was one of the first things she exclaimed. I characterize it as Louis's "snicker"; usually an indicator that he was up to some mischief.

"Oh yeah, Louis got away with anything. Frank and Ed would be fighting, but Lou would be laughing because he knew his father wouldn't lay a hand on him!"

She was also jealous of some of the nifty things that the Fazio boys would get, like "those motorized bikes with Snoopy in the front basket."

Louis

Snoopy was our miniature dachshund who rode in the basket. We'd even throw him up in the air in the family room and catch him in the blanket like a trampoline! Snoopy really enjoyed it. My mom would yell at us, *"Don't do that with Snoopy!"*

Matthias

Besides being afraid of Lou Fazio, Sr., Joanne also mentioned, "Your mom and dad wanted you to do everything the other kids would do. I mean, your dad would let you do everything." At that point, Louis brought up the story of his father even letting him go on the riding lawn mower.

"Your dad kept the lawn *immaculate.* He seeded it, fertilized it, mowed it . . . and your mom, every time of the day, it didn't matter, she kept a beautiful appearance. And the inside of the house . . . it was a museum!" She further said about Louis's mom, "She was strong, stoic, and independent—and she was a lioness when it came to her kids."

Louis

I'm always glad to see Joanne and think of those crazy childhood days; Tall Timber Drive was filled with bitter-sweet memories. As my father had told me when I was little, either he or I would go. He *did* go, for a while, when he attempted to choke my mother to death. And, as Aunt Betty reports, my uncles told him, "Better not do that again, or we'll kill you." I believe they would have. They loved their sister.

After visiting Joanne and Dan, we then went next door to show Matthias a closer view of my childhood home and hopefully to get a view of the pool. As fate would have it, we did! We met the current owner, Loraine, a social worker herself! So, we had that in common right off the bat! She would have showed us the inside, but that was under remodeling.

She was more than happy to show us the pool. This brought back many memories. The dome was long gone. We had taken that down. Loraine spoke of how grateful she was that she met me because we were the original owners, and they were concerned that they were going to lose the pool because it had to be redone. But much to their surprise, it was concrete! They only had to redo the liner of the pool.

That was a great quality of my father. He could design things. He had vision. He was a smart man in many ways. Maybe not book smart, but he was very intelligent. He also was very street smart—a quality I don't possess. Matthias will correct me and say, "You are smart." I appreciate that.

It was interesting that Loraine was wearing a South Carolina sweatshirt, Myrtle Beach specifically. Matthias and I were going to Myrtle Beach to visit Aunt Betty after returning to the States.

This brings us to Pentecost Sunday. I was originally going to meet with one of my newer friends, Braden, but unfortunately, I got sick and ended up dry heaving which was no fun. We figured out that it was likely the magnesium supplements I was taking at Marjorie's suggestion to help me have bowel movements more naturally rather than relying on enemas. In my case, however, this suggestion didn't work. It was doing the reverse of what it should have done.

Due to my dry heaving, Matthias and I stayed a little longer in the hotel. We would change the plan a bit and go see my Uncle Marion and Aunt Barbara and their family before going to the evening Sunday Mass. I sent a text to Ed and Mark, this time including Mark's wife Chrissy.

Louis

Good morning everyone! Happy Pentecost Sunday!
As I mentioned, I am planning on coming over to Mt. Lebanon to visit the extended family and relatives today, looking forward to it. Ed, I truly would appreciate that you do not hold any ill will against any of the family in relation to my visit. This is a pilgrimage of Faith, Hope, and Healing. May God bless you all.

Ed

Louis, live your life and do whatever you wanna do. God Bless your pilgrimage.

On that note, Matthias and I began our drive out to Mt. Lebanon, where my Uncle Marion and Aunt Barbara have lived since the mid-1970s. I was quickly reminded of the difficult terrain that I would need to traverse in order to gain entry into my uncle and aunt's (and Mark and Chrissy's) home. There is a steep, curved driveway, so Matthias wouldn't be able to let me out of the rental van near the house. After parking by the sidewalk, I had to roll up the driveway myself. I got up there fine, but I didn't reach my uncle and aunt's house itself, instead ending up on Mark and Chrissy's patio, who lived next door.

Mark and Chrissy's house was originally my grandmother's, purchased by Uncle Marion for her in the late 1970s shortly after moving there himself from Colorado Springs with Aunt Barbara and their young family. Uncle Marion and Aunt Barbara have four children, Ann, the oldest; Diedra; then Mark; and Justin, their youngest.

Mark's wife Chrissy was the first to greet us. Then Mark came onto the patio, first explaining that Uncle Marion and Aunt Barbara had gone somewhere but showed up later, along with my cousin Ann and her husband John, who is a cardiologist, one of the best in Pittsburgh.

Aunt Barbara asked if I was going to see my Aunt Carole. I told her we were planning on going there the next day. After that exchange, we all sat around their patio table catching up. Things were cordial, and in fact, my cousin Ann contributed to our GoFundMe campaign for the pilgrimage, which I was very appreciative of.

I truly enjoyed seeing everyone. It brought back many emotions. I enjoyed being around the table. I figured that this would probably be one of the last times, if not *the* last time I would see most of these people. I expressed to them all my love and my appreciation.

This reunion was through the grace of God and the empowerment provided by Matthias. If you haven't seen the movie *The Bucket List,* you should. It chronicles two individuals and their journey to ensure that they do the things that they want to do before they pass on. The whole pilgrimage is about healing for me and Matthias. I wanted to make sure that I went back to Pittsburgh. In my mind, this could and probably would be the last time.

Matthias

I wasn't sure what to expect at this meeting; I guess just as unsure as the Vujeviches and Louis were. As the cheese and wine were passed around and the conversation unfolded, I was wondering if they were gaslighting Louis. You see, the only impression that I really had of this section of Louis's family was of how things went after his father's death. Ed had "poisoned the waters" and "assassinated" Louis's character in front of most of these people. Louis later told me that he wondered if Marion and Barbara's delayed arrival was due to their debating whether or not they should come. I don't think they were, but the fact that Louis was wondering is telling about the situation.

When it came to the topic of Louis's "absence" from the family, the response was very warm. Uncle Marion made sure to say, "No, Louis, we never wanted you to feel like you were rejected or anything like that. In fact, we have a great respect for you, especially knowing the struggles that you've faced and how you've dealt with them."

Tears streamed down Louis's face as Chrissy kissed him, communicating her love, with Uncle Marion and Aunt Barbara speaking similarly. Louis managed to say, "Whoa, I never realized . . ." It was powerful to behold.

All the same, the gulf between loyalty to Ed or to Louis was lurking underneath. I think they were deliberately trying to say nice things about Ed and Frank to portray them as good people and preserve Ed's good name with themselves. I don't know. Knowing the way Ed treated (and continued to treat) his own older brother made me worry about how consistently he treats his wife and kids, especially when the other cousins aren't looking. We pray for them.

Aunt Barbara encouraged Louis to reach out to Ed. "I'm sure he'd want to see you," she said. "He told us that he tried to reach out to you but that you turned him down."

I spoke up at that one. "No, that's not true. It's the other way around. Louis has reached out to him multiple times. And when Ed finally did respond, thanks to Mark connecting him and Louis, he flatly refused. He does not want to see Louis." I didn't divulge any further details.

Even still, Louis did send another text to Ed at Aunt Barbara's behest, in the group chat he had started earlier which included Mark and Chrissy.

Louis

> Eddie, are you willing to have lunch with me greatly appreciate it. Love you, brother.

Ed

> No
>
> I'm busy. Catch up maybe sometime down the road. Have a good pilgrimage. God bless!

Louis

After our visit, Matthias and I left Longue Vue Drive and traveled on Washington Road to the downtown area of Mt. Lebanon, where we went to 7:30 p.m. Mass at St. Bernard's. The church is beautiful; it reminds me of a cathedral. It also brought back memories of my mother's funeral and memories of my mother stopping the car per my brothers' and my request for ice cream.

The second reading was from St. Paul's letter to the Galatians:

. . . now the works of the flesh are obvious: immorality, impurity, licentiousness, idolatry, sorcery, hatreds, rivalry, jealousy, outbursts of fury, acts of selfishness, dissensions, factions, occasions of envy, drinking bouts, orgies, and the like. I warn you, as I warned you before, that those who do such things will not inherit the Kingdom of God. (Galatians, 5:19-21)

I later said to Matthias, "Yeah, from what we heard in that reading, Ed's not with Jesus."

"No," said Matthias.

There is still hope though. I do pray for my brother. Both of my brothers. I haven't talked to my brother Frank either. I really hope that someday they come to realize this life on earth is short, compared to the eternal life. Matthias and I both pray for them and their families. If they wish not to see me, that is fine. I don't want to be around the toxicity.

It is kind of interesting because in my early adult years, my mother gave me a book titled *Toxic Parents*.[20] I think she knew. She certainly had her own struggles with abuse. It is a widely held social belief that those being abused become, more often than not, the abuser. However, this claim has also come under some scrutiny and criticism.[21] This is one of the reasons why I am writing this book, and I am fortunate to have Matthias writing it with me. I wanted to expose the abuse, and there have been things that I have done that would put me in the category of abuser. I am aware, self-aware. The only way to stop abuse is to bring it to the light of day.

Matthias and I then went to Eat'n'Park where the text conversation between myself and Ed continued. It got much worse. It got to the point where Matthias exclaimed,

"Louis. I am not going to read this to you anymore. This is disgusting." Attached are excerpts from the continued conversation, for posterity's sake.

Louis

Hi Ed,
Sorry I missed the graduation party . . . I reached out to you because, as I spoke of it, this is a pilgrimage of faith, hope, and healing. I know I won't see you again. I have to come to terms with that. That's why I reached out. But I must tell you, as your brother. I have attempted to reach out numerous times, and Chrissy and Mark are on this text, so they are impartial witnesses. And as God is my witness, I wish you only the best. We have trespassed against each other and we must forgive. Because Ed, no amount of fame or fortune will save us in the afterlife. And there is an afterlife, Ed. I passed over in 2020, when I became very ill. I knew in the spirit then (or soon after) that I must go to Lourdes. At Dad's funeral you told me you did not believe in God. As your brother who loves you—I know we don't always trust each other, that's a mutual thing—as your brother I must love you and I must forgive you. I'm asking for your forgiveness as well. If you can't, that is fine. That is your soul. I cannot do any more than I have done. Yes, I have unique challenges. You were blessed in 1970 when you were two pounds two ounces and two months premature and they thought you were going to die. You were saved due to man's technology. I was grateful. And then again in 1988 when you were involved in an accident that killed a person, that is public record and never served a

> day. I prayed that you did not. So, when you talk about hypocricy, all I want is the best for you, and I am glad you have what you have, Christine and your children.
>
> Like I said to you numerous times now, if you want to see me, I am here til Wednesday. I will move mountains to see you, if you choose. If you don't, I respect your choice.
> Love, your brother

I also explained to Ed why I lost my job with Cox, how they used my sexual orientation to eliminate my position. Ed responded calling me extremely foul names that aren't good for anyone's soul, my own or his. The texting went back and forth until the next day. I did not return his vitriol but instead commended him to God.

Louis

> So I forgive you and release you; you now know my intention.
> Love, your brother

Ed

(dove emoji)

Mon, May 20 at 4:54 PM Chrissy Vujevich left the conversation.

> I release myself as well. Thank you for the memories. And I realize that you won't expect anything of me. I will continue to pray for you as a human. You are my biological brother, you and Frank. But beyond biology, that is it. May God bless you and your family.
>
> Thank you, Mark, please extend that to Chrissy. I will keep in touch with the extended family. That is what we're supposed to do, is love. Noted that Chrissy exited the conversation. Thank you. Love, your cousin

Louis

I was dumped on with quite profane language that Matthias and I omitted for the sake of the reader. It was so dreadfully disgusting. My brother Edward showed that he was hurting. Hurting from years, apparently, of not loving me or himself.

I believe that neither my mother nor father would approve of such hatred. As I mentioned earlier, my mother and I had our disagreements, and I did call her a name that I will regret for the rest of my life. But in the end, she forgave me. We were kindred souls, if you will. She was a caring person. It is hard for me to fathom that such behavior and toxicity would come out of the mouth of an individual who was birthed by the same mother.

I said earlier that domestic abuse is intergenerational. It is hidden. People do not like to admit it. When it is in front of them, they still deny it. I am so concerned for my brothers and their families. Hopefully no domestic abuse occurs in either of my brothers' families. But Edward's behavior toward me leads me to pray for him and his family, and for Frank and his family.

In researching for this book, I have found little on the topic of inheritance and siblings or other family members usurping said inheritance that was slated to be given to the individual family member with a disability. I strongly advocate for those who love someone with a disability to ensure that those whom they leave behind are adequately represented through legal intervention.

On a much happier side of that day, I took Matthias to Primanti Brothers, which used to have only one location in the strip district of the city of Pittsburgh. I had to take Matthias there, and I was ready for a Primanti Bros. sandwich. I got the Reuben, which was not disappointing.

The Primanti Bros.' sandwich is a unique sandwich to the Burg. They were the first known to put everything on the sandwich—and I mean *everything*. The coleslaw and the French fries go right between the two halves of the bread.

It is the greatest experience since the Immaculate Reception of the Pittsburgh Steelers in the 1970s. Matthias was enthralled as well. His reaction was also that of awe and excitement. I also think it was a good respite for us after the mental barrage of the texts by Ed. We had a great waitress, Sage. She was encouraging and a beam of light.

We continued on to my Aunt Carole's home in Mt. Lebanon. She was home. I was so grateful because I hadn't seen her in such a long time. To get into my relatives' homes in Pittsburgh is somewhat of a challenge, because Pittsburgh has a bunch of hills. It was problematic to get into my aunt's house, so we just stayed on the driveway and in the garage. It was a great time of reminiscing.

Matthias heard stories of when I was living with them in Philadelphia-Valley Forge-Phoenixville area. He also heard stories of Aunt Carole and Fluffy the Poodle—like when I went for a walk, and my chair tipped over backward as we were going down a hill. That was rather fun.

My aunt, now in her 90s, is living alone after the death of my uncle Ed a few years back. Her daughter Madeline lives in Phoenixville. Madeline *always* liked Phoenixville, so she lives there with her husband, Dean Caroselli and their two children, Athena and Blaise. I've never had the opportunity to meet either of the second cousins. Maybe someday I'll have the opportunity.

Aunt Carole gave me a big kiss on the lips before we left. This reminded me of the time when I was about 15. She did the same then as she did now. I certainly do love my Aunt Carole and with heartfelt gratitude, I will never forget what she and my uncle Ed did in my most formative of years. They gave me family, family that my father was not willing to give. I believe that he had great respect for my uncle and aunt in this regard. My mother also had a great admiration and thanksgiving for what they were able to do for me.

My beloved Aunt Carole passed on November 6, 2024, a little less than six months after my visit. May she rest in peace.

We then met up with Derrick for dinner at the Cheesecake Factory. I was so glad to see Derrick again; I hadn't seen him since we were about 17 years old. He really hadn't changed much. He was now married and had a family, but he came alone. I was so glad he did. It was good to see him, and I think it would have been awkward if his wife or children were there.

Derrick was another individual in my life whom I loved at a young age. He helped me quite a bit. He would drag me up my parents' stairs so he could give me a shower; at the time my mother was very uncomfortable doing so and my father was away quite a bit. So, Derrick faithfully showered with me. I will never forget the care he showed me. My relationship with Derrick was one of love. I was so happy we reconnected. He also met Matthias.

Tuesday morning, I thought I had a UTI. I had promised to meet my friend Pat from high school that day. Pat also lived in the neighborhood. We were very good friends. My challenge was, I had to go to MedExpress and then meet Pat for lunch. Fortunately, everything worked out. We met for lunch. I was so grateful to get to see him as well. He is doing well. He now has a wife and young adult son. He has a radio show. As it happened, he played *Louie Lou I* on the day we were supposed to meet.

When we met, I asked him, "Did you play *Louie Lou I* on purpose?"

He said, "No, that was already part of the song list, sorry."

I said, "That's okay; I just thought it might be."

We had a great time. We caught up with current events, and I hope we can keep in touch. I'm very happy for him and his family.

Later that same day, we went to the East Hills and Penhurst Drive where I lived with my parents when I was about three years old until they moved to Tall Timber Drive. Penhurst Drive is still a nice area with a rolling hill. That rolling hill is where my dog Fritz and I almost careened off the embankment. We relived those moments when Matthias and I went back to the neighborhood. We tried to find the house, asked a few of the neighbors of the area, but we were never quite certain which one it was.

Our next stop was Mt. Carmel Cemetery, in search of my grandfather's grave, my grandmother's grave (on my father's side), and the graves of my Aunt Sylvia and my eldest brother, Baby Fazio. This was interesting because I had never been to Mt. Carmel Cemetery. I was glad to be there to pay respects to both my grandparents, my aunt, and my older brother.

With the help of Mr. Ed Scott, the operations manager at the Mt. Carmel Cemetery, Matthias located teh grave. Mr. Scott told me, "I don't think you'll be able to go where the infants are traditionally buried." So, he and Matthias went off to the infants' section.

Matthias

Mr. Scott was right; it would not have been safe for Louis to roll down there lest he keep rolling into the bushes. The infant section was situated on the side of the hill. Some of the graves in this area and its near vicinity were very old. There were also many headstones inscribed in Italian.

Mr. Scott had the row and plot number for a certain "Baby Fazio", as recorded in the file he accessed through his laptop. However, the very spot where this was supposed to be, there was nothing, at least above ground. So, we began searching for hints of where the stone *might* be. We spotted a certain glimpse of stone peeking out from the earth. We began to dig. I was at it with my bare hands; Mr. Scott eventually procured a shovel. I uncovered a "B" then the word "Baby . . ." I was getting excited. Finally, we uncovered the whole stone: "Baby Tick."

Tick? I was a little dismayed and chuckled some. Mr. Scott and I continued the search in the area, but to no avail. We returned to the van with Louis awaiting us. We had done our best, and Mr. Scott was resolved to get on the Cemetery's case about cleaning up the infant section. He wasn't too happy with its current dilapidated state.

Louis

While waiting for Mr. Scott and Matthias to return from the infant section, I hoped we would find my older brother. In the same breath, I was glad we found my grandparents and my Aunt Sylvia. I was told that my brother was buried on top of my Aunt Sylvia. So, that could be the case.

After visiting the cemetery, I wanted to show Matthias one of the Inclines on Mt. Washington. We ended up having to walk to the Monongahela Incline, since the Duquesne Incline was not accessible for me. Matthias enjoyed the experience, and I explained to him at that point about the three rivers: the Ohio, the Monongahela and the Allegheny, coming together at Point State Park.

Matthias

The view of Pittsburgh from atop Mt. Washington is glorious. We caught the vista just during sunset, too. With multiple different colored bridges latticing back and forth across the rivers, and the green hills surrounding the skyline, Pittsburgh was a beautiful city to behold.

Louis

This was our last night in Pittsburgh. So, I had to go back to the spot that gave me the most comfort: Rico's Ristorante, atop Rico Drive in the North Hills of Pittsburgh. We hit all the hills, actually. We hit West Hills, where we stayed by the airport. We hit East Hills, where I showed Pennhurst Drive to Matthias. We hit North Hills where I grew up on Tall Timber Drive. And we hit South Hills, where my extended-family relatives still live in Mt. Lebanon.

Matthias also got a taste of our Jewish community by going through Squirrel Hill Tunnel on the way to Churchill and Pennhurst, East Hills. Pittsburgh has a substantial Jewish community, and unfortunately it was the site of the massacre in 2018.

It seemed like our Last Supper—at least for Pittsburgh. I don't see myself returning there ever again, so I had to savor this last meal. Many memories ran through my head. Many thoughts of the week we had in Pittsburgh. And I prayed for my brother Edward quite a bit, silently.

The dinner was fantastic. If you ever get a chance, please go to this charming old-world Italian ristorante. You won't be sorry you did. The cost is worth every penny. I have so many family memories; I am certain that the synergy of family members and the quality of food will be etched in my soul for eternity.

the queen mary 2

may 23 — may 31

Matthias

The shower thoughts this morning of departure were interesting. Louis said, "I am so glad Ed did what he did. The serpent's deceit has been revealed." Louis also noted that he was grateful his brother had the opportunity to get it all out there. But what followed, per his description, was "a wave of sadness," but at the same time, he said it was "freeing". He had been holding onto this for so many years. Now he felt he could put that energy toward people who don't spew back vitriol. He said, "Now you have me, Bro." I told him that I've had him for a while, but perhaps he was now free to be more present to me in ways that he wasn't, yet.

I was grateful that I could be there for Louis during that week and very grateful that this pilgrimage ended up being configured the way it was. In spite of not being able to go with the Order of Malta, I think Our Lord and His Mother knew what they were doing in giving us so many signs that seemed to indicate that we were supposed to go with them.

Frankly, I would have been too reluctant to plan a pilgrimage all on my own. So, once I had been sold on going with the Order of Malta (and how they have the trip already organized, Louis paid for, etc.) I was sold on the pilgrimage itself. Once the Order of Malta denied us, I was too convinced of the divine purpose for the pilgrimage to back down.

Looking back, it was especially providential that we had a week at sea in between our time in Pittsburgh and reaching Europe. After the grueling back and forth with Ed and the stresses of traveling (in the disability time zone, no less), a week at sea with absolutely nothing to do was exactly what we needed to prepare for Lourdes. Louis and I both thanked God and the Blessed Mother time and time again.

Louis

We were on our way from Pittsburgh to New York City to catch the ship that would take us across the Atlantic to the European continent. I hadn't been on a ship in a while; the last time was when I was on a Carnival cruise going to the Bahamas. I was very excited about going on the *Queen Mary 2*. I felt the presence of my mother looking down and smiling.

We landed at La Guardia in New York City, spending one night at the Holiday Inn and then we took the Uber WAV (Wheelchair Accessible Vehicle) to the cruise terminal. Like our trip from the airport, we needed two vehicles: one to transport me and the baggage, another to transport Matthias with the sit-to-stand lift and my shower chair.

On our departure from the hotel to the cruise terminal, some of the hotel staff got out in the middle of the street and bartered with the Uber drivers. As a result, we got much better rates to get to the cruise terminal. I distinctly remember one driver saying, "No no no, too much luggage, too much luggage." And the horns were a-honkin', like we needed to get out of the way. New York City. I think they just like honking their horns.

We got to Brooklyn Cruise Terminal, Red Hook. In the distance, you could see this *big* ship. That was our ocean liner that was going to take us across the Atlantic. We would eventually arrive in Southampton, England and then onto Lourdes, France.

We boarded the ship. It was magnificent. Elegant in a way, but it also reminded me of the movie *Titanic* for a moment. I kept that thought to myself because Matthias had never been on an ocean liner or cruise ship before.

We arrived at our stateroom, and it was terrific. We had an ocean view room on the fourth deck toward the front of the ship. Our stewardess, Ethel, was good as well. She was originally from Zimbabwe and then moved to South Africa. She was very personable and amicable. We told her that we would be coming back on the westward voyage, and she said that she would be on the ship as well. So, knowing that, we made certain that we would get her a small gift of the Lourdes holy water.

We also watched as the ship departed New York Harbor by going underneath the Verrazzano-Narrows Bridge. It was a sight to behold. We left about 4 p.m. that day.

Our first night at dinner, we had assigned times. But after that, we were on what you called "flex time", which meant any time after 5 p.m. up until 8:30 p.m. you could dine in the main dining room, The Britannia.

Matthias and I enjoyed it immensely. We had plenty of relaxation time. Little did we know we would be in for some treats. The first said treat was the fact that we had veterans from World War II, Korea, Vietnam, and Iraq aboard the ship, giving presentations every day of the voyage. They were on their way to Normandy, France, for the 80th-anniversary celebration of D-Day. I felt privileged, considering my work with the Southern Arizona VA. I also thought of the selflessness of these individuals. Most interesting for me were the nurses in the MASH units of Vietnam, where my Uncle Marion served as a doctor.

We also met some entertaining performers and attended shows on a regular basis. On our eastbound voyage, Matthias and I gained a reputation. We were the dancing duo. And that was fun.

We still had to keep up with my UTI on the ship. Fortunately for us, Marjorie, who is very persistent, had contacted the urgent care in Pittsburgh and now the ship doctor to ensure that I was on the right regimen of medication. I am so glad that she did because as it turns out, as it is in many cases with urinary tract infections, I was not on the correct antibiotic. So, I also got to view the medical facilities of the ship.

There was a computer lab which Matthias and I used to submit my care time sheets to John Hancock. We learned after, however, that they don't cover international travel. Oh well. I was glad they covered my care over domestic travel.

We met some fantastic people on our voyage. One such couple was an Orthodox priest and his mother, Fr. Gerasimos and Stella. We met them at daily Mass, celebrated by Fr. John Shea, SJ. We became fast friends and would eat together in the King's Court buffet for lunch. Stella was comical to watch because she would not eat her entire plate and place her food that she felt was extra onto her son's plate, "Oh, I can't eat this, Father," and Fr. Gerasimos would take it dutifully. Matthias and I figured that he knew this would be happening; he seemed to leave ample room on his plate for such things.

Matthias
I greatly appreciated the years of priestly experience that Fr. Gerasimos liberally shared with me, knowing my

vocation. "You never have a day off from being a priest," he said. "Just like you never have a day off from being a mom or dad or a husband or wife, you never have a day off from being a priest. You might get a day off from office and administrative work, but you never have a day off from being a priest." He also told me, having learned from the wisdom of his good bishop and a dear friend to him, "There are very few truly urgent matters, but there are plenty of urgent people."

Stella shared a powerful story, handed on from centuries of Greek Orthodox tradition. I'll do my best to recall it here, because it cast a poignant light on the purpose of our pilgrimage. It went something like this:

There once was a very good and generous man. He lived in the city in the valley, and he spent all of his time and energy helping others. He fed the hungry, helped the sick, took care of the homeless, and would even give his own money away to others. He was tirelessly doing good deeds for other people. Many acclaimed him a very pious man. However, one day, he suddenly became paralyzed, neck down. And the man became very bitter.

He soon demanded, "I need to see the holy man on Mt. Athos!" His friends told him that was impossible. He was a hermit: nobody could see him. The monks up on the holy mountain hardly ever saw him. "I demand to see the holy man on Mt. Athos!" The poor guy was determined.

His friends finally agreed to carry him all the way up the mountain. The monks were surprised to find the crew carrying their crippled friend. They asked to see the holy man, the hermit. The monks sent for him.

They delivered their friend to the holy man's hermitage, and the holy man appeared. "I have been waiting for you. Come in." The friends carried him into the hut and left him alone with the holy man.

"I know why you're here," the hermit said.

"You do?"

"Yes. You're here to ask me why this happened to you, why you have been afflicted with paralysis."

The man wouldn't deny it. "Yes. That's exactly why I am here. I have only been doing good with my life. Why has God done this to me?"

"I will tell you. Get up and walk around the room."

"What? Can you not see that I am paralyzed?"

"Get up and walk around the room."

To his astonishment, the man found strength in his limbs and was able to easily walk around the room.

"You see, God has power over everything. He is very pleased with your efforts to show kindness to everyone and especially the poor. But now, God wants to use you to soften their hardened hearts, so that they are moved to show you the kindness that you have shown them."

The man was astounded; he had never thought of it that way before.

"Get back down."

The man obeyed, and his paralysis returned. However, he retained enough movement with his head and right arm to be able to prostrate himself, cross himself, and venerate the holy icons. He was carried down that mountain a different man.

Stella shared this story with us because she understood that we were looking for a miracle. I had big hopes for one. I shared the story of how Louis's kidney stones all came out after we had gone to the water for three days back in Scottsdale when we were there for his graduation. "Big graces are in store for us," I said, hinting at something spectacular. For all my desires for a supernatural healing of Louis's body, I knew Stella had shared an important lesson with us.

May 30th finally arrived. We had a busy day ahead of us. After disembarking in Southampton, Cunard would shuttle us to London Heathrow Airport. From there we would fly British Airways directly to Toulouse. We would then need to catch the AERO bus from Toulouse Blagnac airport to get to Gare Matabiau, Toulouse's main train station. From there we would catch the train to Lourdes, then walk a kilometer or so to our hotel, the Hôtel Roissy.

Keep in mind, we had 10 pieces of luggage total: two suitcases for clothes, two backpacks for books and personal items, Louis's ventilator, a suitcase of personal items specifically for Louis, the sit-to-stand lift, the shower chair, and another bag for whatever didn't fit in the rest. Being experienced traveling with Louis by now, I had been workshopping various ways to assemble these all together so I could transport them in one movement, a sort of makeshift luggage cart. I call it our "luggage behemoth". So, the plan was to make all these transfers, flights, and train rides wheeling all that stuff around, assembling, disassembling, and reassembling the luggage behemoth at multiple intervals.

Sounds ambitious? You bet. When we had scheduled this all back in April, I was wondering if I was trying to fit too many things into too little time . . . remember, the disability time zone is in effect.

Nonetheless, it was an auspicious arrangement of dates: we would reach Hôtel Roissy after midnight, thus dating our arrival on May 31st, which is the Feast of the Visitation. Now, anxious for miraculous graces, our time in Lourdes would secure the completion of my time with Louis. My Visitation would be complete; Louis would be free of the disability that makes my leaving so complicated and difficult. So I prayed; so I hoped.

Our disembarkation and transfer to London Heathrow were fairly uneventful. It was perfect timing to check in and do all the required paperwork for the wheelchair and oversized baggage (not called "luggage" in England). We had an amazing captain. I really wish I could remember his African name, but he kept it simple, "Oh, you can call me Captain IK."

Studies have shown that we Americans are favorably disposed to "fancy" British accents, even to the point of unfairly attributing more intelligence to "refined" English registers, while attributing stupidity to "less refined" dialects, like a southern drawl. This was no exception; I loved listening to Captain IK's voice. Accent or no accent, he was very professional and helpful with Louis's needs for boarding the aircraft and demonstrated a great deal of confidence. However, I won't deny that his voice and accent only served to reinforce my positive impression of him.

In the States, it is usually the airlines that are required to staff and manage the special transfers that folks like Louis require. When we fly, Louis has to be taken from his power chair into an aisle chair. If you're not familiar, the aisle chair is a narrow, uncomfortable thing on wheels that's just small enough to roll in the aisle between the airline seats and just big enough to support a person sitting on it (with several straps to secure the person in place). Next, Louis has to be lifted from the aisle chair into the airline seat. This usually gets us in the first or second row, which is easiest for everyone involved.

For most transfers, if you want to be safe, you should have four people. Louis's weight and body configuration simply require that. Now, we're fairly accustomed to this drill, usually with the stewards of Southwest Airlines (and sometimes even the ground crew, who tend to have bigger guys and gals that can help). But in Europe, it's not the same way. They contract with a third party to provide special needs transfers of this sort.

Given that, Captain IK insisted upon seeing the ID of each of the third-party folks who were about to handle Louis. He was not going to let them touch him without being absolutely sure he knew who they were and that they knew what they were doing. Louis deeply appreciated this.

It's a short hop of a flight over the channel to Toulouse. Now it was time to scramble toward the bus station outside the airport (after going through customs, collecting all our bags, and reassembling the luggage behemoth) and cross our fingers that enough people would understand some English along the way. I know enough Latin, Spanish, and Italian, as well as some of the basic mechanics of French to guess my way through most French vocabulary and get the gist of French writing, but I don't speak French, and I certainly don't understand spoken French. It was an excellent opportunity to start learning, which I knew I would enjoy, despite the frustrations of the language barrier we would certainly experience.

We missed the first AERO bus by minutes. It was another 25 minutes until the next one. I wasn't too worried. *There's still time. And the Blessed Mother wants us to make it.*

The next bus arrived. Thankfully, Louis *and* the luggage behemoth were able to fit on the bus without too much fenagling. The driver didn't mind, so we were happy. I looked at my phone. *Time is getting closer . . . and we have a lot of stations to go before Gare Matabiau . . .* I was beginning to lose confidence that we could reach the train station on time. We were driving through downtown Toulouse at 6 p.m. or so, and traffic was heavy. I kept praying. Not only that we would make it, but that I would trust.

"Prochain arrêt: Gare Matabiau . . ."

Bless the Lord! Time to get off. I glanced at my phone. 6:45 p.m. The train for Lourdes was scheduled for 6:55 p.m. *C'mon . . .*

I wheeled the luggage behemoth out of the bus, and Louis rolled out after. A kind young man who spoke a little English offered his assistance with the behemoth; I gratefully accepted. We entered the station. We had to go down the elevator to get under the platform. The elevator was too small for Louis and me both to fit with all the baggage, so I went first. Then the elevator went back up. Louis got on. The elevator went back down. *How many minutes does each elevator ride take?*

We rolled across the lower level, trying to make sense of which elevator to take up to the proper platform. Our helper dashed up the stairs to look. He ran back down, and we selected the elevator for platform D. I got on and rode the elevator up, then Louis got on and rode the elevator up.

It was 6:58 p.m. Our train was nowhere to be seen. We were too late.

There were no more trains to Lourdes that Thursday evening, so we figured we had two options: 1) check into a hotel in Toulouse and take a train tomorrow (there were at least three of them at different times, so that wouldn't be too complicated. 2) Take the train to Tarbes, departing at 8:55 or so, and try to find a taxi to get us to Lourdes. Tarbes is only about 10 miles north of Lourdes. Louis, not 100% well at the moment given he was still recovering from the UTI and side-effects from the antibiotics, favored the more conservative option to stay in Toulouse (Toulouse is a bigger city, more resources, and so forth). I, zealous to reach our divinely inspired destination, favored boarding the train to Tarbes. I also really didn't want to unpack everything for a night in Toulouse and repack it all the next morning. Perhaps if

Louis hadn't been dealing with the UTI and antibiotics, he would have been firmer, but I ended up winning this one.

We did the rounds with the elevators again and began searching for a section of the platform that might be level with a train door. The conductor stepped outside to see if he could help us. Philippe spoke a little English, enough to ascertain our intentions:

"You want to go to Lourdes?"

"Yes."

"You realize this is the train to Tarbes?"

"Yes."

"Are you sure you want to take this train?"

"Yes."

I suppose he had pity on us poor, confused Americans and summoned for the ramp to be brought out. We boarded. Amazingly, the luggage behemoth was able to make it on without being dismantled, though not without boxing in a fellow passenger, also bound for Tarbes. She didn't mind.

After a few minutes, Philippe came back to talk with us. "Do you know how you will go from Tarbes to Lourdes?"

We explained that we were hoping to get an accessible taxi.

"Do you have one yet?"

"No."

"Can you call?"

"No. We don't have French cell service. Would you be able to call for us?"

To our humble amazement, Philippe proceeded to place several phone calls on our behalf. It was truly an act of mercy.

He came back 20 minutes later. "We have problem. You see, at Tarbes, there is . . . *travaux*. How do you say . . ."

I had no clue what "travaux" might have meant, and Philippe soon went through Google translate. "There is work at the station." Louis and I figured there must be some sort of construction.

"Your friend in the wheelchair cannot get off the train at Tarbes station. The *travaux* . . . it is impossible. You will have to get off at the station before Tarbes."

We said that would be alright. By this point, Philippe and I discovered that we both spoke Spanish. He said he spoke better Spanish than English, and I don't speak French at all, so we found our happy medium.

Another half hour went by. Philippe returned. "*Cambio de historia* . . ." Turned out, there was *travaux* at this other station, too. "You will have to get off at Lannemezan. I have called a colleague there, and he will help you find a taxi. Good luck."

We thanked Philippe profusely. By 11 p.m., we reached Lannemezan. As promised, his colleague (whose name we never caught) was there to greet us and help me wheel the luggage behemoth across the tracks and onto the station. It was dark, cold (mid to low 40s Fahrenheit), and the station was closed. We were not really dressed for the conditions.

At this point, I felt pretty stupid. I got down on my knees to pray, begging God for mercy in spite of my pride (I absolutely *insisted* on going to Lourdes tonight). I should have been more cautious and willing to change plans (such as staying the night in Toulouse, where there are more resources, another train to Lourdes, etc.), especially in light of Louis's current condition: he was still recovering from the UTI and experiencing side effects from the antibiotics. I apologized to Louis, and he gave his forgiveness with his usual merciful lightheartedness.

Even worse, I feared that my prideful rashness would lessen the possibility of God granting a miraculous healing for Louis. I knew this was an unhealthy (and theologically problematic) attitude; you don't "earn" miracles. You don't "produce" them. God works, and He chooses to work through human instruments. Of course, having the right disposition is helpful, so I was worried about having an unfavorable disposition for facilitating a miraculous healing. I was putting a lot of pressure on myself to perform. And, at least in this moment, I felt I was performing poorly. If Louis was healed (on the third day of going to the water, mind you), we wouldn't have to worry about the struggle for personal care anymore; I wouldn't have to worry about complications or delays for my timeline to enter religious life. Hence, the pressure.

Nevertheless, in my moments of stress and undue preoccupation with myself, I knew God's mercy is greater than my misery. No matter how much I might mess things up, God can (and *does*) still work through poor human instruments. With faith in this God of Mercy, I found some peace.

Louis needed to pee, so I helped him, right there on the train platform. Louis suggested I dump it on the train tracks. I declined to do so (that would be disrespectful to SNCF, the French rail company). I found some suitable shrubbery away from the tracks to mark Louis's territory.

We asked the SNCF representative (who was still looking for a taxi for us) if we could enter the train station because of the cold. He allowed us in. We promptly used the vending machine to get a drink for Louis to take his medications, plus an additional snack.

A few minutes later, the representative returned. Good news and bad news. The bad news: he had no authorization to allow us into the train station, and upon conferring with his supervisor, he had to kick us back outside. The good news: he had found a taxi, and it would arrive around midnight.

As we were ushered out onto the parking lot, Louis asked, "What do we owe you for the taxi?" To our amazement, he replied, "Nothing. It's on us." Louis's and my jaws dropped. We thanked him profusely. He told us not to worry about it, and he wished us good luck. He got into his car and left. We had another 40 minutes or so in the cold until midnight.

Louis

Well, by this time Matthias and I were out on the parking lot, and I felt bad for both of us because we were both cold. I also had another thought enter my head, *I wish that little brother of mine would listen to me next time, otherwise we wouldn't be out in the cold, we would be in a bed in Toulouse!* And, as we would find out later, the taxi that they were so graciously sending for us came from Toulouse! So, all in all, I think my idea was better.

Matthias

Louis was beginning to shiver. Despite his protests, I removed some of my own layers and pulled some from our suitcases to drape over him. I was cold, but I could run around and warm up (plus I had no UTI or antibiotics' side effects to contend with). Every sound of a car going by or the glimpse of headlights in the distance aroused our hope . . . and then said car would appear, clearly too small to be an accessible taxi, and drive on. I think this is the single period of time that saw the most instances of Louis asking, "What time is it?" in the stretch of one hour.

This past month in particular I had been taking a little bit more physical space from Louis. I wasn't hugging him as much and was even no longer holding his hand during the Our Father (or even hugging him for the Sign of Peace). I needed space to recalibrate. However, this was a different scenario. The occasion called for us to warm up, penguin-style.

Louis

In order for us to warm up, we had to hold each other, which I knew for Matthias during this time was going to be interesting. This circumstance required us to be quite intimate for a prolonged period. So, I was very mindful of the situation. I enjoyed holding Matthias. I always do, but I know when he is in the mindset of needing his space, how important that is to him (and me, frankly).

I again was saying to myself, *Well, I'm grateful I have the brother that I do,* and *Thank you, God,* as I often do. I just appreciated being with him.

The experience always reminds me that we are both human and that the adventures we go on are never predictable because I would have never predicted that we would be in Lannemezan, France, stuck in a parking lot at 11 p.m. and holding each other intensely for about 40 minutes. I guess we both needed that at that particular moment in time.

Matthias

Our penguin time was interspersed with our Angelic Warfare Confraternity prayers and the Divine Mercy Chaplet, as well as a break during which I ran several laps around the parking lot. We had to pass the time and keep as warm as we could.

Finally, around 12:15 a.m., a beautiful, wonderful, glorious black taxi arrived in the parking lot. Eloï, our driver, was cheerful and ready to help out. I don't think he was prepared to fit all of our stuff (plus Louis in his powerchair) into his vehicle, but he embraced the challenge. I am grateful. We managed to fit most of the luggage *and* the sit-to-stand and shower chair in the space between the front seats and the wheelchair section (it was a rear-entry vehicle).

Louis was all smiles seated there in the back of the van. *It was heated.* He fell asleep on the way from Lannemezan to Lourdes. I struck up a pleasant conversation with Eloï and discovered to my amazement, the French *tac-tac-tac* (pronounced roughly "tuck-tuck-tuck"). Eloï would mutter this way when stalling over an idea or thinking. It was delightful.

Louis

When we boarded the taxi to Lourdes, I was grateful that Matthias and I were finally in the warmth of the vehicle. I was just glad to begin experiencing France. I was waiting with great anticipation to see what tomorrow would bring. By this time, it *was* tomorrow, so I began really looking forward to lounging around the hotel, in silent appreciation for our trip.

Matthias

It was past 1 a.m.; we finally arrived at the Hôtel Roissy. We checked in, lugged up the luggage (behemoth reassembled in the lobby), and began the night routine. The ordeal was over; we finally made it.

And then I messed things up *even worse*.

CHAPTER 34

Lourdes

may 31 – june 6

Matthias

Louis fell asleep instantly. All that remained was for me to do my toiletries, plug in the powerchair for the night, and go to bed myself. However, there was an issue: where would I plug in the powerchair? Louis had used up a lot of battery yesterday, getting off the *Queen Mary 2*, getting to London Heathrow, and traveling through Toulouse then Lannemezan. He charges it every night anyway, but it was especially needful this night.

Now you see, Jerry, Louis's wheelchair tech from American Mobility, gave us very specific instructions about charging Louis's chair while abroad. He explained to us that we would need a voltage converter for the European outlets or else we would risk damaging the charger, or worse, damaging the electronics of the chair itself. We duly ordered a voltage converter from Amazon well ahead of our flight to Pittsburgh. However, aboard the *Queen Mary 2*, I discovered that this "converter" was virtually useless. I don't know if it was a scam or if I misread the product label. Whatever the case may be, it was no good for helping us charge Louis's chair, and I knew that going into Lourdes.

So, there I was in the hotel room, not a suitable outlet to be found. European outlets have a voltage output of about 230 to 240 Volts, whereas American outlets put out about 120 Volts. What to do?

I looked around and found one American outlet in our whole hotel room. It was in the bathroom, probably for hairdryers or electric razors and the like. Further, it *explicitly* stated, "240 V". I plugged in Louis's electric toothbrush charger. Didn't seem to cause any problems. Then I recalled our conversations with Jerry about this. *And I ignored it.* Flying in the face of Jerry's instructions and my better judgment, I plugged Louis's charger into the wall.

The lights on the charger all flashed once. I next plugged the charger into the chair. Nothing happened. I decided to unplug from the wall and use a simple adapter to plug Louis's chair charger into one of the wall outlets. I reasoned that the wall outlet might have a lesser voltage than the bathroom outlet that explicitly stated "240 V". This time, the charger flashed on, and the light remained on indicating that the charger was receiving power. *This is good.*

I plugged the charger into Louis's chair. The indicator light went out. *This is not good.* After sitting for a couple minutes, I finally unplugged the charger. *This is really not good.* I tried re-plugging and unplugging the charger a few more times, but to no avail. I was confident I had just fried Louis's charger. I prayed and finally went to sleep with a really bad feeling in my stomach.

We hadn't set any alarm. I awoke to brilliant mid-morning sun. Louis was still sleeping heavily. I then did what I really needed to do next. I prayed the Rosary. It was Friday, the 31st of May, but instead of praying the Sorrowful Mysteries (traditional for Friday), I prayed the Joyful Mysteries, because it was the Feast of the Visitation. What I had seen before as a divinely arranged and triumphant arrival had gone sour. Not only was this something I had been investing so many of my hopes, efforts, energies, and prayers into (let alone Louis's), but many many people had invested *thousands* of dollars to support us in this trip. This trip where we prayed for healing, that Louis might walk, that we might have great spiritual renewal. And I kicked it off by effectively chopping Louis's legs off. I needed some capital J Joy right then.

Sometimes when I pray the Rosary, especially in times of need, Mary will, in the Spirit, give me very specific words, phrases, or ideas for me to meditate on for each mystery. This was a time of need. I got out on our hotel room balcony (fourth floor, I think) and began my Rosary.

The First Joyful Mystery, the Annunciation. Mary's message: *Do not lose hope.*

I needed to hear that. I was so fearful that my foolish behavior would lose us the chance for healing (again, this is problematic thinking, I know). But I took Mary's words as an exhortation to abandon myself to Divine Mercy. No matter how much I might mess things up, God still works.

The Second Joyful Mystery, the Visitation. Mary's message: *Show great courage.*

You bet I needed courage. I would need courage to face the challenges of the broken charger situation, and I would especially need courage to tell Louis.

The Third Joyful Mystery, the Nativity of Jesus Christ. Mary's message: *Joy.*

Not a verb or phrase, just the noun: *joy.* Okay, sure, Jesus was born, and the Incarnation of the Son of God saved all of humanity. Yeah, I should be joyful about that in spite of my present unpleasant circumstance. Then it hit me: *Matthias, you made it! You guys made it to Lourdes! You're HERE!* Yes, there were serious challenges in front of us, but by golly, WE MADE IT TO LOURDES!

The Fourth Joyful Mystery, the Presentation. Mary's message: Okay, this was actually a private one that I will not share, but it involved St. Joseph.

The Fifth Joyful Mystery, the Finding of the Child Jesus in the Temple. Mary's message: *Seek and you shall find.*

I took My Dearest Mother's messages all to heart and made extra sure to jot some notes down so I would remember. I had received the strength and encouragement I needed to break the news to Louis.

Louis

I awoke our first day in Lourdes, in a meditative state. As fate would have it, my love was tested again. This time, in electrifying ways. I thought, *Matthias is acting strangely sheepish.* He asked me how I was, and in my groggy voice, I was like, "Yeah, I'm good."

We usually tell each other we love each other. I'm usually the one that starts. This particular morning, he was more—shall we say—noncombative, if you will? Usually, we discuss some topic. We started off with prayer as we usually do. Always good, because we begin the morning routine without interfacing with the power wheelchair. I got a sense that he had something to tell me. I wasn't quite sure what it was because he seemed to be in a more solemn mood, almost mournful. Like someone had died or something.

He finally mustered up the courage to tell me the news. It went something like this, "I have something to tell you."

I thought, *Hmm. What might that be?* Again, his mood was depressive. *Must be something sad. Did someone die who we both knew mutually? Were his parents ill? Did something happen to one of the siblings?*

No, it was nothing like that, thankfully. It was the fact that he had done some electrical work. We affectionately call my powerchair "Peri" (it is made by Permobil). Turns out, someone did die. Matthias killed Peri's charger, which disabled me *and* Peri.

The reason that Matthias was so concerned about telling me of his situation was because, by nature, I'm Italian and Croatian. He probably was wondering which one of the two natures was going to react first. The Italian or the Croatian? In this case, the Italian reacted first, and I basically said, "How the heck could you do that?!"

Words cannot adequately capture my ire. I traditionally do not get mad at Matthias. He will tell you so. But on this particular occasion, I was fairly inflamed—while remembering: *personal regulation,* from my Social Work Master's program.

Bottom line: I think I handled it fairly well. Whenever Matthias is up to something, he is similar to Dennis the Menace. He doesn't actually mean to cause great issue because he usually thinks logically about it and if he thinks it's a good idea, he'll do it. I think that's what happened when he fried the charger and disabled both myself and Peri. I think he thought it was a good idea. What ensued is similar to what happens to Dennis the Menace. It created a whole adventure in and of itself, sending Mr. Wilson (AKA Louis) into heartache.

So begins our first day in Lourdes.

I said to Matthias, "Well, what are we going to do now?"

Of course, I wasn't expecting much from Matthias at this point because we had just been stuck in a parking lot because of his lack of paying attention to what I had suggested in the first place. As he says, if asked, "I pay attention. But I do not necessarily follow." Hmm. So, he paid attention to my assertion and question of what we were going to do.

He had no answer at this point.

So, I said, "What we should do, is go down the elevator to the restaurant and eat something."

This was our first exposure to French bread. God bless the French, because I was able to put something in my mouth other than Matthias's head. This calmed me down a little more. The French do have good bread. Matthias's head can smell.

Yes, just like the Romans with the Christians, I was going to send my brother to the lions. But, unlike the Romans, I loved my brother unconditionally—even when he kills my charger and cuts off my legs. I save him from the proverbial guillotine out of heartfelt compassion.

So, it was now up to myself and Matthias to figure out how we were going to keep me moving. We had no manual chair. We could have gotten one, I'm sure, there are plenty around Lourdes, but that wouldn't answer how we were going to handle the rest of the voyage (and for that matter the rest of the pilgrimage). One thing that I have learned about my brother Matthias is that he is sensitive. Similar to when my grandfather Pappap said to me in his bedroom, "If you're going to survive in this family, you'd better toughen up." Those were prophetic words because maybe I'm still sensitive, and maybe that's why I didn't last in that family. So, when it comes to Matthias, I realize he's sensitive, and I'm very careful because I don't want to hurt him, not intentionally anyway.

We worked together as we always do, and Matthias came up with glee at one point during the day and said, "You know what, Bro? I found a charger on the ground!"

And I was like, "Really?"

He was like, "That's Providence."

And I was like, "Yeah." I was about ready to believe anything at that point. I said to myself, *Well, we are in Lourdes . . .*

The charger was a 2-amp charger which was great because it could get us at least around the hotel. I didn't tell Matthias at that time, but I was thinking that if we had to, we could go to the grotto that way; it wasn't that far. However, it would be a lot of charging and recharging, and actually, we'd need to carry the minifridge with us because the charger would have heated up so fast. We learned this by trial because in the hotel, we had to occasionally put the charger in the refrigerator to cool it down.

Nevertheless, I was just so grateful. I wasn't really certain how the charger showed up. Matthias made it sound like it fell out of Heaven. Frankly, I was grateful it didn't hit anyone on the head, but I sorta figured, from my business perspective, *nah, there has to be a further connection to this.*

Sure enough, there was. There was a company delivering scooters with their chargers for pilgrims who were staying at the various hotels around Lourdes. It seemed to me to be a great service and a profitable business in a town of 15,000 individuals, but it probably swells to 60,000 to 100,000 with all the pilgrims! So, needless to say, it's a great business.

I am so grateful that Brother is as he is, because he immediately tried to figure out, in French, where the owner of these scooters and chargers resided. He went for a walk himself while I was in the hotel room keeping up with international news. Matthias is not much for news. Nor is he much for elections. But I'm attempting to let him know that he should be keeping up and emulating his youngest brother, Nicholas, who is so up-to-date with current events and politics. I admire that quality about Nicholas immensely and encourage Matthias to follow in his youngest brother's footsteps.

Anyway, he journeyed out and he couldn't find where this business was. He came back to the hotel. Before he came up to the room, he also engaged with the hotel clerk about the fact that there were other chargers, realizing that these other chargers were higher amperage (my lately deceased charger was 10 amps). He found a charger that was 6 amps, which was fantastic. I'm sure he was elated.

Matthias

Earlier, I had spoken with the clerk about the 2-amp charger which we had unceremoniously and clandestinely taken. He said that was all right, no problem. I don't think he understood what I really meant; his English only went so far. So, having found a 6-amp charger downstairs, I proceeded to unplug it with the intention to swap it with the 2-amp charger. The clerk came out, "No no no, this belongs to the business." I apologized and left it alone.

I was still stymied. When I had gone searching for the business, all I could find at the address (posted on their website) was an Irish pub. I went back upstairs, and Louis brought forward again the idea of contacting the business and renting a higher amperage charger from them.

Louis

I asked Matthias, "Bro, have you considered that the Irish pub could be where they're running the business out of?" *Eureka!*

Matthias was like, "Maybe."

"Let's call." So, we did. My 22 years of management experience with Cox Enterprises paid off in France. My company is an international company, even though I don't think they have any auto auctions in France.

We called. They didn't pick up. Matthias contacted one of the owners through WhatsApp. He said that he had a higher amp charger and that we could meet him at the business. We were both excited. One would think that you would be excited about going to the Grotto on the second day of being at Lourdes (it was Saturday now). No, we were excited about going to a pub to get a charger.

Matthias

I guess Louis was excited, but I was in a different sort of way. You see, Saturday is the Marian day of the week. So, it has a special emphasis on Marian devotion which I like to observe. Every night in Lourdes there is a Marian procession at 9 p.m. which starts at the Grotto and processes toward the Basilica. That night, you could see thousands of pilgrims streaming through the streets toward the sanctuary with their candles in hand. You could even hear some of the Marian hymns in the distance. Yet against this crowd, you could have spotted the *only two people* going the opposite direction. Instead of going to pray in procession before the Blessed Mother *on Saturday, IN LOURDES* . . . we were going to an Irish Pub to get a chair charger. I felt it was deserved, but it still broke my heart.

Louis

I felt bad for Matthias, but I knew that we had to do it. I was grateful that we found the Irish pub. It was getting dark. I thought to myself, *Once again, Matthias has us in the dark . . . in a strange city. First Lannemezan, and now Lourdes, of all things, looking for an Irish pub!*

This was the first time I had gone into the town of Lourdes. I was dutifully following my brother because, on occasion, the way we both operate, we can lose each other quite easily in crowds. I did not want that to happen. I think we were more attuned to each other's whereabouts this night.

We finally found the pub. We had to go into a back alley to get in and when we got in, it was *Allez!* I was like, *Oh my goodness, what is this?* to myself, just in awe of the environment. We spoke to a man, I assumed one of the co-owners, Declan. He was one of the nicest guys. I think he was a father because there was this young girl who was also in the pub and she was precocious and feisty. The mother was also working there, so it was a family affair, it appeared.

He said, in Irish-accented English, that he would rent us a charger for 15 euros a day. Without hesitation, I said, "We'll take it!" That was my freedom to see Lourdes. He apologized for having to charge, but he explained that he had to because he couldn't rent out the scooter as long as I had the charger that accompanied it. Being in management, I understood. Again, Cox experience came to the rescue!

We finally had a charger! I was elated. And then, Sunday, the Feast of Corpus Christi, we could finally relax and *go to Lourdes.*

Matthias

In case Louis's description of the scene did not make it clear, we had received our first full immersion into the European football experience. My younger brothers later explained to us that the people at the pub were watching the Champions League final match. Another interesting note: the alley we had to go up to enter the pub from the back was named *Rue Saint-Dominique,* Saint Dominic Way. I thanked St. Dominic for his intercession on our behalf, and Louis and I both profusely thanked Declan, and then Jesus, God, and the Blessed Mother. We were too late to join the procession, but getting pizza and going to bed was enough for the night.

Louis

So, we awoke to go to English Mass at 11 a.m. Fr. Martins Obikara was the priest who concelebrated. Matthias was asked by Fr. Obikara to lector. Matthias and I sat in the front row, off to the side. We were so pleased and honored to be there among our fellow brothers and sisters.

During the homily, it was expressed by the priest that the miracles at Lourdes were not necessarily at the Grotto, but they are also during the time of the Eucharist. It was encouraged that we attend the procession of the Eucharist. I said to Matthias, "We need to go." Matthias agreed.

Matthias

As the lead celebrant preached the homily regarding Christ's Body and Blood and the importance of the Eucharistic procession, a message came back to my mind from my spiritual director, Fr. JP: "Oh, Matthias. Yes, Lourdes is about healing for Louis, but it's also *for you.*" I knew that intellectually. Fr. JP (and many others, for that matter) had told me this, more than once, but this time it finally hit my heart because I knew I needed healing, too.

If you are not familiar with the Catholic practice of Eucharistic procession, allow me to explain: Catholics believe Jesus at His word when He says, "This is my body" and "This is my blood" (Matthew 26:26, 28), and when He states, ". . . my flesh is true food, and my blood is true drink" (John 6:55). We believe that the bread and wine, when consecrated by the priest during Mass, indeed become the Body and Blood of Jesus. They are His real presence with us on earth, and we partake of Him in the most intimate way. When there is a Eucharistic procession, the consecrated host is placed in a monstrance, a cross-shaped display, usually fashioned from precious metals. The priest will carry the monstrance for worshippers to adore and venerate.

God is always communicating with us, but very often, we set up a lot of obstacles. I often am like a big, opulent mansion, with complex corridors and mazelike halls leading to obscure rooms all over the place. Just the kind of place that makes it very hard for God to reach me. But in that moment, with the priest's preaching and Fr. JP's reminder in my mind, a single, direct hallway to the very center of the building, that is, to my heart, opened right up; all the doors that had been locked swung wide open. It was as if God was telling me, *I have direct access to you, always, and I am here for your healing, too. Healing your WHOLE being.* My heart trembled in joy and in fear. Unlike the miraculous intervention I was feverishly hoping for (on the third day of going to bath/bless/rinse in the Lourdes water, of course), this was a healing I wasn't expecting. However, I knew with my whole heart: *The Eucharistic procession tonight: you're expected.*

Louis

On the day of the Feast of Corpus Christi, the Body of Christ, we attended the Eucharistic procession. I was in awe during that first procession of the Eucharist because not only were we processing above ground, we also processed beneath the ground into the underground Basilica. This basilica was huge; it had the capacity to seat 25,000 pilgrims.

During this first Eucharistic procession, we ended up sitting in the very front row, after being directed by ushers to do so. This is a common practice in Lourdes, to ensure that individuals with any type of disability or illness are seated as close to the front as possible.

In our case, we were blessed to be in the very front. In the Spirit, it was told to both of us that we needed to be at this procession. So, we both knew that we had the grace of divine intervention. What we didn't know was what would transpire. What transpired was in its own way a miracle.

I was in the front row, and Jesus was taken by the priest down into the crowd. Jesus, at that moment of His entrance into the crowd, was taken directly to me, as close as inches away. In fact, this surprised Matthias to such a degree, as he was kneeling. It surprised me as well. I was in a state of prayer, and I could feel the Holy Spirit.

At that same time, I remembered what the priest said at Mass earlier in the morning, that the miracles do not necessarily happen at the Grotto, but they also happen at the Eucharistic procession. When I thought about it as well, I knew that Matthias and I were there at the Feast of Corpus Christi. This was an internal miracle for my soul. It began the work of putting my soul to rest from what I had experienced throughout my life: my institutionalization as a child, the conflict within my immediate and extended family as it related to my disability, my samesex attraction, the issues of ensuring that I had proper help for getting out of bed and into bed, working for Cox Enterprises, the loss of my job, finding myself after the loss of my job, going to graduate school, and then finally the challenges ahead of me, as I aged with a disability and finding the place where I could age with dignity.

All those things flashed before my eyes in that moment of having Jesus inches away from me physically but intimately connected in my heart. At that time, I didn't really realize who was beside me, who was around me. It was just me and Jesus. That was the first healing at Lourdes.

Matthias

After all the heartache, frustration, and confusion of my mishandling Louis's charger, which ate up our first two full days in Lourdes, the Lord prepared this special moment to give me the encouragement I desperately needed. You see, all of the other times we would go to the Eucharistic procession, we did not get so close to the front (there are hundreds of other folks in wheelchairs who get priority sitting), nor would we ever be in the same place. And neither would the priest begin with the same position to bless the pilgrims! Only this time, that Corpus Christi Sunday, did the priest take Jesus in the monstrance directly from the altar, right down to be right in front of Louis and me. It was the most epic sign of the Cross ever made over me. Indeed, we were expected. The Lord delivered on His promise to my heart. *I am here.*

I have returned to this prayer again and again in the months after this; it is one of those moments that fuels you again and again. God is good.

Louis

After attending the Eucharistic procession, I knew I had begun to change. I knew as well that that evening we would be going to the Marian procession. I felt thankful that we no longer had to worry about the mechanical aspects of having a power wheelchair that was fully charged. We still had to tackle the aspect of leaving Lourdes and having a charger, separate from Declan and his company in Lourdes. We accomplished that previous Friday by diligently coordinating with American Mobility to have a new charger shipped from the U.S.

to us in Lourdes. The catalyst behind that was Mary. Matthias and I found that to be interesting: her name was Mary! She was the one ensuring, on her own free time, that we would receive a charger in Lourdes, due to arrive to us Wednesday. That was a blessing in and of itself because we would be leaving Lourdes on that next Friday. So, we found that there was divine intervention once again, or shall we say angels, like Mary at American Mobility, that made sure we had the resources needed.

Matthias

Though greatly encouraged by Jesus' Eucharistic presence (and His special favor to us), I was still anxious for the miracle. Just like Louis's kidney stones, which came out last December on the third day of us going down to the water at the pool in Scottsdale, just like Joseph and Mary finding the child Jesus in the Temple on the third day searching for Him in Jerusalem, and just like Jesus resurrecting on the third day, so too Louis would rise and walk (I prayed) upon the third day of us going to the waters of Lourdes.

Simple enough, right? What was I to be worried about? It's not like we had anything else to do in Lourdes. However, I was worried, because doing anything that *I* plan to do is never straightforward with Louis. Not only are we in the disability time zone, but I have zero control over what Louis may want to do in any given moment. He's his own person, of course, but I also know that there's always *something* that can get Louis to change plans. I knew that directing Louis (and therefore both of us) to go down to the Grotto and anoint ourselves with the water on three different days would be like trying to herd cats.

Part of this conflict is my tunnel vision: if I have a plan, I zero in on it like nothing else exists (Groceries?

Who needs those?). I think I've grown in that regard, at least some. However, I also know that no matter what real needs we have or don't have, Louis can always find *something* that can suddenly take priority (especially something I really don't care about).

For instance, any time we pass by one of those little tourist/souvenir stores (there are hundreds in Lourdes), the odds Louis will stop to check it out (doesn't matter how many times we've already been there) are pretty high. If Louis goes inside, he's like a kid in a candy store.

Blessed be God, because Louis is the perfect person to teach me to let go of control! If I want to respect Louis's autonomy and free will, while at the same time fulfill a mission I believe we're both called to fulfill, I have to abandon myself to blind confidence in God.

It can also be tricky, because if Louis wants to do something, more likely than not, he'll need my help to do it. So, it's not like it may be with able-bodied friends, where, if they want to do something you're not too interested in, they have the ability to do it all themselves, and you can meet up later. Louis and I can sometimes have those split-off moments. But especially in a foreign country, if Louis wants to do anything that I don't particularly care for, I'll have to go with him anyway (if I want him to have the freedom to do it). It certainly pushed me, but I knew that these are some of those little sacrifices of love that Jesus asks us to make.

I'd be trying my best to fight it, but each day, I was so nervous that we wouldn't make it to the water. I would get anxious if we started walking by the shops (is that another precious hour that we might lose looking for gifts?). For me, nothing else mattered; we had to get to the water so that Louis could be healed. All the while, I was fighting to follow the lesson God had taught me with

Lannemezan and the frying of the powerchair charger: *It's not you, Matthias. It's Me.*

Another crucial aspect of healing is healing from sin. In the Gospels, Jesus' physical healings are always part and parcel with a spiritual, inner healing. He says to the paralytic, "Your sins are forgiven you," and then He tells him, "Rise, take up your mat, and go home." Ministers and lay leaders well versed in miraculous healings know that attachment to sin can block the path of healing.

Further, miraculous healings are never ends in themselves. They are *always* directed toward faith in Jesus Christ. As Jesus tells the Jewish authorities regarding the paralytic, "Which is easier? To say to the man, 'Rise, take up your mat, and go home?' or 'Your sins are forgiven you?' But so you may know that the Son of Man has authority to forgive sins, I say to you [the paralytic], rise, take up your mat, and go home." (see Mark 2:1-12)

So, confession would also be crucial before we completed the triad of three days' visits to the miraculous water of Lourdes. This regrettably helped increase my worry. *What if we* don't *get to confession and make it to the water for three days?* I originally envisioned Louis and I going to confession before we would start going to the water. However, the way it panned out, we ran out of time on the first day we wanted to go to the water. Louis was able to make confession, but there wasn't enough time for me to go. We went to the water, and we followed the Blessed Mother's instructions to St. Bernadette: "Drink the water and wash in it." I had brought some plastic cups, so I drew some water from the spigot and gave it to Louis to drink. Then I grabbed a cup, poured my portion, and gulped it. It was cool and refreshing, tapped directly from the spring. Next, I removed Louis's shoes. I applied some water to my fingers, then anointed Louis's feet, his hands, and his forehead. Louis then anointed my forehead, and I took the rest from the cup to pour it over my temples. It felt like a little re-baptism (so to speak).

I was very conscious of not doing a full-on foot washing, as Louis and I once had the custom of doing. I knew that if we crossed that boundary, it would disturb my interior peace.

The next day came. This time, instead of merely drawing water from the multiple spigots outside, we lined up for the baths. Before COVID, pilgrims could enter the baths and get fully immersed in the holy water. This has not been allowed since COVID. What they do now is a "water gesture". Louis and I were escorted to one of the rooms; the bath was right in front of us. Two sanctuary volunteers remained in the room with us and invited us to pray. They gave us some time for silent prayer. Next, they gave us cups to drink the water. Louis took a cup; I took a cup; we drank. After we'd drunk, they took a pitcher of the water and poured it out however we liked. I facilitated the pouring of the water on Louis's head and subsequently doused myself on the head as I had yesterday. It was very peaceful.

After this, we had plenty of time for me to go make my confession. At Lourdes, an entire building is set aside for pilgrims' confessions. Different slots of time are allocated for pilgrims of different languages. The English slot was open, with plenty of time to spare. I openly choose to share some of what I gained from the priest's counsel: "God chose the foolish to bring low those who think they are something in this world . . . None of it, our foolishness, or even our sin which tries to get in the way of God, none of it matters: all I care about is the love of God . . . You know, I lost my phone the other day, my umbrella today, but all I care about is the love of God."

It was exactly the confession I needed and at the time I needed it. I received the lesson: *My timing, Matthias, not your timing.* Of course, God is right: His timing was much better than what I was originally hoping for.

Finally, our third day to go to the water came. We didn't go to the baths directly again; we just went to the spigots outside like we had the first time we went to the water. The whole day leading up to this, I imagined every aspect of the personal care and wheeling around as our final times. Henceforth, I wouldn't have to get Louis out of the bed. I'll have learned the meaning of purposeful suffering in this season. Simon of Cyrene will be complete with his post helping Jesus carry the Cross. Such were my thoughts throughout the day.

This time at the water, I said Louis should wash my feet.

"Are you sure?"

I paused for a good moment. I sat down on the curb opposite the spigots for a good five minutes. I had a very strong impression from the Spirit: *You don't have to do this.*

But I did it anyway. And only moments into the foot washing, I knew I had made a mistake. Just like plugging that 120 Volt charger into a 240 Volt outlet, I had plugged a 120 Volt Matthias into a 240 Volt activity. I spoke with Louis about it, and he told me, as he's said time and time again, "Bro, that's why I ask. You need to tell me."

I still hoped for the miracle, in spite of my trying to grab it (as if doing the more intense, full-on foot washing would usher in God's miraculous intervention). However, I stood fast by Fr. JP's words, "If something is going to happen, and you need to do something, *it will be very obvious.*" So, I refused to try to summon a miracle and waited for something very obvious. It never came.

We attended the Marian procession that evening at dusk. This, in my mind, was the last opportunity for something very obvious to happen. Nothing happened. After the conclusion of the Rosary and procession, I told Louis I needed some time to pray. I spent about an hour in front of the mosaic of San Juan Diego and Our Lady of Guadalupe. My prayer was basically a drawn-out version of the following:

"What gives? You set me up for this!" and "Your will be done . . . but I really wanted it that way . . . Your will be done."

The message I received back was what was written on the mosaic. Our Lady's words to San Juan Diego were her words to me: "Am I not here, who am your mother? Do not fear the present illness, do not let your face be downcast." I did my best to take these to heart, but I needed the time to process.

In that time, Louis went to the late night 10:00 Mass and was unable to find me upon returning to the plaza. He met up with Francine and ended up waiting at the hotel while she went out to look for me. Well, I finally got up and started looking for Louis in the plaza, at the Grotto, up on the platform of the upper Basilica (I took the opportunity to take some night photos of the plaza), but to no avail.

I finally resolved to search at the hotel. On my way up the steep road from the sanctuary, a blinding pair of headlights greeted me: Francine in her Permobil. She stated that Louis was quite distressed at my absence and that I should get to the hotel as soon as possible. I thanked her, and I did.

As I was getting Louis ready for bed, he seemed to have recovered from the distress that Francine had described.

He told me, "You know, I really wanted to be healed for you."

"It's okay."

I was puzzled by this at first. *Why wouldn't you want it for yourself?* But a moment's reflection led me to this: Louis was at more peace with his disability than I was. I appreciated his words that night. I held on to no illusions that we somehow "didn't perform" or "messed up" so as to prevent a miracle. I knew that it just wasn't the will of God. As I had prayed multiple times leading up to the pilgrimage, "Lord, please grant full healing for Louis. But if such healing would diminish the amount of love that could be grown with his disability, please don't do it."

The following two weeks of our pilgrimage, I was certainly more sober. My affect was a bit flatter, and my previous anxiety for a miracle had mostly subsided. It was a calm that paved the way for greater graces than I could have expected. The next night, as I was caring for Louis, showed that to me front and center. I saw the face of God.

We were going about the night routine, and as I saw Louis there in the bed, completely dependent on my care, it occurred to me that many souls would greatly envy the opportunity to love that I have. If Louis had been healed, I wouldn't necessarily have the opportunity to love him in this way. As I looked upon him again, calm, though in some pain there on the bed, I saw the face of Jesus. That is, my heart was filled with Mary's love as she would take care of her baby Jesus.

My great sin, my great error, was like Moses' error again: striking with his staff one time too many. I allowed Louis to wash my feet and dry them, even though I knew it would be pushing my comfort limits AND I was clearly warned in the Spirit.

But the fact that I blundered at that moment and that Louis received no healing was highly, highly crucial for me. Why? Because it teaches me, like no other event or person can teach me, that I must not compromise anything because I think it will promote a miracle. *You are never called to compromise your integrity for the sake of some perceived good—even a great spiritual good.* I had made an idol out of my desire for Louis's physical healing. I needed to be healed of this misprioritization because it is at the root of many of my errors concerning boundaries and how I have allowed myself to be abused.

Did I really need a $17,000+ pilgrimage, traveling halfway across the world, and *messing up* at the climax of this trip to get this lesson through to me? I guess I did. If that's what I needed to learn this, then I bless God. I bless Him for His mercy and the generosity of many, many people who helped me receive this grace.

Now, I am free. I know in a way I couldn't have learned otherwise that there is no need to compromise my personal and psychological integrity for any goal, no matter how charitable such a goal may appear. That night, my heart was taken aback by how much of Jesus' love was flowing through me. For Louis there, he was depending on me like the child Jesus depended on His mother Mary and St. Joseph.

Truly, it is a great, great privilege to be able to show Louis this love. It is a privilege few are envious of on Earth, but I believe many are jealous of on the other side. This is a mystery that strengthens me like no other: when I care for Louis, I care for Jesus.

Louis

I think Matthias had such expectations of Lourdes, but some were unattainable because they weren't to be. The Blessed Mother and Jesus were there, though, because no matter what, Jesus could heal at any time and so could the Blessed Mother. This was difficult for Matthias at times. I think I was there for him as much as he was there for me.

When Matthias asked me to wash his feet, I agreed. I wasn't sure it was going to make the difference he wanted it to, but I was more than willing because I love him. I knew that we were there with Jesus and the Blessed Mother, so I left it up to them.

It's so interesting because Matthias wanted me to be healed in a physical sense, but a lot of internal healing was going on. I was still dealing with demons and doubts, but there was an internal healing. I have dealt a lot with demons and doubts throughout my life. However, after meeting Matthias, it has lessened. I still dealt with evil thoughts, but they too have lessened.

I think that is the gift of Lourdes. I didn't have a miraculous physical healing, not one that I know of, anyway. I met people like Francine, a lady from Switzerland who comes to Lourdes on an annual basis by train and has cerebral palsy and utilizes a Permobil wheelchair like I do. That was part of the healing at Lourdes. So, I know for certain that I had an internal healing. I just know and I am more equipped to handle the demons that have plagued me throughout my life from a young age. Knowing and accepting that there doesn't have to be a miraculous physical healing is key; you can also have just as miraculous an internal healing. I think that's what I had. That is the gift of Lourdes for me, the internal healing and acceptance of where I am on this earthly journey and the fact that I am a child of God.

I think it was significant for our time in Lourdes that Matthias and I thought of my earthly mother. Ann V. Fazio was devoted to the Blessed Mother, as devoted to the Blessed Mother as she was to her earthly children, even her stillborn child.

There are large clusters of votive candles that pilgrims can light just outside the Grotto to pray for loved ones and other intentions. As I carried the candle to honor my mother, there was a distinct feeling that I was recognizing my mother's own pilgrimage. Some in the family say that she made it to Lourdes. I'm not certain but my Uncle Marion said she had.

One thing I do know, whether she made it to Lourdes or Fatima (because I know she did make it to Fatima), those are earthly places of memorial, of sightings of the Blessed Mother. I know for certain that Mom is with the Blessed Mother on the other side of the veil. It brings one to think: *How important is it to make it to holy places? Or, Is it more important to make it to the other side of the veil?*

I think the Bible tells us that it is more important to make it to the other side of the veil than it is to make it to these earthly holy places. Not to diminish their importance on this side of the veil, but as I write this portion of the book, that revelation is coming to me. It's more about making it to the other side. Whether you're a religious or a lay person, I think that should be our goal. These are markers of the divine life. They are not the true reality of the divine life. I think we look for that in hope, but our hope should not be placed entirely on these religious sites. Our hope should be more internal, to ensure that we achieve what Jesus and God want us to hopefully achieve, and that is our eternal life.

Matthias

When I wasn't so absorbed with my own worries or expectations, I really enjoyed the Marian processions. They started at the Grotto with a large statue of the Blessed

Mother (crowned as Queen) wheeled ahead of the crowd to wind its way around the avenue and then back to the front of the main basilica in the massive plaza. The Rosary is prayed during the procession. Speakers line the whole procession path, so we could always hear the voice of the prayer leader. Priests led the opening and closing prayers and Our Fathers in Latin. The intervening Hail Marys (all 53 of them) were recited by various pilgrims who prayed the first half of the prayer in their own tongue, followed by the crowd reciting the second half.

This really touched me. As a linguist, I enjoyed the variety. As a Catholic, I enjoyed this expression of the universality of the Church. There were different languages depending on who was there for each day, but in all I counted no fewer than 15 languages from all the processions we attended: French, English, Spanish, Italian, Polish, Vietnamese, German, Dutch, Portuguese, Tagalog, Arabic, Japanese, one or two I can't recall (Flemish and/or Irish Gaelic?), and at least two I could not identify.

This is what true world unity looks like. Here were all these different peoples, cultures, and languages, all here because we love the same Mother and her Divine Son. The mystery of Mary's coronation as Queen of Heaven and Earth is something I can grasp (to some extent) intellectually, but here it entered my heart in a new way, surrounded by thousands honoring her Queenship with me. We were with our Mother. We all love her and she loves all of us. I agree with Louis: these places are markers for the divine life. This was a foretaste of Heaven.

Louis

Our final full day in Lourdes happened to be D-Day, June 6, 2024. That was the 80th anniversary of when our

American troops stormed the beaches at Normandy for our freedom against our foes of Nazism and oppression. This is a time to invoke the prayer and the spirit of the Blessed Mother to save us from current political leaders who seem to wish to turn the clock back; we must look ahead. We must remember those who fought at D-Day and what their purpose was and what they sacrificed for this nation. Matthias and I came to Lourdes for my freedom from the chair, but these veterans paid for our freedom and are now in chairs.

My hope is that whether you make it to Lourdes or not, healing can take place. I think we put so much expectation in holy places that we overlook the healing that has already transformed us. As Jane Lacovara said to me and Matthias upon our denial in going with the Order of Malta, "Healing can also take place in just filling out the application."

Not to say that going to Lourdes is a waste of time. No. That isn't the case either, but I think what I have learned is healing comes from the mindset of the person. I am coming to believe that too often we wish and hope for external force. God made us, gave us free will, and the ability to have intellect. Not all have intellect due to circumstances beyond themselves. But they have a type of intellect, they have an innocence of intellect. I think what Lourdes attempts to show us is the innocence of intellect. Are we willing to turn our minds off to allow our faith to heal us? Or, must we keep our minds on because we lack trust?

There are days when I definitely keep my mind on because of my lack of trust. I would be a liar if I were to say, "Oh, upon my return from Lourdes, I totally trust." No, in my case that is not the case. In my case, I have a better propensity to trust in my Heavenly Father and my Blessed Mother.

The goal for all humanity, whether you are the president of the United States or a person with a disability who is an average citizen, is the trust in your Maker must be childlike. If I and my fellow humanity can achieve this, I think that is healing. I wish that for all, including myself.

london and the return voyage

june 7 – june 15

D ay 24 of our pilgrimage began on the Feast of the Sacred Heart of Jesus. This day was the day that we would leave Lourdes and travel back to Toulouse to catch our British Airways flight back to London.

For me, this was a time to pinch myself. Matthias and I traveled with greater confidence this time. We boarded the train at the Lourdes station and took it to Toulouse (Gare Matabiau), this time not so sheepishly, this time with some minimal experience under our belts. The trip was uneventful, which I was grateful for.

We boarded British Airways and saw our favorite captain, Captain IK, who remembered us and said, "Oh Louis and Matthias! So good to see you!"

We were glad to see him as well. We flew from Toulouse to London Heathrow where we again had to take our famous configuration of various pieces of luggage and various disability related items ("the luggage behemoth") onto a bus, in search of our hotel. We arrived in London later in the evening.

Matthias
We deplaned without much issue, but . . .

We traveled across multiple terminals to get to Terminal 2 where the Hilton Garden Inn was supposed to be. Louis was hungry. We arrived. Turns out, there's more than one Hilton Garden Inn London Heathrow Airport. The Hilton Garden Inn we had booked was at Terminal 4. We would definitely miss the hotel's dinner hours so we turned around. We tried to access the Piccadilly Line of the Tube (London's subway system), but the staff at the stop advised us to take the bus because Hatton Cross, our required stop, has no lifts. Off we went across the airport again.

The bus was packed. The driver, a young, short-haired Asian woman whose accent revealed she was not a native of London, calmly informed us (as we tried to cram our luggage and Louis and me into said bus) we couldn't travel on the bus. "Too big, too much a safety hazard."

I told her that we didn't have a choice; the Tube told us to come here. She insisted, and fellow passengers were growing impatient. "That's not just a wheelchair, that's a trolley!" one yelled. They didn't understand that this was medical equipment we couldn't travel without.

The driver called her supervisor and shut the bus down while one kind gentleman (and several others as their position on the bus enabled them) helped us break down the luggage "cart" to satisfy the driver.

We eventually took off, and she did not charge us the fare. I was very grateful that she had kept her composure and tried to thank her as profusely as I could. Other passengers who deboarded at Hatton Cross were kind enough to help manage the luggage while I put it all back together. Some of the folks apologized on behalf of the impatient and rude people on the bus who had been clamoring for us to get off.

It was funny: two times our Guardian Angels gave us hints to go to Terminal 4 instead of 2. There was one gentleman who initially pointed us to Terminal 4, and after we had made up our minds based on other information to go to Terminal 2, Louis started going toward the T4 train until I stopped him. I blessed God that we finally made it to our hotel at Terminal 4 safe and sound.

We ordered Chinese through Uber Eats.

Louis

When we finally arrived at the correct Hilton Garden Inn, I was impressed with our hotel room. It actually had a powered door. I've stayed at a lot of hotels, and none of the Hilton Garden Inns in the Continental US have powered doors for guest rooms, or any other brand of hotel that I know of. The other thing was that the hotel room was very spacious. So, our time in London started out very well (minus the few things that Matthias spoke of). By now, we were used to those types of hiccups, and it was just part of the adventure.

We decided to tour around the city of London going downtown. I was very impressed with London. The people were very nice. We crossed paths with someone wearing an Orlando hat, which made for a pleasant conversation.

I enjoyed rolling through the city and the different neighborhoods. I had to pinch myself a few times again because, frankly, I couldn't believe I was rolling through London! I wondered if maybe Winston Churchill had walked—which I'm sure he had—on these same streets.

Or, if the citizens of London during World War II scampered for the underground as the German *Blitzkrieg* bombs fell. I immediately thought of the men and women who'd fought with us on those streets. I think that was because Matthias and I had been on the *Queen Mary 2* with all those D-Day veterans and some British citizens.

It just showed me how we are all interconnected, no matter what continent you're on.

Matthias

Louis had been talking about seeing Big Ben and Buckingham Palace for *months* before we even scheduled everything for the trip to Lourdes. However, our one full day in London, that Saturday, it didn't look like we were going to have much time to visit these places between waking up late (we slept in after the previous night's shenanigans) and going to the Saturday Vigil Mass at Westminster Cathedral (not to be confused with Westminster Abbey, which is Anglican). We finally found our way to the Piccadilly Line to get to downtown London and attend Mass. It was a beautiful liturgy, and the church's magnificent Neo-Byzantine architecture only helped accentuate that.

Louis

When we went to the Westminster Cathedral, I was in awe. I don't look at the same things Matthias does. The first thing I usually look for is a bookstore. I'm not as much into the paintings quite honestly, if they're from this era or that era, or if they're Byzantine or Roman Catholic. It doesn't really matter to me. I do look at the architecture, but nine times out of 10, unless it's the Blessed Mother or Jesus, I ask Matthias to read the placard because I can't read it, even with my glasses on. My ophthalmologist, Dr. Louis, says cataracts are on the way. So, for me, I am grateful that Matthias is there when I exclaim, "Can you read that? I can't see it," and he dutifully does.

The Cathedral was just magnificent though. I was so honored to be there for the Vigil Mass. I was praising Jesus in the Cathedral, in one of the greatest cities of the world, London England. What more can you ask for? I was just so thankful that we did the GoFundMe.

With all that in my memory, I realized that this whole experience was a gift, over and over again. I thank all who contributed to our GoFundMe (or donated directly to us). It was also a gift to go to London. It was a gift to be with those veterans who fought so selflessly and now, the individuals who helped make our trip and pilgrimage possible, came to the forefront of my mind when I was in the Cathedral. I really held onto the uniqueness of this pilgrimage. The uniqueness was due to the fact that it was for myself and Matthias, who, in many respects, I am a mentor to.

After Mass, we went a few blocks east and had a lovely dinner at The Ivy. Many have said that the food isn't as good in England. I didn't find that to be the case; I found it to have a bit of its own pizzazz, if you will.

Matthias

Per the recommendation of British pilgrims we had met in Lourdes, we considered taking the newer, more accessible Elizabeth line all the way back to our hotel, instead of the Piccadilly Line. It was getting late; we did not want to be late *at all* for our transfer to Southampton the next day to board the *Queen Mary 2* again.

I pulled up the Elizabeth Line on Google Maps. However, it was not nearly as close to us at The Ivy as the Piccadilly Line was. However, the walking path that Maps chartered for us suggested some interesting turns.

"Well well well," I said. "Would you look at that?"

Louis said, "Look at what?"

I feigned yawning, "It just looks like, if we want to take the Elizabeth Line, we have to walk through Buckingham Palace."

Louis was enthralled. "Let's go!"

So, we did. It was pretty sweet.

We didn't get to see Big Ben (but there was a cute "Little Ben" near Westminster Cathedral). So often, when Louis wants to add things to the agenda that I don't necessarily consider essential, I am vulnerable to getting frustrated or stressed out, trying to accommodate Louis's whim. This time, however, I was very grateful to be able to help fulfill Louis's desire to see the great Buckingham Palace. He had calmly and quietly accepted that it was probably not in the cards for us, but it now suddenly became possible.

Curiously, we also passed by a juvenile Tyrannosaurus. I was delighted and made sure to send a photo to my father. Of the many things he has passed down to me, a great love for dinosaurs is one.

Louis

I was delighted to see Buckingham Palace. The flag was up, indicating that the King was in residence. I decided not to see if he would answer the door. After taking pictures at the Palace gates, we walked and rolled through Green Park on our way to the Elizabeth Line. We got to see the small memorial honoring Princess Diana in the park.

The next day, it was time to board the *Queen Mary 2* for our westbound voyage. Fr. John Shea SJ from Fordham University joined us on our way back, and we went to confession. We also attended the daily Masses.

We had an emergency on the ship, the first night of the voyage, where Captain Hashmi came over the PA system at 3 a.m. I thought, *Wow, this must be important.* Sure enough, it was. He explained to us that they were going to have to turn a bit off course so that the British Coast Guard could evacuate one of our fellow passengers, who was now referred to as a "patient", due to severe medical emergency. We were instructed not to go out of our staterooms. I had no plan to do so. I had my portable ventilator mask on. Matthias and I did not speak, but I am certain we both realized the importance and urgency of this situation.

The only person whom we knew from the eastbound voyage who remained with us was Ethel, our stewardess from South Africa. Matthias and I had gotten Ethel holy water from Lourdes. She was very appreciative of our thoughtfulness. We were glad to see a familiar face.

We really did not interact with other passengers as much as we did on the eastbound voyage. We did not dance, so no one knew of our dance. For me, that was OK. I had a sense that I wanted to be more reclusive.

Matthias and I took time to work on the book. We also spent more time apart, which I think we both needed. I spent more time in the library and the bookshop, which I enjoyed immensely. Those are two of my addictions that I'm proud of. They don't *usually* get me into any trouble.

On the eastbound voyage we had the veterans of D-Day. On the westbound voyage, we had *Tiano*. *Tiano* was a duo of men who played the piano and sang tenor. They were fantastic to listen to and lots of fun. For two of our nights, Shimi Goodman (tenor) and Chris Hamilton (piano) showed their skills individually to the audience. But then, on the last night of the voyage, it came to a crescendo, if you will, where they came together as *Tiano*. And, according to their bio, they were referred to as "the love child of Liberace and Pavarotti" (sorry, Scott Thorson). Considering I have same-sex attraction (and literally sat on Liberace's lap at the age of nine), I was like, *Yeah, I could see that. I wonder if they're a couple.* I think I even mentioned it to Matthias, who's become quite more accustomed to my inquisitiveness in relation to things of this nature.

Matthias

I saw Shimi Goodman's individual performance as well as the *Tiano* finale with Chris Hamilton. I can't deny I was wondering the same things Louis was. The energy was there.

Louis insisted on getting photos with the dynamic duo, and they were very warm and welcoming to us both. Louis was disappointed that they don't play in the United States (or at least not very often) because of the expenses incurred for foreign musicians; neither are U.S. citizens. Nonetheless, Louis was sure to buy several CDs.

In the middle of our westward crossing, I noticed an unusual rumbling below our cabins. Unlike our first crossing, we were now toward the aft (back) of the ship, which put us closer to the motors and propellors. I could even feel the rumbling a little bit. I began going through a mental checklist of what to do if things got extreme. I mentally confirmed that I remembered the location of the life vests, and thought about the procedure I would use to wake Louis and get him into his chair in case we needed to get to the lifeboats. I assumed Louis's chair would get left behind, and fellow passengers and/or crew would have to hoist Louis into a lifeboat. It probably wasn't *too* consequential. I soon fell back to sleep.

Louis

It *was* consequential. This time, it was the ship itself, due to some technological issues. At 8 a.m., alarms sounded on the bridge, and our Captain came on the PA system. This was highly unusual, so I knew right away that we were going to hear of something that was of vital importance to all. Captain Hashmi let us know that the ship had to be stopped overnight due to these alarms and that he wasn't quite certain how long this would delay our arrival into New York, and he would let us know later that afternoon.

Around noon, he made an announcement that we would be four hours delayed into the port of Brooklyn. This was problematic for those who were catching planes or some type of transportation to wherever their homes were.

For Matthias and me, it didn't much matter because Brooklyn was our next stop. To us, it was actually a bonus because instead of coming into Brooklyn port at the wee hours of the morning under the cover of darkness, we came into the port during the early hours of the morning under the bright sunlight, and we could see in the distance the Statue of Liberty, the Verrazzano Narrows Bridge, Ellis Island, and the Manhattan skyline. That was absolutely spectacular.

We had gotten ready that morning; we needed to be out of our stateroom by 9 a.m. preparing to disembark.

It was beautiful. We had breakfast in the Britannia, which I became fond of. Matthias wasn't so much so. He was more into the buffet because whether he admits it or not, he likes to pack it away when he can. For now, Matthias is skinny, but I always tell him, "Beware my Brother, the metabolism will slow down, and you won't be so skinny anymore."

new york, south carolina, texas— what a state of affairs!

June 16 – July 7

Where's the hotel?

The *Queen Mary 2* arrived at the Brooklyn Cruise Terminal. For those who have not been on cruise ships, when you arrive on a ship, you don't immediately get off. There is a procedure that one must follow in order to have orderly disembarkation. I'm certain that y'all are wondering if everyone was orderly. If you said that they were and everyone followed directions, you would be incorrect. For those of us that *do* follow directions, it delays the disembarkation process.

Almost immediately, when the first color was called (it's done by color groups, in our ship's case), the Purser's Office came over the PA to let us know that people weren't so good about following directions and got off the ship before their color was called and urged all of us to remain on the ship in the ship's lounges so that it could be done orderly.

You see, if you entered the cruise terminal, that's where you would have to wait with no seating, and it certainly wasn't as comfortable. So, all in all, after waiting for those individuals and their impatience which clogged up the process, no matter what country they came from, we were then able to disembark with ease.

Matthias

It's a wonderful feeling being surrounded by familiar kinds of strangers again. After several weeks of sailing, being in France and England, the sounds of brusque Brooklyn accents and Latin American Spanish were very comforting. We were back in our home country.

It was about 1:30 p.m. when we were ready to arrange our ground transportation from the cruise terminal to our hotel. I figured I was a pro at this by now. All we had to do was hail two separate Uber WAVs, one for Louis and the greater part of the luggage, and another one for me, the sit-to-stand, and the shower chair. Simple enough. I hailed one from Louis's phone and another from my phone. Keep in mind: there are hundreds of other passengers also hailing Ubers, Lyfts, and waiting for taxis.

Louis's Uber WAV arrived first. I was confused as to why the driver sent us a text in Georgian characters (not the American state, mind you, the beautiful Georgian script looks like this: მამა ჩვენო, რომელი ხარ ცათა შინა. We soon learned he was from Georgia—the country. He was polite and had no trouble loading Louis with nine pieces of luggage. And off they went.

My driver came about 10 minutes later. He was a kind man from Bangladesh. We had an adventure fitting the sit-to-stand and shower chair into his vehicle, but he didn't mind. I texted Louis to let him know that we were about 10 minutes behind them; I then called the hotel to ask if they could send someone to help unload Louis's Uber upon their arrival without me.

After our pleasant conversation, my Bangladeshi driver dropped me off at 300 Schermerhorn Street and assisted me unloading the medical equipment. We said goodbye, and I pushed the sit-to-stand and shower chair (a skeletal version of the luggage behemoth) into the hotel lobby. But Louis—and the other 9 pieces of luggage—were nowhere to be found.

I texted him. "Arrived! Still in traffic?"

He texted back, "Yeah, I'll explain when I get there. I'm glad you're there."

Louis

One would think that if Matthias was 10 minutes behind me, that I would be the first to arrive at our hotel, the Holiday Inn Brooklyn Downtown. That was not to be, as you can see from the text. My driver was utilizing Google Maps which told him that there was some type of work or construction ahead. And for some reason, he could not figure out how to get around that particular work or construction. So, what ensued could only happen, in many cases, to me because, as I explain this, if you know me, you will say, "Yes, that would only happen to Louis."

Here's what happened. My Georgian driver (not from *y'all* country) proceeded to tell me that he could go no further. We were on a street in New York City, somewhere between Schermerhorn and the cruise terminal. To my right, there was a set of rowhouses. I began to exclaim, in very simple English, "Where hotel?" And then my Georgian driver said, "You must get out." And I was like, "Excuse me?" He said, "You must get out."

So, I rolled down the ramp once he put it down in the rear and said to a guy sitting on the balcony of his rowhouse, "Hey Bro, can you help us?" And he was like, "Yeah." I said, "The driver doesn't know how to get to Schermerhorn Street around construction." He then wanted me to take the luggage out of the car. I exclaimed, "Where hotel?" even more vigorously and explained we weren't taking any luggage anywhere—except to Schermerhorn Street!

Now we had my Georgian driver talking up to the man sitting on the balcony of his rowhouse. Finally, the man sitting on his rowhouse balcony explained to the driver how to get around the construction. I, of course, had no idea where I was, not being from New York City, let alone being from Brooklyn. My only phrase that I kept repeating at opportune times was, "Where hotel?"

Finally, thanks to the man sitting on the balcony of his rowhouse, we made it to the Holiday Day Inn Brooklyn Downtown.

When we arrived, Matthias of course was like, "Where were you?"

"I'll explain it to you once we check in. It will be too complicated to explain on the fly." I then said to myself, *only in New York City,* and was hopeful that the rest of the trip in New York would not be so eventful—at least from a transportation perspective.

We got settled into our Brooklyn hotel and Matthias called Cella and Mike to let them know, along with Fr. Gerasimos and his mother Stella, that we had arrived. However, none were the wiser about the "where hotel?" adventures. We figured we would keep that for face-to-face audiences.

Cella and Mike did suggest that we go and check out the New York subway system to see if we could get around. In true Matthias-and-Louis fashion, we already experienced some of New York (Brooklyn, anyway) because we went out and got pizza, which meant we had to take the subway to get there. So, on the first night, we realized that yes, we could get anywhere we needed to, if we paid attention. We also got set up with a transit pass for me and a regular pass. Mine was discounted, thank you to the city of New York, and I paid for regular fare for Matthias's. So, it certainly helped us.

The pizza was good; it was Little Italy. I was grateful to eat. I thought of all the people who don't have the ability to have food, and I was thankful. I was also thankful for my Georgian driver in getting me to connect with Matthias, but I don't think any time soon I'll forget my experience of "Where hotel?"

Settling in for the evening, we prepared to get up for Mass the next Sunday morning at St. Patrick's Cathedral, which was a beautiful church. I pinched myself once again. I was grateful to be there, and I was grateful as well to have Matthias. I thanked God and the Blessed Mother for our trip and the fact that he was my brother.

I thought back to my two biological brothers, who are now, for all intents and purposes, not connected, in an operational sense, if you will. I pray for them daily because Jesus says pray for your enemies (Matthew 5:43-48, Luke 6:27, 28, 32-36). On this pilgrimage it became very clear to me through my brother Edward's actions and statements that he would be my enemy and that I must pray for him. That was the position he was taking. I can't speak for my other brother so succinctly and exactly because I have tried to reach out to him as well, with no response. They have made their choice. And I was so thankful that I had Matthias as my gift from God.

At the Cathedral, we had to utilize the restroom facilities which meant Matthias and I had to experience whether or not the restrooms were an afterthought or truly accessible. Unfortunately, the door was so narrow that I could barely get in. Thank God Matthias is skinny! I don't know what we're going to do once he hits middle age and his metabolism slows, because we definitely won't fit in the St. Patrick's Cathedral bathroom in New York!

"I'm gonna write the Pope. He needs to make a papal encyclical that mandates ALL churches around the world be accessible. In the US and the UK, there are laws, but there aren't the same protections in other places." I think this could be a fantastic way of inclusion from a social justice perspective. Wouldn't it be amazing, wouldn't it be a gift from the Blessed Mother, from Jesus, if the Pope, whether that is Pope Francis or any successor, had the forethought to consider making things accessible, Churchwide and globally, even in places that don't have those protections? Would it not be a beginning to include and be inclusive to all? All of us, if we are graced and blessed to live with purposeful suffering, would benefit from such an action by our Pope.

Matthias and I anxiously awaited our reunion with our newfound friends, Fr. Gerasimos and his mother, Stella. We had so much fun listening to Stella tell Fr. Gerasimos that she couldn't eat such and such and then place it on his plate. He was a dutiful son, the Father was, and he ate what his mother placed on his plate.

I learned from Stella that her other son was not as gracious with her, nor as caring. So, it reminded me of my brothers versus Matthias. We had an enjoyable dinner at a Greek restaurant. We ended up not going too far from our hotel so we didn't have to take the subway.

Fr. Gerasimos was a gracious host along with his mom, who absolutely insisted that we eat whatever we wanted and as much as we wanted. I felt so cared for by their kindness.

Stella told us how important it was that we had each other and to remain in touch with each other even as Matthias goes into the Dominican Order and the priesthood. I reflected upon that, and I know that we will do so because we truly are brothers now, in the truest sense of the word. I think we're closer than you can be biologically in some respects. That has been proven to me by my biological brothers. So, I pray that I am correct in this assertion.

I think individuals such as Stella, who have years of wisdom, know the importance of family, friendship, and the concept of being one's brother. Again, it goes back to the subtitle of the book: *My Brother's Keeper.* For Matthias and me, this time with Stella and Fr. Gerasimos brought a sense of the interconnectivity of the title of my book and the folks that God was placing before me.

Interestingly for me, there are many challenges with the relationship that Matthias and I have, not due to our intimacy or our love for another as brothers, but from our paths and how those paths can stay connected. As Matthias will tell you, I have expressed on more than one occasion our need to stay together, even if we are thousands of miles apart. While we are together, it is important for us to embrace that togetherness. As Matthias does for me, I would do for him. Whether that was cleaning him from head to toe or whatever he needed. I think he's coming to accept that about our relationship. It's beyond just being friends; at the core we were always family; we just didn't know each other. Because we belong to God.

Matthias

I was eager for Stella and Fr. Gerasimos's company again (not to mention the great food at Underhill Café we would be enjoying with them). They were people of deep faith with whom we had the privilege of sharing portions of our pilgrimage, before and after Lourdes. They are the only people (minus Ethel, and our delightful servers Judgeman and Agus aboard the *Queen Mary 2*) who had such a role for us. I knew being with them again after Lourdes was important for me.

I'm sure this was to no one's surprise, but there were at least a few stories that Stella told again, as if she had never told them before. When Fr. Gerasimos pointed this out to her, she acknowledged it, and proceeded as if she still hadn't told it before. Interestingly enough, the main story she did tell again was about the very generous man who became paralyzed. The message hit home once again: God puts some of us in positions of great vulnerability so that others, moved to help them in their need, are moved to love. This time, I was much more sober in my attitude toward healing and Louis's continuing disability. The very lesson of that story (repeated in detail, in case we missed anything) I could accept and receive with a larger heart than before.

I also found myself accepting and receiving their hospitality with a larger stomach than before. Fr. Gerasimos said at the beginning, "I'm a practical guy. If you need seven plates of food, I don't mind, eat seven plates of food. But don't push yourself, you know?" Well, toward the end, I said, "I'm at my limit." His response was quick: "Oh, you can finish it off." He was right. I'm glad our hotel was over a mile away to walk some of it off. It was *good*.

I couldn't help but reflect, as I know Louis did, on the parallels between Fr. Gerasimos pushing his mother in her walker and of myself walking alongside Louis in his powerchair. Our female inverse counterparts, Bethany and Gwen, were the first pair whom I met who I could seriously compare ourselves, in terms of a caregiving dynamic. Having first met them, the loneliness of being a caregiver becomes a little less lonely because you know that there are others out there, just as able-bodied and capable as you, but who are willing to make the sacrifices for others who are less so.

No matter the food, and no matter how many times the stories (I'm sure I've repeated a few myself), I was deeply grateful for Fr. Gerasimos and Stella's company. Their love and their commitment to the Lord are a quiet, beautiful witness to the love of God; they are a little icon of the Holy Trinity.

Louis

After leaving Fr. Gerasimos and his mother Stella, I felt profoundly grateful that we met people on our journey who understood how important faith was. It was very important to me that Matthias received support because I knew that he was sad. I knew that he thought about me not being healed. I thought about this as well in the coming days. *Did I do something wrong? Or did I do something that was inauthentic, thus not creating the environment for physical healing? Considering I struggle with demons on a regular basis, did the demons that I struggle with preclude me from a complete healing?*

I had to remember that it's about, at least from what I know, self-surrendering. So, again, I thought about our Dominican chastity prayers that we say regularly. The 14th Hail Mary accompanies a prayer for the grace of self-surrender, and I had to self-surrender.

I think the idea of self-surrendering is a very common theme in these last few months. If you are willing to self-surrender, you gain peace. This was another aspect of our relationship with Fr. Gerasimos and his mother, Stella: the peace of self-surrender.

Monday came, and we got to see Cella and Mike. I was so looking forward to this because I enjoy both Cella and Mike like I do the rest of the Mahoney brothers.

We enjoyed the start of our time together by going to Ellis Island and the Statue of Liberty. This was great because we could see where some of our distant relatives entered the United States. For me, it was my grandfather Vujevich, whom we couldn't find in the records. But my guess is that he arrived somewhere around 1916 when he was about 19 years old, as the story goes. He returned to Yugoslavia some time thereafter and brought my grandmother to the U.S.; the assumption was through Ellis Island.

My father's parents were born here, so my great-grand parents on my father's side were the ones that immigrated. And as the story goes, they changed the name from De Fazio to Fazio, upon arrival.

It was interesting to attempt to find the relatives of the past that we were connected to. Again, we're all connected through Jesus, but this human connection I think is important for all of us. Where did we come from as far as our earthly journey is concerned?

We then went to the Statue of Liberty. Matthias and I saw this from the Hudson River on the *Queen Mary 2*. It was a fantastic sight to behold. I also thought about, *Isn't it interesting? We just came from France, and now we're looking at a statue, Lady Liberty, that the French gave to America.* And we did this in the 21st century; the French gave the Statue of Liberty to America in 1886.

When I looked up at the Statue from my vantage point, I looked from the lens of a person who lived and suffered with a disability. The French gave us that statue as a gift of freedom. As I saw Lady Liberty up close (we couldn't go into the statue because we didn't get tickets in time), it reminded me of what it means to be a citizen of the United States of America, and also what type of role we play for other countries. It reminded me of when we celebrated the 80th year of our veterans storming the beaches of Normandy in France to save the French from Nazi Germany and further occupation.

Freedom. What does it mean? What does it say? How do we express it?

The next day we experienced freedom in a different way at the 9/11 Memorial & Museum. As an American with a disability, what did 9/11 mean to me? I worked that day, heading to work on the Florida Turnpike, heading southbound, when I heard over the radio that there was an attack on the World Trade Center, the Twin Towers. The first one had been hit by an airplane; it was thought to be an accident. The second plane, we knew as a collective nation and worldwide, this was an act of terror; this was an act of war.

When you enter the museum, you are entering a piece of history, in my case, that was a lived piece of history. In Matthias's case, he only knows of the 9/11 attack from secondhand accounts. You knew where you were the day the World Trade Center towers came down in a ball of flame. You know what you felt and what you saw. I knew that I was walking (or rolling, in my case) on hallowed ground. I knew that we won't forget. I knew as well of a woman who had a disability and was carried by two strangers down from the 68th floor, chronicled in the book written by Michael Benfante: *Reluctant Hero: A 9/11 Survivor Speaks Out About That Unthinkable Day, What He's Learned, How He's Struggled, and What No One Should Ever Forget.*

We met Mel, a docent at the museum. He was on his way to work on Tuesday, September 11th, 2001. He got off the No. 1 subway beneath the World Trade Center. He called his wife, and his wife said, "Don't go up the elevator." Everyone was running down yelling, "There's been a fire, there's been a fire."

That fire was due to the plane hitting the North Tower only 30 minutes prior. She urged her husband to leave, and he did so through the Survivor's Staircase. There, from the subway platform, people could escape to the north side of the plaza. This staircase was moved to the museum. The damage on the staircase was not caused by the 9/11 attack, but from the movement of the staircase from its original location.

The 9/11 Museum allowed me to remember the meaning of our country. There are many who want to see us fail as an experiment of freedom. There are many who want to restrict our freedoms. There are many who want the United States as a whole to fail. But it also reminded me that there are many who want us to succeed. It is up to us and our fellow humanity to cry out for freedom, cry out for justice, and cry out to God so that we can transcend enemies of humanity.

Matthias

Fr. Gerasimos gave me a call while we were underground in the 9/11 Museum. He fervently wanted to remind me about the recent film that had come out in anticipation of the Catholic Eucharistic Congress, *Jesus' Thirst: the Miracle of the Eucharist*. He apologized for interrupting our museum experience, but he also said something that stuck with me: ". . . Visiting the museum is like a pilgrimage of its own."

I think he's quite right. I have heard that whether or not you remember 9/11 is the distinguishing line between Millennials and Gen Z. I'm at the very edge of that line. I was only one and a half when it happened; I have no recollection. So, I knew, that as one unmarked by the memory of the tragedy, I had to absorb every moment in that museum as best I could. I let my heart take in as much of the sorrow and suffering that occurred on that day and the following days as I could. That way I could join it to Jesus' suffering and offer my presence there as a prayer.

I was especially keen to see material about Fr. Mychal Judge, numbered the first victim from the attacks. He was the legendary Franciscan friar/chaplain of the Fire Department of New York. After tireless years serving AIDS victims, the FDNY, and parishes around New York, he gave the final testament of his life going right into the wreckage to offer spiritual help.

I hope, when the day comes (Lord willing) I am ordained a priest and sent into ministry, that I can emulate his courage and tireless devotion to God's people. His example, like that of Fr. Emil Kapaun, who died in a North Korean POW camp, will forever remain engraved on my soul.

Later we got dinner with Cella and Mike at Parm, a nice Italian restaurant nearby. We had brought our complimentary bottle of champagne from the ship to share. After our perfectly portioned, hearty pasta bowls, the waiter was kind enough to look the other way and provide us champagne flutes to enjoy our libation on our final night all together.

The next day, we would fly to South Carolina.

Originally, during our several hours' layover at Chicago Midway, Louis and I agreed to split up for a while: he would do some perusing around the shops, and I would go find the chapel. I finally did find it, and to my delight, it was established by a Catholic priest a few decades ago, and as such, there was a small tabernacle, with a red sanctuary lamp (= candle) lit above it. This meant that Jesus, in the consecrated host, under the veil of bread was present. Jesus was here!

I took a little more time to pray alone with Jesus, then ran to get Louis. This was too good of an opportunity. "Louis!" I finally shouted upon seeing him. "They have

Jesus in the chapel!" There was only a little more time before boarding, so we had to get a move on.

Louis

We did have some prayer time together which strengthened our pilgrimage even more before it was time to board our flight to Myrtle Beach; Little River was close at hand.

We got to Myrtle Beach Airport and the transportation we had arranged picked us up. She was such a nice person. We attempted to get a rental car, but there was nothing available. She told us to give a call in the morning to see if a rental car could become available. I prayed to Jesus for a way to get a car so that Matthias and I could go to Aunt Betty's and at least have dinner with her at home, with my second cousin, Ike and his girlfriend, Alyson.

Jesus answered my prayer, and by the end of that day, we had a van. It was a rear-entry vehicle. I loved that van! It was nothing to write home about for most people, but it was everything for me.

Myrtle Beach and Little River were our oyster. We had to go to the local Home Depot to get some wood planks so that I could get into Aunt Betty's home. My cousin Ike was there to help us with the planks. After a terrific dinner together, we reminisced and Aunt Betty showed Matthias pictures of my mother and pictures of my childhood, when little Lou, as I was commonly called back then, was five. How time flies!

Aunt Betty was not an aunt by blood; my Uncle Steve was her second husband. Carl was her first, I do believe, who was quite ill, and she took care of him dutifully. My Aunt Betty was someone I wanted to pay respects to while she was living; she had just turned 91 the week before we arrived. I think it's important for us to remember, at least in our American culture, don't wait until the person passes; tell them you love them while they're still here and can hear the words and the joy that love brings.

Matthias

Even though Aunt Betty, Alyson, Ike, and Louis made for a much smaller party than that of his extended relatives in Pennsylvania, you could feel the difference in the air. With Louis's Uncle Marion, Aunt Barbara, and cousins Mark, Chrissy, Ann, and John, you could feel the tension; there was warmth, but there was a hesitancy about them (or at least enough of them) because of their loyalty to Ed and Frank. They had not stood up for Louis when Ed maligned him and disenfranchised him from what their parents had intended to leave for him. And we all knew it.

Here, in the smaller, humbler room with Aunt Betty, Ike, and Alyson, the love was almost palpable. We didn't even plan on seeing Ike; apparently, he and Alyson had completely independently planned to see Aunt Betty in the same time frame we did. That was the one possible night, before they took off again for Cleveland, Ohio, that we would have been able to see them. And we did. That's Divine Providence. This was true family love. We all knew that Aunt Betty had stood up for Louis. She didn't care about the cost to her personally for doing so. There was no hesitancy or tension; it was free.

This was the first time I got to see what I had only caught snatches of from Louis's phone conversations with her or saw memories of his meeting with his Aunt Carole. It was the first time I saw Louis with family, his own family, in the true way family is supposed to be. I don't want to discount the love shown by Uncle Marion, Aunt Barbara, John, Ann, Chrissy, and Mark; but I can't deny the limit to that love when we were at their homes that Pentecost Sunday.

I was amazed to learn that the piano in Aunt Betty's living room was the very piano Louis had grown up around in Uncle Ed's home when he was at the Home of the Merciful Savior. The piano Louis saw (and I'm sure played—or banged on) as a little boy every other weekend during his institutionalization, the piano beloved by his Uncle Steve later, I had the privilege to play. I don't know what effect this had for those hearing me (other than Aunt Betty remarking it was probably the first time in a while a real song was played on it; many grandchildren had treated it as little grandchildren are apt to do), but it certainly left an impression on me. I was playing in the footsteps of many others who had loved Louis well.

Louis
Our time in Myrtle Beach and Little River caused me to feel as though I was back in West Orange County, Florida. Matthias once again noticed that my southern drawl came back in full swing; not intermittent, according to Matthias the linguist, it was on full bore. I said hello to everyone, and most people in South Carolina are extremely friendly. I also introduced Matthias to Publix supermarkets, one of the few supermarket chains that is entirely owned by its employees. They also have the best subs of any supermarket that I know of.

We also took Highway 17 down to the beach, which reminded me of Daytona Beach, Florida. I felt nostalgia for my time in Orlando and the surrounding area, along with many trips to the beach during my twenty-two-year residency. Matthias and I enjoyed fish at my Aunt Betty's favorite restaurant where she would take my uncle, who didn't eat fish. But after going to Captain Nance's Seafood, in Calibash, North Carolina, he was hooked, and so was his nephew and his nephew's beloved friend and brother, Matthias.

After several games of Mexican Golf, a card game, Aunt Betty told Matthias privately, and semi-publicly (because my Aunt Betty is about as candid as I) that she knew what I was doing. I was saying my goodbyes in person.

We truly had a great experience also in going to the North Myrtle Beach Aquatic Center. When I was living in Orlando, I would sometimes fly to South Carolina to visit Aunt Betty and Uncle Steve. He would take me to the Aquatic Center (which he had in fact helped design). I would be swimming with him, reminiscing about the times when I was younger and he would take me into the water.

Matthias

It was quite the un-accidental accident that we were able to go to the Aquatic Center therapeutic pool on three different days. Opportunities had arisen to modify our trip, by either going to visit a care facility that Louis might move to in Austin OR going to visit Tony in Milwaukee. Louis and I went back and forth a lot, booking and cancelling flights to both places. In the end, we had to stay a few more days in Myrtle Beach and decided to fly to Austin to spend some time with my family before returning to Tucson. Because of this hemming and hawing, we got exactly three days to go into that pool at the North Myrtle Beach Aquatic Center. It was uncanny.

I said to God, *Don't play with me, please . . .* I wasn't expecting the miracle from Lourdes to finally occur here in South Carolina, but I knew that this set of three-times-in-the-water was something He really wanted me to pay attention to.

Being in the Aquatic Center pool made me think back to another time I knew Louis was in a pool. When I had prayed the Rosary that morning, it was Wednesday, so I prayed the Glorious Mysteries. For the first glorious Mystery, the Resurrection, Mary gave me this one word: LIFE! In spite of travel and care fatigue, I knew that Louis and I were supposed to enjoy life in the pool today. I was to give Louis an opportunity to live with freedom of movement he typically can't enjoy.

During and after our trips to the Aquatic Center, he would tell me, "Uncle Steve is smiling." But I thought back to a different man who would exercise Louis in the pool: his father. Fifty-one years before, the man apparently tried to kill Louis by having him drown in their own pool and have it look like a tragic accident. I felt that I was, in a way, making up for this evil in the pool in North Myrtle Beach. One man thought to bring death, I had come to bring life. Where one man struggled to accept Louis as family, his own son, I welcomed him and took joy in sharing life with him.

Of course, it's not like I haven't struggled to understand what my familial commitment to Louis fully means and how much it demands of me. I have trepidation at Louis's joy in calling me "my gift" and "my brother" every time. I know part of my trepidation is fear of getting too sucked in and stuck, too enmeshed in caring for Louis's needs, unable to leave and live my own life—namely, to finally enter religious life.

I don't know exactly what made Louis's father tick or what he feared, but I do know what I have that he needed more of: deep, trusting faith. Only true faith will enable someone to genuinely accept the challenges of caring for another; only true faith and trust in God's Providence and promises will enable someone to nobly struggle with these challenges. And I know the Blessed Mother's promise to me in my heart: "Do you want to enter religious life? I will bring you there." She is the same one who encouraged me, "Do not be afraid to take Louis on."

I know that I am in the right place and that I will be in the right place—even though it isn't the original timeline I envisioned. When I remember this, when I trust this, I am free to love Louis boldly and generously without fear. When I do not trust this, when I believe I am not where I am supposed to be, i.e., that Louis is an obstacle, charity wanes, and I become irritable and vindictive, and often defensive.

But that day, Wednesday June 26th, Mary spoke to me a word of life, and life is what I shared with Louis. I took delight in the whole aquatic exercise process. Louis's father had desperately hoped that bringing Louis to the water would get him to walk one day. I had feverishly hoped that bringing Louis to the waters of Lourdes would get him to walk. But here we were, in the water again. Now, I was content that Louis was walking there, as he only could in a pool. More truly he was walking with a free spirit: one that knows that he is loved and that he loves. The opportunity that Louis's father had passed up, I was now enjoying.

In the course of these three days of going to the water, we had our final days with Aunt Betty. Her words to me left profound impressions. Not only was she close to Louis, and one of the few who stood by him when Ed had ditched him, she was also an experienced caregiver. She understood the struggles well.

After our second to last dinner together, Aunt Betty said to me privately, "I thank you for what you do for Louis. I know it's a thankless job. You have been a great blessing for him in his life; I hope he has been a blessing for you . . ."

I said, simply, "Yes."

"I love you."

"I love you, too."

Her words, though simple and short, had a very great impact on me. Her words are her love and are truly precious. Truly precious indeed.

She said something else that caught my attention, too. Louis was talking about Ed and Frank, and Aunt Betty flatly said, "Don't worry about them. Matthias is more your brother than they ever were."

Louis later told me that this freed him. He said, "This was confirmation to release myself from the toxicity of the family and embrace your gift without fear or reservation. I don't feel like I'm betraying them." Aunt Betty, the truest representative of his family, by saying that about me, legitimized Louis's embrace of my family and my embrace of him. For me, it was an objective confirmation that my gift had been received. Family dynamics are never solo affairs; Aunt Betty had received me. She further demonstrated this when Louis asked her to pray for us. She said, "Oh, I do. Every night when I say my prayers, I pray for Brenda, Marie, Roger . . . and you. And now I pray for Matthias, because he needs it to put up with you." My gift had been received.

Louis

It was time to say goodbye to Aunt Betty and Little River. I carried with me the memories that she gave and put together: photo albums of memories, memories since I moved from Salt Lake to Tucson. I now had photos of my mother and other members of the family. Even though Aunt Betty was acknowledging the passing of the torch to Matthias, and ultimately to Matthias's nuclear family, I still had the foundation in photos from where I had originated, at least earthly. But eternally, I knew that I was a child of God.

Off to Austin. After talking with Marjorie, there were potential placement opportunities for me in Austin. So, we decided to travel there, to check them out personally. If there is one thing I would suggest to the reader and/or anyone whom you may be placing in our long-term care system, it is a good idea to diligently check your options. The challenge with our system in today's market is that it is highly driven by money and profit. Beware; buyer beware.

On our way to Austin, we flew Southwest; it was uneventful, until we began to descend into Austin's airport. Upon commencing our descent into the airport, Matthias was snoozing, as he usually does, or zoning things out.

Matthias

I told Louis that I was going to "check out" and try to take a nap. This had been interrupted by the snack cart and beverage service, a high-priority activity that not even naps could supersede. Thereafter, I announced my return to "nap" mode. I didn't manage to *really* fall asleep, as I almost had before the beverage service, but I was intent on zoning out and staying that way.

A good while later, I heard Louis's voice, "Bro, are you awake?" I was not keen on being awake, and thought to myself, *What kind of question is that?* So, I continued to "be asleep."

He asked again, "Bro, are you awake?"

Seriously? I told him I wanted to take a nap.

I continued my feigned (or attempted) napping. For all I could tell, everything continued as normal.

Louis

What happened next was right out of the Smithsonian Channel's *Air Disasters*. We were on Flight #4084, from Baltimore BWI to Austin AUS, originally scheduled to arrive at 11:25 p.m. However, we were delayed to arrive at midnight. Matthias's father Bob graciously waited for us with Nicholas at Austin's airport. The chosen family is now very accustomed to disability time, so Bob and Nichol understood.

What happened next upon our descent was interesting, to say the least. The front cabin flight attendant, Stephanie, was in her seat as we descended into Austin. All of a sudden, she and I locked eyes because we both had the same thought, I am certain. *What was that noise?*

The next thing I knew, Stephanie retrieved a gentleman to the front who was an off-duty pilot for Southwest who happened to be on the airplane connecting in Austin.

There was a noise coming from the right-side door. Well, my mind began to recall recent episodes of *Air Disasters*, and I remembered that Southwest had had some issues with their doors' maintenance. Fortunately, Southwest only has two types of planes: the 737-700 and the 737-800 (and a few 737 MAX 8s), so their fleet is very limited, but they have a very good maintenance record, for the most part. But I remembered that there had been a Southwest Airline flight in 2018 that was featured on *Air Disasters* where a woman, Jennifer Riordan, was partially sucked out as fellow passengers feverishly tried to bring her back into the aircraft. They had to make a rapid descent and reroute to Philadelphia International Airport. I thought, *Oh my gosh. Please God protect us.*

The off-duty pilot, Stephanie, and I were the only ones on the aircraft (beside other crew) who were aware of the potential severity of the issue. Once they surveyed the situation, the off-duty pilot stated, "We should be OK. It needs to be noted for maintenance once we land in Austin." I breathed a sigh of relief, and thanked God. I knew that my fellow passengers, myself, and Matthias were safe.

Matthias was none the wiser because he was in happy land until we got to Austin when I said to Stephanie, "Great job." I commended the pilot as well and let him know what Stephanie did with precision. Her training came through without a hitch. I told her that I would write Southwest. That was my intent. We were fortunate to have such committed flight attendants and pilots in our country and within the aviation industry.

Matthias

I felt a little silly after Louis explained why he was trying to get my attention during my nap time. He didn't want to speak in such a way as to alarm any fellow passengers, so he opted for the calm, benign question of, "Bro, are you awake?" He wanted me to scoot over toward the middle seat so that I would be further from the windows and the door in front of us, on the other side of the thin wall partition (we were in the very front row, right side of the aisle). In retrospect, I'm not sure how much safer that move would have truly made me if the situation became drastic, but I was sorry to have ignored my brother in his concern for my safety.

Louis

In Austin, we checked out two facilities, Tech Ridge Oaks and Juniper Estates at Spicewood Springs. Neither facility met all of my care needs. However, the care search wasn't really the focus of our time. We spent time with Matthias's family; Fourth of July was upon us so we got together with the extended family while celebrating the values of our American culture.

Unlike our Christmas visit, we did not get stuck in the mud at Nonit's and Carolyn's. Though when we called David, the owner of Wheelchair Accessible Transportation, he said, "Oh yeah. I certainly remember you. You're the one that got stuck in the mud and damaged my fender!"

Matthias

While we were at Nonit's, Louis and I gave a presentation about our pilgrimage to my extended family. We went through (almost) all of the photos that were taken on Louis's phone and my phone. We told many of the stories. We also showed some of the photos that Aunt Betty had given us. I distinctly remember my cousin Sarah remarking about Louis's mother, "Wow, she's beautiful," and the giggles elicited by the photo of five-year-old Louis. He's got those same big hands and that same smile, very reminiscent of his Uncle Steve. I could only pour out my gratitude to God for these moments.

I didn't realize it would line up this way, but the last media to be shown was the video of Louis swimming in the pool at the North Myrtle Beach Aquatic and Fitness Center. I told an abbreviated version of the three-days-to-fulfillment story . . . but this time, the conclusion of the three days ended right there in that room, Nonit's living room. "Here," I said, with the family. Is this not, then, the fulfillment of my covenant? That is, the realization of that which I could not promise on my own ("You are in my family now"), but only my whole family could bring about? I did not see another way I could say of myself, "I am my brother's keeper," unless Louis was truly integrated into the family.

As I prayed that night, I had again the peaceful conviction that Louis should come here—and come here to stay. I was not always comfortable with the idea of Louis coming to live in Austin. But, seeing us all together in Texas, I thought in my heart that that was what I would want for him the most.

Three days in the pool at Scottsdale, three times at the waters of Lourdes, three days in the pool at North Myrtle Beach . . . and three times now that Louis has come to Austin to be with my family.

We all wanted it for him—Mom wanted it for him, searching tirelessly for assisted living placement options like Tech Ridge Oaks and Juniper Estates. The family loves him. My goodness, my little cousin Yuna (about five years old or so) referred to him as "Uncle Louis."

"If two of you agree on earth about anything for which they are to pray, it shall be granted to them by my heavenly Father . . ." (see Matthew 18:19-20) I prayed that the Lord would show us in our hearts and our desires what His will was.

The next day we learned that neither Juniper nor Tech Ridge Oaks could work for Louis. I was devastated. The following morning, we were busy packing, preparing to return to Tucson. When I finally took my shower, I began to cry bitterly. I was so sorry that I couldn't do more for Louis. I couldn't facilitate healing at Lourdes; I couldn't even find a way to get him to move to Texas to be close to my family. I felt like I couldn't leave him in a better state than I found him. It is St. Joseph's Cross.

Yet there was a beautiful peace that came with that pain: a tear-filled peace, the peace of calm after a fire burns out. I felt defeated and heartbroken, but I felt a deep peace in its place because I knew that I was loving and giving my all, truly desiring the best for Louis.

Louis

I am grateful that I have chosen family. As Matthias mentioned earlier, my Aunt Betty had passed the torch and my brother's comments, no matter how disturbing you may find them, was his truth. He had exclaimed it, which I was grateful for. Now, I have peace because I know that people truly do care. They aren't being paid to care. They care from their hearts. I left Austin with a feeling of thankfulness. It was an unexpected stop, but it was grace-filled.

On the plane to Tucson, Matthias lamented how he still wanted to see the Blessed Mother "deliver the fulfillment". I said to him, "Bro, there was the fulfillment. I have your family, chosen family—that's the fulfillment! Even if I can't live close to the family, Matthias, I know that I have them. Even if I'm all the way across the country, I know that they care about me, that they're concerned about me. I know that they love me, just to love me. I have chosen them as family and they have accepted that. That's it, Bro. Even if I didn't live in Texas, I know that they care about me."

brothers in the order of preachers

When we came back to the Newman Center, our pastor, Fr. JP, said upon seeing me, "You look different."

Upon reflection, I could identify five things about the pilgrimage that caused me to feel different.

When I released my brother and released myself. I was carrying a weight. The Blessed Mother saw that. She was like, "Nuh-uh!"

The monstrance, when the priest brought Jesus right up to me at Lourdes. That was Jesus.

When we went to the water at Lourdes. I wasn't physically healed, but just like in baptism, I was transformed.

When Aunt Betty told us, "Matthias is your brother."

Visiting Austin. We weren't supposed to go to Texas. It wasn't on the itinerary. But we *were* supposed to go to Austin. To see the chosen family.

That's what Fr. JP saw. The Blessed Mother's hands were all over it. Jesus knew what my brother would do before we knew. The Blessed Mother knew.

In 2022, Matthias went to the Monastery of Christ in the Desert. When he described it to me, I was like *we have to go there.* I use that phrase a lot with Matthias. He is my travel companion, which I thoroughly enjoy. It gives me freedom. I haven't had such freedom since college.

I was grateful for what I had in the materialistic world, but as the years have progressed, I have yearned for more. What do I mean by that? I mean something that is beyond the materialism of our U.S. society. There has been a yearning inside of me.

Matthias and I left Tucson and headed for Abiquiu, New Mexico. Abiquiu is home to the Monastery of Christ in the Desert. The Monastery is down a road that takes you back in time, nestled between the Chama Canyon walls and the Rio Chama, which runs through the canyon. It hearkened me back to the road to Emmaus, the road that Jesus walked. We spent two weeks there, reflecting and writing.

There was a couple we met at the Monastery whose son, Ru, had an accident that left him a quadriplegic. Ru is a resident of the Inglis House nursing home in Philadelphia. Inglis House is a not-for-profit nursing home, but most recently, that status was threatened. Ru has a background in business. Many of the residents there cannot speak for themselves due to some type of mental condition, but some can, so he spearheaded a protest which was featured a few years ago in *The Philadelphia Inquirer*. The protest was over the nursing home going from a not-for-profit to a profit motive endeavor. This nursing home has been in existence for over 100 years as a non-profit, and due to Ru's efforts, they have so far thwarted all attempts to become a for-profit nursing home.

There are many good things in our American culture, but one of the most nasty, deplorable, and despicable is when individuals profit off the backs of the most vulnerable and summarily turn their backs in so doing. These types of situations need to be brought to the attention of the American people and our allies. Belonging doesn't mean exploitation of one's vulnerability.

Many in America tend to look at our disabled and those of us who are aging as commodities for profit. This does not mean you should not pay competitively. To the contrary, the individuals helping others need to be paid well. The challenge is, there are those organizations, like the nursing home lobby, who lobby legislatures and provide perks or money for their votes. This should be against the law and those that promulgate such behavior should be censured.

We need to remember that the Americans with Disabilities Act is just a beginning, not an end. I had written to President George Herbert Walker Bush on his birthday in June, prior to his death in 2018, thanking him for the legislation, and for the courage to sign such legislation. He responded back in a note (and I am paraphrasing), "So nice of you to write a note on my birthday. I also wanted to let you know that Barbara and I utilize aspects of the ADA ourselves." This indicated to me that he realized how important that piece of legislation was, not only for the disabled, but for those who become disabled because of the aging process.

One of the monks at the monastery told us something quite interesting. He said, "Those who are in nursing homes have a type of monastic lifestyle, if you will. But it's forced upon them. Those in monastic life choose to do so. Those individuals in nursing homes or assisted living"—or anything institutional, I would say—"are forced into a lifestyle not of their choosing."

I'm trying to avoid going into any institutionalized setting myself, so why not volunteer for monastic life instead? The monastic environment offered me something that spoke to the yearning in my heart for more. Sure, even monasteries must deal with the day-to-day drudgery of paying bills, but I hoped that religious life could transcend these kinds of worldly concerns. I dictated a seven-page letter to Matthias, outlining my request and vision for the monks to accept me as a brother. I would give all my resources to the Order, as written in Benedict's rule. I wondered, *Will the Church be innovative? Will the Church be willing?*

Fr. Thomas, the vocations director for the Monastery, sat down with me to discuss my intention to become a monk. He was very kind but said honestly, "We're not big enough to handle you. We had an elder priest and one brother who have since passed, but it cost us $56,000 in that year to take care of the priest. We tried to do what we could, but we had to call in outside help. Even though you don't need as much as the priest did, we just don't have the resources."

I understood their dilemma because that's what Matthias and I are faced with when it comes to my care, as I am now 61. But it seems as though, from the experience they had with this priest (who used to be a Dominican) and their other brother, they weren't willing to take the risk. In fact, the vocations director stated, "It's not only us. But it's the diocese, the bishop . . . We would have to go through those hoops." Fr. Thomas explained that they had learned from caring for their two aging brothers that the personal care commitment also took away from the monastic lifestyle for those who were caring for them.

Again, I understood their dilemma. As I said, I face it, with the help of God. But I was saddened. It is sad that the monastery needs to be placed in that position of caring for their elder monks from a perspective of dollars and cents. Further, Matthias and I were speaking with a brother monk the day before who was from the Congo in Africa. He said, even though it is war-torn in certain regions (his was one; that's why he got out), they are overflowing with vocations. Africa, India, and Vietnam are overflowing. There are waiting lists, basically.

I thought to myself, *Wow. What a difference in culture.* It saddened me that our American culture has affected our American monasteries, or at least the mindset. Yes, it costs money, but there are ways you can make it work. There are nurses or certified caregivers that I'm certain would help on a voluntary basis or as an apostolate. I thought about the Western Province of the Dominican Order. I know that there is a specific friar who coordinates the medical needs of the friars for the whole province. They recently created his position, Vicar Provincial of Healthcare. This is innovative. The Dominican Order might just have something, but the Benedictines could as well.

There is a disconnect here in my view. We have a shortage of vocations, but yet we are told that you can't. I don't like that word: *can't.* And neither should the Church. I wish to challenge our Church. Now, I realize that the sex scandals of the '90s and even more recently have rocked the Church but that doesn't mean we sit on our laurels and say, "Oh my god, what are we to do?" God would want us to move forward, and He would want us to sin no more. I said *us* because the man without sin, let him cast the first stone (see John 8:1-11).

What would Jesus think of all this? I don't think He would be too happy. I think He might turn over a few tables.

Matthias and I recently watched the film *Cabrini.* By no means was everything in that film accurate, because as we all know, Hollywood does take some liberties with the truth, but the basic premise holds true: we had a sister who was willing to work within the framework of the Church in obedience but still created social change. She went over the head of the bishop to the Pope more than once, as chronicled in the movie. But she did it in such a fashion that it did not go against the bishop's directives. We need more Cabrinis. And that's what I was attempting with my thought of becoming a professed religious at the monastery.

I was so excited about the prospect of becoming a monk and taking the vows. I saw those vows as similar to what I released myself from with my brothers Edward and Frank. I made it known to them that it was a two-way release. I release them from responsibility and I also release myself. I believe that that's what I was hopeful for with the monastery. I was going to give it my all.

As my supervisor at SACASA stated, "You are a hard worker, Louis." That was also stated by many at Manheim Orlando, that I was a hard worker. That is one thing my mother and my father gave me: my work ethic. If someone or an entity takes an interest in me, I will do everything in my power to do the best I can. That's what I sought at the monastery, but it wasn't to be. However, I did find belonging in a different religious community.

I was actually already in formation for the Dominican Third Order (Lay Dominicans) before we went to the monastery. However, after Matthias and I left New Mexico and returned to Tucson I began to pursue the option with greater resolve. The Dominican Order (officially titled "Order of Preachers") is comprised of brothers, sisters, and friars. The Order of Preachers is one of the oldest democracies still functioning, since 1216 A.D. Friars are priests and religious brothers of the "First Order" who take vows of poverty, chastity (celibacy), and obedience. This is what Matthias aspires to become. The "Second Order" refers to the contemplative Dominican nuns who support the friars by their prayers. The "Third Order" refers to celibate non-cloistered religious sisters who take vows OR laity (married or unmarried) who make "promises" (not as wide in scope as the vows) of poverty, chastity, and obedience, according to their state of life. This last group is also called the "Lay Dominicans" and is usually what people refer to when they say "the Third Order". Friars, nuns, and lay brothers and sisters are part of the same family of St. Dominic, subject to the authority of the Master of the Order, who resides in Rome.

I also looked at other orders, specifically the Carmelite Third Order. The Monastery of Christ in the Desert also offered me the opportunity to become an "oblate", somewhat akin to a Third Order for laypeople who wish to emulate the Benedictine lifestyle in the world and be affiliated with the monastery. However, in the Spirit, these paths just didn't seem to fulfill my eternal longing. Not to say the Carmelites or the Benedictines aren't connected to our Eternal Father, but each individual has the freedom to choose. The Church is made up of many parts. This is the definition of what it means to be Catholic, from my perspective. It's a truth of universality. The Dominican Order flourishes in that truth.

It's interesting to me because Jesus gave all of us a choice to be free. That is also what the Dominican Order reminded me of. It is our choice to be free. That freedom is through our Heavenly Father. He sacrificed, so that we may be free.

I was honored to be received into the Third Order on February 11, 2025. Gilbert, who is the lay moderator of the St. Martin de Porres Chapter of Lay Dominicans at the University of Arizona Newman Center, picked that date, not with any influence from me. Matthias and I firmly believe that the Blessed Mother had her hand in the decision. February 11th is the feast of Our Lady of Lourdes.

I was determined to have Fr. Tom DeMan, OP be present and be the celebrant of my reception into the Order. The Blessed Mother granted my request, and Fr. Tom was in fact the celebrant of the Mass and was present as Fr. JP welcomed me into the Order. Fr. Tom reminded all present of our longstanding friendship in faith, spanning some 40 years. My reception was one of joy for me, one of family, a family that was part of God's family. For me, this meant there would be no need to concern myself about abandonment.

I did reflect in prayer about when Jesus said to the Father, "My God, why have you abandoned me?" (Matthew 27:46, New Century Version translation) Was there a purpose for my abandonment from my biological family that was beyond earthly comprehension?

For me, this reflection at the time of my reception into the Third Order helped me once again to answer the question, "Who is my brother's keeper?" realizing as well that there is a privilege to being part of the Third Order. Not everyone achieves their desire to become a Third Order Dominican or, for that matter, a First or Second Order Dominican. It is a privilege and a calling from God.

As a Lay Dominican, I have the privilege to be buried in the Dominican habit. I will hopefully be alongside my brother and sister Dominicans at St. Dominic's Cemetery in Benicia, California. This is where Matthias would also be buried, together with the rest of the friars of the Western Province. I hope that as I continue as a Dominican, that upon my death, in the halls of the most ultimate democracy within the heavenly kingdom, Jesus will say, "Good job, my faithful servant. Now you may truly rest in your eternal home."

Matthias

Still to this day I don't believe I can fully wrap my mind around what I actually signed myself up for when I told Louis back in 2020, "You're in *my* family now." Boy, how little did I realize God would vindicate this declaration!

In my time with Louis these past six years, I have discovered a treasure beyond price, a rose I shall not ever acquire elsewhere. Not even in either of my dating relationships did I spend so much time with one individual. Not even with my brothers or sister have I had the opportunity to so regularly share so much of myself, my thoughts, my frustrations, my hopes, my dreams. In a word, never have I had such regular *intimacy* with another individual. Never has someone else had such regular intimacy with me. Yes, that intimacy of deeply knowing another person and being familiar with some of one's deepest desires and longings, but also that everyday intimacy, a kind so often only found in marriage or truly tight-knit families.

Louis and I can simply pray together; this is one of my most cherished types of time that we share. I can tell Louis out of the blue, "Hey, let's pray for so-and-so, he really needs help right now," and we would pray right then and there, on the spot. I love that. I can do this with a few more of my close friends, too, and for that I am very grateful.

Perhaps even more than this, Louis's love is constant. His readiness to forgive me always humbles me, and his concern for *my* concerns astounds me. Of course, there are myriad times where I feel *Oh, he's not paying attention, oh he just wants something for himself* . . . but I know his is a faithful love. I could disappear for twenty years, suddenly show up, and know that he will have my back. With him there is a home I can always return to, even if I haven't always felt at home there. Yes, I know that I must move on to religious life, but it is truly good to have so much good to give up.

Our friendship is a unique treasure that has taken ahold of my heart—as one priest observed, I have fallen in love in a way. I have invested so much of my heart, so I know my departure will leave a very big hole in it. I am often afraid of facing that hole. But I have come to accept that it is indeed God's will for me to carry this hole in me as I progress toward religious life. This is space carved out such that I may pour myself out from a greater heart in the future as a religious and a priest. Living with Louis, being a caregiver and intimate friend, being a brother, is so demanding, I've often feared that being in priestly ministry would be too cushy in comparison, that not as much of my heart would be pushed to grow. Our Lady reassured me in prayer one time, regarding this concern: *Don't worry. All of your heart will be called for.* I'm sure any experienced priests reading this will laugh.

Now, as I surrender myself to the call Our Father has placed on my heart, I must also surrender my brother to the care of the One who Loves him more than I do and takes far better care of him than I could ever do. Yes, prudence and wisdom are called for as we look for new caregivers to take my place and "succeed" me. There will be suitable arrangements—good, not just passing—as I depart. But there can be no looking back, only forward.

Several months after his reception into the Lay Dominicans, Louis made his first profession of promises on August 12, 2025. He promised to live the life of a Lay Dominican for three years, after which point he would be eligible to make perpetual promises. I was so proud of him, watching him consecrate himself to Jesus and Our Lady as he professed membership to the family of the Order of Preachers. I was also stunned. Had I not delayed again and entered the Dominican Order that year, August 12th would have been the day of my arrival at their doorstep. The friars traditionally have their postulants invested (clothed in the habit) as novices on or around August 15th, the feast of Mary's Assumption into Heaven. Instead of arriving for my entry to the Dominicans, here was I watching Louis's entry as a layman into the same Order.

I could have been resentful for what I have given up helping bring Louis this far. How much time, how many setbacks, how much heartache, how much confusion and frustration. But imagine me looking the crucified Jesus in the eye, shaking my fist at Him, demanding, "Why do I have to give up so much?" Wouldn't that be kind of silly? Thankfully, I didn't do that. I was grateful because, by grace, I have come to understand something about purposeful suffering.

Nothing we could possibly suffer could compare with the self-emptying love that God already IS in Himself, the love with which He loves His Son. Whatever is taken from us can never measure up to how much God has already freely given away. This was finally revealed to us in the voluntary surrender of His Son, His *Son*, His beloved, to death. Looking at Jesus on the Cross, my fist-shaking demands wouldn't only make me look silly— they would show me to be a fool and an ungrateful brat.

Now, it's not like God sacrificed his beloved Son to death because He doesn't mind the pain or because He likes the pain or just because He's God so He's tough enough to take the loss. No. Jesus' sacrifice was assiduously prepared for, millennia, eons, in the making. An entire religious tradition, an entire priestly people, a nation, was raised up by God so that the whole world could be witness to and recipient of this voluntary surrender. Prophecy upon prophecy, patriarch after patriarch pointed to His arrival. The stars, the moon, earthquakes, all carefully, exactly timed to highlight this sacrifice. And all this with a purpose: to save us and restore us to God's love, His friendship. And *then* the Son was brought *back* from the dead.

God the Father only willed to freely hand over His only dearly beloved Son to ultimate suffering and death with a meticulous, masterfully thought-out plan, with a clear, lifesaving purpose, and with the full intention to completely restore everything which would be lost—and then some. Only on such conditions did Our Father hand over His Son to death.

So, can we but open our hearts, even if just a little, even if we can't understand HOW, to at least understand *that it is the case that* not a single suffering that God has sent our way or anything or anyone that God has taken away is not part of a meticulously, carefully measured design, with a noble, life-saving purpose, and that He will restore it in a more wonderful way than we could possibly imagine?

So too, I accept the suffering I have suffered these past six years. I have suffered a lot because of Louis's wounds, his needs, my immaturity, my naïveté, my own vices, his actions, my actions, my weaknesses, my inactions . . . I have suffered a lot.

This could have been avoided, I suppose. I could have never entered into such a deep relationship with such a wounded, vulnerable, and complicated man. I could have avoided making myself so vulnerable by never getting so close.

But God put me here to save that man's soul. And He put that man here—and gave him the option to stay here in 2020 instead of passing on—to teach me some soul-saving lessons. I can only imagine the disasters I would have gotten myself into if I hadn't learned what I have learned in my relationship with this man. If I imagine myself as a priest without such formation and experience, I can see a steep learning curve—with far steeper consequences.

When I am tempted to be bitter, impatient, or to "just get out of here" so I can move on—which, indeed, I must do—it's because I've lost sight of that bigger picture. Oh, how many people's words, even if well intentioned, have been daggers in my heart, dragging me into deeper disdain! "It's about time you left Louis and moved on." "Man, I would be really frustrated and angry if I were you and still with Louis." "I just want to see you out of there." "He's taking advantage of you."

Yes, I have been really frustrated. I have just really wanted to get out of this. I have wanted to throw in the towel. I have questioned whether or not Louis was taking advantage of me. Many times, I have told myself, "It's time, it's time," when it wasn't yet time.

But time and time again, Our Blessed Mother has made it quite clear that Louis's healing—the restoration of his identity as a son of God—is an integral part of his call to be a Lay Dominican brother, and that this brotherhood is very purposefully bound up with my call to be a Dominican brother and priest, the way I am called to live out my identity as a son of God.

Sure, I could have avoided all that suffering. But God put that man there so that I could be a part of his story and he a part of mine, so that his story could be a part of my priesthood and his person a part of my heart.

Though my time living with Louis and being his primary caregiver and protector is coming to a close, our connection as family in Jesus, His Blessed Mother, and St. Dominic shall continue, in this life and the next. I honestly don't know what that's supposed to look like. I do know that we'll be praying the Divine Office and Angelic Warfare Confraternity Prayers together, even if disjointed in time and space. But it's often difficult for me to understand the proper place our relationship will have as *all* of my ties (biological family, friends, everyone) are radically reprioritized in my surrender to religious life. Jesus Himself says, "If anyone comes to me without hating his father and mother, wife and children, brothers and sisters, and even his own life, he cannot be my disciple." (Luke 14:26)

Detaching with love is hard for me and the navigation of that love in real time in the years ahead will certainly come with its challenges. But that's okay. I know that the Lord holds all of this together in a marvelous unity, the tapestry that we can only dimly see the back of. I'm willing to accept the gift I have been given in Louis in the present time and as our lives continue, even if I don't fully understand what that means and still have some trepidation.

Sometimes I get worried because when Louis talks about us being together forever in Heaven, my response is, "Uh, that's not how I imagine Heaven." But that's because of all the imbalances and wounds we still have on this side. I do pray that I am there to send Louis off when Our Father does finally call him home. I want to be there to hold his hand and shout, "Run! Run through the field, and don't look back!" And when Louis is waiting to welcome me, he won't be overbearing in Heaven (he's still getting better here on earth) and I *won't* be doing his personal care. He'll be giving me piggyback rides as we run through the field and on to the everlasting hills.

We'll be singing the Rosary together before Our Blessed Mother, worshipping Almighty God, alongside countless others of every race and tongue, just like we did at Lourdes—this time with Louis's mom, Teresa Romano, Grandma and Grandpa Vujevich,

Brian Eckert, Uncle Steve and Uncle Ed, my Great-grandpa William Aloysius . . .

I say all these things to tell you my response to Cain's sarcastic question to God: I *am* my brother's keeper. So I was, so I am, and so shall I ever be.

a talk with momma

Louis

Jesus himself cried out to His Father and asked *why*. I hope that by telling my story in the most organic way possible I pose for the reader the question of "why", whatever that "why" may be. When we ask the question "why", we then begin the collective process of change. I hope my memoir and story have changed your thoughts, your views, your biases, your person, and your faith, to show that all of us are each other's brother's keeper. Maybe and hopefully, this will not only be an idea, but it will actually become ingrained within the fabric of our souls.

When I was visiting my mother's mausoleum, I turned and saw Calaizzi's beauty shop, via direct line of sight. I thought right at that moment, *Momma, your son, my brother Edward, did such a good job in capturing the essence of you. Every Tuesday you went to that beauty shop for years on end, and hardly ever missed an appointment. That was your time; that was your space. My brother honored you by ensuring that you rested in peace while still having your hair done.*

I was and still am in awe of your beauty. Not only as a person that I was privileged to have as my mother, but as a person who was concerned for others. You told me of a story when you were a schoolteacher and you came to find out that one of your student's homes had only dirt floors. I remember that you helped that student to make his learning environment better, since you understood that he was coming from an underprivileged background. This also answers the question of "Who is my brother's keeper?"

When I began to consider writing this book back in 2007/2008, I had the sense that you didn't want me to write it. For years I wondered why. After writing this book, I came up with a plausible explanation. You were proud. You were strong. You were elegant. You were forceful. As many have said, the one thing you didn't mess with was Ann Fazio's children: Baby Fazio, me, Frank, or Edward. I believe you did not want to expose to the world the domestic violence we all had to endure at the hands of the patriarch of our family.

I have wondered something, ever since learning that Lou Fazio Sr., my father and your husband, was married before you. The woman he was married to, petitioned for, and received an annullment. I've since wondered: Why did she seek annulment. Was it because she saw the signs of domestic abuse and quickly exited? You always told me, "I can change your father." In the end, you took care of our father, your husband. Again, the question was answered, "Who is my brother's keeper?"

In 1977, that dreadful Christmas season night, when the life was almost choked out of you, you were saved only by Frank's entrance into your bedroom. Again the question was answered, "Who is my brother's keeper?" Or the day when Uncle Marion came and you all went down to the basement, where he told our father, your husband, that if he ever touched you again, they, he and the rest of your brothers, would kill him. This story was relayed by Uncle Steve and Aunt Betty, to a man now not of 13 years, but to a man much older. That man was me. Again, who is my brother's keeper?

Or the time at my home off Bridgewood Trail, when you said, "You are much more patient than your father." I was stunned, because I could see the hurt in your eyes as you uttered those words.

Or in 2001, when my father, your husband, had a massive stroke, disabling him to the point of almost a vegetable, the doctor came to me at North Allegheny Hospital and said, "Who are you?" I responded by saying, "I am his son." Because he had responded from his comatose state and once again, I was asked and I pondered the question, "Who is my brother's keeper?"

Your devotion to the Blessed Mother showed me and helped me realize that in my sinfulness, as when I called you a name that I should have never uttered, I received grace. I too now devote my life to the Blessed Mother, allowing me to see exactly who my brother's keeper is. Momma, you have helped me realize, through the other side of the veil, that my brother's keeper is the Trinity: the Father, the Son, and the Holy Spirit.

When I take my last breath upon the hour of my death, I will rise in life anew, awaiting you to greet me far beyond the earthly bound and I will embrace you saying, "I love you, Momma."

ACKNOWLEDGEMENTS

Louis

I would like to acknowledge my chosen brother, Matthias Jeffery Mahoney, for his tireless work on the completion of my biographical memoir. I wish as well to acknowledge my friend, Dr. Kevin Kuper, who also helped me begin the process of writing, and Mr. Robert J. Mahoney, who graciously provided his input in relation to the mechanics in the writing and editing of the initial manuscript.

I also graciously would like to acknowledge the gift of W. Brand Publishing, led by JuLee Brand, who saw the value of my story. JuLee's flexibility and belief in my story provided the opportunity and motivation to never lose hope in its publication. I would also like to thank her developmental editor, Virginia Bhashkar. Her suggestions and comments truly helped polish the manuscript to capture the essence of the words within.

Sue Kroeger, who is currently Associate Professor of Practice, Disability and Psychoeducational Studies and Adjunct Assistant Professor, as well as a member of the Graduate Faculty at the University of Arizona, was an individual that reminded me of the importance of this story, and that if the story was not told, how it would be lost to unspoken or unwritten history.

I also wish to extend my gratitude to all those who pledged their monetary support via Kickstarter, especially Gerardo Garcia, Dr. Brian Hutcheson, Dr. Kevin and Kelly Kuper, Mike and Cella Conaway, Nathaniel and Camila Mahoney, Donald and Krisann Traicoff, Giacomo Lucertini, Jess and Tyson Cisneros, Bruce and Char Steenson, and finally Nicole Traicoff, for her willingness to help with the distribution of copies after Matthias's departure for religious life. Your generous support created a critical foundation of investment for getting the publication off the ground. Thank you.

I would also like to thank Dr. Danita Applewhite, for her willingness to bring my work to a larger audience prior to its official release, on her podcast, *ASK DR. APPLEwhite.*

Further, I wish to acknowledge those of us within our American society that triumph on a daily basis in conquering their physical, emotional, or mental challenges. The word "disability", if you remove the prefix, is "ability", at its core. Everyone in our society, no matter their circumstance, has ability. I hope this book helps us all see that inevitability.

I wish also to acknowledge all of my friends who have acted as my caregivers, along with those that have performed caregiving for me as professionals. I further wish to acknowledge all those who have touched my life since my birth in 1964. Whether you are friend, foe, or just someone that I happened to meet along my journey.

I wish to acknowledge the omnipresent gift of the Holy Trinity in my earthly existence. This partnership has served me in my darkest and brightest times on my earthly journey.

In relation to my earthly father, Lou Fazio, Sr., I humbly ask and hope that his soul is with his Heavenly Father.

Lastly, I wish to thank Teresa Romano, in memoriam, for her strength during my darkest hour. May she rest in peace.

Matthias

I will not repeat, but I add my deepest heartfelt "thank you" for each person whom Louis mentioned above.

I wish to extend my particular gratitude firstly to Louis, for his willingness to share his life's story with me so early on in our friendship. I would also like to acknowledge his patience with me and my sometimes excessive zeal to push through the writing process. But more importantly, I wish to acknowledge his greater patience with my person. His unconditional love continues to humble me and amaze me. Thank you.

Dad, thank you for sharing from your lifetime's experience in writing, in editing, and in the book-writing biz. Thank you for making your copy of the initial draft bleed with red ink. Your suggestions and insight gave Louis and me much needed direction in the early phases of the book's development. Thank you for being a good dad. And I thank you for being a good professional patient, which gave me much needed foundation to support Louis in his needs.

Mom, thank you for your tireless witness of care, especially toward Dad, your children, granddaughter, and so, so many others—as a wife, as a mother (and now grandmother!), as a doctor, and as a friend. Whenever people compliment my patience, I say that I got it from you, because you have a lot of them. Thank you for your suggestions from reading the initial draft.

Godmother Donna, Ralph, and Kathryn: I thank you for your witness of unconditional and persistent love. I can't imagine how many favors your prayers have earned for me.

I would also like to thank Eve Tushnet and Wesley Hill. Their stories gave me invaluable wisdom for navigating my relationship with Louis and sharing intimately about it. I extend further thanks to Eve for her prayer, encouragement, and willingness to help promote the manuscript.

I must also extend my thanks to all those who have supported us through their prayers over days, weeks, months, and years to see this book come to completion. I cannot fathom the totality of the graces you have gained for us to help us along the way.

Finally, I must give God the glory. He's writing the story; I'm privileged to tell it. I must say thank you to the holy ladies in Heaven whose advocacy and examples have inspired so much of the good in my life and given me the strength to walk this path with Louis. Dear St. Faustyna, Secretary of Divine Mercy, thank you. My Dearest Mother, Our Queen, you have delivered the fulfillment again. Together, let our souls proclaim the greatness of the Lord.

The Almighty has done great things for me, and holy is His name.

ENDNOTES AND REFERENCES

1. The Home of the Merciful Savior for Crippled Children was opened in 1882 by Helen Innes. She and her husband, an Episcopal minister, had a young boy with disabilities in their custody. Unable to find a suitable home for him, she set about founding one herself and soon began providing a home for children from any city and any state for no fee. The Home of the Merciful Savior (HMS) since then had expanded to include a school. The focus of HMS has evolved in its mission and purpose over the decades. During the '40s and '50s, HMS was especially serving children with polio, but as the Salk vaccine became more available, their focus shifted to children with Cerebral Palsy. By the '80s, as powerchairs were becoming more user-friendly and more widely available, the HMS was an innovator in communication programs and "augmentative approaches to traditional speech" and took the name "HMS School for Children with Cerebral Palsy". During my residency, the name (The Home of the Merciful Savior for Crippled Children) was indicative, in my view, of American society's perception of disability at that time.

2. *Catechism of the Catholic Church.* (2023). (2nd ed.). Libreria Editrice Vaticana.

3. Albom, M. (1997). *Tuesdays with Morrie: an old man, a young man, and life's greatest lesson.* Doubleday.

4. Van der Kolk, B. (2014). *The Body Keeps the Score.* This book was important for practitioners and laymen alike, reminding us of the importance of paying attention

to your body. You can avoid a lot of ailments by just paying attention to your body.

5. One notable counterexample which I included in the original (unabridged) email to Sr. Angélica was St. Anne's Catholic Church in Garden City, NY. (Parish Social Ministry. (2025) *Church of St. Anne.* http://www. stannesgc.org/Parish-Social-Ministry
See also their page directly addressing parishioner needs: Are You in Need? (2025). *Church of St. Anne.* https://www.stannesgc.org/About-Our-Parish/Are-You-In-Need Need?

6. Tushnet, E. (2014). *Gay and Catholic: Accepting my sexuality, finding community, living my faith.* Ave Maria Press.

7. Hill, W. (2010). *Washed and Waiting: Reflections on Christian faithfulness and homosexuality.* Zondervan.

8. Hill, W. (2015). *Spiritual Friendship: Finding love in the Church as a celibate gay Christian.* Brazos Press.

9. See Lev 20:13, 1 Cor 6:9-10. See also Catechism of the Catholic Church, 2357-2359.

10. Schmitz, M. [Steubenville Youth Conferences]. (2016, August 3). *Fr. Mike Schmitz | Love and Same Sex Attraction.* [YouTube]. https://www.youtube.com/watch?v=fWZ171V0wEQike Schmitz | Love and Same Sex Attraction

11. Shapiro, J. (2018). The Sexual Assault Epidemic No One Talks About. *All Things Considered, Special Series: Abused and Betrayed.* National Public Radio. https://www.npr.org/2018/01/08/570224090/the-sexual-assault-epidemic-no-one-talks-about

12. Christensen, D., et al. (2014). Prevalence of cerebral palsy, co-occurring autism spectrum disorders, and motor functioning - Autism and Developmental Disabilities Monitoring Network, USA, 2008. *Developmental medicine and child neurology 56*(1), 59-65. doi:10.1111/dmcn.12268 (Note: the Autism and Developmental Disabilities Monitoring Network is a branch of the Center for Disease Control.)

13. Crist, J.D., Woo, S.H., & Choi, M. (2008). A Comparison of the Use of Home Care Services by Anglo-American and Mexican American Elders. *Journal of Transcultural Nursing 18*(4). https://doi.org/10.1177/1043659607305190

14. Statista. (2025). *Countries with the largest number of prisoners per 100,000 of the national population, as of February 2025.* Statista.com https://www.statista.com/statistics/300986/incarceration-rates-in-oecd-countries/

15. See, for example: Moscrip, A.N. (2020, September 20). *Generation Z's Positive and Negative Attributes and the Impact on Empathy After a Community-Based Learning Experience.* Morning Consult. https://morningconsult.com/2020/09/29/gen-z-biggest-issues-polling/

16. Tomasa, L., et al. (2024). *Sexual Violence Told Through Lived Experiences of Survivors, Families, and Professionals: The impact of sexual violence on people with intellectual and developmental disabilities.* The University of Arizona College of Medicine Tucson, Sonoran University Center for Excellence in Disabilities.

17. Schmitz, M. [AscensionPresents] (2018, Nov 8). *Why We Need Boundaries.* [Video]. YouTube. https://www.youtube.com/watch?v=nISpzukXrZ0

18. The text of St. Joseph's alleged words to Sr. Mary Ephrem was featured in this excellent consecration devotional: Bottaro, G., & Settle, J. (2021). *Consecration to Jesus through St. Joseph: An integrated look at the Holy Family.* Catholic Psych Press.

19. Gaitley, M.E. (2011). *33 Days to Morning Glory. A Do-It-Yourself-Retreat In Preparation for Marian Consecration.* Marian Fathers of the Immaculate Conception of the B.V.M.

20. Forward, S., with Buck, C. (1989). *Toxic Parents.* Bantam.

21. See, for instance Middleton, W., Sachs, A., & Dorahy, M.J. (Eds.). (2018). *The Abused and the Abuser, Victim-Perpetrator Dynamics.* Routledge. doi: 10.4324/9781351213981

www.ingramcontent.com/pod-product-compliance
Lightning Source LLC
Chambersburg PA
CBHW051127130726
47988CB00005B/1731